P9-DVZ-296

My
Samsung Galaxy S®5

Steve Schwartz

800 East 96th Street,
Indianapolis, Indiana 46240 USA

My Samsung Galaxy S⁵

Copyright © 2015 by Pearson Education

ISBN-13: 978-0-7897-5349-6
ISBN-10: 0-7897-5349-9

Library of Congress Control Number: 2014940441

Printed in the United States of America

Second Printing: September 2014

Trademarks

Warning and Disclaimer

Special Sales

For information about buying this title in bulk quantities, or for special sales opportunities (which may include electronic versions; custom cover designs; and content particular to your business, training goals, marketing focus, or branding interests), please contact our corporate sales department at corpsales@pearsoned.com or (800) 382-3419.

For government sales inquiries, please contact governmentsales@pearsoned.com.

For questions about sales outside the U.S., please contact international@pearsoned.com.

Editor-in-Chief
Greg Wiegand

Acquisitions Editor
Michelle Newcomb

Development Editor
Charlotte Kughen

Managing Editor
Kristy Hart

Senior Project Editor
Betsy Gratner

Indexer
Emily Glossbrenner

Proofreader
Williams Woods
Publishing Services

Technical Editor
Christian Kenyeres

Editorial Assistant
Cindy Teeters

Cover Designer
Mark Shirar

Compositor
Tricia Bronkella

Contributor
Craig Johnston

Contents at a Glance

Extra content is available on the book's website, www.informit.com/title/9780789753496. (Look on the Downloads tab.) The bonus content includes formatting and removing a memory card, installing and replacing the SIM card, checking for system updates, troubleshooting, and performing a Factory Data Reset.

Table of Contents

xii   My Samsung Galaxy S®5

19 Powering Other Devices **587**

Creating a Mobile Hotspot for Wi-Fi Devices 587
Tethering the Phone and a Computer 592
USB Tethering for Windows PCs 592
Bluetooth Tethering 594
Mirroring the Phone on an HDTV 596

20 Optimizing and Troubleshooting **601**

Managing Memory 601
Conserving the Battery 603
Configure and Enable Power Saving Mode 603
Configure and Enable Ultra Power Saving Mode 606
Tips for Manually Conserving the Remaining Charge .. 608
View Battery Usage by Features and Apps 610
Managing Talk Time and Data Usage 612
Checking Current Usage 612
Manage Data Usage 613
What's Cheaper? 616
Can This Call Be Made Later? 617
Prorated Features 617
Faster Downloads with Download Booster 617
Viewing and Expanding Storage 617
View Used and Available Space 618
Adding a Memory Card 619

Index **621**

Extra content is available on the book's website, www.informit.com/
title/9780789753496. (Look on the Downloads tab.) The bonus content includes
formatting and removing a memory card, installing and replacing the SIM card,
checking for system updates, troubleshooting, and performing a Factory Data
Reset.

About the Author

Steve Schwartz got an early start as a computer industry writer and author. Immediately after buying an Apple II+ in 1978, he began writing regularly for the computer magazines of the day. Since then, he has written hundreds of articles for major publications, including *Macworld*, *PC World*, *InfoWorld*, and *Computerworld*. He is also the author of more than 60 books on technology, game, and computer topics, including guides to business/productivity software (Microsoft Office, Access, and FileMaker Pro), Internet software (Internet Explorer, Outlook Express, Entourage, and Gmail), and graphics/image-editing software (Picasa, Picture It!, Digital Image Suite, and CorelDRAW). Following his best-selling *My Samsung Galaxy S III* and *My Samsung Galaxy S 4*, this is Steve's third book in the *My* series.

Before becoming a full-time writer in 1990, Steve served as editor-in-chief for *Software Digest* and technical services director for Funk Software. He also authored the first trade paperback on the then-new Nintendo phenomenon: *Compute!'s Guide to Nintendo Games*.

Steve has a Ph.D. in psychology, consults on game design, database design, and technology issues, and lives in the fictional town of Lizard Spit, Arizona. You can see the complete list of his books at www.siliconwasteland.com/misc.htm.

Acknowledgments

I'd like to extend my special thanks to the following individuals:

- The talented, dedicated, hard-working Que editorial and production team: Michelle Newcomb, Todd Brakke, Betsy Gratner, Charlotte Kughen, Tricia Bronkella, and Emily Glossbrenner

- Margot Hutchison and Carole Jelen of Waterside Productions

- *My…* series author, Craig Johnston

- Lucas Wymer for assisting in testing phone-to-phone transfers

- Shepard and Emileyne for ensuring that Jethro was entertained while we tested

We Want to Hear from You!

As the reader of this book, *you* are our most important critic and commentator. We value your opinion and want to know what we're doing right, what we could do better, what areas you'd like to see us publish in, and any other words of wisdom you're willing to pass our way.

We welcome your comments. You can email or write to let us know what you did or didn't like about this book—as well as what we can do to make our books better.

Please note that we cannot help you with technical problems related to the topic of this book.

When you write, please be sure to include this book's title and author, as well as your name and email address. We will carefully review your comments and share them with the author and editors who worked on the book.

Email: feedback@quepublishing.com

Mail: Que Publishing
        ATTN: Reader Feedback
        800 East 96th Street
        Indianapolis, IN 46240 USA

Reader Services

Visit our website and register this book at quepublishing.com/register for convenient access to any updates, downloads, or errata that might be available for this book.

Introduction

About This Book

Welcome to *My Samsung Galaxy S5*, a book about using, customizing, maintaining, and troubleshooting your Samsung Galaxy S5. It attempts to be a comprehensive guide to "all things Galaxy S5," but it concentrates on the apps and features that you're most likely to use. To make it easy for you to follow along, procedures are presented in step-by-step fashion, each illustrated by an image of what you'll see onscreen. Although much of this book's information is also applicable to other recent Android phones and tablets, it will be most helpful to those of you who either own or intend to get a Samsung Galaxy S5.

If you have a previous phone in the Galaxy S family, you might want to check out my other titles in this series: *My Samsung Galaxy S III* and *My Samsung Galaxy S 4*.

The Need for a Book

If this is your first smartphone, you'll quickly discover that learning to use your Galaxy S5 has a much steeper learning curve than mastering an ordinary phone. Actually, it will probably help you to think of your phone as a handheld computer that you can also use to place and receive phone calls. For many users, the calling capabilities of the S5 are secondary to all the other wonderful things you can do with it.

What distinguishes this book from competing titles is its attention to detail. Although each carrier offers a free, downloadable manual with *general* explanations of how their phone works and how to use the standard applications (or *apps*), the manual seldom provides sufficient information to enable you to comfortably use your phone's many features or to understand the impact of setting particular options. Much of the work and "figuring out" is left to your experimentation or reading books such as this one.

One direct result of providing detailed, step-by-step instructions for the most commonly used apps and features is that this book is almost twice as long as other S5 books. For example, rather than simply telling you how to launch Camera and which button to tap to snap a picture, you also learn about configuring Camera for different lighting conditions and shooting situations, applying filters, sharing your photos with friends and social networking sites, and creating slideshows. *Rest assured, however, that you don't have to read everything!* Save the extra detailed information for those occasions when you really *need* to reconfigure an app or determine how its more advanced features work.

In addition to furthering your education about your marvelous new smartphone, it's my hope that this book will provide an additional immediate and long-term benefit to you. *It will save you time.* You won't have to waste hours experimenting, performing fruitless Google searches, and watching an endless stream of YouTube video reviews and tutorials in an effort to figure out how an app or one of its features works. I've done my best to do that for you.

How to Read This Book

Although the chapters are presented in what is intended to be a logical order (based on *what* I think you need to know and *when* you'll need to know it), it may sometimes feel like you have to understand *everything* about the phone before you can do *anything* with it. Placing a call, for example, requires you to know how to interact with the touchscreen and, optionally, how to select a phone number or person's name in Contacts.

You'll do well to at least skim through the entire book. But to avoid being overwhelmed by that "need to know everything at once" feeling, I recommend that you start by working your way through the basics provided in Chapters 1 through 3 and only then jump to whatever chapter covers the topic you want to tackle next.

Extra content is available on this book's website, www.informit.com/title/ 9780789753496. (Look on the Downloads tab.) The bonus content includes information on formatting and removing a memory card, installing and replacing the SIM card, checking for system updates, troubleshooting, and more.

Smartphone "Facts of Life"

When reading this book, there are some important facts you should know:

- At its launch, six major U.S. carriers carried the Galaxy S5: AT&T, Metro PCS, Sprint, T-Mobile, Verizon, and U.S. Cellular. From a hardware perspective, each of these phones is identical.

- On a software basis, however, there are occasionally differences between the carriers. First, most carriers add their own applications (*apps*) to the standard ones that come with every S5, and they sometimes make small modifications to the standard apps, too.

  Second, the names of Settings icons can vary slightly among carriers, as can the manner in which *operating system* (OS) updates are performed.

  To be applicable to every carrier's S5, this book explains how to use the software that they all have in common; there's little discussion of carrier-specific apps. For such information, you should refer to the carrier's downloadable manual and support information.

- App and OS updates can be delivered or downloaded whenever the app developers and your carrier, respectively, see fit. Thus, like all Android cell phones, the S5 is a *moving target* and subject to change. This book, on the other hand, is static text—correct at the time it was written. When a new version of the OS is applied to your phone, the steps to perform some procedures, what you see onscreen, and the options available in certain Settings categories might change slightly. However, based on past OS updates, even if this happens to an app here or a procedure there, the material in this book should still be sufficiently relevant for you to determine how to work with and use the new features and options. In other words, you're still far better off with this book in your hands than without it!

Status or Notification Bar

Widget

Google
Search

App
shortcuts

Home screen
page indicator

Primary
shortcuts

In this chapter, you become familiar with the basics of setting up and operating your new phone. Topics include the following:

→ Familiarizing yourself with the phone hardware, operating system, interface, and customization options

→ Performing basic phone operations

→ Running the setup wizard

→ Adjusting the display and volume

→ Using a headset or headphones

→ Setting up voicemail

→ Creating or registering Gmail, Samsung, and Dropbox accounts

→ Using Wi-Fi networks and printers

Galaxy S5 Essentials

In this chapter and Chapter 2, "Understanding the Android/ TouchWiz Interface," you become familiar with the fundamentals of operating and interacting with your new Android-based phone. In Chapter 3, "Making the Phone Your Own," you find out how to customize your phone to make it look and work the way that you prefer.

About the Galaxy S5

As the latest entrant in Samsung's all-star lineup of Galaxy S-series phones, the Galaxy S5 is a fast, feature-laden smartphone. This section discusses the phone hardware, the Android operating system that powers the S5, the interface you use to interact with it, and available customization options.

The Hardware

To create a powerful, flexible smartphone, Samsung equipped the Galaxy S5 as follows

- 2.5GHz quad-core processor, running the Android 4.4.2 (KitKat) operating system
- HD Super AMOLED, 1920 × 1080-pixel, 432 ppi, 5.1" touchscreen display
- 2.0-megapixel front-facing camera; 16-megapixel rear-facing camera with UHD (4K) and HD video recording
- 16 or 32GB internal memory; 2GB RAM; and support for up to 128GB of additional memory with a microSDHC card
- 4G/LTE network support
- Wi-Fi (802.11 a/b/g/n/ac) on 2.4 or 5 GHz, USB 3.0, Bluetooth 4.0, and NFC connectivity
- GPS (global positioning system)
- Accelerometer, gyro, proximity, compass, barometer, Hall sensor, RGB ambient light, gesture, fingerprint scanner, and heart rate sensor
- IR (infrared) remote; MHL 2.1; IP67 dust- and water-resistant

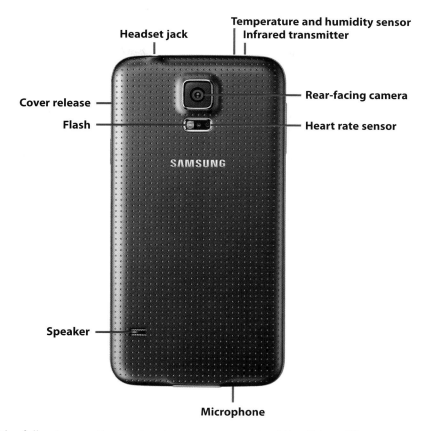

Temperature and humidity sensor
Infrared transmitter

Headset jack

Rear-facing camera

Cover release

Flash

Heart rate sensor

SAMSUNG

Speaker

Microphone

The following are the key hardware components of the Galaxy S5:

Power/Lock button. Press the Power button to turn the phone on or off and to manually darken (lock) or restore the screen.

Volume control. Press this context-sensitive hardware control to raise (top part) or lower (bottom part) the volume of the current activity, such as conducting a call or playing music.

Microphones. Speak into the bottom microphone when participating in a call, giving voice commands, or using the phone's speech-to-text feature. The top microphone is used for noise cancellation and stereo recording.

Earpiece/receiver. When you're not using a headset, call audio is transmitted through this front speaker. The external speaker on the back of the phone is used to play music, ringtones, and other audio.

Headset jack. Port for connecting a compatible 3.5mm wired headset or headphones; enables 5.1 channel sound when playing media.

Front-facing camera. Low-resolution (2-megapixel), front-facing camera for taking self-portraits and participating in video chats.

Rear-facing camera. High-resolution (16-megapixel), rear-facing camera for taking pictures and high-definition movies.

Flash. Illuminates photos shot with the rear-facing camera (unless you've disabled it for the shot).

Heart rate sensor. Used in conjunction with health apps (such as S Health) to measure your pulse.

Touchscreen. Touch-sensitive screen; displays information and enables you to interact with the phone.

Recent Apps, Home, and Back keys. Press these hardware keys to interact with the operating system and installed applications.

USB charger/accessory connector. Enables the phone to be connected with the supplied USB cable to a computer for file transfers or to the charger head and a wall outlet to charge the phone's battery.

LED status or indicator light. Displays a flashing or steady light to indicate that the phone is performing its startup sequence, denoting notifications (such as newly received email or text messages), or showing the charging status.

Ambient light, proximity, and gesture sensors. The ambient light sensor enables the screen's brightness to adjust to current lighting conditions. The proximity and gesture sensors detect how close an object is to the phone and whether particular gestures are occurring. During calls, the proximity sensor determines when your face is pressed to the screen and locks the keypad to prevent accidental key presses.

Infrared transmitter. With the appropriate apps, enables you to control infrared devices, such as flat-screen televisions, DVRs, and set-top boxes.

Adding a Memory Card

In addition to using the S5's built-in memory for storing email, photos, music, apps, and other material, you can purchase a memory card (up to 128GB) to increase the phone's available storage—much like adding a second hard disk to your computer. For information on installing, formatting, or removing a memory card, see "Viewing and Expanding Storage" in Chapter 20, "Optimizing and Troubleshooting."

The Android Operating System and TouchWiz

Just like a computer, every smartphone has an *operating system* that controls virtually every important activity that the phone can perform, as well as the ways in which you interact with it. On the Galaxy S5, the operating system is Android 4.4.2 (KitKat).

Like many of the other major cell phone manufacturers, Samsung has customized the Android operating system to differentiate its phones from those of competitors. Samsung's TouchWiz interface is that operating system customization. Although phones from other manufacturers run Android 4.4.x, TouchWiz ensures that Galaxy S5 phones operate in a similar—but never identical—fashion to those phones.

Note that operating system updates are periodically made available to phones through the carriers.

The Interface

Much of what you do with the phone involves using its touchscreen. The Home screen consists of a series of customizable pages that you can optionally expand to seven. On these pages, you can place shortcuts to the applications (*apps*) that you use most often, as well as small applications called widgets that run directly on the Home screen. To interact with the touchscreen, you tap app icons to launch programs, flick up or down to scroll through lists, pinch and spread your fingers to change the current magnification, and so on. Chapter 2 explains in detail how to work with the touchscreen interface.

Easy or Standard Mode

If you're new to cell phones (or just to Android phones), you can elect to use a Home screen variant called Easy mode. Although the material in this book is based on Standard mode, you may want to use Easy mode until you're comfortable with the phone. See "Set the Home Screen Mode" in Chapter 2 for instructions and information about switching modes.

Customization

One of the main reasons for buying a smartphone such as the Galaxy S5 is that you can do considerably more with it than you can with an ordinary telephone or cell phone. Much as you can do with a computer, you can customize your phone by populating the Home screen with custom arrangements of widgets and app icons, change the Home and lock screens' background (*wallpaper*), install additional useful apps, and set preferences (*settings*) for the system software and installed apps. When you're comfortable with the phone's basic operations and are ready to start customizing it, read Chapter 3.

>>>Go Further

CHANGING SYSTEM SETTINGS

To change certain operating system features (such as choosing a new Wi-Fi network or adjusting the screen timeout interval), you need to access the Settings screen by doing either of the following:

- On any Home screen page, tap the Apps icon, and then tap Settings.

 —— **Settings icon**

- Open the Notification panel by dragging the status bar downward, and then tap the Settings icon.

—— **Settings**

—— **Quick Setting buttons**

The top of the Notification panel also contains a row of scrolling icons called Quick Setting buttons. By tapping these icons, you can quickly enable or disable important features, such as Wi-Fi and Bluetooth. For information about using and customizing the Quick Setting buttons, see "The Notification Panel" in Chapter 2.

Because there are now so many icons in Settings, you can elect to display them in several different ways. To change their display, open Settings, tap the menu icon, and choose Grid View, List View, or Tab View.

Charging the Battery

The Galaxy S5 includes a two-piece wall charger that consists of a special USB 3.0 cable and a charger head. You charge the phone's battery by connecting the assembled wall charger to the phone and a standard wall outlet. It's recommended that you fully charge the phone before its first use. Note that it isn't necessary to wait until the battery is almost fully discharged before charging.

Connecting to a Computer

The battery also charges while the phone is connected to a computer by the USB cable. The included cable is compatible with computers with USB 3.0 or 2.0 ports. If you have an older computer with USB 2.0 ports, you don't need a different cable to connect the phone to your computer—for any USB task, such as charging the battery or transferring data. See "Manually Transferring Files over USB" in Chapter 16, "Transferring and Sharing Files," for instructions on making the phone-to-computer connection.

1. Gently flip open the USB cover on the bottom of the phone.

2. Plug the end of the USB cable with the single rectangular connector into the charger head.

3. Plug the other end of the cable (with the pair of connectors) into the bottom of the phone.

4. Plug the charger head into a wall outlet. The LED indicator light glows while the phone charges.

5. When the LED changes color, the phone is fully charged. Disconnect the USB cable from the wall outlet and phone. Replace the USB cover on the bottom of the phone.

Charging While the Phone Is On

If you need to complete a call or use apps when the battery is almost drained, you can continue to use the phone while it charges.

Powering On/Off

Although many people prefer to simply leave their phones on, you can turn yours off whenever you like—to conserve the battery, for example.

- To turn on the phone, press and hold the Power button until the phone vibrates and begins its normal startup sequence.

Power button

- To turn off the phone, press and hold the Power button for about 2 seconds. In the Device Options dialog box that appears, tap Power Off, and then tap OK to confirm that you want to shut down your phone.

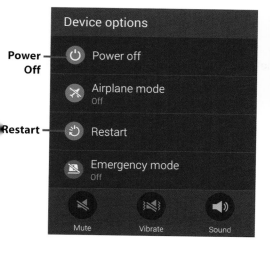

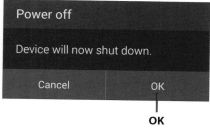

Restarting the Phone

You can also *restart* the phone from the Device Options dialog box. If you've been running the phone continuously for several days, periodically restarting clears *memory fragmentation*—enabling you to start again with a clean slate.

Running the Setup Wizard

The first time the phone is turned on (and after a Factory Data Reset), the setup wizard automatically launches and displays its Welcome screen. You can respond to its prompts to set up some essential services, such as creating or signing in to a Google account and Samsung account, configuring your Wi-Fi settings, and adding an email account. The pages referenced in the following task explain how to establish these basic settings manually—without the wizard's assistance.

Now or Later?

It doesn't matter whether you use the setup wizard to immediately set up the phone or configure it manually when it's more convenient. For instance, if a salesperson sells you the phone and runs the wizard, you won't be able to select your particular Wi-Fi network until you go back home or to work. All important options in the wizard can be manually reconfigured whenever—and as often as—you like.

Run the Setup Wizard

1. On the wizard's opening screen, select a default language. (See "Changing the Default Language" on page 44 to manually choose a new default language.)

2. *Optional*: If you have hearing, vision, or dexterity issues, tap Accessibility to review or modify Accessibility settings, such as the size of the display font. To manually configure these settings, tap Settings, Accessibility.

3. Tap Start (on the opening screen) or Next (on the Accessibility screen) to continue.

4. If you have a Wi-Fi (wireless) home or business network, ensure that the Wi-Fi slider is On, select the network's name, enter your network password (if any), and tap Connect. Tap Next to continue. (See "Connect to a New Wireless Network," later in this chapter, for details.)

Where's My Network?

If your wireless network doesn't appear in the list, ensure that it's active (by checking your router or modem's lights) and that you're reasonably close to it. Tap Scan to refresh the list of nearby networks.

---

5. Read the End User License Agreement (EULA), and tap the I Understand... box.

6. Read the Consent to Provide Diagnostic and Usage Data information, select Yes or No Thanks, and tap Next.

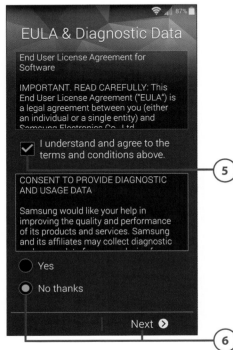

7. A Google/Gmail account is essential for accessing a variety of Android services and apps with the S5. Do one of the following:

- If you already have a Google/ Gmail account and you'd like to register now, tap Yes and enter your account information (see "Gmail and Your Phone," later in this chapter, for instructions).

- If you'd like to create an account or would rather register an existing account later, tap No. Then tap Get an Account (see "Create a Gmail Account," later in this chapter, for instructions) or Not Now, respectively.

8. Set Google location preferences by tapping check boxes. Tap Next.

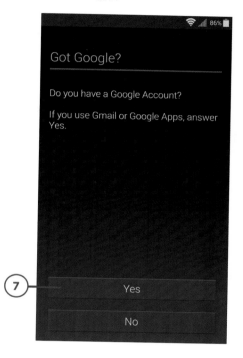

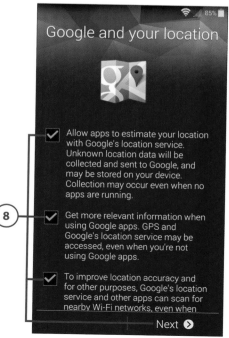

9. Personalize your phone by entering your name. Continue by tapping the right arrow icon at the bottom of the screen.

10. Certain Samsung apps require a free Samsung account. Do one of the following:

    • Tap Sign In if you already have a Samsung account that you'd like to register now. Enter the email address that you associated with the account and your Samsung password.

    • Tap Create Account if you'd like to create a Samsung account (see "Creating a Samsung Account," later in this chapter, for additional details).

    • Tap Skip to ignore this option.

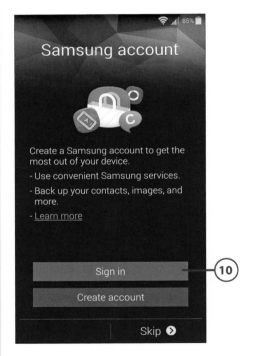

11. Some carriers offer a 50GB Dropbox account—free to Galaxy S5 users for the first two years. You can use the remote Dropbox servers to store your videos, photos, and other files, and access and share them among your devices and with others over the Internet. Do one of the following:

   - Tap Sign In if you already have a Dropbox account. Enter the email address that you associated with the account and your Dropbox password, and tap Sign In.

   - Tap Create Account to create a Dropbox account (see "Creating a Dropbox Account," later in this chapter, for additional details).

   - Tap Skip to ignore this option.

12. *Optional*: Edit the name that will be used to identify the phone.

13. *Optional*: If you're new to Android phones, you might want to enable Easy mode to present a simpler inter-face for your S5 (see "Set the Home Screen Mode" in Chapter 2). Note, however, that instructions presented in this book assume that you're using Standard mode rather than Easy mode.

Easy Versus Standard Mode

When you're ready to experience the Android operating system and TouchWiz interface in its full glory, you can restore Standard mode by tapping Apps, Settings, Easy Mode.

14. Tap Finish to dismiss the wizard. Depending on your carrier, addi-tional options and dialog boxes may appear as the wizard configures your phone for initial use.

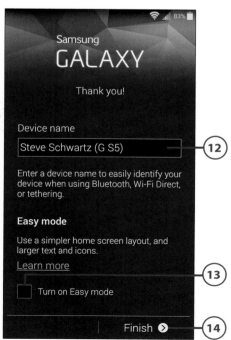

>>>*Go Further*

SAMSUNG SMART SWITCH

If the S5 isn't your first cell phone, you may be able to ease the transition from your old phone by visiting www.samsungsmartswitch.com and downloading the free content-transfer program. In addition to various iPhones and Samsung Galaxy devices, support is provided for transferring data from an LG, HTC, Sony, BlackBerry, or Huawei phone to your new Galaxy S5. (Click the FAQs link for the current list of supported phones and devices.)

When you run Smart Switch, selected content is backed up from the old phone to your computer and then transferred to the S5. If you're an iPhone user, Smart Switch can even transfer your iTunes music, videos, and podcasts, as well as recommend Android apps that are similar to the iOS apps installed on your iPhone.

Darkening and Restoring the Display

Depending on your screen timeout setting, the display automatically turns off during periods of inactivity. In addition to waiting for this timeout to occur, you can manually darken the display to conserve the battery or maintain privacy by pressing the Power button on the right side of the phone.

Restore a Dark Display

1. Press the Power button on the right side of the phone to make the lock screen appear. (The lock screen also appears when you turn on the phone.)

Dimmed, Not Dark

The display momentarily dims for a brief period before it turns black. To restore a dimmed display, tap any blank spot on the touchscreen.

2. Swipe in any direction to dismiss the lock screen.

Working with a Locked Phone

You can secure the phone by other methods, such as assigning a password, to require more than a simple swipe to dismiss the lock screen. See "Securing the Lock Screen" in Chapter 18, "Securing the Phone," for instructions.

Lock screen

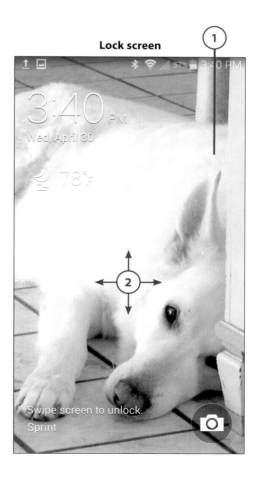

Set the Screen Timeout Interval

1. On the Home screen, tap Apps, followed by Settings.

2. In the Sound and Display section of Settings, tap the Display icon.

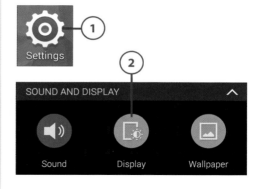

3. Tap Screen Timeout.

4. In the Screen Timeout dialog box, select a new timeout interval or tap the Cancel button to retain the current setting.

③ **Smart Stay enabled**

Smart stay
Screen stays on as long as you are looking at it. ☑

Screen timeout
30 seconds

It's All About Trade-Offs

Substantial juice is needed to power the phone's gorgeous display, so the sooner it dims during idle periods, the longer the current charge will last. The key is to select a screen timeout that enables the phone to sit idle as long as possible before dimming and still have sufficient charge to meet your daily calling and app requirements.

To avoid timeouts when you're reading or viewing material onscreen, enable the Smart Stay setting. (In Settings, tap Display and ensure that Smart Stay is checked.) If the front-facing camera detects that you're looking at the screen, it prevents the normal timeout from occurring. Smart Stay works best when you hold the phone upright, the lighting is adequate, and you aren't wearing glasses (which can make it more difficult for the camera to detect that you're looking at the phone).

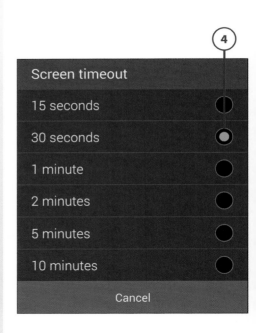

④

Screen timeout

15 seconds

30 seconds

1 minute

2 minutes

5 minutes

10 minutes

Cancel

Adjusting the Volume

You can press the volume control on the left side of the phone to adjust voice volume during a call, media playback volume, or ringer volume (when you're neither playing media nor participating in a call). The volume control is context-sensitive instead of being a general volume control; what is affected when you press the control depends on what you're doing.

1. To change the volume, press the volume control on the left side of the phone. A context-sensitive control appears.

2. To raise or lower the volume, drag the slider. You can also press the top part of the hardware volume control to raise the volume or press the bottom part to lower the volume.

3. *Optional*: To adjust other common volume settings, tap the Settings icon and drag the sliders that appear.

Same Settings, Different Presentation

You can also open Settings to adjust the various volumes. From the Home screen, tap Apps, Settings, Sound, and Volume. Adjust the volume sliders by dragging and tap OK.

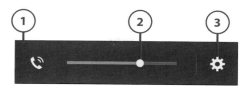

Volume settings

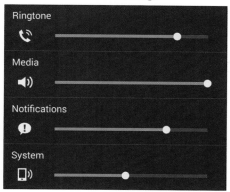

Volume dialog box

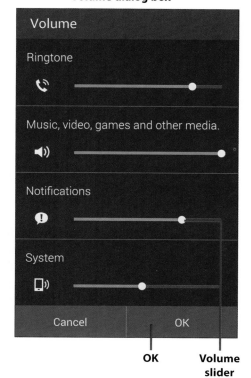

OK   Volume slider

Using a Headset or Headphones

By connecting the headset that's included with the Galaxy S5 (or any other compatible 3.5mm wired headset or headphones), you can improve the phone's audio quality. For example, the Music app supports 5.1 channel sound when a headset is connected. And a wired or a wireless (Bluetooth) headset is great for making hands-free calls.

Wired Headset or Headphones

1. Plug any compatible headset or headphones into the jack at the top of the phone.

2. Adjust the volume for whatever you're currently doing (taking a call, playing media, and so on) using the phone's or the headset's volume control. For instructions on the former, see "Adjusting the Volume," earlier in this chapter.

Bluetooth Headset

Although a few Bluetooth headsets support stereo (making them suitable for listening to music), most are mono devices intended primarily for hands-free phone calls. With a maximum range of 30 feet, using a Bluetooth headset enables you to place the phone nearby and conduct a conversation. Unlike using a speakerphone, the audio is routed directly to your ear and the headset's microphone won't pick up as much ambient noise.

Working with a Bluetooth headset involves two steps: pairing the headset and phone (a one-time procedure) and using the headset for calls. The procedures for pairing and answering calls are specific to your headset and are explained in the headset's instructions. As an example, the following tasks illustrate how to use a Jabra EasyGo Bluetooth headset with the Galaxy S5.

Pair the Headset with the Phone

1. On the Home screen, tap Apps, followed by Settings.

2. Tap Bluetooth in the Network Connections section of Settings.

3. Enable Bluetooth by dragging the slider to the On position.

4. Make the phone visible to the headset by ensuring that the check box is selected. Turn the Bluetooth headset on.

Check Your Headset's Manual

Your Bluetooth headset may require more than simply turning it on to enter pairing mode. The Jabra EasyGo, for example, can be paired with two devices. You must hold down the Answer button for 5 seconds to initiate the second pairing. Similarly, if your headset is already paired with one or more phones, it may be necessary to manually release the pairings to initiate this new pairing.

---

5. *Optional*: Tap the Scan button if the headset doesn't appear in the Available Devices list.

6. Tap the headset's name in the Available Devices list to pair it with the phone.

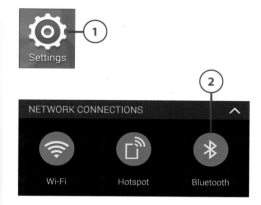

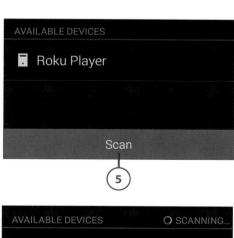

7. A confirmation appears when pairing is successful.

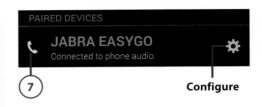

Configure

Future Headset Sessions

When you later use your headset for making and receiving calls, the Bluetooth Settings screen will list the headset as a paired device. You can tap the settings icon to the right of the headset's name to configure or unpair it from your S5.

Use the Headset for Calls

1. Turn on the headset and place it in your ear. If Bluetooth isn't currently enabled, open the Notification panel by dragging the status bar downward. In the Quick Setting buttons, tap the Bluetooth icon to enable it.

When the Headset Won't Connect

If a previously paired Bluetooth headset refuses to connect to the phone, open the Notification panel, and then disable and re-enable Bluetooth.

2. To place a call, dial using any of the methods supported by the phone (see "Placing Calls" in Chapter 4, "Placing and Receiving Calls").

3. To receive an incoming call, tap the headset's Answer/End button or drag the green Accept Call icon to the right.

Adjusting the Volume

While on a call, you can adjust the volume by pressing the volume control on the left side of the phone or on the headset.

4. Tap the headset's Answer/End button or tap the End Call icon on the phone when you're done with the call.

Bluetooth enabled

>>>Go Further

IN-CALL OPTIONS

During a call, you can freely disable or enable the headset by tapping the Bluetooth icon. In addition, your headset may support a variety of in-call options. For example, you can also use the Jabra EasyGo to reject incoming calls, redial the last number, mute the microphone, and place the current call on hold to switch between two conversations (if you have call waiting). Refer to your headset manual for instructions.

Setting Up Voicemail

After your phone is activated, one of the first things you should do is set up voicemail. Doing so identifies the phone number as yours and ensures that callers have an opportunity to leave a message when you're unavailable.

Carriers Differ

Note that the exact process of setting up and using voicemail is specific to each provider. They may even include their own app that you can use to review and manage your voicemail. See "Checking Voicemail" in Chapter 4 for instructions on accessing voicemail and changing your settings.

1. On any Home screen page, tap the Phone icon.

2. On the Phone keypad, press and hold 1 (the speed dial number reserved for voicemail) or tap the Voicemail icon.

3. When prompted, record your name, enter a password, and select or record a greeting. When you finish reviewing voicemail options, tap the End Call icon.

Gmail and Your Phone

Your phone runs on Android, the Google operating system. To use and connect to any Google service (such as Google Play, a source for Android apps that run on your phone), you must have a Google (Gmail) account. Gmail is Google's free email service. If you don't have an account, you should create one now. The final step is letting your phone know your Gmail account username and password, enabling it to access Google services.

Do It the Easy Way

Although you can create a Gmail account using your phone, a lot of typing is required. It's easier to use your computer's web browser (as described next). On the other hand, if you don't have access to a computer or would prefer to create the account using your phone, open Settings and tap Accounts, Add Account, Google, New. You can have more than one Google account, if you like.

Create a Gmail Account

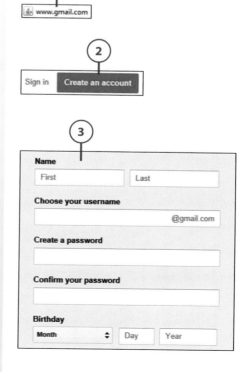

1. On your PC or Mac, launch your web browser: Internet Explorer, Safari, Firefox, or Chrome, for example. Type www.gmail.com in the address box and press Enter/Return.

2. Click the Create an Account button in the page's upper-right corner.

3. Enter the requested registration information on the Create a New Google Account page.

>>>*Go Further*

ACCOUNT-CREATION TIPS

The most common, desirable Gmail usernames are taken. To get one based on your name or your company's name, try adding numbers at the end (sschwartz972), separate words with periods (steve.schwartz), or combine two or more unusual words (hamstringwarrior). Your username can be any combination of letters, numbers, and periods.

Your password must contain at least eight characters and can be any combination of uppercase letters, lowercase letters, and numbers. The Password Strength rating indicates how secure your proposed password is.

If possible, resist the temptation to use your Internet service provider (ISP) account password for Gmail, too. If you use one password everywhere on the Internet and someone learns it, all your accounts could be compromised. The most secure passwords combine uppercase letters, lowercase letters, and numbers (such as hA73rTv91).

Register Your Gmail Account

If you just created a Gmail account using your computer's browser, you need to add the account to your phone.

Once Will Suffice

To see if the account is already registered, open Settings and tap Accounts. If Google is listed in the My Accounts section, the account is registered, and you can skip the following task.

Registered Google (Gmail) account ——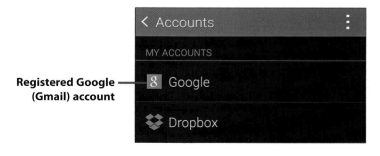

1. Open Settings, and then tap Accounts.

2. Tap Add Account at the bottom of the Accounts list.

3. Tap Google.

4. On the Add a Google Account screen, tap Existing. (If you don't have a Google/Gmail account, tap New and follow the onscreen prompts, or perform the steps in the "Create a Gmail Account" task.)

USER AND BACKUP

Accounts   Cloud   Backup and reset

S Health account

+ Add account

< Add account

S Samsung account

❖ Dropbox

@ Email

8 Google

Existing

New

5. Enter your Gmail username and password. Tap the right-arrow icon to continue.

6. Tap OK to agree to the terms of service. An attempt is made to sign into the account.

7. Decide whether you want to receive news and offers from Google Play. Tap the right-arrow icon to continue.

By signing in, you are agreeing to the Google Terms of Service and Privacy Policy, Chrome Terms of Service and Privacy Notice, and Google Play Terms of Service.

Cancel | OK

8. Enter payment information for purchases that you may later make in Goggle Play, or tap Not Now to skip this step. The phone attempts to sign into your new account.

9. On the Account Sign-In Successful screen, the check boxes determine the types of important phone data that will be regularly synced with your Gmail account. Ensure that each box is checked or unchecked according to your preference, and then tap the right-arrow icon. An account sync is automatically attempted.

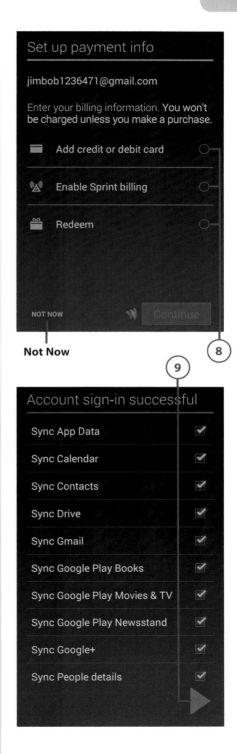

Not Now

Not Now

Set up payment info

jimbob1236471@gmail.com

Enter your billing information. **You won't be charged unless you make a purchase.**

📇 Add credit or debit card

📶 Enable Sprint billing

🎁 Redeem

NOT NOW   Continue

Account sign-in successful

Sync App Data   ✔
Sync Calendar   ✔
Sync Contacts   ✔
Sync Drive   ✔
Sync Gmail   ✔
Sync Google Play Books   ✔
Sync Google Play Movies & TV   ✔
Sync Google Play Newsstand   ✔
Sync Google+   ✔
Sync People details   ✔

Creating a Samsung Account

Certain Samsung applications that are supported on the Galaxy S5 require you to sign up for a free Samsung account. Having a Samsung account also enables you to easily back up some types of data, such as your phone logs and messages. If you didn't create the account or log into an existing one when you ran the setup wizard, you can create the account now—or the first time you use an application that requires an account.

1. Open Settings, and then tap Accounts.

2. Tap Add Account at the bottom of the Accounts list.

3. Tap Samsung Account. (If the account's status dot is green, you've already added a Samsung account to this phone and can skip the remaining steps.)

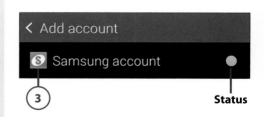

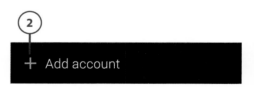

4. Tap Create Account.

5. Create the account by entering an email address and password to use for the account, as well as the other requested information. Tap the Sign Up button.

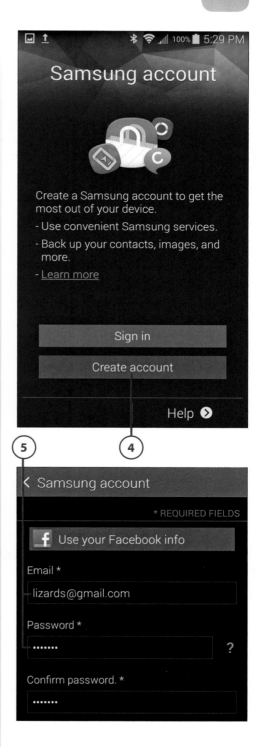

6. Review the Terms and Conditions, Special Terms, Privacy Policy, and Data Combination information by tapping each entry. Tap the check boxes, and then tap the Agree button.

7. Open the account verification email message on your phone or computer and follow the account activation instructions. When you finish, the Samsung account is marked with a green dot on the Add Account screen, indicating that it's recorded on your phone.

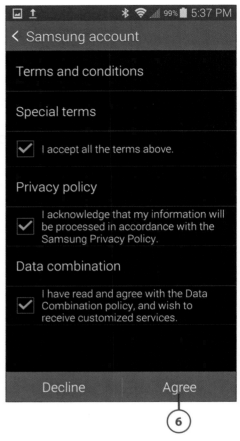

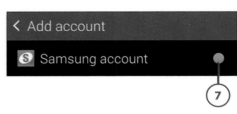

Creating a Dropbox Account

With Dropbox installed on your phone, tablet, and computers, you can use cloud storage to share your videos, photos, and other files among your devices and with other users. Normally, a free Dropbox account provides 2GB of online storage. If your carrier is one of those participating in the Galaxy S5 promotion, you're eligible for an upgrade to 50GB—free for the first two years.

Getting the App and Desktop Versions

If the Dropbox app isn't preinstalled on your S5, you can download it from Google Play. You can get versions for PCs, Macs, tablets, and other devices from the Dropbox website at www.dropbox.com. Instructions and tutorials for using Dropbox are there, too.

1. To create a free Dropbox account, do either of the following:

   - From any Home screen, tap Apps and then Dropbox.

   - Perform Steps 1 and 2 of "Creating a Samsung Account," and then tap Dropbox.

   The Dropbox Welcome screen appears.

2. Swipe repeatedly until you reach the last page. Tap Sign Up. (If you already have an account, tap Sign In and provide your log-in information.)

Welcome!

Swipe to learn about Dropbox

Already have an account? Sign in!

Your stuff, anywhere

Sign Up

Already have an account? Sign in!

Sign In

3. Enter your first and last name, an email address with which to associate the account, and a password for the Dropbox account. Tap Create Account.

4. Review the Terms of Service, and tap I Agree.

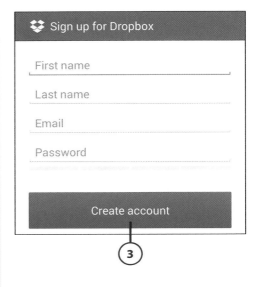

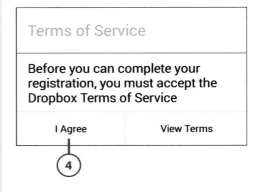

5. To instruct Dropbox to automatically back up photos and videos that you take with the phone, tap Turn On Camera Upload; otherwise, tap Skip This. (You can enable this feature within the Dropbox app whenever you like.)

6. The Dropbox account is marked with a green dot on the Add Account screen, indicating that it's recorded on your phone.

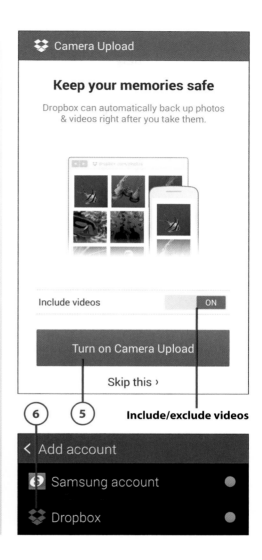

Include/exclude videos

Working with Data

Any activity that transmits data to and from your phone over the cellular network counts toward your plan's data limit. The same data transmitted over Wi-Fi, on the other hand, doesn't count. By tapping icons in the Notification panel, you can manually control the method by which data transmissions occur, ensuring that the least expensive and fastest method is used. In this section, you learn how to enable and disable Wi-Fi, as well as how to connect your phone to a wireless (Wi-Fi) network.

Connection Methods

At any given time, only Wi-Fi or 2G/3G/4G can be the active data connection method. When Wi-Fi is enabled and you're connected to a network, 2G/3G/4G is automatically disabled. When Wi-Fi is disabled or unavailable and you perform a data-related activity, 2G, 3G, or 4G is automatically used, depending on what's available at your current location. (Note that there's an exception to the Wi-Fi or cellular connection rule. if your carrier is one of the few that supports the Download Booster feature, Wi-Fi and a cellular connection can be *simultaneously* active, enabling you to improve download speeds for files larger than 30 MB.)

You can also use Bluetooth to exchange data directly between the phone and any Bluetooth-capable computer or laptop. For instructions on using Bluetooth for data transfers, see Chapter 16.

Manually Set a Connection Method

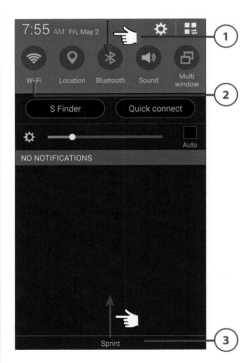

1. Open the Notification panel by touching the status bar at the top of the screen and dragging downward.

2. The Wi-Fi icon toggles between a Wi-Fi and cellular (2G/3G/4G) data connection. Wi-Fi is enabled when the icon is green; a cellular connection is active when the Wi-Fi icon is dim. Tap the Wi-Fi icon to toggle its state.

3. Close the Notification panel by touching the bottom of the panel and dragging upward.

Which Wi-Fi Network?

In Settings, Wi-Fi shows the Wi-Fi network to which you're connected, as well as other available networks. Open Settings and tap Wi-Fi, or press and hold the Wi-Fi icon in the Quick Setting buttons. You can tap any network name to view its speed and signal strength.

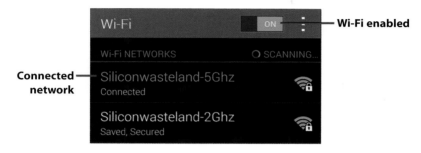

Wi-Fi enabled

Connected network

Monitoring Data Usage

If your data plan isn't unlimited, you can use the Data Usage setting to monitor your usage and warn when you're close to the limit. See "Managing Talk Time and Data Usage" in Chapter 20 for details.

Connect to a New Wireless Network

Because it's free and often a faster connection than using a 2G, 3G, or 4G cellular connection, it's advantageous to use a Wi-Fi connection whenever it's available. After you successfully connect to a given network (such as your home network or one at a local coffee shop), your phone can reconnect without requesting the password again.

1. To go directly to the Wi-Fi screen, open the Notification panel, and then press and hold the Wi-Fi icon in the Quick Setting buttons. (Alternatively, you can open Settings and tap the Wi-Fi icon.)

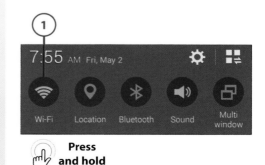

Press and hold

2. Ensure that Wi-Fi is enabled by dragging its slider to the On position.

3. A list of nearby networks appears. If a network to which you've previously connected is found, the phone automatically connects to it. If no network is automatically chosen or you want to connect to a different network, tap the name of the network to which you want to connect and continue with Step 4.

4. Do one of the following:

   • If the network is unsecured (open), tap the Connect button. No password is required to connect.

   • If the network is secured (password protected), enter the requested password, and then tap the Connect button.

Show Password

When entering a lengthy or complex password, you may find it helpful to tap the Show Password check box. Otherwise, each character in the password is only momentarily visible as you type it.

5. If successful, the Settings screen shows that you're connected to the network.

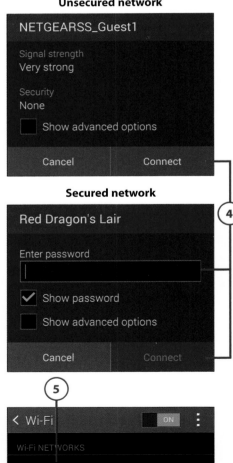

Unsecured network

Secured network

>>>*Go Further*

WI-FI NETWORK TIPS

If you have occasion to connect to more than one Wi-Fi network, here are a couple of tips you may find helpful:

- To forget a network to which you've previously connected, press and hold the network name in the Wi-Fi Networks list, and then tap Forget Network.

Forget this network ———

- To view information about the network to which you're connected, tap its name in the Wi-Fi Networks list. If there are multiple unsecured networks within range, you can connect to each one and compare their signal strength and speed.

Network properties

Changing the Default Language

If English isn't your native language, you can change the phone's default language to another supported language.

1. On the Home screen, tap Apps, followed by Settings.

2. In the System section, tap the Language and Input icon.

3. Tap Language.

4. Tap the desired language. Icon names, display text, prompts, dialog boxes, and other text change to reflect the selected language.

Change the Input Language

Options for the default language are limited. Although it won't affect system text, such as prompts and dialog boxes, you can still change the *input language* (text that you type or speak) to your native tongue. See the "Typing Tips" sidebar in Chapter 2 for more information.

Current default language

Wireless Printing

If you own or have access to a wireless printer, you can print from any app
that provides a Print command, such as Gallery and Internet. Prior to printing, you must install print service software for your printer. You'll also need
to know the IP (Internet protocol) address of the printer on the wireless network. See the printer manual for this information. (If you know your router's
IP address, you can turn on the printer, enter the router's IP address in your
browser, and discern the printer's IP address.)

Install the Print Services Software (First Time Only)

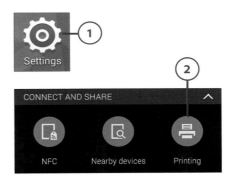

1. On the Home screen, tap Apps,
   followed by Settings.

2. In the Connect and Share section,
   tap Printing.

3. If a print service plug-in isn't listed
   for your printer, tap the plus (+)
   button. Play Store launches.

4. In the list that appears, locate a print service app from your printer's manufacturer. Tap to select the software.

5. Review its description, ensure that your printer model is supported, and tap Install.

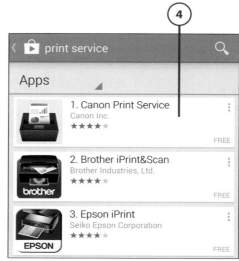

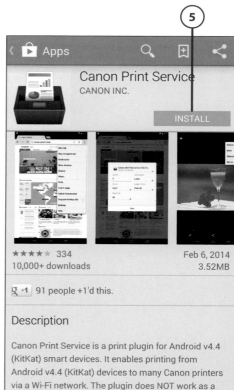

6. When installation finishes, press the Back key repeatedly until the Printing screen reappears. The new print service software is added to the list. Tap its name to enable and configure it.

7. When you print from an app, select your wireless printer from the Available list.

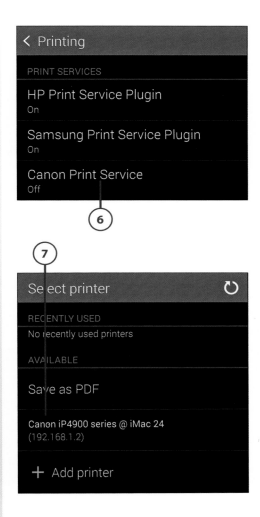

Recorded text

Voice input
language

Recording
indicator

In this chapter, you become familiar with the Samsung Galaxy S5 interface and how to interact with it. Topics include the following:

→ Understanding the Home screen and its components
→ Using the three hardware keys below the touchscreen
→ Working with the Notification panel
→ Tapping and interacting with touchscreen elements
→ Using the onscreen keyboard and voice input to enter and edit text
→ Searching for material on the phone and on the Web

2

Understanding the Android/TouchWiz Interface

The Galaxy S5 has a touch-sensitive screen (or *touchscreen*) that can detect location, pressure, and motion on its surface. The Android operating system and Samsung's TouchWiz modifications to it determine how the phone and its applications react to various touches. Even if you've previously owned an Android phone or another touch-sensitive device, such as an iPod touch or a tablet, you need to be familiar with the information in this chapter. Read on for the essential methods of interacting with the touchscreen and the hardware keys below the screen, techniques for entering and editing text, and methods of conducting searches for material on the phone and the Web.

The Home Screen

The Home screen is Command Central for your phone. You launch *apps* (applications) from this screen, view the latest information presented on widgets (such as the local weather from AccuWeather.com), and initiate phone calls and messaging sessions.

The important parts of the Home screen include the status or Notification bar, the main area (equivalent to a PC or Mac desktop), Home screen indicator, and icons for five primary shortcuts.

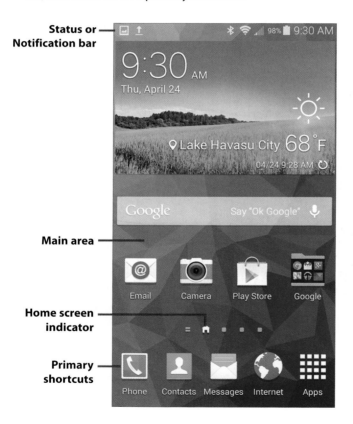

Status or Notification bar

Main area

Home screen indicator

Primary shortcuts

The Status or Notification Bar

The status or Notification bar at the top of the screen serves two functions. First, icons on the right side of the bar show the active communication features (such as Wi-Fi, 4G, Bluetooth, and GPS) and display status information (such as the current battery charge and Wi-Fi signal strength). Second, the left side of the bar displays notification icons for important events, such as new email, new text messages, missed calls, and downloaded or uploaded items.

Although it might be tempting to do so, you can't interact with the bar; tapping its icons does nothing. To change the active features or respond to notifications, you use the Notification panel (described in "The Notification Panel," later in this chapter).

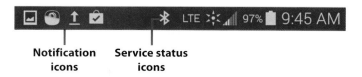

**Notification   Service status
icons   icons**

Main Area

The Home screen is yours to embellish as you like. As you can see, you can place widgets and shortcuts wherever you want, as well as choose a custom background (*wallpaper*) for it, as explained in Chapter 3, "Making the Phone Your Own."

Extended Home Screen

The Home screen can consist of up to seven different screens or pages, each represented by a Home screen indicator—plus an indicator for My Magazine, a personalized magazine of web content and social networking feeds. As with the main Home screen page, you can add different widgets and shortcuts to each page. To move from one page to another, do any of the following:

- Press the Home key to go directly to the main Home screen page (marked by the house icon).

- Tap the Home screen indicator of the page that you want to view.

- Swipe left or right to flip to the desired page.

- Drag a Home screen indicator to the left or right to see a visual and numeric representation of each Home screen page.

Dragging an indicator

Home screen page indicator

- To view My Magazine, tap the equal sign (=) Home screen indicator or continue swiping to the left past all Home screen pages.

As explained in Chapter 3, you can rearrange the Home screen pages, add new ones (up to the maximum of seven), and delete unwanted ones.

Other Screen Indicators

The indicator dots in Apps and Widgets work in the same manner as they do on the Home screen pages. Each dot represents a screen or page of icons. The lit dot indicates the screen or page that you're viewing.

>>>*Go Further*

EASY MODE

To make it easier for new smartphone (or Android smartphone) users to become comfortable with their Galaxy S5, the Home screen can be changed from Standard mode (which is the focus of this book) to the simpler Easy mode. Easy mode provides:

- Three simple Home screen layouts with larger icons and text
- Large, easy-to-read text in important apps, such as Contacts, Calendar, and Phone
- Fixed shortcuts to 12 essential apps and the option to add 3 more of your choosing
- Three fixed widgets (time, date, and temperature)
- Access to additional apps as a scrolling alphabetical list

Main Home screen (Easy mode)

Set the Home Screen Mode

You can switch between Standard and Easy mode whenever you like. Customizations that you've made to the Home screen pages in either mode are restored when you return to that mode.

1. On the Home screen, tap Apps, followed by Settings. (Or use one of the other methods for opening Settings described in "Changing System Settings" in Chapter 1, "Galaxy S5 Essentials.")

2. In the Personalization section of Settings, tap Easy Mode.

3. Select Easy Mode, select up to 12 important apps that you want to display as Home screen shortcuts, and tap Done.

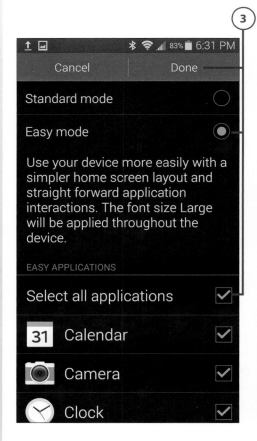

4. On the first Home screen page, you can add contact icons for people that you frequently call or text. Tap a placeholder, and select a person from Contacts or create a new record from scratch. To later call or text the person, tap his or her icon.

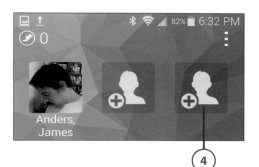

Adding an app

5. To add or edit your Home screen app shortcuts, do either of the following:

• *Adding app shortcuts.* You can add app shortcuts to the second or third Home screen page—as long as there are empty spots marked with plus (+) placeholders. Tap a placeholder and select an app from the list of all installed apps.

Removing an app

• *Removing app shortcuts.* Display the Home screen page from which you want to remove one or more app shortcuts, tap the menu icon, and choose Edit. To remove an app shortcut, tap its icon. (App shortcuts that can be removed are marked with a minus (–) symbol.)

Restoring Standard Mode

If you later decide that you're ready to try Standard mode, tap the Easy Settings icon (or open Settings by another means). Tap the Easy Mode icon, select Standard Mode, and tap Done.

>>>*Go Further*

KIDS MODE

In addition to Standard and Easy modes, the S5 has yet another mode. When you want to entrust your $650 smartphone to a young child or grandchild, you can enable Kids Mode. To install Kids Mode, add the Kids Mode widget to any Home screen page (see "Add Widgets" in Chapter 3), tap the widget, and follow the instructions. To later enable Kids Mode or exit from it, you must enter a PIN.

Primary and Other App Shortcuts

Beneath the indicator dots on every Home screen page are icons for Phone, Contacts, Messages, Internet (or Chrome), and Apps. These are known as the *primary shortcuts*. With the exception of the Apps shortcut, you can remove, reorder, or replace the first four. If, for example, you seldom use Messages, you can replace its shortcut with one for Email, Settings, or another app that you constantly use, such as Angry Birds or Facebook. See "Reposition and Remove Home Screen Items" in Chapter 3 for instructions.

Depending on your carrier, you may see additional app shortcuts above the indicator dots on some Home screen pages. Like the primary shortcuts—as well as other shortcuts that you add to any Home screen page—you can freely remove, reorder, or replace these shortcuts.

Primary shortcuts

Using the Hardware Keys

There are three ever-present hardware keys located directly below the touch-screen: Recent Apps, Home, and Back. When pressed, each key performs a function related to the operating system (when you're viewing the Home screen) or the app you're currently using.

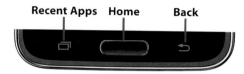

Recent Apps   Home   Back

Recent Apps Key

When you press the Recent Apps key, a list of recently run and active apps appears. Tap any app thumbnail to launch or switch to that app. To remove an app from the list, swipe it horizontally off-screen. To remove all items from the list, tap the Clear All icon. Tap the Task Manager icon if you want to force stop one or more running apps (see the "About Force Stop" sidebar in Chapter 20, "Optimizing and Troubleshooting," for more information).

Recent Apps

Task Manager   Clear All

The Missing Menu Key

In previous iterations of the Galaxy S, the first hardware key was the Menu key. To display an app or Home screen's menu on the S5 (if there is one), tap the three stacked dots—frequently found in the upper-right corner of the screen. This is the universal icon denoting an Android menu. (Note that you can also use the Recent Apps key to open certain menus by pressing and holding the key.)

Home Key

The Home key has multiple functions, depending on whether you're on the Home screen or using an app. You can also use it in combination with the Power button to take screen shots (as described shortly).

Within an app. Press the Home key to exit the app and return to the most recently viewed Home screen page.

On the Home screen. When you press the Home key while viewing any Home screen page, it displays the main Home screen page—the one marked with the house icon. If you quickly double-press the Home key, S Voice is activated (see Chapter 15, "Using Voice Services," for information about using S Voice). Finally, with some carriers, pressing and holding the Home key launches a Google app, such as Google Now.

Within an app or on the Home screen. If you simultaneously press and hold the Home key and Power button, the phone performs a screen capture, creating a graphic image of the screen. All captures are saved in the Screenshots folder and can be viewed in Gallery. You can also perform a screen capture by dragging the side of your hand across the screen.

Screenshots folder

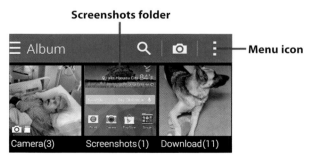

Menu icon

Back Key

You use the Back key within apps to return to the previous screen or—if on the app's initial screen—to exit to the Home screen.

Within an app. Press the Back key to return to the previous screen. If you press it on the app's initial screen, you exit the app and return to the most recently viewed Home screen page.

Within Internet and Chrome. Press Back to display the previous web page. The Back key has the same function as pressing Backspace (Windows) or Delete (Mac) when using a web browser.

Within a dialog box or an options menu. Similar to pressing the Escape key in many computer programs, you can press Back to exit a dialog box or options menu without making a choice.

When typing. Press Back to dismiss the onscreen keyboard.

Within the Notification panel. Press Back to close the panel.

The Notification Panel

When new notifications appear in the Notification bar announcing received email, text messages, software updates, and the like, you can display the Notification panel and optionally respond to or clear the notifications.

1. Open the Notification panel on the Home screen or within most apps by touching the status bar and dragging downward.

2. Tap a notification to respond to or interact with it. For example, tapping a New Email notification launches Email and displays the Inbox. When you respond to a notification, it's removed from the Notification panel.

3. To remove a notification without responding to it, drag it off the screen to the left or right. To simultaneously remove all notifications, tap the Clear button.

4. To close the Notification panel, touch the gray bar or carrier designation at the bottom of the screen and drag upward. Pressing the Back key also closes the panel.

>>>*Go Further*

QUICK SETTING BUTTONS

At the top of the Notification panel is a horizontally scrolling string of icons called *Quick Setting buttons*. By tapping these icons, you can quickly enable or disable system features, such as Bluetooth, GPS, or Wi-Fi. When a feature is enabled, its icon is bright green. Swipe left or right to scroll through the icons until you find the one you need, and then tap the icon to toggle the feature's state. If you need to configure a feature (connecting to a new Wi-Fi network, for example), press and hold its Quick Setting button to open its section in Settings. To display all the icons as an array, tap the grid icon. To customize the icons and their order, see "Customize the Quick Setting Buttons" in Chapter 3.

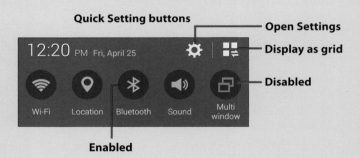

Interacting with the Touchscreen

Your phone has a touch-sensitive screen that you interact with by tapping, touching, and making other motions with your fingers or hand. In addition, within many apps, the phone can optionally recognize and respond to the angle at which it's being held or its proximity to nearby objects.

Using Your Fingers

You can interact with the touchscreen by doing any of the following:

- *Tap.* To launch an app, open a
  document, choose a menu command, select an item in a list,
  activate a button, or type characters on the onscreen keyboard,
  tap the item lightly with your
  fingertip. (A tap is equivalent to a
  mouse click on a computer.)

- *Touch and hold, press and hold,
  or long-press.* You can interact
  with some items by touching and
  holding them. The result depends
  on the particular item or active
  app. For example, you can use
  touch and hold to move or delete
  a Home screen item, select a word
  in a text message that you're composing, or select an item in a list.
  Long-pressing a few items, such
  as a link on a web page, causes a
  contextual menu to appear.

- *Flick.* Scroll up or down through
  a lengthy menu, a vertical list
  of items (such as a message list
  in Email), or a long web page
  by making light, quick vertical
  strokes.

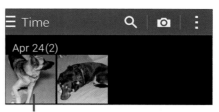

Tap a thumbnail to view a photo (Gallery)

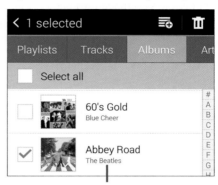

**Touch and hold an album in
Music to select the album**

**Flick
up or
down**

- *Swipe.* A swipe is the horizontal equivalent of a flick. Swipe to flip through images in a Gallery folder, view different Home screen pages, or move through the Apps and Widgets screen pages.

- *Drag.* To move an item (such as a widget or app icon on the Home screen), press and hold the item, and then drag. Don't release it until it's in the desired position— on the current screen page or a different one.

- *Spread/pinch.* To zoom in or out (increasing or decreasing the magnification) when viewing a photo or web page, place two fingers on the screen and spread them apart or pinch them together, respectively.

Try a Double-Tap

In certain apps (Gallery, Internet, and Chrome, for example), you can also double-tap the screen to zoom in or out. Spreading and pinching, however, provides more precise control over the amount of magnification.

Current image

Swipe left or right (Gallery)

Drag a Home screen item to change its position

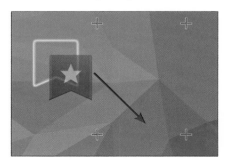

It's Not All Good

Inconsistent Touch and Hold Behavior

On previous phones in the Galaxy S line, long-pressing an item in a list, such as a song in Music, a photo in Gallery, an email message, or a record in Contacts, almost always resulted in the appearance of a contextual menu—similar to right-clicking an item on a PC or Mac. In most—*but not all*—S5 core apps, touching and holding (also known as long-pressing) the same item types now causes the pressed item to be selected, enabling you to select additional items within the list so you can simultaneously move or delete them all, for instance. Long-pressing is now a shortcut to choosing the Select command from the app's menu, while marking the pressed item as your first selection.

In addition to causing you to make additional, less convenient taps to perform an action, touch and hold behavior is now inconsistent between apps. Sometimes it results in selecting the item, whereas a contextual menu appears in other apps. You'll have to experiment to see which behavior occurs in which situations.

Rotating the Screen

In many apps, you can rotate the screen to change from portrait to landscape orientation and vice versa. It's extremely useful when viewing photos in Gallery, when reading web pages, and when using the onscreen keyboard, for example.

Portrait   **Landscape**

In order for the S5 to automatically rotate the screen when you rotate the phone, Screen Rotation must be enabled (its default state). To enable or disable Screen Rotation, tap its button in the Quick Setting buttons or in Settings, Display.

>>>*Go Further*
USING MOTIONS AND GESTURES

In addition to tapping, flicking, swiping, and pinching, you can perform certain activities using other actions. For example, when Motions and Gestures Settings are enabled, tilting the phone or waving your hand over it are treated as commands. After mastering the basics of controlling the phone and apps via touch, you should explore motion, air-based, and other options in Settings (see "Motions and Gestures Settings," "Air View," and "One-Handed Operation" in Chapter 3) and decide which ones, if any, you find helpful and want to enable.

Entering Text

In addition to simply viewing and listening to content on your phone, much of what you do involves entering text. You can enter text using the onscreen keyboard or by speaking into the phone.

Using the onscreen keyboard, there are two methods of typing. You're familiar with the first in which you tap letter, number, and punctuation keys as you would on a computer keyboard or typewriter. The second uses software called *Swype*, in which you drag your finger over the keyboard—gliding over the characters needed to spell each word.

Keyboard Variations

Depending on the current app, you may notice some minor differences among the keyboards. For example, the Internet app's keyboard has additional keys in its bottom row that make it easier to type URLs.

Use the Keyboard: Tapping

1. Tap to select a text field or box, such as the Internet address box, a password field, or the message area of a text message. The onscreen keyboard appears. A blinking text insertion mark shows where the next typed character will appear.

2. Tap keys to type.

Entering Non-Alphabetic Characters

Tap the SYM key. The key above it is now labeled 1/2, and the layout displays numbers, currency symbols, and common punctuation. Tap this key (1/2) to cycle to the symbol (2/2) layout. To return to the alphabetic layout, tap the ABC key.

3. To dismiss or hide the keyboard, perform the action necessary to complete your typing (such as tapping Send) or press the Back key. To make the keyboard reappear after pressing Back, tap in the text box or field again.

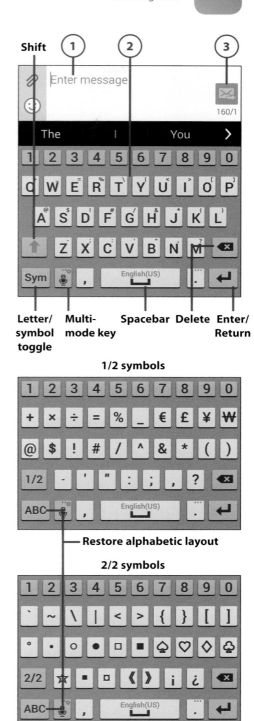

Shift (1) (2) (3)

Letter/symbol toggle Multi-mode key Spacebar Delete Enter/Return

1/2 symbols

Restore alphabetic layout

2/2 symbols

Capitalization

When you begin entering text into a field or are starting a new sentence, the first character is typically capitalized automatically. Subsequent capitalization is determined by the state of the Shift key. Tap the Shift key to toggle it among its three states: lowercase, capitalize next letter only, and capitalize all letters.

Lowercase	**Capitalize** **next letter**	**Uppercase** **(Shift Lock)**

Use the Keyboard: Swype

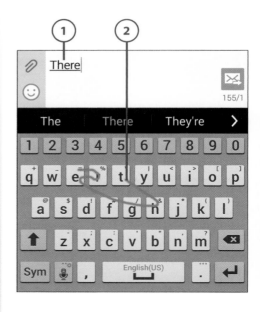

1. Tap to select a text field or box, such as the browser's address box, a password field, or the message area of a text message. The onscreen keyboard appears. A blinking text insertion mark shows where the next entered character will appear.

2. To type each word, drag over its letters—in order. Complete the word by briefly lifting your finger from the screen and then drag over the letters needed to form the next word. A space is auto-matically inserted between each pair of words. Tap punctuation where it's needed.

Duplicate Letters

If a letter is repeated in a word, such as *l* in follow, make a loop over the letter or scribble over it to indicate that it's repeated.

>>>Go Further

TYPING TIPS

Although the basics of typing are straightforward, the following tips can help you fine-tune this sometimes difficult process.

- *Try landscape mode.* To use a larger version of the keyboard, simply rotate the phone to landscape orientation. (For this to work, the phone's auto-rotate feature must be enabled. Open Settings, tap Display, and ensure that Rotate Screen is enabled. Unless you've changed the default Quick Setting buttons, you can enable or disable Rotate Screen there, too.)

Landscape keyboard (Internet)

- *Multiple languages.* When typing in Samsung Keyboard mode, the active language is shown on the spacebar. If you have more than one language enabled, swipe across the spacebar to switch languages.

- *Change the input method.* The phone supports typed or traced text input (Samsung Keyboard and Swype), as well as voice input (Google Voice Typing). To switch input methods while entering text, open the Notification panel, tap Choose Input Method, and select an alternative method in the dialog box that appears.

Why Choose?

When Samsung Keyboard is the input method and the Auto Spacing setting is enabled, you can freely switch between typing and Swype—even within the same sentence.

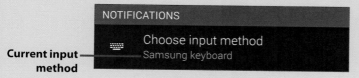

Current input method

- *Explore the Language and Input settings.* By tapping the settings icons in Language and Input settings, you can configure each of the three input methods. In the Samsung Keyboard settings, for instance, you can specify whether to display predictive text and enable the insertion of boilerplate text (My Shortcuts) when you long-press an assigned number key. By tapping Default, you can change the default input method. You can view onscreen help for typing by tapping the Samsung Keyboard settings icon, opening the menu, and choosing Help. For help using Swype, tap the Swype settings icon, Help, How to Swype.

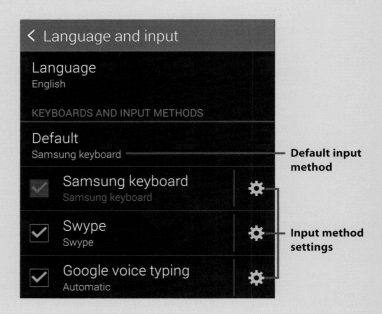

Default input method

Input method settings

- *Change the language.* If English isn't your native or preferred input language, you can select a different one. In the Language and Input settings, tap the Samsung Keyboard settings icon, followed by Select Input Languages. Select a language from the Downloaded Languages list. If the desired language isn't shown, tap the menu icon, choose Update List, and then download the desired language by tapping its name in the Available Languages list.

- *Use Predictive Text.* As you type or trace, the phone presents a scrolling list of suggestions (predictive text) for the word it thinks you're typing. If you see the correct one, tap it to use it as a replacement for the current word.

You can also tap the arrow icon—when it's presented—to view additional replacement words.

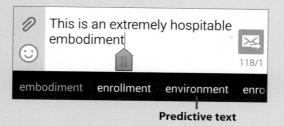

Predictive text

Fine-Tuning Predictive Text

You can improve the predictive text suggestions by allowing your S5 to study what you type in Facebook, Gmail, Twitter, Messages, and Contacts. In settings for the Samsung Keyboard, tap Predictive Text and review the options. If you don't find predictive text helpful, you can disable it by dragging its slider to the Off position.

- *Character preview.* You can type secondary characters (such as the symbols above some letter keys) without leaving the main alphabetic keyboard. If you press and hold any key, its secondary characters, if any, appear. If there's only one secondary character, release the key to insert the character into your text. Pressing and holding other keys results in a pop-up menu of characters, numbers, and/or symbols for the key. Slide your fingertip onto the one that you want to insert or do nothing to insert the currently highlighted character.

Secondary characters for t

Press and hold

- *Other input options.* When entering text, you can switch input methods at any time, using any combination that you find convenient. To change methods, press and hold the multi-mode key and select the new input method. Or just tap the key to switch to the input method that's pictured on the key. Some typical options include voice input, handwriting, inserting material from the Clipboard, normal keyboard, and a floating keyboard that you can reposition by tapping its tab and dragging. (When using the floating keyboard, tap its icon again to revert to the normal keyboard.)

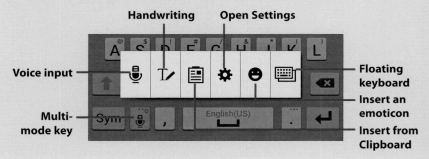

Handwriting   Open Settings

Voice input

Floating keyboard

Insert an emoticon

Multi-mode key

Insert from Clipboard

Use Voice Input

If you're abysmal at using the onscreen keyboard and are unwilling to take the time to master it, voice input (also called *voice typing*) might be more to your liking. You speak or dictate what you want to type, and it's translated into text.

1. To enable voice input, press and hold the multi-mode key and select voice input—the microphone. If the key already displays the microphone, simply tap it.

Switch Using the Notification Panel

As explained earlier in the chapter, you can also switch input methods by opening the Notification panel, tapping Choose Input Method, and selecting Google Voice Typing in the dialog box that appears.

Voice input

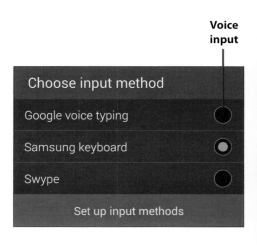

2. A recording indicator appears. Speak the text, saying punctuation (such as comma, period, question mark, and exclamation point) where it's needed. The text is transcribed as you speak.

3. When you finish recording, tap the recording icon and then tap the keyboard icon. (After a sufficiently long pause, recording ends automatically.)

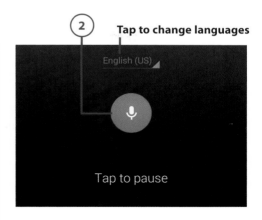

Tap to change languages

Poor Results

If a transcription is unacceptable, you can reject it by tapping Delete.

4. Any instance of questionable transcription is marked with a faint gray underline. If the underlined text is incorrect, tap it to review possible corrections. You can select a replacement from the suggestions, tap Delete to remove the entire word or text phrase, or dismiss the suggestions by pressing the Back key and then manually edit the text.

Getting Better All the Time

Voice input is great for converting straightforward, common speech to text and every update includes improvements. However, the need for some after-the-fact editing isn't unusual. To determine if voice input will work for you, test it. Say some normal text and try reading a few sentences from a book or magazine. Whether it's a winner for you will be determined by how accurate it is and the amount of cleanup you typically need to do.

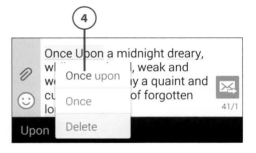

>>>*Go Further*

CHANGE THE VOICE INPUT LANGUAGE

Just as you can configure the keyboard to type in languages other than English (see Chapter 1), you can configure Voice Input in the same manner.

1. Tap the language indicator above the recording icon and select a language. If the desired language isn't shown, go to Step 2.

2. Choose Add More Languages.

3. Remove the check mark from Automatic, select the language(s), and press the Back key to return to Step 1. (If you ever want to revert to the original language for voice input, check Automatic again.)

Editing Text

Typos, incorrect capitalization, missing punctuation, and bad guesses in Swype or voice input are common in entered text. Instead of just tapping Send and hoping your message recipient will *know* what you mean, you can edit the text by doing any of the following:

- At the blinking text insertion mark, you can type or paste new text or press the Delete key to delete the character to the left.

- To reposition the text insertion mark for editing, tap in the text. If the text insertion mark isn't positioned correctly, carefully drag the blue marker to the desired spot.

- To select a single word for deletion or replacement, double-tap or long-press the word. To delete it, tap the Delete key; to replace it, type over it.

- To select a specific text string (a word, sentence, or paragraph, for instance), start by selecting a word at the beginning or end of the text that you want to select. Drag the selection handles to highlight the desired text. Then select a command from the pop-up menu above the selection (to cut or copy it to the Clipboard, for example), press the Delete key, or overtype the selected text. (Note that the command icons, their appearance, and whether they're labeled can vary from one app to another. If there are more icons than can be shown at once, they scroll horizontally.)

Messages

Command icons —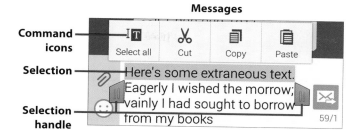

Selection

Selection handle

• To paste the most recently copied or cut text into a text box, set the text insertion mark, tap the blue marker, and then tap Paste in the pop-up that appears.

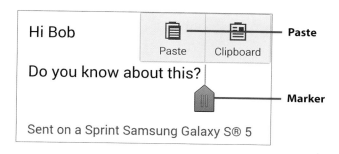

Pasting Other Material

If you select Clipboard from the pop-up menu rather than Paste, you can paste *other* material—images, for example—that you recently copied or cut. Tap the item that you want to insert. To remove an unwanted item from the Clipboard, press and hold the item, and tap Delete from Clipboard.

Clipboard

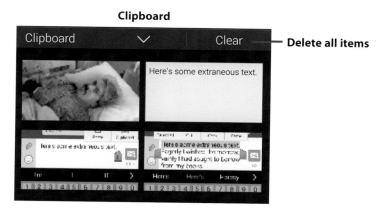

- When entering and editing text in Email, you can tap icons on the formatting toolbar above the message area to insert images, apply character and paragraph formatting, or undo the most recent change.

Email

Show/hide toolbar

Copying Text from a Web Page

You can also use editing techniques to copy text from a web page. Press to select the first word, and then drag the handles to select the material to copy. In the toolbar that appears, tap Copy to copy the material so that you can paste it elsewhere or tap Share Via to copy the material directly into a new email, text message, or Google+ post, for example.

Selection

Handle

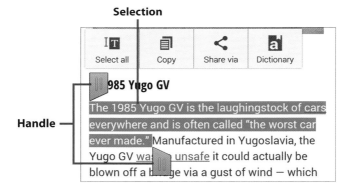

Searching for Items on the Phone and Web

Rather than relying on your memory or a lengthy series of taps to find buried Settings, launch apps, open contact records, and so on, you can use the S5 search features to quickly locate material of interest.

Use S Finder

As you type, paste, or speak a search word or phrase, S Finder displays a scrolling list of potential matches arranged by category, such as email messages, contacts, phone calls, and Settings names or sections. Matches can be the names of items or text contained somewhere within the item—in a text message, email, or Word document, for example. And if you know even part of an app's name, S Finder can double as a program launcher.

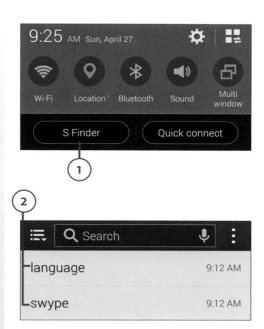

1. Open the Notification panel and tap the S Finder button.

2. A scrolling list of recent searches is shown. To repeat a search, tap its entry and go to Step 4; otherwise, continue with Step 3.

3. Enter a search term or phrase in the text box. As you type, a suggestion list appears. Tap one of the suggestions or continue typing.

Precision Counts

Potential matches must include your search term or phrase (or a simple variation of it). Searching for *privacy*, for example, will not consider references to the lock screen to be matches—unless *privacy* is used as a word in the description or help text.

---

4. Scroll through the various match categories until you find the correct item, and then tap its entry.

Search the Web

To perform a web search for the term or phrase, scroll to the Web Search section of matches and tap the Search icon.

Search term or phrase

Perform a Google search

Search in Settings

Settings categories and options seem to grow exponentially with every major Android release. When you're searching for a particular setting or option, you can restrict the search to Settings only.

1. Open Settings by tapping its icon in the Notification panel or using one of the other methods discussed in Chapter 1.

2. Type the search icon at the top of the opening Settings screen.

3. Enter your Settings search term or phrase in the text box. Matches are displayed as you type. (Only Settings or options that contain the search term/phrase in their name or description are considered matches.)

4. When you see the desired setting or option, tap its entry to go directly to that Settings screen.

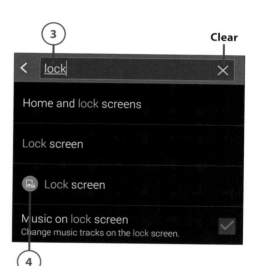

Starting Over

If a search fails, you can try again by tapping the Clear icon (X) and entering new search text.

Use Google Search

You can use Google Search to perform a text-based or voice search of the Web. The first time you use the Google app or the Google Search widget, you'll be asked to enable Google Now.

Enable Now, Disable Later

If you later decide that Google Now isn't for you, launch the Google app, tap the menu icon in its lower-right corner, and choose Settings from the menu that appears. Drag the Google Now slider to the Off position. Although Google Now will be disabled, Google Search will continue to function normally.

Text-Based Search

1. Tap in the Google Search widget or tap Apps, Google.

2. Type the search term or phrase in the text box that appears. As you type, potential matches are shown.

3. If you see an appropriate suggestion, tap it to perform that search. Otherwise, continue typing the search term or phrase, and tap the search key when you're ready to perform the search.

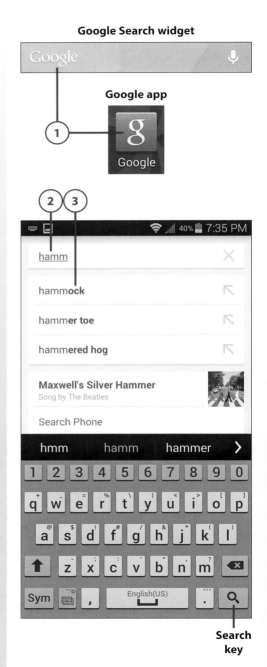

Google Search widget

Google app

Google

Search key

Voice Search

1. Display the Home screen page that contains the Google Search widget, or tap Apps, Google.

2. Initiate a voice search by tapping the microphone icon or by saying "OK, Google."

3. Speak the search term or phrase. The results are presented as a series of links.

Google Search widget

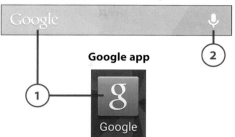

Google app

One-Handed Operation mode

Favorite apps

Favorite contacts

Restore display

Resize window

Favorite apps

Recent Apps   Home   Back   Volume Down   Volume Up   Edit favorite apps or contacts

In this chapter, you find out how to customize your phone by populating the Home screen with widgets, shortcuts, and folders; change the default wallpaper; organize your Apps pages and create folders; set default and contact-specific ringtones; and configure and enable special system settings, such as Blocking mode and One-Handed Operation. Topics include the following:

3

→ Customizing the Home screen with new wallpaper, shortcuts, folders, and widgets

→ Setting the Apps view

→ Changing system settings

Making the Phone Your Own

Nothing prevents you from using the phone exactly as it was when you first opened the box—keeping the default wallpaper, installing no additional widgets, downloading no new apps, and ignoring Settings for the operating system and apps. But the fun of having a powerful smartphone is in *customizing* it—personalizing the phone in ways that make it easier, more efficient, and fun to use.

Customizing the Home Screen

The easiest and most obvious way to personalize the phone is to customize its Home screen. In fact, many of the Home screen customization options, such as changing the wallpaper, adding widgets, and adding shortcuts to your favorite apps, are what users do first with their new phones.

Select Wallpaper

The simplest way to customize the phone is to change its Home screen background (called *wallpaper*) by selecting an image that's aesthetically pleasing, amusing, or touching. Wallpaper can be a static image or a *live*, moving image. The image you choose is applied to all Home screen pages.

1. On the Home screen, press and hold the Recent Apps key and tap the Wallpapers icon at the bottom of the screen.

Wallpaper Shortcuts

As alternatives, you can press and hold any empty spot on a Home screen page or pinch your fingers together on an empty spot, and then tap the Wallpapers icon.

2. Tap Home Screen, Lock Screen, or Home and Lock Screens—depending on the screen(s) for which you want to select a new wallpaper image.

Using a Photo as Home Screen Wallpaper

Photos make excellent lock screen wallpaper but so-so Home screen wallpaper. When a photo is used as a Home screen background, it's obliterated on most pages by widgets and shortcuts. When placed on the lock screen, on the other hand, you'll actually be able to see your treasured photo. You'll probably be happier with a pattern, color, or another simple wallpaper as the Home screen background.

3. Scroll through and tap thumb-nails to view the available types of wallpaper. Options include More Images (a cropped area of a photo or other image that's stored on the phone or in an online account), personal images you've previously used as wall-paper, static images provided by Samsung and your carrier, and live wallpaper.

4. To apply an image or live wall-paper shown in the scrolling list, select its thumbnail and tap Set Wallpaper. If you want to use a photo or image that *isn't* in the Wallpapers list, continue with Step 5.

Static Versus Live Wallpaper

Live wallpaper contributes more to battery drain than a static wall-paper design or personal photo. If you find that you're running out of power too quickly, consider replacing your live wallpaper with static wallpaper.

5. Tap the More Images thumbnail.

6. If a Complete Action Using dialog box appears, select an app or image source, and tap Just Once.

7. Open the folder that contains the image. Tap the thumbnail to open the image for cropping, resize and move the selection rectangle as necessary to select the desired area, and tap Done.

Select an app or source

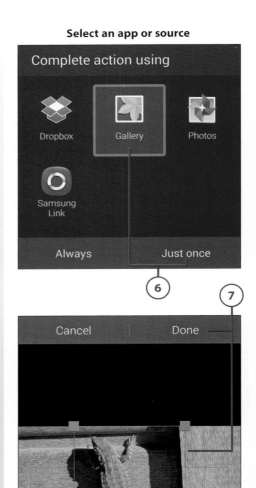

Managing Personal Wallpaper Images

Each time you try out a personal image as wallpaper (Step 5), an image thumbnail is added to the scrolling Wallpapers list. To remove any image that you don't intend to reuse, perform Steps 1–2, press and hold one of the images to select it, select other images that you want to remove, and then tap the Trash icon at the top of the screen.

Selecting personal images to remove

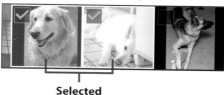

Selected

Rearrange, Remove, and Add Home Screen Pages

The default Home screen has four horizontally scrolling pages, plus a special page dedicated to My Magazine/Flipboard—a news and social networking aggregator. You can rearrange the pages, remove ones that you don't need, or add new pages (up to the maximum of seven).

1. On the Home screen, press and hold the Recent Apps key, or press and hold (or pinch) an empty spot on a Home screen page.

My Magazine | Active page
Main page

2. *Move a page.* To change the position of a page, press and hold it, and then drag to the left or right. As you drag, affected pages automatically slide out of the way to make room for the page. Release the page when it's in the correct position.

3. *Designate a different main page.* The main page (marked with a house icon) can be *any* Home screen page, not just the first one. Whenever you're on the Home screen, pressing the Home key always takes you to this main page. To set a *new* main page, tap the house icon at the top of the page.

New main page position

4. *Delete a page.* Press and hold a page's thumbnail, and then drag it onto the Remove icon at the top of the screen. If the page contains one or more items, a confirmation dialog appears. Tap OK to confirm the deletion.

Effects of Deleting a Page

As indicated in the confirmation dialog, deleting a page also removes the items on that page, such as widgets and shortcuts. Of course, you can add those items to the remaining or new pages, if you want.

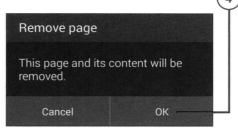

5. *Add a new page.* You can have a maximum of seven Home screen pages. To create a new page, scroll to the last page (marked with a plus (+) symbol) and tap the symbol. After adding a new page, you can optionally change its position (see Step 2).

6. When you finish editing, complete the process by pressing the Back key, pressing the Home key, or tapping the thumbnail of the Home screen page that you want to view.

Home Screen Settings

Another option that can affect the number of Home screen pages is found by tapping the Home Screen Settings icon (see the figure for Step 1). You can elect to remove the My Magazine/Flipboard page and specify a transition effect to use when flipping through the Home screen pages.

Add Shortcuts

You can place shortcuts to your favorite apps on the Home screen. When you tap an app shortcut, the app that it represents launches. An Android *shortcut* is the equivalent of a Mac alias or a Windows shortcut.

1. Navigate to the Home screen page to which you want to add the shortcut, ensure that it has an open space for the shortcut, and tap the Apps icon. (You can add the shortcut to any page, but the current one is initially offered as the destination.)

2. Find the app for which you want to create a shortcut.

3. Press and hold the app's icon, drag it into an open spot on the current Home screen page, and release the icon.

Repositioning or Removing a Shortcut

After creating a shortcut, you can reposition it on the current or a different Home screen page. Press and hold the shortcut, and then drag it to the desired position.

To remove a shortcut that you no longer want, press and hold it, and then drag it onto the Remove icon at the top of the screen. Removing a shortcut doesn't affect the item it represents.

Creating a Bookmark Shortcut

You can also create shortcuts to your favorite web pages. In the Internet or Chrome app, open the page or site for viewing. In Internet, tap the menu icon and choose Add Shortcut to Home Screen. In Chrome, tap the menu icon and choose Add to Homescreen, edit the name, and tap Add. The bookmark is added to a Home screen page.

Bookmark shortcuts

Internet ———  ——— Chrome

Add Widgets

A *widget* is an application that runs on the Home screen. Many, such as Weather, aren't interactive or are only minimally so. For example, you can tap the refresh icon on the Weather widget to force an update of the weather info. Otherwise, such widgets simply provide continuously updated information. Other widgets, such as Music, are designed for interaction. By tapping its buttons, you can pause or restart playback, and skip to the next or previous song.

You can add a widget in any free space on a Home screen page, as long as there's room for it. Widgets come in a variety of sizes, from one- or two-section widgets to full-screen ones. In addition to the widgets supplied with your phone, downloaded applications sometimes include their own widgets.

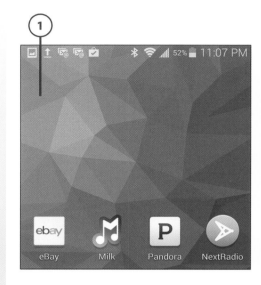

1. Navigate to the Home screen page to which you want to add the widget and ensure that it has an open space for the widget.

2. Press and hold the Recent Apps key, and then tap the Widgets icon.

3. Find the widget that you want to install. Above each widget is the number of screen sections (horizontal × vertical) it requires. To assist in your search, you can do any of the following:

- Navigate the widget pages by swiping left and right or by tapping navigation dots.

- Search for a widget by tapping the menu icon and choosing Search Widgets. Enter part of the widget's name. As you type, matches are displayed. To dismiss the search box, tap the less than (<) icon on the box's left edge.

- Any widget followed by a greater than (>) icon is a *widget group*. To view or select one of its widgets, tap the > icon.

Remove search box   **Search text**   **Clear**

Widget group   **Tap**

Expanded widget group

4. Press and hold the widget, and then drag it into position on the current (or another) Home screen page.

>>>Go Further
WIDGET SHORTCUTS

Shortcuts in Android provide great flexibility because they can be direct links to a variety of things other than apps, such as files, records, and operating system elements. For instance, you can create a Direct Dial shortcut that automatically dials a person's phone number when you tap it. After adding the Direct Dial widget to a Home screen page, you select the person's Contacts record to link it to the shortcut.

Here are some other widget-based shortcuts you can add:

- *Book.* Links to a downloaded ebook.

- *Bookmark.* Links to a web page in Internet or Chrome.

- *Contact.* Links to a person's record in Contacts, enabling you to easily call, message, email, or locate the person.

- *Direct Dial.* Automatically dials the specified number, based on a selected record in Contacts.

- *Direct Message.* Enables you to create a new text or multimedia message to a specific person in Contacts.

- *Directions.* Provides turn-by-turn navigation to a single specified destination.

- *Dropbox Folder.* Enables you to open a specific folder in your Dropbox account.

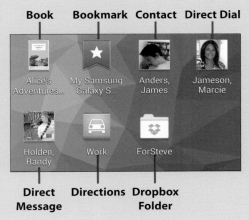

Book   Bookmark   Contact   Direct Dial

Direct   Directions   Dropbox
Message   Folder

Create Folders

To help organize your Home screen shortcuts, you can add folders in which to store them.

1. On the Home screen, navigate to the page to which you want to add a folder. Press and hold the first shortcut that you want to add to the folder and drag it onto the Create Folder icon at the top of the screen.

2. Type a name for the folder in the text box.

3. To populate the folder, do one of the following:

- Tap the Done key. When desired, you can add other shortcuts to the folder (or any other folder) by long-pressing each shortcut and dragging it onto the folder icon.

- Tap the + (plus) icon, select apps by tapping each one's icon, and then tap Done. A shortcut is created for each checked app and inserted into the folder.

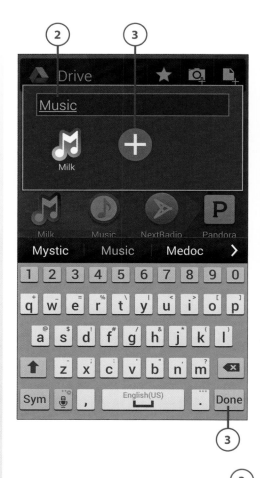

>>>Go Further

WORKING WITH FOLDERS

Of course, creating a folder is just the first step. Adding and organizing shortcuts within the folders is what makes them useful. Here's how to use, organize, and manage folders and their contents.

- Tap a folder to view the items it contains. In the pop-up window that appears, tap an item to launch or open it. To reposition an item in the folder, press and hold it, and then drag it to a new position. To close an open folder, tap anywhere outside of the folder.

- To change a folder's background color, open the folder, tap the menu icon, and then tap a color swatch.

Change background color

- To remove an item from a folder, tap the folder to open it, press and hold the item's icon, and then drag it to any location outside of the folder. (To *delete* an app shortcut that's in a folder, drag the shortcut out of the folder. Then press and hold the shortcut, and drag it onto the Remove icon.)

- Finally, like other Home screen items, you can reposition a folder by pressing and holding its icon, and then dragging it to a destination on the current or a different Home screen page.

Reposition and Remove Home Screen Items

Part of the fun of setting up your Home screen pages is that you can freely rearrange items. Because many items are shortcuts, removing them from the Home screen has no effect on the actual items they represent. Follow these steps to reposition or remove Home screen items.

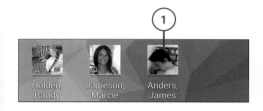

1. On the Home screen page, press and hold the item you want to reposition or remove.

2. *Remove* the item by dragging it onto the Remove icon that appears at the top of the screen. When you release the item, it is removed.

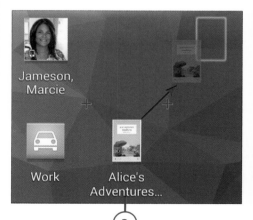

3. *Reposition* the item by dragging it to an empty or occupied spot on the current or another Home screen page. If the destination is occupied, items will shift to make room (if possible). When you release the item, the move is completed.

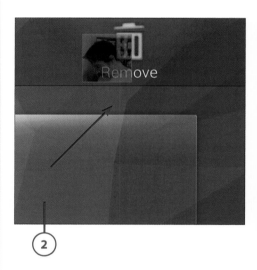

Moving Between Pages

When moving an item between Home screen pages, don't let up on the finger pressure until the destination page appears. If you inadvertently release the item on the wrong page or in the wrong spot, press and hold the item again and finish the move.

>>>Go Further

REARRANGING AND REPLACING THE PRIMARY SHORTCUTS

At the bottom of every Home screen page are the five primary shortcuts: Phone, Contacts, Messages, Internet (or Chrome), and Apps. If desired, you can rear-range, remove, or replace any of the first four.

- To *rearrange* the primary shortcuts, press and hold the one you want to move, drag it to the left or right, and then release it when it's in the correct position.

- To *remove* a primary shortcut, press and hold it, and then drag it to the Remove icon at the top of the page. If you want to remove the primary shortcut from the bottom of the screen but keep it on the page, drag it to any blank spot on the current Home screen page.

- To *replace* a primary shortcut (or add one, if you have less than four), drag the replacement or addition from a Home screen or Apps page onto the pri-mary shortcut you want to replace or into position between a pair, respec-tively.

New primary shortcuts

Setting the Apps View

The default method of viewing your installed apps is an alphabetical, multi-page grid. Because you'll spend a lot of time in Apps, you may prefer to change this display to show your apps as a custom grid that you've arranged in a fashion and order you prefer.

1. On the Home screen, tap the Apps icon.

2. Tap the menu icon and choose View As.

3. In the View As dialog, select one of the following:

   • *Alphabetical Order.* This is the default display style, presenting and maintaining all app icons alphabetically. Whenever you install a new app, it is automatically inserted into the correct spot.

   • *Custom.* This option enables you to create additional grid pages and arrange the app icons however you like, such as putting all games or image-editing apps together and placing your most frequently used apps on the first page.

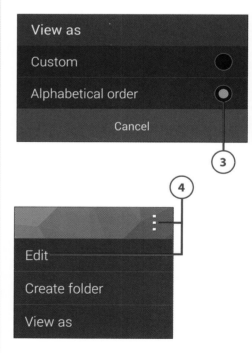

Change Is Constant

In previous versions of the Android operating system, you could also display your apps as a scrolling alphabetical list. That option is no longer supported. Another big change is that folders can be created and used in *either* view—not just Custom. Folders are always displayed on the last Apps page.

4. In either view, you make most changes in Edit mode. To enable Edit mode, open the menu and choose Edit.

Edit Mode First!

Most modifications you make to the Apps pages require that you first switch to Edit mode. If you neglect (or forget) to do this, changes are made to Home screen pages rather than Apps pages. If you mistakenly find yourself on the Home screen while dragging an app or folder, drag the item onto the Cancel icon at the top of the screen.

5. *Alphabetical Order view.* Although you can't rearrange the apps, you can use Edit mode to create folders, view an app's App Info screen (normally accessed by tapping Settings, Application Manager), and uninstall or disable certain apps. Press and hold an app and then drag it onto the appropriate icon at the top of the screen.

Alphabetical Order view

Command icons   5

Uninstalling and Disabling Apps

As explained in "Uninstall, Disable, and Hide Apps" in Chapter 10, "Installing and Using Applications," whether you can uninstall, disable, or do neither with an app depends on the app. Apps that you downloaded can normally be uninstalled. Certain Android, Samsung, and carrier-provided apps can be uninstalled or disabled, whereas others—especially critical system apps—must remain on your phone and cannot be disabled. When you press and hold an app, only the allowable action is presented as an icon: Uninstall, Disable, or neither icon.

6. *Custom view.* In addition to the Edit mode actions in Step 5, you can rearrange apps by dragging them to new positions. You can also create additional app pages by long-pressing an icon you want to add to the new page, and then dragging it onto the Create Page icon at the top of the screen.

Custom view

Command icons   6

No Blank Spots or Pages

When rearranging apps, blank spaces are only allowed at the end of each Apps page. Similarly, if a page is blank after you finish your edits, the page is automatically removed.

7. When you finish making changes to the Apps pages, exit Edit mode by tapping the Back icon or by pressing the Back key.

Creating and Working with App Folders

As mentioned, folders are now supported in both Apps views and are automatically placed on the last Apps page. The purpose of creating folders is to reduce app clutter and impart additional organization to the Apps pages, grouping similar apps in one convenient location. When an app is added to a folder, its icon is removed from the Apps grid.

Create App Folders

1. To create a folder in Apps, do one of the following:

   - Open the menu and choose Create Folder.

   - Press and hold an app that you want to move into the new folder, and drag it onto the Create Folder icon at the top of the screen.

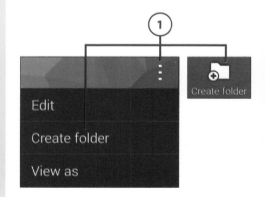

2. Name the folder.

3. During the folder-creation process, you can optionally select
apps to populate the folder. Do
one of the following:

- To immediately add apps to
the folder, tap the plus (+)
icon, tap the check box of
each app you want to add,
and tap Done. The added
apps are moved into the
folder.

- To create the named folder
without adding other apps at
this time, tap the Done key
on the keyboard.

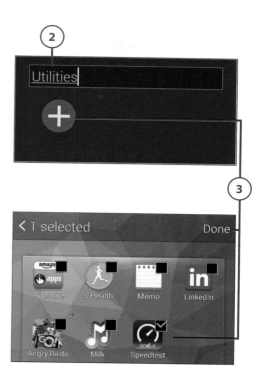

Manually Adding Apps to a Folder

To manually add apps to a folder,
enable Edit mode and then drag
app icons onto the folder. You
can add and remove apps from a
folder whenever you want.

Work with App Folders

After creating a folder and adding some apps to it, you can do the following:

- *Launch an app.* Scroll to the last page of Apps, tap the folder to open it,
and then tap the icon of the app you want to launch.

Closing the Folder

If you decide not to launch an app, you can close the open folder by tapping
any blank space inside the folder or by pressing the Back key.

- *Change the background color.* Open the folder, tap the menu icon, select a color, and then tap anywhere in the folder. You set the background color individually for each folder. You can change the color even when Edit mode isn't active.

Select a color

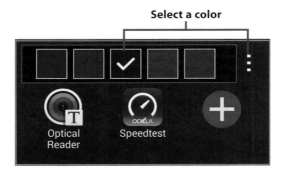

- *Remove apps from a folder.* Enable Edit mode, tap the folder to display its contents, and then drag the app out of the folder onto any Apps page— other than a folders page. If you release the app on a folders page, it's assumed that you want to *create* a folder to enclose the app.

- *Rearrange folders (Custom view only).* Enable Edit mode, press and hold a folder to select it, and then drag it into a new position on a folders page. As is the case when rearranging apps, no blank spaces are allowed within a folders page.

- *Remove a folder.* Enable Edit mode, press and hold the folder, and then drag it onto the Remove icon at the top of the screen. Tap OK in the Remove Folder confirmation dialog. Apps within the deleted folder are restored to the Apps pages.

Changing System Settings

By changing preferences in Settings, you can make the phone look and work to match your needs. Although system and app settings are discussed throughout the book, this section points out some that aren't mentioned elsewhere but are important in customizing your phone.

To access system settings, go to the Home screen and tap Apps, Settings. You can also tap a Home screen Settings shortcut (if you've created one), or you can open the Notification panel and tap the Settings icon at the top. (An advantage of the latter approach is that you can go to Settings no matter what you're doing without first having to return to the Home screen.)

To access an app's settings (for those that provide them), launch the app, tap the menu icon, and choose Settings.

System settings (Grid view)   **App settings (Gallery)**

 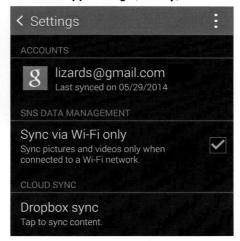

Different Views of Settings

There are three different methods of of displaying Settings: Grid, List, and Tab view. To switch views, tap the menu icon and choose a new view. If what you see onscreen looks substantially different from the figures in this and other chapters, it's probably because you've set a different view. Most Settings figures in this book show Grid view—the default view for a brand new S5.

It's Not All Good

Quick Setting Buttons Versus Quick Settings

You've undoubtedly noticed that—in addition to the Quick Settings in the Notification panel—the first section of Settings is labeled Quick Settings. Imagine my surprise when I discovered that the icons in Settings weren't the same as the ones in the Notification panel! Unfortunately, although the two sets of icons have essentially the same name, they're *different* features. (Nice programming, guys.)

The icons in the Notification panel are properly called *Quick Setting buttons;* the icons in the first section of Settings are the *Quick Settings.* Customizing both sets are discussed in the following sections—separately, of course.

Quick Setting buttons (Notification panel)   **Quick Settings (Settings)**

Customize the Quick Setting Buttons

At the top of the Notification panel is a horizontally scrolling string of icons called *Quick Setting buttons*. By tapping these buttons, you can quickly enable or disable system features. If you press and hold most of these buttons, you go directly to that feature's screen in Settings. You can customize the Quick Setting buttons by selecting different settings to display and changing the order in which they're listed.

1. Open the Notification panel by swiping the top of the screen downward.

2. Tap the Grid View icon to display the entire array of Quick Setting buttons.

3. Tap the Edit icon.

Notification panel (top)

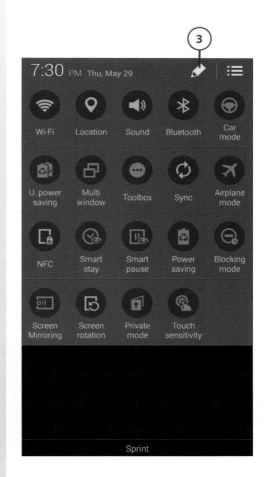

4. The Quick Setting buttons are divided into two sets: Active Buttons (those currently in use in the Notification panel) and Available Buttons (other buttons that can be moved into the Active Buttons set). You can edit the Quick Setting buttons in these ways:

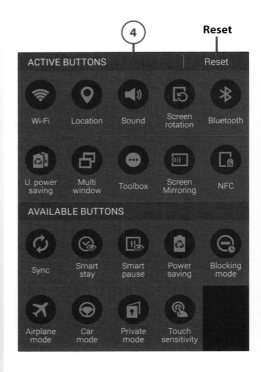

- Swap any pair of buttons by long-pressing a button in one set and dragging it onto a button in the other set. (The final set of Active Buttons can contain either nine or ten buttons.)

- Change the order of the Active Buttons by long-pressing a button and dragging it to a new position. The two buttons swap places.

- Restore the original Quick Setting buttons and their order by tapping Reset.

Customize the Quick Settings

Whenever you open Settings, the first section—regardless of the view you've set (Grid, List, or Tab)—is always Quick Settings. The purpose of the Quick Settings is to make a dozen of your most frequently used settings easily accessible without having to remember the Settings section in which each one can otherwise be found.

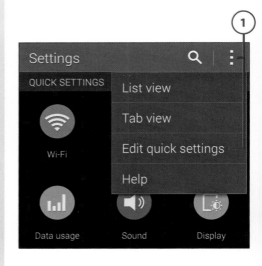

1. Open Settings by tapping Apps, Settings (or any other method previously discussed) and choose Edit Quick Settings from the menu.

2. Quick Settings can contain only a dozen settings. To change the current settings, tap those you want to eliminate (removing their check marks) and then tap the settings icons that you want to use as replacements.

3. Tap Save when you're done making changes.

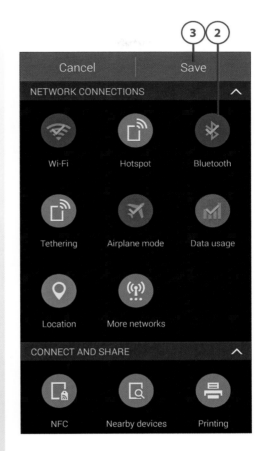

Motions and Gestures Settings

You can selectively enable Motions and Gestures settings to control phone features by making special movements with the phone or gestures that are sensed by it. Many of these settings are very helpful; others… well, you be the judge.

1. Open Settings, and tap the Motions and Gestures icon (in the Motion section).

2. Each of the Motions and Gestures settings operates as an on/off toggle. They work as follows:

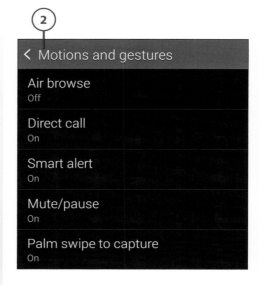

- *Air Browse.* When enabled, you can wave your hand over the sensor at the top of the phone to instruct it to scroll in various apps, such as Gallery, Music, Email, and Internet.

- *Direct Call.* When viewing a person's contact record, log entry, or message conversation, you can move the phone to your ear to automatically call the person.

- *Smart Alert.* When you pick up the phone, it vibrates to notify you of missed calls or messages.

- *Mute/Pause.* When enabled, you can specify methods that can be used to pause media playback and mute alarms or incoming calls. Unlike the two natural motions for silencing the phone, Smart Pause relies on the front camera to detect when you're looking at the screen. If it senses you've looked away, video playback is automatically paused. It restarts again when it detects that you're looking at the screen.

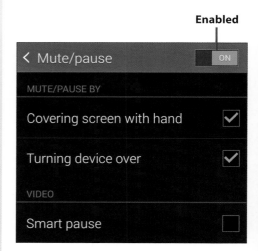

- *Palm Swipe to Capture.* When enabled, you can create screen captures by placing the edge of your hand on the screen and dragging across it. Captured screens are saved in the Screenshots folder. (You can also create screen captures by simultaneously pressing the Home key and Power button.)

Air View

When enabled, Air View instructs certain apps to respond when they sense that your finger is hovering slightly above the screen. For example, Calendar can pop up an event's details and Phone shows the person and number associated with a speed dial number. To enable or disable Air View, open Settings and tap the Air View icon (in the Motion section).

Air View (Speed Dial Assignments)

One-Handed Operation

If you sometimes need to operate the phone entirely with one hand, you can enable One-Handed Operation. When enabled, the screen is reduced in size and shifted so it's closest to the operating hand. To avoid the need to press the hardware buttons at the bottom of the phone and other essential controls, onscreen controls are added to the reduced display within reach of your thumb.

1. Open Settings and tap the One-Handed Operation icon (in the Sound and Display section).

2. Enable One-Handed Operation mode by moving the slider to the On position.

3. Follow the onscreen directions by sliding your thumb from the outer edge to the center and then back. When successful, the screen will reduce in size.

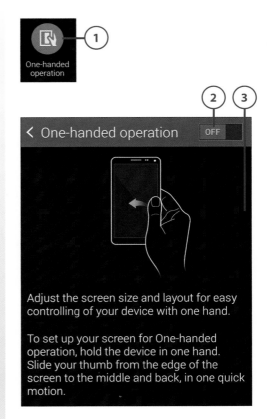

Adjust the screen size and layout for easy controlling of your device with one hand.

To set up your screen for One-handed operation, hold the device in one hand. Slide your thumb from the edge of the screen to the middle and back, in one quick motion.

4. To configure and use the reduced screen, you can do any of the following:

- Drag the upper-right corner to adjust the display size.

- Tap icons at the bottom of the screen rather than trying to press the keys they represent.

- Tap icons at the top of the screen to display your favorite contacts or favorite apps on the right edge of the window. With the contacts or apps icon selected (dark), you can tap the Edit icon to modify the listed contacts or apps. To hide the favorites, tap the same icon at the top of the screen again.

5. When you're done using One-Handed Operation, repeat Steps 1 and 2 to disable it.

One-Handed Operation mode

Restore display   Favorite Resize
     Favorite contacts   apps   window

Recent   Back   Volume Up Edit favorite
 Apps   Home   Volume Down   apps or
                                     contacts

It's Not All Good

A Cool, Finicky, Undocumented Feature

One-Handed Operation is an *exceptionally* cool feature. It's obvious that a tremendous amount of work went into creating it. However, it's difficult to enable, largely undocumented, and automatically disables itself now and then as explained here.

- Try as I might, it frequently takes me dozens of thumb-swiping attempts to enable this mode. I have no idea whether success is determined by the position of the hand, palm, or thumb; using the flat or side of the thumb; the section of the screen one should swipe; the speed of the swipe; the pressure applied; or some combination of these. To make matters worse, *you must repeat this process every time you want to re-enable it*. This should be a setting that's stored by the S5.

- One-Handed Operation is virtually undocumented. There are many factors to the proper enabling, operating, and customization of this feature. It's sufficiently complex so that users shouldn't be expected to simply *discover* how it works.

- Finally, this feature screams for configuration settings. You should be able to dictate whether/when it automatically reverts to the normal screen. (In fact, when this happens, it *might* still be operating. I managed to restore to the reduced screen once, but have no clue how I did it.) An option to add One-Handed Operation to the Quick Setting buttons in the Navigation pane—to *quickly* enable it—would be helpful, too. (This assumes that after you've successfully enabled it once, it could be re-enabled by simply toggling the slider.)

Hopefully, One-Handed Operation is a feature that's tweaked and improved in updates—rather than one that quietly disappears.

Ringtones

A *ringtone* is an audible event notification, such as a sound effect or snippet of music. You can specify default ringtones for incoming calls and text messages, as well as set person- or group-specific ringtones.

Set the Default Incoming Call Ringtone

Unless overridden by a personal or group ringtone, the default ringtone plays to notify you of an incoming call.

1. Open Settings and tap the Sound icon (in the Sound and Display section).

2. Tap Ringtones.

3. The Ringtones dialog box appears, showing a scrolling list of all built-in, created, and downloaded ringtones. Tap a ringtone to play it. When you're satisfied with your choice, tap OK. (For an explanation of the Add button, see the note at the end of the "Assign a Ringtone to a Contact" task.)

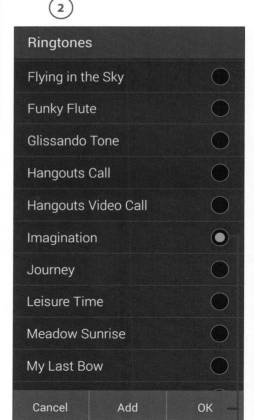

Set the Default Notification Ringtone

Unless overridden by a personal or group ringtone, the default notification ringtone plays to signify a new email, new text message, missed call, waiting voicemail, or upcoming Calendar event. Unlike call ringtones, notification ringtones are brief and less intrusive.

1. Open Settings and tap the Sound icon (in the Sound and Display section).

2. Tap Notifications.

3. The Notifications dialog box appears, showing a scrolling list containing all the notification ringtones. Tap an entry to play it. When you're satisfied with your choice, tap OK.

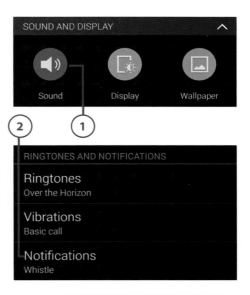

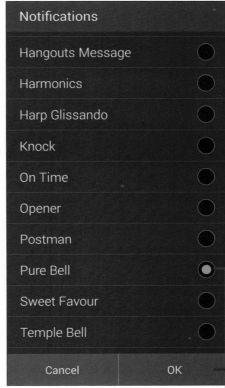

Assign a Ringtone to a Contact

To make it easy to quickly recognize an incoming call from a person, you can associate a distinctive ringtone with his or her record in Contacts.

1. Open Contacts by tapping its Home screen icon or by tapping Apps, Contacts.

2. With the Contacts tab selected, find the person's record by scrolling or searching. Tap the record to open it.

3. Tap the Edit icon.

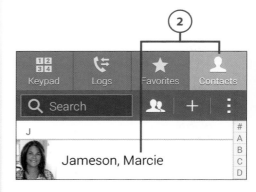

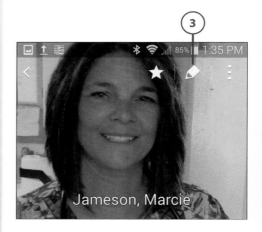

4. Tap the Ringtone entry.

5. Select the ringtone that you want to use and tap OK. Select Default Ringtone (at the top of the list) if you prefer to use the default ringtone for this contact.

6. Tap the Save button.

7. The selected ringtone is associated with and displayed on the person's contact record.

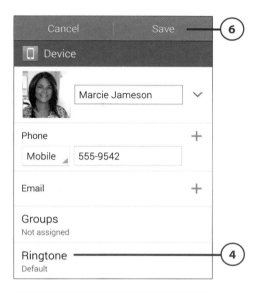

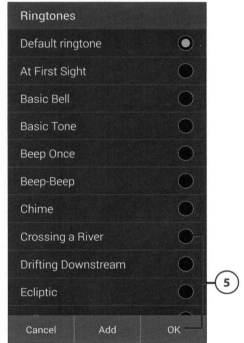

Chapter 3

Using Sound Files and Songs as Ringtones

If the ringtone you want to use isn't listed in the Ringtones dialog box, tap Add. If a Complete Action Using dialog box appears, select the app that you want to use to specify the ringtone (such as Sound Picker, for example) and tap Just Once. Navigate to the ringtone, sound, or music file; select it; and tap Done or OK.

Selecting a song with Sound Picker

Assign a Ringtone to a Contact Group

You can also assign a distinctive ringtone to all members of a contact group. (To learn about groups, see "Working with Contact Groups" in Chapter 5, "Managing Contacts.")

1. Open Contacts by tapping its Home screen icon or by tapping Apps, Contacts.

2. Select the Contacts tab, and then tap the Groups icon to display the list of defined groups.

3. Open a group by tapping its name.

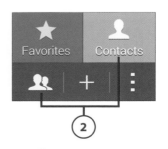

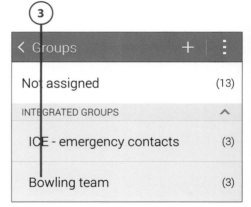

4. Tap the menu icon and choose Edit Group.

5. Tap Group Ringtone and select a ringtone as described in Steps 5–7 of the previous task ("Assign a Ringtone to a Contact").

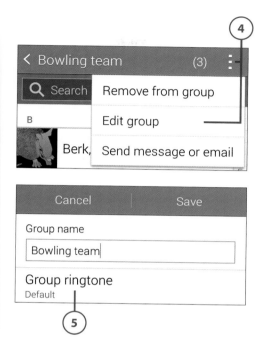

>>>Go Further

WHICH RINGTONE HAS PRECEDENCE?

After reading the material in this section, you might be wondering what happens when a person is associated with *multiple* ringtones. For instance, although Bob may have been assigned a personal ringtone, he may also be a member of a group that has a different ringtone. The answer is that *a contact record ringtone always has precedence*.

Thus, if a caller has no personal ringtone and doesn't belong to a group with a ringtone, his calls are announced by the default ringtone. If the person belongs to a group with a ringtone and he doesn't have a personal ringtone, the group ringtone plays. Finally, if a person belongs to a group with a ringtone *and* also has a personal ringtone, the personal ringtone plays.

Assign a Message Notification Sound

In addition to selecting a sound to announce new text and multimedia messages from within the Messages app, you can set one in Sound settings. In this task, you learn to use this second approach. The technique can also be used to specify a sound or ringtone to announce incoming calls, new email, or calendar events.

1. Open Settings and tap the Sound icon (in the Sound and Display section).

2. Scroll to the Samsung Applications section of Sound Settings and tap Messages. (Note the entries for other apps and features.)

3. Ensure that Messages is On, and then tap Notification Sound.

4. Select a sound from the scrolling list and tap OK. (If you'd rather not have a messaging sound, select Silent.)

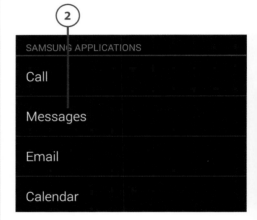

Sound

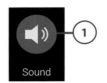

SAMSUNG APPLICATIONS

Call

Messages

Email

Calendar

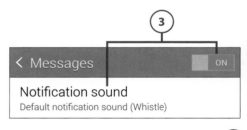

< Messages   ON

Notification sound
Default notification sound (Whistle)

Pure Bell

Sweet Favour

Cancel   OK

Create Ringtones from Songs

Here's another method for creating a ringtone from a song.

1. Launch Music, and select the song by pressing and holding its title.

2. Open the menu and choose Set As.

3. Tap From the Beginning or Auto Recommendations to specify the part of the song to use as the ringtone.

4. In the Set As section, tap Phone Ringtone to use the song as the default ringtone for incoming calls. Tap Caller Ringtone to play the song whenever you receive a call from a particular person. Tap Alarm Tone to use the song as the alarm tone for an alarm you're about to create in the Clock app.

5. Tap Done.

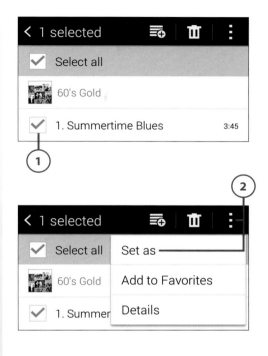

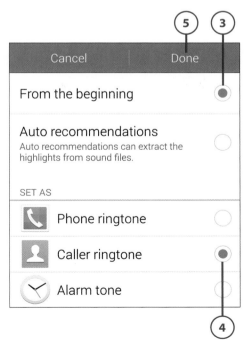

6. If you selected Caller Ringtone or Alarm Tone in Step 4, select the person's record in Contacts or create the alarm to which you want to link the song.

Caller Ringtone

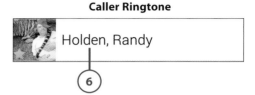

Holden, Randy

Blocking Mode

If you enable Blocking mode, you can elect to receive only certain types of notifications while blocking others. Blocking can be set for a period of time (to silence notifications during an important meeting, for example) or permanently enabled for certain features.

1. Open Settings and tap the Blocking Mode icon (in the Personalization section).

2. Enable Blocking mode by dragging its slider to the On position.

3. In the Features section, check each feature that you want to block.

PERSONALIZATION

Easy mode   Accessibility   Blocking mode

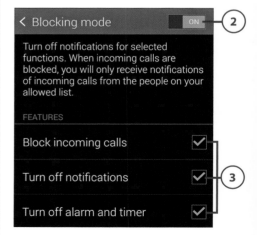

< Blocking mode   ON

Turn off notifications for selected functions. When incoming calls are blocked, you will only receive notifications of incoming calls from the people on your allowed list.

FEATURES

Block incoming calls   ✓

Turn off notifications   ✓

Turn off alarm and timer   ✓

4. In the Set Time section, do one of the following:

- Tap the Always check box to enable blocking of the selected features indefinitely—until it's turned off.

- Tap the From and To time settings to set a specific period during which blocking will be active.

5. In the Allowed Contacts section, specify people you want to treat as *exceptions*; that is, those whose notifications will *not* be blocked. Tap Allowed Contacts and select an option: *None* (no exceptions), *All Contacts* (anyone with a Contacts record), *Favorites* (any person saved as a Contacts favorite), or Custom (create a custom list from selected Contacts records).

6. Blocking will be in—or go into—effect for the designated period, covering the specified features, and with the selected exceptions. When you're ready to turn blocking off, perform Steps 1–2 and disable Blocking mode.

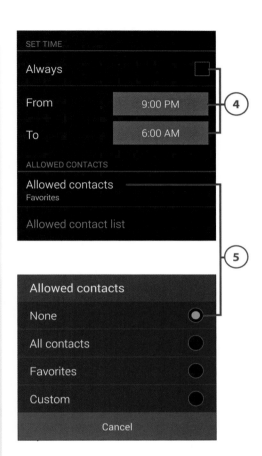

A Blocking Mode Shortcut

You can also disable Blocking mode by opening the Notification panel and then tapping its notification entry or its Quick Setting button. (If the button isn't one of the primary buttons, tap the Grid View icon to access it.)

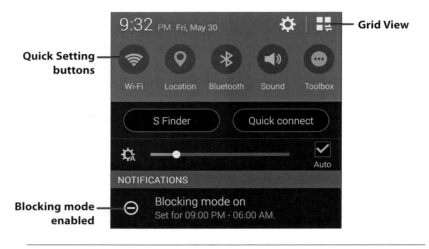

Safety Assistance Settings

When enabled, Safety Assistance settings provide a way for you to secretly summon help in an emergency situation—other than or in addition to placing a 911 call. After specifying 1–4 primary contacts, you quickly press the Power button three times to send them a text message that requests help and includes a URL to Google maps that shows your location. Pictures from both cameras and a sound recording can also be transmitted. (Note that this feature is best for temporary, short-term use due to its high battery consumption.)

Plan Ahead

Before designating someone as a primary contact, it's a good idea to inform them, describe what will happen if you use the phone to request assistance, and discuss what they should do in response.

1. Open Settings and tap the Safety Assistance icon (in the System section).

2. If you haven't designated at least one primary contact, tap Manage Primary Contacts; otherwise, go to Step 4.

3. Tap the plus (+) icon. Tap Create New Contact or Select from Contacts and then create or select an emergency contact. If desired, continue creating or specifying contacts up to the maximum of four. Press the Back key or tap the Back icon to return to the Safety Assistance screen.

Check the Phone Number

Be sure to examine the phone number of each primary contact to ensure it's the correct one. To be of use, the recipient's phone needs to be able to receive text and multimedia messages. To change the number, tap the person's entry on the Primary Contacts screen, edit the number, and tap Save.

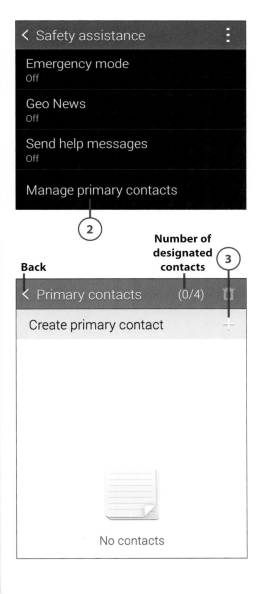

4. When you think you might be entering or are already in a dangerous situation, tap Send Help Messages. Drag the slider to the On position, set options, and then press the Back key or tap the Back icon.

5. *Optional:* Enable Emergency mode (a special power-conserving mode) by tapping its text and moving its slider to On.

6. While Send Help Messages is On, you can request assistance and execute the options selected in Step 4 by quickly pressing the Power key three times in a row.

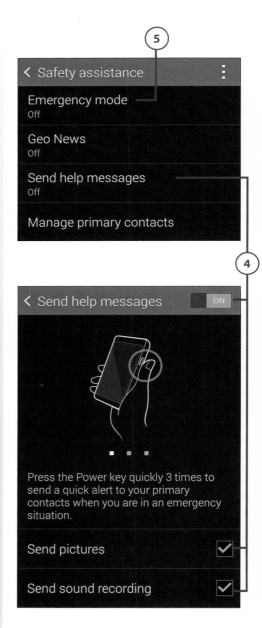

Clearing Emergency Declared Mode and Send Help Messages

After you request emergency assistance and determine that you're safe, clear the Emergency Declared mode by tapping its entry in the Notification panel. Then return to the Safety Assistance screen and disable Send Help Messages.

You should disable Send Help Messages as soon as it's convenient in order to avoid unnecessary battery drain.

>>>*Go Further*

REVIEW THE ACCESSIBILITY SETTINGS

Although the Accessibility settings (in the Personalization section) are designed to assist people with visual, hearing, or dexterity deficits, several are worth exploring by everyone. Here are some that you might want to consider:

- *Vision, Font Size.* Increase or decrease the standard font size used by the operating system and apps.

- *Hearing, Sound Balance.* When listening to media while wearing earphones, you can adjust the left/right balance.

- *Hearing, Mono Audio.* Convert stereo sound to mono when using a single earpiece to listen to media, such as a typical Bluetooth headset.

- *Dexterity and Interaction, Press and Hold Delay.* If the S5 is interpreting some of your taps as long-presses, you can lengthen the press and hold delay.

In this chapter, you learn to use the phone to place and receive calls. Topics include the following:

→ Dialing calls

→ Summoning help with an emergency call

→ Setting up a three-way conference call

→ Speed dialing

→ Receiving incoming calls

→ Using call waiting and call forwarding

→ Using in-call options, such as the speakerphone and a Bluetooth headset

→ Checking your voicemail

→ Enabling Mute, Vibrate, and Airplane mode

→ Configuring call settings

Placing and Receiving Calls

With all the functionality that your smartphone provides, it's easy to forget that you can also use it to make and receive calls. But smartphone power comes at a price. To optimize your use of the phone as a phone, you should learn the various calling procedures and the different options for performing each one.

Placing Calls

The Galaxy S5 provides many convenient ways for you to make calls. You can manually enter numbers, dial a number from a contact record, use the call logs to return missed calls and redial numbers, call embedded numbers in text and email messages, create and use speed dial entries, and make three-way and emergency calls.

With or Without the 1

When dialing a number, you need to add the dialing prefix/country code only when you're calling a country that uses a *different* code. As a result, most numbers that you dial manually, as well as ones stored in Contacts, can either omit or include the dialing prefix. Similarly, local numbers (in the phone's area code) can usually omit the area code, too.

Manual Dialing

You can use the Phone app's keypad to manually dial numbers. The procedure differs slightly if the number you're dialing is also associated with a record in Contacts.

The Phone/Contacts Relationship

Although you'll generally launch Phone to make calls, Phone and Contacts are essentially two parts of the same app. Within Contacts, you can make a manual call by selecting the Keypad tab. Within Phone, you can work with your contact records by selecting the Contacts tab. Thus, it doesn't matter which app you run when you're ready to call someone.

Dial Someone Without a Contacts Record

1. Tap the Phone icon at the bottom of the Home screen.

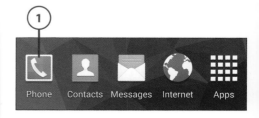

2. Select the Keypad tab if the keypad isn't displayed. Then tap the digits in the phone number.

Dialing International Numbers

To make an international call, press and hold **0**. A plus symbol appears as the first character in the number. Enter the country code, followed by the phone number.

Mistakes Happen

If you make a mistake, you can press the Delete key to delete the last digit entered. To remove the entire number and start over, press and hold Delete. You can also use normal editing techniques to position the text insertion mark within the number and make changes, such as inserting the area code.

3. *Optional:* To create a new contact record for this number or add the number to an existing contact record, tap Add to Contacts and then select an option.

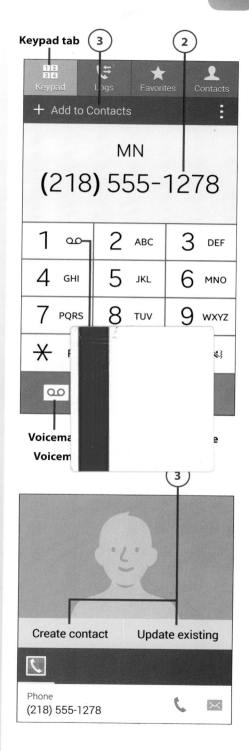

4. Tap the green phone icon to dial the call. Tap the red End Call icon to disconnect when you finish talking.

Dial Someone with a Contacts Record

1. Tap the Phone icon at the bottom of the Home screen.

2. Tap the Keypad tab if it isn't auto-matically selected. Then type any of the phone number's digits. You can start at the beginning or with any consecutive string of digits that you remember. As you enter digits, potential matches from Contacts and from num-bers you've previously dialed are shown.

Dial by Name

If you can't remember a person's number but are sure he has a Contacts record, use the keypad to spell part of the person's name, company, or any other informa-tion that you know.

3. Do one of the following:

   • Select the main suggestion by tapping the person or company's name.

   • View additional matches by tapping the numbered down arrow and selecting some-one from the Search Result list.

   • Continue entering digits until the correct match is suggest-ed, and then tap the person or company's name.

4. Tap the green phone icon to dial the call. Tap the red End Call icon to disconnect when you finish talking.

Keypad tab

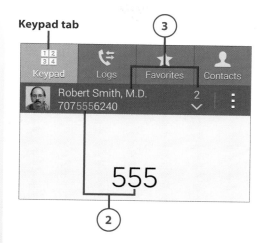

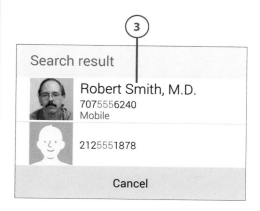

Dial from a Contact Record

Many of your outgoing calls will be to people and companies that have a record in Contacts. Rather than typing part of their name or number, it is often faster to find them in Contacts.

1. Open Contacts by tapping its icon at the bottom of the Home screen, tapping the Phone icon on the Home screen and then selecting the Contacts tab, or accessing Contacts from another app, such as Messages.

2. Tap the Contacts tab if it isn't already selected. Find the record by scrolling or searching, and then tap the entry to view the full record.

3. Tap a listed phone number or its green telephone icon to dial that number.

4. Tap the red End Call icon to disconnect when you finish talking.

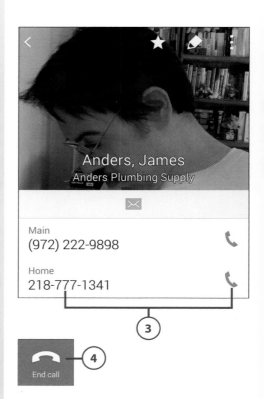

Dialing from the Call Logs

Every incoming and outgoing call is automatically recorded in the Logs section of Phone and Contacts. By viewing the logs, you can determine which calls need to be returned, as well as initiate the calls.

Return and Redial Calls

By selecting a particular log, you can see whom you've called and who has called you. You can then dial any log entry.

1. On the Home screen, launch Phone by tapping its icon.

2. Tap the Logs tab at the top of the screen.

3. Select a log to view by opening the menu above the log and choosing an option. (If you don't select a log, the last one viewed displays.)

4. To call a person without leaving the Logs screen, swipe his entry to the right. The displayed number is automatically dialed.

5. To text a person, swipe the log entry to the left. A new message window in Messages appears.

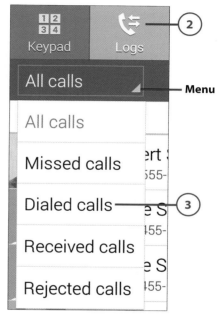

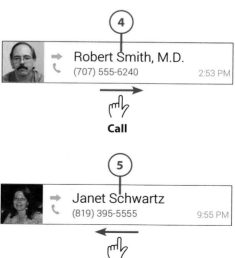

Tap Versus Swipe

If swiping isn't your thing or you want more control over what happens, tap the log entry. On the screen that appears, you can call the person by tapping the phone icon. To send a text or multimedia message to the person, tap the message icon.

Message

Call

>>>*Go Further*

PHONE LOG ICONS

In each log entry, icons provide information about the call (see Table 4.1). The icon beside each person, company, and number shows the type of call, as well as whether it was incoming or outgoing.

Table 4.1   Phone Log Icons

Icon	Meaning	Icon	Meaning
	Incoming call		Rejected incoming call
	Outgoing call		Auto-rejected incoming call
	Missed incoming call		

>>>*Go Further*

OTHER PHONE LOG OPTIONS

Using the logs to return calls is often more convenient than dialing manually or searching for the person's contact record. Here are some other actions you can take when viewing a log:

- Press and hold a log entry to select it. You can tap the Delete icon to delete this single entry or select additional entries prior to tapping Delete.

- With a log item selected, open the menu and choose a command. *View Contact* displays the individual's record, *Copy to Dialing Screen* enters the person's phone number on the dialing screen, *Send Number* embeds the person's name and phone number in a new text message, and *Add to Reject List* causes any future calls from this number to be automatically sent to voicemail.

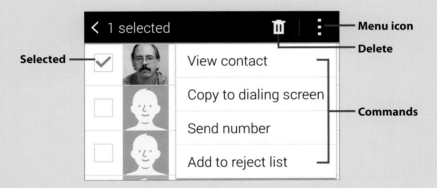

- Another way to delete old, duplicate, and unwanted entries is to choose an appropriate log from the left-hand menu, tap the menu icon (on the right), and choose Delete. Select all log entries that you want to remove (or tap Select All), tap Done, and then tap OK in the confirmation dialog box.

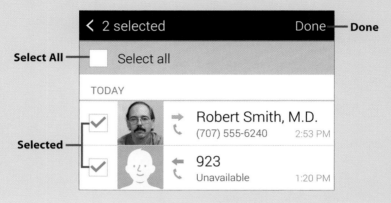

Dialing a Number in a Text or Email Message

A phone number in an email or text message acts as a *link* that, when tapped, can dial the number.

Text Message Links

1. In Messages, display the received or sent message that contains the phone number, and then tap the number.

2. Tap Call in the dialog box that appears. Phone launches and dials the number.

Email Message Links

1. In Email, display the received or sent email message that contains the phone number, and then tap the number.

2. The number appears in the Keypad section of Phone. If necessary, you can edit it (adding or removing the area code, for example) using normal editing techniques.

3. Tap the green phone icon to dial the number.

>>>*Go Further*

QUICK DIALING TECHNIQUES

For people and companies with a record in Contacts, you can also call them using a voice command, such as "Call Janice Gunderson." For information about using voice apps, see Chapter 15, "Using Voice Services."

Dialing with S Voice

You can quickly call anyone whose name appears in the Contacts, Logs, or Favorites list of Phone/Contacts or with whom you've recently exchanged messages in Messages.

- Locate the person or company in the Contacts, Logs, or Messages conversations list and swipe the item to the right. The Phone screen appears, and the person or company's number is automatically dialed.

- Locate the person or company's entry in the Favorites list and tap it to automatically dial the number.

Emergency Calling

Where available, the Galaxy S5 supports *e911* (Enhanced 911), enabling it to connect to a nearby emergency dispatch center regardless of where in the United States or Canada you happen to be. (The equivalent emergency number is different in other countries. In the United Kingdom, for example, it's 999.) When you place a 911 call, your position can usually be determined by the phone's GPS or by triangulating your position using nearby cell sites.

As a safety feature, you can even call 911 from a locked phone. To learn about other options for summoning assistance in an emergency situation, see "Safety Assistance Settings" in Chapter 3, "Making the Phone Your Own."

Call 911

1. Do one of the following:

   - Tap the Phone icon on the Home screen.

   - If the lock screen is displayed and the phone is protected with a pattern, password, PIN, or fingerprint scan, you can go directly to Phone by tapping the Emergency Call text.

2. On the normal Phone or the Emergency Dialer screen, respectively, enter **911** (or your country's equivalent number) and tap the green phone icon to dial the number.

Lock screen (bottom)

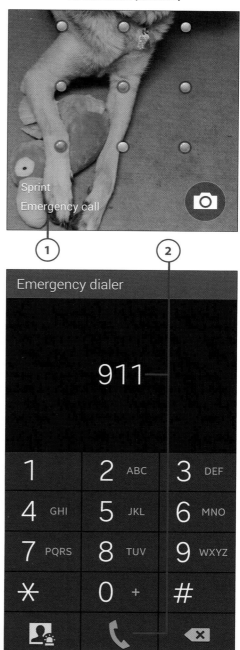

Emergency Calling Tips

Keep the following in mind when seeking emergency assistance:

- Even if you've disabled the phone's location/GPS functions for all other uses, these features remain available for 911 use.

- Not all emergency dispatch centers support e911. Instead of assuming they've determined where you are based on GPS or triangulation, be prepared to state your location.

- Some emergency dispatch centers use an automated voice menu that prompts you to enter numbers. According to Sprint, for example, "If you encounter a prerecorded message instead of a live operator, wait for the appropriate prompt and say 'EMERGENCY' instead of pressing 1. Not all wireless phones transmit number tones during a 911 call."

Other Outgoing Call Options

The Galaxy S5 also supports some additional outgoing call options: speed dialing, blocking your caller ID information, three-way calling, and inserting pause and wait commands.

Speed Dialing

To make it easy to dial your most important numbers, you can assign a *speed dial number* to anyone with a record in Contacts. The digits 2–100 are available as speed dial numbers; 1 is reserved for voicemail.

The New, Simplified Version

In previous implementations of Speed Dialing, you could replace a slot's contact with someone else, as well as swap the positions of any two entries. On the Galaxy S5, you can only assign and remove individual speed dial numbers.

Access the Speed Dial Screen

1. Launch Phone or Contacts by tapping an icon at the bottom of the Home screen.

2. Display the Speed Dial screen by selecting the Keypad or Contacts tab, tapping the menu icon, and choosing Speed Dial.

What Next?

When you reach the Speed Dial screen, jump ahead to the section that describes the task you want to perform.

Keypad tab

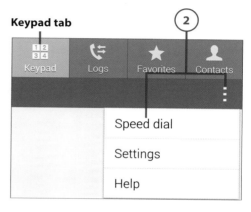

Assign a Speed Dial Number

1. On the Speed Dial screen, tap a currently unassigned number—that is, one that says Add Contact.

2. Tap the name of the person or company with which to associate this speed dial number.

3. If the contact record contains only one phone number, that number is automatically used. If the record contains multiple numbers, select the number to use.

4. The contact's phone number is assigned to the speed dial number.

Removing Speed Dial Entries

An X appears beside each assigned speed dial entry. To remove an entry, tap the X. The speed dial number is now unassigned and labeled Add Contact.

Dial a Speed Dial Number

1. Launch Phone by tapping its icon at the bottom of the Home screen.

2. With the Keypad tab selected, enter the speed dial number. Press and hold the final digit.

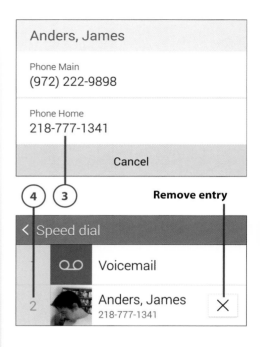

3. The phone dials the person or company associated with the speed dial number. Tap the red End Call icon to disconnect when you finish talking.

Dialing from the Speed Dial Screen

If you can't remember a particular speed dial number, you can initiate a call or message from the Speed Dial screen. Scroll to find the person or company's entry, tap the person's picture or placeholder, and then tap the Call or Message icon in the dialog box that appears. (If the person or company has multiple numbers, flick up or down in the list to find the number you want to call.)

Temporarily Blocking Your Caller ID Information

If you want to prevent your caller ID information from displaying on an outgoing call, precede the number with *67, such as *675591234 for a local call or *672145591234 for a long-distance call. The recipient's phone should display Private Number rather than your name, city, or number. Note that *67 is the correct prefix in the United States and Canada only; other countries have a different prefix.

If you want to prevent your caller ID information from displaying on *every* call, contact your service provider for assistance.

Three-Way Calling

By making a three-way call, you can talk to two people at the same time. (If you don't have an unlimited minutes plan, check with your service provider to determine how three-way calls are billed.)

1. Launch Phone and dial the first number.

2. When the first person answers, tell him to wait while you call the second person. Tap the Add Call icon and dial the second number. The first person is automatically placed on hold.

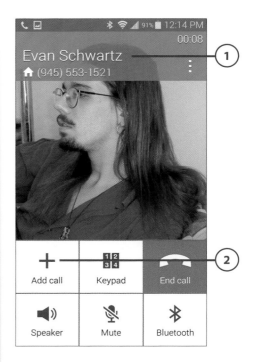

First call

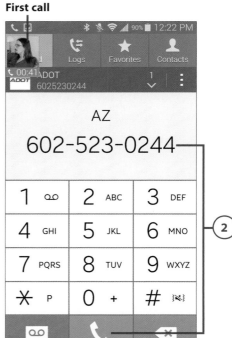

3. When the second person answers, tap the Merge icon.

4. The display shows that you're all connected to a conference call. When the call is completed, tap End Call. Any person who is still connected will be disconnected.

Second call

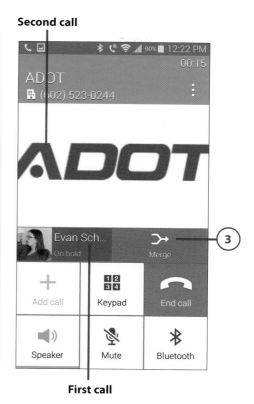

First call

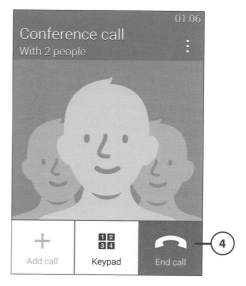

Inserting Pause and Wait Commands

If you're fed up with listening and responding to the automated answering systems used by banks, insurance companies, telephone companies, and cable systems, you might consider programming their Contacts record to automatically tap the correct keypad digits in response to their menus. For instance, 2145527777,,1,2,6310,,43 might take you to your Internet provider's technical support group.

In addition to digits, each phone number can contain commas (,) and semi-colons (;). Each comma represents a 2-second pause (you can string together multiple pauses), and each semicolon instructs the phone to wait until you enter any number or press a key. Creating a number that responds correctly to voice prompts requires trial and error. For example, if you don't wait long enough (using pauses) before the next number is entered, the process fails.

As you enter or edit a phone number, tap the menu icon and choose Add 2-Sec Pause or Add Wait to insert a pause or wait. The best numbers in which to use pauses and waits are the simple ones, such as those for which the initial prompt is for an extension. Complex, multilayered menus take much longer to program, and your efforts will "break" if the answering system's menu structure changes.

>>>Go Further

WI-FI CALLING (T-MOBILE AND METRO PCS)

T-Mobile and Metro PCS customers can optionally make calls over a Wi-Fi net-work rather than using their normal cellular service. This can be very useful when you live or work in a place that has a weak cell signal and, hence, poor call qual-ity. Note that Wi-Fi calling doesn't cost extra, but it does use plan minutes. And if you want to make out-of-country calls, you still must have an international plan.

To turn on Wi-Fi calling, ensure that Wi-Fi is enabled and that you're connected to an available network. Then open Settings, tap More Networks, and move the Wi-Fi Calling slider to the On position. If you want to set calling preferences, tap Connection Preferences and make a selection (such as Wi-Fi Preferred).

Receiving Calls

The other half of the phone call equation is that of receiving and responding to incoming calls.

Respond to an Incoming Call

1. When a call comes in, the caller is identified by name and number (if he has a Contacts record), by number (if there's no matching Contacts record), or by Private Number (if he has blocked his caller ID).

2. You can respond in any of the following ways:

   - *Accept call.* Drag the green phone icon in any direction.

   - *Reject call.* Drag the red phone icon in any direction, sending the caller to voicemail.

   - *Ignore call.* Do nothing; let the phone ring. After a number of rings, the caller is transferred to voicemail.

   - *Reject with explanation.* Drag Reject Call with Message upward and select a text message to transmit to the caller. (Note that if the caller doesn't have a messaging plan or is calling from a landline, the text message might not be delivered.)

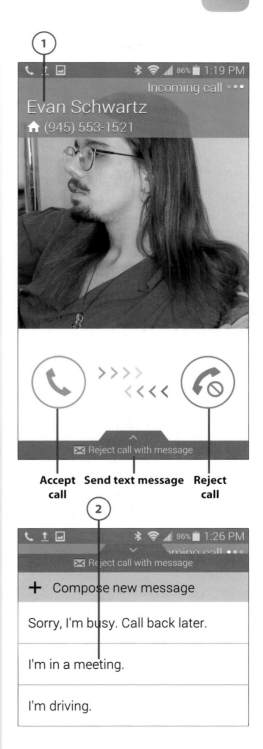

3. Tap the red End Call icon to disconnect when you finish talking.

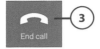

>>>*Go Further*

MORE WAYS TO ACCEPT AND END CALLS

In addition to the normal methods described in this chapter, the Answering and Ending Calls settings provide novel ways to accept and end calls. To view or change these settings, launch Phone, press the menu key, choose Settings, and tap Call, Answering and Ending Calls. Options include the following:

- *Pressing the Home key.* Press the Home key to answer an incoming call. This can be more convenient than dragging the green Accept icon, especially in the dark or when driving.

- *Voice control.* Incoming calls are announced by caller name or number. You can say "Answer" to accept the call or "Reject" to send the caller to voicemail.

- *Waving hand over device.* Wave your hand back and forth over the phone to accept a call.

- *Pressing the power key.* You can press the Power key to end a call.

‹ Answering and ending calls
ANSWER CALLS BY
Pressing the Home key ✓
Voice control ✓ Answer calls with voice commands.
Waving hand over device ✓
END CALLS BY
Pressing the power key ✓

Call Waiting

Call waiting enables you to answer an incoming call when you're already on a call.

1. Answer the new call by sliding the green phone icon in any direction.

2. The initial call is automatically placed on hold while you speak to the new caller. To switch between callers, tap the Swap icon. The active call is always shown in green at the top of the screen.

3. Tap the End Call icon to end the active call. The other call becomes active, ringing your phone if necessary.

Incoming caller's info

Active call

On hold

Call Forwarding

Depending on your carrier, you can have all or only particular kinds of calls that your cell phone would normally receive automatically forwarded to another number. Forwarding works even when the Galaxy S5 is turned off. To restore normal calling, deactivate call forwarding when you're finished. (Check with your service provider or review your plan to determine the cost of using call forwarding.)

The following are two of the simplest implementations of call forwarding: Sprint and Verizon. Enabling and disabling call forwarding with other carriers is often handled by tapping Phone's menu icon, choosing Settings, and then tapping Call, Additional Settings, Call Forwarding. Consult your carrier's website for specific instructions.

- *Sprint.* To activate call forwarding, launch Phone and dial *72, followed by the number to which calls should be forwarded. When you're ready to deactivate forwarding, dial *720. When activating or deactivating call forwarding, a tone signifies that the change has been accepted.

- *Verizon.* Launch Phone, tap the menu icon, and choose Settings. To enable or disable call forwarding, tap Call, Call Forwarding, and then choose Turn On Call Forwarding or Turn Off Call Forwarding, respectively.

In-Call Options

While on a call, you can access common in-call options by tapping icons and choosing menu commands. Additional options are available via hardware controls and the Notification panel.

Menu commands. Tap the menu icon and choose one of these commands:

- *Contacts, Memo, or Messages.* View information in Contacts, take notes in Memo during the call, or send a text message to the other party.

- *Personalize Call Sound.* Choose an audio equalizer setting for the current call. Before you can use this feature, you must set it up as described in the "Personalize Call Sound" sidebar later in this chapter.

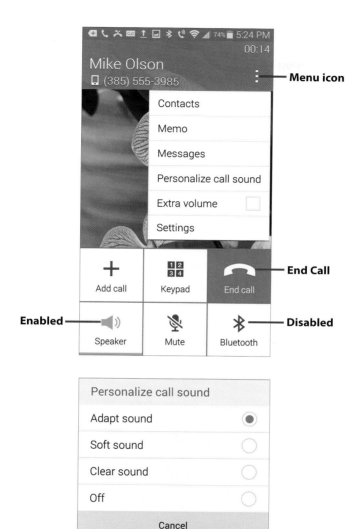

- *Extra Volume*. You can boost in-call volume above the normal maximum when this command is checked. Tap it a second time to disable the volume boost.

Onscreen icons. You can tap the following icons during a call. When an icon-based option is enabled or active, it is green.

- *Keypad*. If you need to enter an extension or information to respond to a voice prompt, tap the Keypad icon to display the dialing keypad. The icon's label changes to Hide. To dismiss the keypad, tap the Hide icon or press the Back key.

- *Speaker*. Tap the Speaker icon to toggle between normal and speaker-phone modes.

- *Mute*. To temporarily turn off the phone's microphone so that the other party can't hear you, tap the Mute icon.

- *Bluetooth*. To use a Bluetooth headset on the current call, tap the Bluetooth icon. To resume using the built-in earpiece, tap the icon again.

- *End Call*. Tap End Call to "hang up," disconnecting from the other party.

Other options. Two other important options are available during calls that aren't represented by icons.

- *Volume adjustment*. To change the volume, press the hardware Volume control on the left side of the phone. An onscreen volume indicator appears. Press the top half of the hardware Volume control to raise the volume; press the lower half to lower the volume. You can also adjust the volume by dragging the onscreen slider.

- *Notification panel controls*. You can drag down the Notification panel to access the Speaker, Mute, and End options. This is especially useful if you exit the Phone screen during the call in order to run other apps.

Notification panel in-call controls

Phone Call Multitasking

You can indeed run other apps while on a call. Return to the Home screen by pressing the Home key and then launch the apps. You can also open Phone's menu to launch Contacts, Memo, or Messages. To indicate that you're still on a call, the status bar turns neon green, a phone icon is added to the status bar, and a call progress icon is displayed. You can drag the call progress icon to a new location if it's in your way.

If you want to return to Phone, tap the call progress icon, tap the picture or placeholder icon in the Notification panel, or launch Phone. When you're ready to end the call, launch Phone or tap the End icon in the Notification panel.

Active call indicator

Call progress icon

Checking Voicemail

Using your service provider's voicemail, people can leave messages for you when you're unavailable or the phone is turned off. When voicemail is waiting, a voicemail icon appears in the status bar and an entry is added to the Notification panel.

Voicemail Password

If you set up voicemail to require a password, you'll be asked to enter it each time you contact voicemail. When prompted, tap each digit in the password and end by tapping the pound sign (#)—or follow whatever instructions your carrier provides. Refer to Chapter 1, "Galaxy S5 Essentials," for instructions on setting up voicemail.

You can check your voicemail in two or more ways:

1. Connect to your carrier's voicemail service by doing one of the following:

   - Drag down the Notification panel and tap a voicemail entry. The carrier's voicemail is automatically dialed or its voicemail app launches (if one is provided).

   - Launch the Phone app. Press and hold 1 (the speed dial number assigned to voicemail) or tap the voicemail icon. The Phone app dials the carrier's voicemail.

   - Launch your carrier's voicemail app (if one is provided).

Voicemail indicator

2. You connect to the carrier's voicemail system. Because the voicemail menus require you to enter numbers to choose options, tap the Keypad icon to reveal the keypad (if it's currently hidden). Listen to the menu options and tap numbers to indicate your choices.

3. Tap the End Call icon when you finish using voicemail.

Changing Voicemail Settings

You can change your voicemail settings (such as your greeting, password, and notification methods) whenever you want. Connect with voicemail and respond to the prompts.

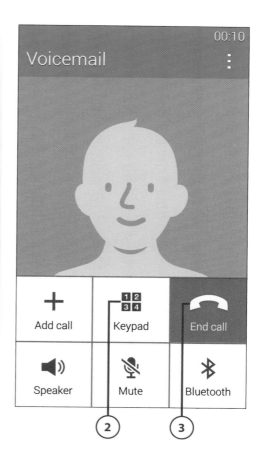

Enabling Mute, Vibrate, or Airplane Mode

Your phone has three special settings that you'll occasionally find useful: Mute, Vibrate, and Airplane mode. Enable Mute when your phone *must* remain silent, such as when you're in a meeting or place of worship. Vibrate also silences notifications, but denotes them by vibrating the phone. Enable Airplane mode during flights to quickly make your phone compliant with government and airline regulations by disabling the ability to place or receive calls, as well as transmit data.

Mute and Vibrate

When Mute is enabled, all sounds except media playback and alarms are disabled. Incoming calls cause the Phone app to launch—even when the screen is dark—but no sound or vibration occurs. Vibration has the same silencing effect as Mute, but important events are signaled by vibration.

1. To enable muting or vibration, do one of the following:

   • Press and hold the Power button until the Device Options menu appears, and then tap the Mute or Vibrate icon.

   • On the Home screen, press and hold the Volume down key until the onscreen volume control shows that Mute or Vibrate is enabled. (Lower the volume all the way to enable Mute. When the Mute icon is shown, you can quickly switch to Vibrate by tapping the Volume up key once.)

   • Open the Notification panel. Repeatedly tap the Sound button to toggle between its three states: Mute, Vibrate, and Sound.

2. When Vibrate or Mute is active, a matching indicator displays in the status bar.

3. Restore normal sound by selecting Sound in the Device Options menu, enabling Sound in the Notification panel, or increasing the volume.

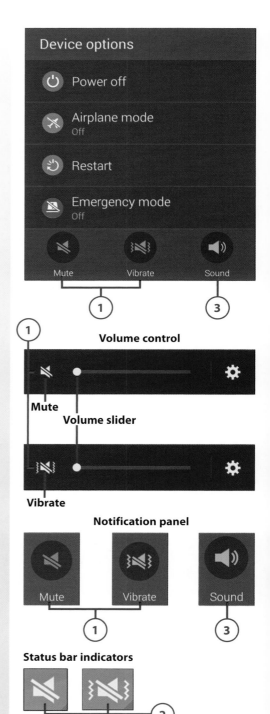

Volume control

Mute

Volume slider

Vibrate

Notification panel

Status bar indicators

Airplane Mode

When flying, you can quickly set your phone to Airplane mode, disabling its ability to place or receive calls and to send or receive data. Other functions operate normally.

1. To quickly enable Airplane mode, do one of the following:

   - Press and hold the Power button until the Device Options menu appears. Tap Airplane Mode.

   - Open the Notification panel, scroll the Quick Setting buttons to the right, and tap Airplane Mode. When enabled, the button is green. (If the button isn't visible, tap the Grid View icon and *then* tap the Airplane Mode button.)

   - Open Settings, tap the Airplane Mode icon (in Network Connections), and move its slider to the On position.

Device Options

Notification panel

Grid View

Airplane mode settings

2. In the Turn On Airplane Mode dialog box, confirm by tapping OK. The Airplane mode indicator appears in the status bar; cellular connections, Wi-Fi, and Bluetooth are automatically disabled.

3. Restore normal calling and data transmission functionality by disabling Airplane mode by reversing any of the actions described in Step 1. Tap OK in the Airplane Mode dialog box.

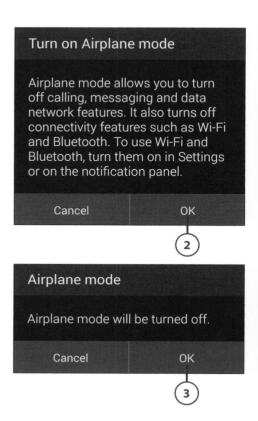

Configuring Call Settings

You can set preferences for many phone operations in Call Settings. Although the default settings will suffice for most calling situations, you should still familiarize yourself with them.

To review or change the settings, launch Phone, tap the menu icon, choose Settings, and tap Call. Or you can open Settings and tap the Call icon (in the Applications section). Here are some of the most useful Call Settings:

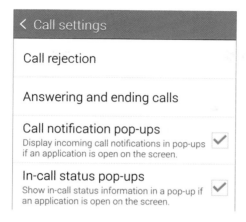

- *Call Rejection.* Enable/disable Auto Reject mode for blocked callers (or to temporarily reject *all* incoming calls), as well as add or remove numbers from the Auto Reject List. Rejected calls are sent straight to voicemail. You can also create or delete call rejection text messages. These can optionally be sent when manually rejecting an incoming call by dragging Reject Call with Message upward (at the bottom of Phone's main screen).

- *Answering and Ending Calls.* See the "More Ways to Accept and End Calls" sidebar, earlier in this chapter.

- *Call Notification Pop-ups.* When this setting is enabled, rather than com-mandeer your entire screen whenever there's an incoming call, a smaller, less intrusive pop-up window appears. You can tap a button to answer or reject the call, expand the window to its normal full-screen view (in order to view additional information or reject with a text message), or drag the pop-up to a different screen location.

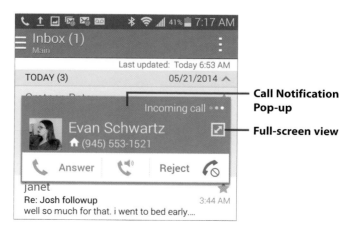

- *In-call Status Pop-ups.* When you dial a number or receive a call, a window above the Accept and Reject icons shows your most recent interactions with the person or company (as a reminder of when you last talked, for example).

In-Call Status Pop-up

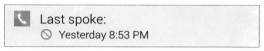

- *Call Alerts.* Specify whether the phone vibrates when the call recipient answers and when the call ends, whether tones denote each call connection and end, and whether alarms and new message notifications are active during calls. When Minute Minder is enabled, the phone beeps twice whenever another minute of connect time passes.

Call Alerts Settings

< Call alerts

CALL VIBRATIONS

Vibrate on connection to netwo..

Call-end vibration

CALL STATUS TONES

Call connect tone   ✓

Minute minder

Call end tone   ✓

ALERTS ON CALL

Notify during calls   ✓
Allow alarms and notifications to sound/
vibrate during calls.

- *Call Accessories.* Configure the phone for use with a Bluetooth headset. You can enable the headset to automatically answer incoming calls and specify a delay period prior to answering. Outgoing Call Conditions determines whether calls can also be initiated with the headset when the phone is locked.

- *Additional Settings.* Configure settings for the deaf and those who wear hearing aids.

- *Ringtone and Sound Settings.* Specify the sounds that announce an incoming call and govern call sound quality. Tap Ringtones and Keypad Tones to select or create a ringtone for incoming calls (see "Ringtones" in Chapter 3), change the vibration pattern, enable or disable vibration when ringing, and enable or disable the playing of tones when tapping numbers on the keypad. Tap Personalize Call Sound to adapt the call audio to your needs (see the "Personalize Call Sound" sidebar at the end of this section). Enable Noise Reduction to suppress background/ambient noise during calls.

RINGTONE AND SOUND SETTINGS
Ringtones and keypad tones
Personalize call sound Adapt sound
Noise reduction Suppresses background noise from your side during calls.

- *Voice Privacy.* When enabled, this setting causes your calls to be encrypted using Enhanced Encryption (when available).

>>>Go Further

PERSONALIZE CALL SOUND

To improve audio quality during phone calls or while listening to music, you can enable the Adapt Sound feature. Based on a hearing test, the phone adjusts sound so it's optimal for you. If you haven't already set up Adapt Sound from within the Music app, you can do so now.

1. Launch Phone, tap the menu icon, choose Settings, and tap Call.

2. Scroll down and tap Personalize Call Sound.

3. Plug in your earphones and, following the instructions, take the audio test.

4. At the test's conclusion, tap icons to compare unaltered (Original) audio in the left, right, and both ears with that of the Adapt Sound (Personalized) audio.

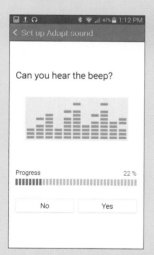
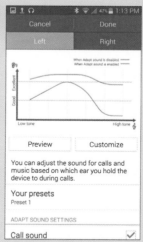
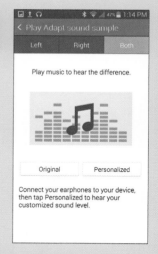

5. Set options in the Adapt Sound Settings section of the screen. To enable Adapt Sound during calls and listening to music, tap their check boxes. Tap Frequently Used Side to specify the side of your face that you typically use when speaking on the phone.

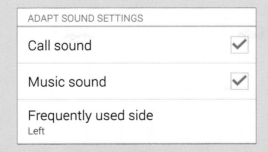

ADAPT SOUND SETTINGS

Call sound   ✓

Music sound   ✓

Frequently used side
Left

6. Tap Done.

During a call, open the menu in Phone, choose Personalize Call Sound to disable or enable the feature, and then select Adapt Sound (for your personalized setting) or one of the other audio options. When using earphones to listen to songs in Music, you can enable or disable Adapt Sound by opening the menu, choosing Settings, and tapping Adapt Sound. (Without earphones, Adapt Sound is automatically disabled.)

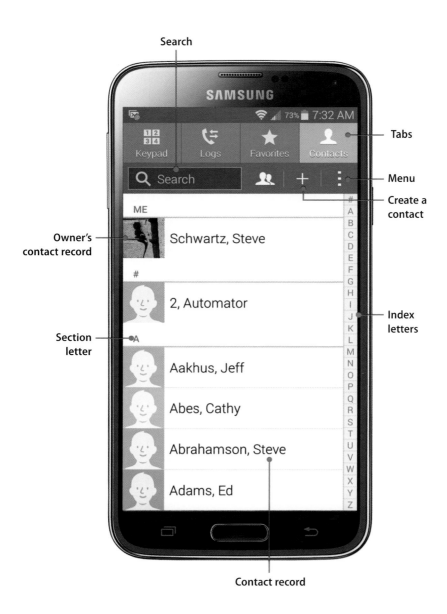

Search

Tabs

Menu

Create a contact

Owner's contact record

Index letters

Section letter

Contact record

In this chapter, you find out how to use the Contacts app to create and manage your business and personal contacts. Topics include the following:

→ Understanding the Contacts interface

→ Creating, viewing, and editing contact records

→ Joining multiple contact records for the same person

→ Defining and working with contact groups

→ Backing up your contacts to built-in memory or a memory card

→ Exporting contacts from Outlook (Windows) and Contacts/Address Book (Mac) and importing them into Google Contacts

→ Setting display options for the Contacts record list

Managing Contacts

Contacts is the built-in address book app on the Galaxy S5. It's populated by contact records created on the phone, in your Google Contacts account on the Web, and in other information sources that you sync to it, such as Facebook, LinkedIn, and Exchange Server accounts. The Contacts app links to Phone for dialing numbers, Email for selecting email recipients, and Messages for selecting text and multimedia message recipients.

Verizon and Other Carriers

The tabs across the top of the Contacts screen are slightly different for Verizon phones. Verizon users will see a Recent tab, whereas everyone else will see a Logs tab. Both tabs and their uses are discussed in this chapter, but the figures shown are a mixture of Verizon and non-Verizon ones.

The Contacts Interface

Contacts has four sections, each represented by a tab at the top of the screen. Here's what you can do in each section:

- *Keypad.* Tap the Keypad tab to switch to the Phone app to make a call. (Phone and Contacts are linked; you can quickly switch between them by tapping the appropriate tab. Chapter 4, "Placing and Receiving Calls," covers the Phone app.)

Section tabs (Verizon)

Section tabs (non-Verizon phones)

- *Logs (all carriers other than Verizon).* Tap the Logs tab to view your call records (dialed calls, missed calls, received calls, and rejected calls), enabling you to easily return calls and assign numbers to your Auto Reject List.

- *Recent (Verizon only).* Tap the Recent tab to view a list of people and companies that you frequently call but have not marked as favorites.

Non-Verizon Phones

If Verizon isn't your carrier, you can view the people you frequently call by selecting the Favorites tab and scrolling to the Frequently Contacted section.

- *Favorites.* Tap the Favorites tab to view a list of only those contact records that you've marked as favorites. To add or remove someone as a favorite, open the person's record for viewing in any list and tap the star icon at the top of the record. For more information about favorites, see "Mark Contacts as Favorites," later in this chapter.

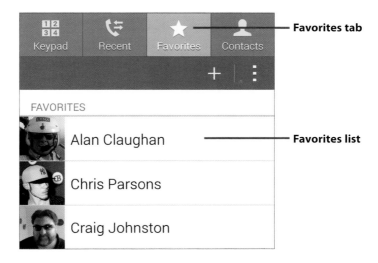

Favorites tab

Favorites list

- *Contacts.* The default tab is Contacts. It displays a scrolling list of your contact records. You can tap a person's name to view her contact record. This section of Contacts can optionally be displayed by Phone, Email, and Messages to enable you to select a call, email, or message recipient. The Contacts list is discussed throughout this chapter.

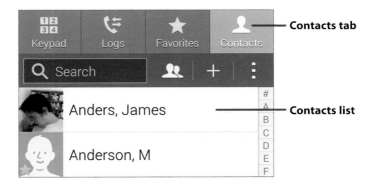

Contacts tab

Contacts list

Creating a Contact Record

In addition to creating contacts in Google Contacts or another address book utility that you're syncing with your phone, you can create new contact records directly on the phone.

1. Tap the Contacts icon on the Home screen or select it in Apps.

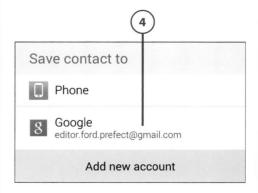

Other Contacts Launch Options

You can also launch Contacts by tapping the Contacts tab in the Phone app or the Contacts icon in Email or Messages when selecting message recipients.

2. Tap the Contacts tab if it isn't already selected.

3. Tap the + (plus) icon to create a new contact record.

4. *Verizon only:* Choose where the new contact will be created. Select Phone for a contact that will reside only on the phone. Select a specific account from your installed accounts to share this record with the account's contact list. (Other carriers specify where the record is created in Step 6.)

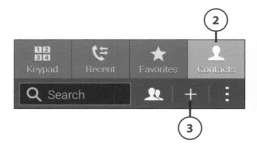

Adding Accounts

Chapters 1, "Galaxy S5 Essentials," and 6, "Using the Calendar," provide examples of adding accounts to the phone.

5. The screen for creating a contact appears, ready for you to enter the person or company's contact information.

6. The top entry shows the account in which the contact will be created and shared. Tap the entry to change the location.

Storage Location and Sharing

To create and store the record only on the phone, choose Phone (Verizon) or Device (carriers other than Verizon).

7. Enter the person's name. You can type the full name in the Name field or—to enter more detailed name information, such as a prefix, suffix, or middle name—tap the expand/collapse arrow beside the field. When you finish entering the name components, you can collapse the name by tapping the same arrow.

8. Enter a phone number for the person in the Phone field. If the label (Mobile, for example) is incorrect, tap the label and select the correct one from the drop-down list. (Select Custom—at the bottom of the list—if you want to create your own label.)

Add more numbers by tapping the Phone field's plus (+) icon. To remove an unwanted or blank number, tap its minus (–) icon.

Text Messaging

If you intend to send text or multimedia messages to this person, you must enter at least one number that's designated as Mobile.

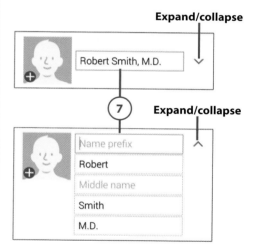

Expand/collapse

Expand/collapse

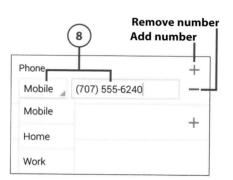

Remove number

Add number

9. Tap the + (plus) icon beside the Email field to record an email address for the person. Use the same process as you did for the Phone field (see Step 8).

10. Add fields that aren't currently shown by tapping Add Another Field at the bottom of the screen. As an example, Steps 11–12 explain how to add an Address field to the record.

11. Select Address in the Add Another Field dialog box and tap OK.

12. Use the same method that you used to enter Phone and Email information. Address is a composite field with separate entries for Street, City, State, ZIP Code, and Country. To add other elements, such as P.O. Box and Neighborhood, tap the expand/collapse icon.

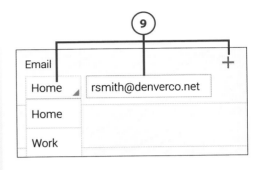

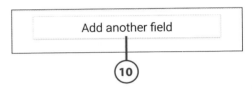

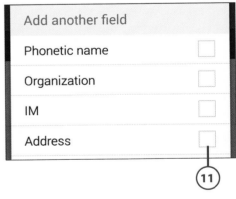

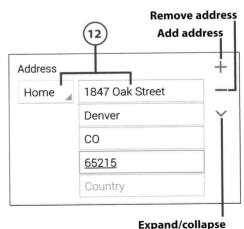

13. *Optional:* You can assign the person to one or more contact groups. The advantage of using groups is that you can text or email all members of the group by addressing a message to the group rather than to each member. To assign the person to groups, tap the Groups field, select the check box of each appropriate group, and tap Save. (To learn how to create and use groups, see "Working with Contact Groups," later in this chapter.)

14. *Optional:* To specify a distinctive ringtone that will announce calls from this person, tap Ringtone, select an option in the Ringtones dialog box, and tap OK.

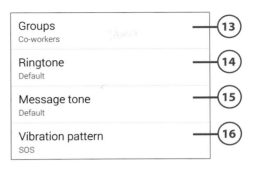

Specifying a Ringtone

You can select ringtones from those provided with the phone (Ringtones) or use any audio file—such as a downloaded ringtone or a complete song—that you've stored on the phone. To assign such a custom ringtone to the record, tap the Add button and locate the audio or music file. Ringtones are discussed in detail in "Ringtones" in Chapter 3, "Making the Phone Your Own."

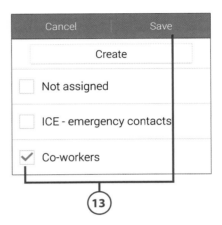

15. *Optional (Verizon only):* To choose a distinctive alert for messages from this contact, tap Message tone, select an alert tone in the Message tone dialog box, and tap OK.

16. *Optional (Verizon only):* To assign an identifiable vibration pattern to the contact, tap Vibration Pattern, select a pattern in the Vibration Pattern dialog box, and tap OK. To create a custom vibration pattern, tap Create, and then touch and release the screen with varying lengths of time to create the pattern on the Create Pattern screen.

17. When you finish entering the initial information for this contact, tap the Save button at the top of the screen or tap Cancel to discard the record.

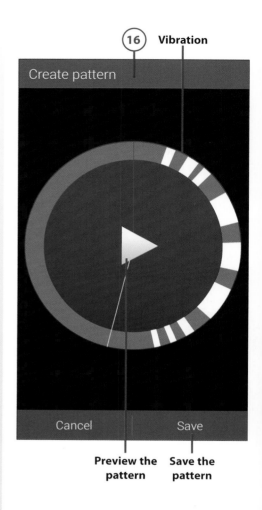

16 **Vibration**

Preview the pattern **Save the pattern**

17

Adding a Photo to a Contact Record

To help identify a contact, you can add a photo to the person's record. You can use any photo that's stored on the phone or use the phone's camera to shoot the picture.

1. Associate a photo with the contact by tapping the photo placeholder in the upper-left corner while creating or editing the contact record. (If the record already has a photo, you can tap it to replace it with a new photo.)

2. Select the appropriate option in the Contact Photo dialog box. Tap Image to use a photo stored on the phone. Tap Tagged Pictures to use a previously shared image. Tap Take Picture to use the phone's camera to shoot the picture now.

3. If you tapped Image or Tagged Pictures in Step 2, Gallery launches. Tap the folder that contains the photo, tap the photo's thumbnail, and go to Step 5.

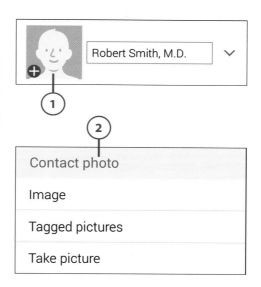

Image (Gallery app)

4. If you tapped Take Picture in Step 2, Camera launches. Tap the Camera button to take the person's picture. If you don't care for the shot, tap Discard and try again; otherwise, tap Save.

5. On the cropping screen, move and resize the blue cropping rectangle to select the area of the photo that you want to use, and then tap Done. The cropped photo is added to the contact record.

6. If you're done creating or editing the record, tap the Save button at the top of the screen.

Viewing Contacts

The bulk of what you do in Contacts involves finding and viewing individual contacts so you can call, email, or text them.

1. Launch Contacts by tapping its Home screen icon.

2. With the Contacts tab selected, contacts are displayed in an alphabetical scrolling list. By default, all contacts from all sources are listed. You can restrict contacts to a single source (LinkedIn, for example) and set other display options by following the instructions in "Setting Display Options" at the end of this chapter.

Add contact

Search

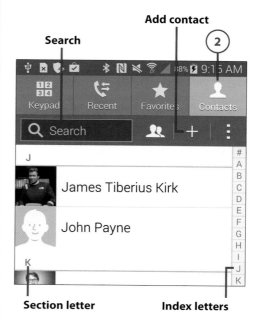

Section letter   **Index letters**

3. To find a particular contact, you can use any of the following techniques:

   - Flick up or down to scroll the list.

   - Tap an index letter on the right edge of the screen to go to that approximate spot in the alphabetical list.

   - Press and drag in the index letter list. As you drag, a large version of each index letter appears. Remove your finger when the correct letter is shown. For example, to find a person whose last name is Jones, release your finger when J appears.

   - Search for someone by tapping the Search box and entering any element of the person's record, such as first or last name, street name, or email address. As you type, a list of likely matching contacts appears. When you see the correct record, tap the person's entry.

4. When you find the contact, tap it to view the person's record. Depending on the information recorded for the contact, you can dial any listed number by tapping the green phone icon, send a text message to the person by tapping the orange envelope icon, or address a new email to the person by tapping an email address' envelope icon.

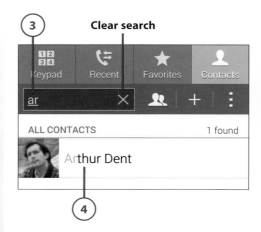

Clear search

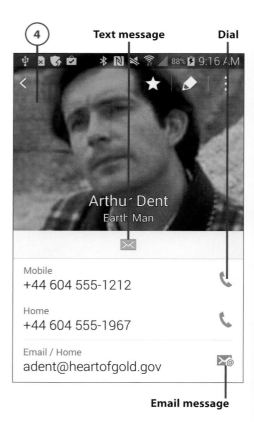

Text message   Dial

Email message

Editing Contact Records

Contact records sometimes require editing. You might have to add or change an email address or phone number, or you may want to substitute a better picture. Editing a contact employs the same techniques that you use to create contact records. In this section, you discover several ways to edit records, as well as delete them.

Edit Contacts

When changes to a record are necessary to bring it up to date, here's what you need to do:

1. Select the record that you want to edit in Contacts. The complete record displays.

2. Tap the Edit icon.

3. Using the techniques described in "Creating a Contact Record," make the necessary changes to the person's information.

4. Tap Save to save your edits, or tap Cancel if you decide not to save the changes.

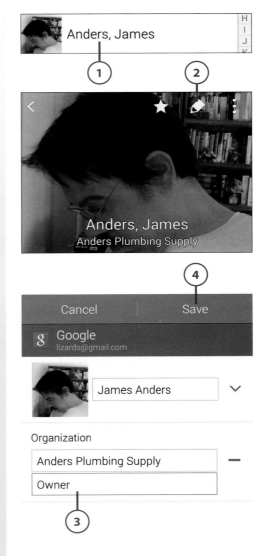

Set Defaults for a Contact

Several contact fields can have multiple entries. For example, a record can have several phone numbers, email addresses, IM usernames, and mailing addresses. For some of these fields, you can optionally specify a *default entry*—that is, one that you want to treat as primary.

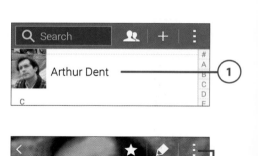

1. In any Contacts list, select the record for which you want to view, set, or change defaults. The complete record displays.

2. Tap the menu icon and choose Mark as Default. All items for which you can set a default are displayed.

3. Tap a radio button to set an entry as a default. If necessary, scroll to see any additional items.

4. Tap Save to set the new defaults for the record.

5. Whenever you view the record, default entries are denoted by a blue check mark.

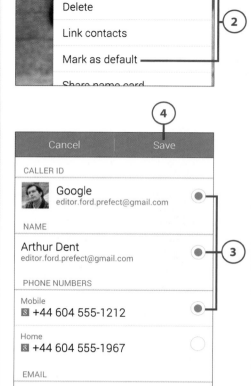

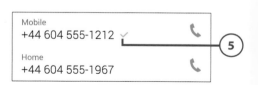

Link and Unlink Contacts

Your contact records probably
come from multiple sources. Some
are created on the phone; others
might originate in Google Contacts,
LinkedIn, an Exchange Server
account, or a social networking site.
As a result, when you scroll through
the entries in Contacts, you may find
some duplicates. You can use the
Link Contacts command (formerly
known as Join Contact) to merge the
duplicates for a person into a single
contact record.

1. In the Contacts list, locate a pair
   of records for the same person by
   browsing or searching. This example uses a person with a record
   that was created on the phone
   and another created in Gmail. Tap
   the record that you want to serve
   as the primary record.

2. Tap the menu icon and choose
   Link Contacts. The Suggested
   Contacts list appears.

3. If the list includes the person's
   other record, select it and tap
   Done. Otherwise, scroll down to
   locate the record, select it, and
   tap Done.

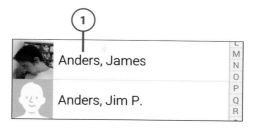
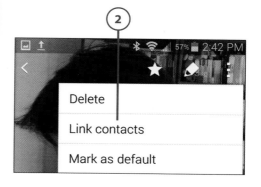
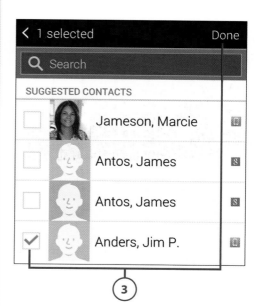

4. The two records are linked to create a single record. If you view the record, you can see the sources of the linked records. If more records exist for this person, you can link those as well by using the Link Contacts command again.

Google

Connected via

Device/Phone

④

Unlinking Contacts

If necessary, you can unlink records, re-creating the original, individual records. Open the linked record, tap the Link icon (which looks like a chain link) or choose Unlink Contacts from the menu, and tap the minus (–) sign beside one of the listed records.

Mark Contacts as Favorites

To make it easy to quickly find people with whom you're in regular contact, you can mark records as *favorites*. Doing so adds those people to the contacts in your Favorites list.

1. In a Contacts list, tap a contact name.

2. Tap the star icon at the top of the screen to add the contact to your Favorites. When marked as a favorite, the star is gold. If you subsequently need to remove the contact from Favorites, open the record and tap the star icon again.

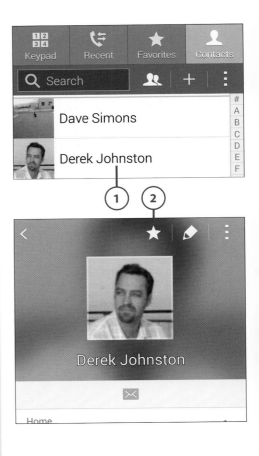

Simultaneously Removing Multiple Favorites

To remove *multiple* contacts from Favorites, select the Favorites tab, tap the menu icon, and choose Remove from Favorites. Tap the check box of each person that you want to remove, and then tap Done. (When removing favorites, you can also remove people from the Frequently Contacted list by tapping their check boxes.)

Selected contacts

Grid Versus List View

If you've added photos to your favorite contacts, tap the menu icon and choose Grid View to display favorites as photo thumbnails. (To restore the Favorites scrolling list, open the menu and choose List View.)

Delete Contacts

People leave your personal and business life for many reasons. When you're certain that you no longer need certain contact records, you can delete them.

1. To delete one or more records while viewing any Contacts list, press and hold any of these records. (Alternatively, you can open the menu and choose Delete.)

2. Select other contacts that you also want to delete, if any. Selected contacts have a green check mark.

3. Delete the selected contacts by tapping the Trash icon or Done, respectively (depending on the technique employed in Step 1). Tap OK in the Delete Contact confirmation dialog box.

Deleting an Open Record

You can also delete a record while you're viewing it. Tap the menu icon, choose Delete, and tap OK in the Delete Contact confirmation dialog box.

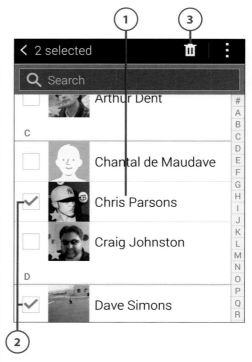

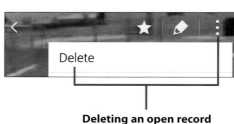

Deleting an open record

Working with Contact Groups

A *group* is a collection of contacts that have something in common, such as membership in a parents' organization, employees in a company department, or high school friends. Because each group is a subset of Contacts, you can use groups to quickly find every important person of a particular type. You can also use a group as the recipient for an email or text message, automatically sending it to all members. You can create groups and define their memberships from scratch, as well as use the built-in groups (Family and Friends, for example) and ones created for you by websites, such as LinkedIn.

Create a Group

1. In Contacts, tap the Groups icon.

2. Tap the plus (+) icon to create a new group.

3. *Optional:* Specify the account of which this group will be a subset by tapping Create Group In.

4. Enter a name for the group.

5. *Optional:* Specify a ringtone that will announce calls from group members.

6. *Optional:* Specify an alert for text messages from group members.

7. *Optional:* Specify a vibration pattern that will announce calls or text messages from group members.

8. *Optional:* Tap Add Member to set the initial group membership. Select members by tapping their names and then tap Done. (Note that you can add members at any time.)

9. Tap the Save button to save the group name, membership, and settings. The group name is added to the Integrated Groups list. Whenever you want to view the group's membership, tap the Groups icon (refer to the figure for Step 1) and tap the group's name in the Integrated Groups list.

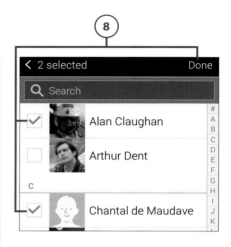

Changing a Group's Definition or Membership

You can quickly change a group's settings or membership. Tap the Groups icon, tap the group's name, and then open the menu and choose Edit Group. When you finish making changes, tap Save.

A Hidden Groups Feature

Below the Integrated Groups list are two categories labeled Accounts and Organizations. Tap Accounts to view contacts grouped by account, such as your LinkedIn associates. Tap Organizations to view all people affiliated with the same organization, such as all Microsoft employees. If you aren't great at remembering names, opening an organization group might be just the help you need to find the name, phone number, or email address of the person you're trying to contact.

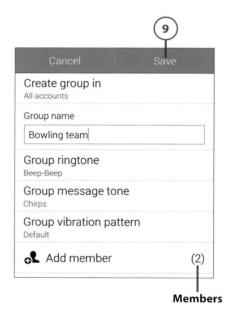

Members

Quickly Removing Members from a Group

In addition to adding new members to a group, you can easily remove one or more members. Open the group to display its membership. Then tap the menu icon, choose Remove from Group, select the members that you want to remove, and tap Done.

Change a Person's Memberships

1. With the Contacts tab selected, tap a person's name to open her record.

2. Tap the Edit icon.

3. Tap the Groups entry.

4. Add or remove check marks to assign or remove the person from the listed groups. Tap Save to save the changes. (Note that a person can be a member of multiple groups.)

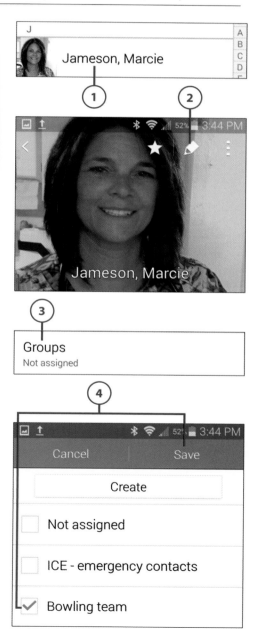

Email or Text a Group

1. In Email or Messages, tap the Compose icon.

2. Tap the Contacts icon to select email or message recipients.

3. In Contacts, tap the Groups tab and select the group that you want to email or message.

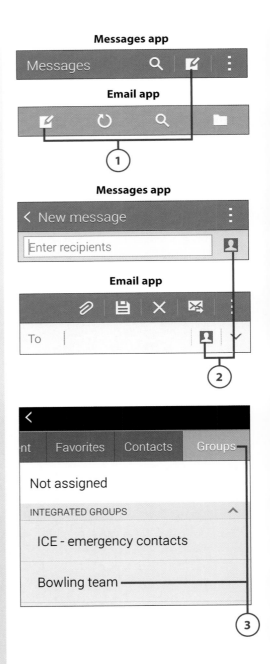

4. Select the individual group members that you want to email or message, or tap Select All to include the entire group as recipients.

Multiple Choice

If a selected individual has multiple email addresses or mobile phone numbers, a dialog box appears in which you must select the correct address or number.

5. Tap Done to transfer the selected members' email addresses or mobile numbers to Email or Messages, respectively. Complete your email or compose your message as you normally do.

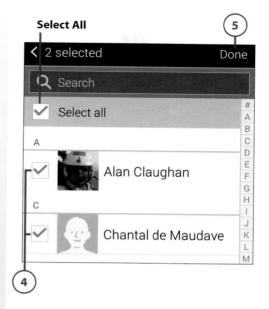

Select All

Start an Email or Text Message from Contacts

You can also initiate a group email or text message from within Contacts. Tap the Groups icon, tap the group name, tap the menu icon, and choose Send Message or Email. Indicate whether you want to send a message or email, select recipients, and tap Done. (Another way to perform this procedure is to choose the Send Message or Email command with the Contacts tab selected, and *then* select a group and specify members who will be recipients.)

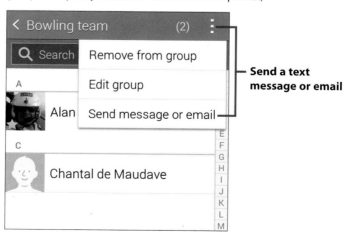

Send a text message or email

Reorder the Groups

1. Tap the Groups icon, and then open the menu and choose Change Order.

2. Change a group's position by dragging the group up or down by the dot pattern on its right edge. Release the group when it's in the desired spot. Repeat for other groups whose positions you want to change.

3. Tap Done to save the new group list order.

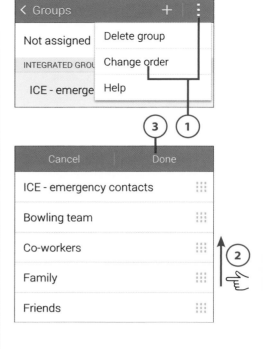

Delete a Group

1. Tap the Groups icon, and then open the menu and choose Delete Group.

2. Select the groups you want to delete by tapping check boxes, and then tap Done.

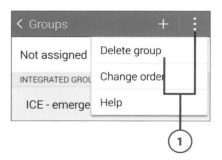

3. Indicate whether you want to delete only the selected group(s)—leaving the associated contact records intact—or the group(s) *and* member contact records.

4. Confirm the deletion(s) by tapping OK or tap Cancel if you've changed your mind.

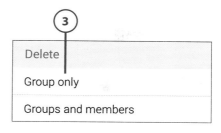

Deleting a User-Created Group

To quickly delete a group that you created, press and hold its entry in the groups list and tap the Trash icon.

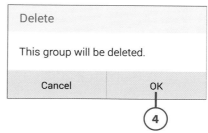

Backing Up/Restoring and Exporting/Importing Contact Records

As security against phone-related disasters or in preparation for switching to a new phone, you can back up your Contacts data to a memory card or built-in memory, or you can merge the data with your Google or Samsung account.

Exporting To and From the SIM Card

Some carriers also allow you to export Contacts data to and from a phone's SIM card. However, because only a record's name, phone number, and email address are exported, backing up to the SIM card is considerably less useful than any other method described in this section. Furthermore, only some carriers support this feature.

To export contacts to the SIM card, select the Contacts tab and tap the menu icon. Choose SIM Management, Copy Contacts to SIM or choose Settings, Contacts, Import/Export, Export to SIM Card, depending on your carrier. To restore contacts from the SIM card, select the Contacts tab and tap the menu icon. Choose SIM Management, Copy Contacts from SIM or choose Settings, Contacts, Import/Export, Import from SIM Card.

You can also use export/import procedures to manually move copies of contact records from your computer-based email and address book utilities into Contacts. For information about and strategies for syncing your contact data with its various sources, see Chapter 17, "Synchronizing Data."

Carriers Differ

Each carrier decides the Contacts backup and restore procedures that it supports, as well as the steps required. However, regardless of which carrier you have, you should find several procedures in this section—occasionally with small variations—that are applicable to *your* phone.

Backing Up Contact Data

Regardless of your carrier, there are multiple options for backing up your Contacts data.

Merge with Google Contacts or Your Samsung Account

1. With the Contacts list displayed, tap the menu icon and choose Merge Accounts.

2. Tap Google or Samsung Account, as appropriate.

3. Tap OK in the confirmation dialog box. When you open and view individual contact records, you see that all are now marked as Google contacts or as Samsung contacts.

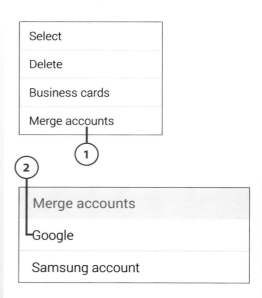

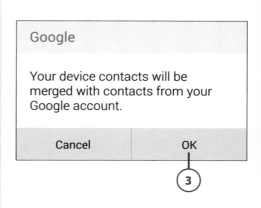

Only the Device (Phone) Records Merge

If you merge your phone's contacts with the Samsung account that you created during the phone's setup, only those contacts created with Device or Phone as the source are merged; Google contacts are left unchanged.

To Merge or Not to Merge

Think carefully before performing a Merge with Google or—to a lesser degree—Merge with Samsung Account, especially if your contact records have many different sources and you want to keep those sources intact. Unlike the other backup and export procedures described in this section, the Merge commands modify the records by changing their creation source. Thus, use Merge with Google only if you're committing to using Google/Gmail as the repository of *all* your contact data.

Back Up to a Memory Card

1. With the Contacts tab selected, tap the menu icon and choose Settings. (Note that you *must* have a memory card installed in the phone to export your Contacts data using this procedure.)

2. Tap Contacts.

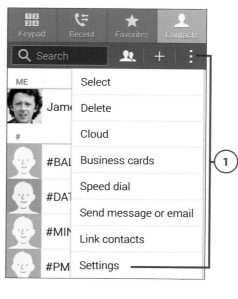

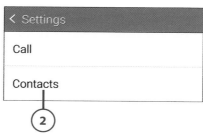

3. Tap Import/Export.

4. Tap Export to SD Card.

5. Tap OK in the Confirm Export dialog box. The data is exported to the displayed vCard filename (.vcf) and location. The extSdCard in the file pathname indicates that your add-in memory card is the destination.

Multiple Backups

As time passes, you can export *multiple* backups of the Contacts database to your memory card. Each new backup increments the filename by 1 over the highest-numbered backup on the card. For example, if there's already a Contacts.vcf, the next backup will be Contacts_002.vcf.

Exporting to USB (Built-In Memory)

If you don't have an add-in memory card, you can export your contacts to a vCard file in the phone's built-in memory (USB Storage). From there, you can copy the file to your computer or store it in an online storage service. In Step 4 of this task, select Export to USB Storage, and then tap OK in the Confirm Export dialog box.

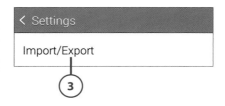

< Settings

Import/Export

③

Import/Export contacts

Import from USB storage

Export to USB storage

Import from SD card

Export to SD card

④

Confirm export

Your contacts will be exported to: / storage/extSdCard/Contacts.vcf.

Cancel | OK

Filename and path ⑤

>>>Go Further
BACK UP *EVERYTHING!*

Before you begin experimenting with contact importing/exporting or syncing, it's extremely important to have current backups of *all* your contact data sources on your computer, the Web, and company servers, as well as the Contacts data on your phone. If you're a Mac user, for example, that might mean backing up Microsoft Outlook contacts, Address Book or Contacts, and Google Contacts. If something goes wrong (such as ending up with duplicates of every contact), you can delete all contacts in the affected applications and then restore the original data from the backups.

Restoring Contacts from Backups

If something happens to the Contacts database on your Galaxy S5 or you get a new phone, you can restore the data from one or more backups.

Restore Contacts from a Memory Card Backup

If this is a new phone, install the memory card in the phone to which you want to restore your Contacts database. (See "Adding a Memory Card" in Chapter 20, "Optimizing and Troubleshooting," for instructions.)

1. Launch the Contacts app. With the Contacts tab selected, tap the menu icon and choose Settings.

2. Tap Contacts.

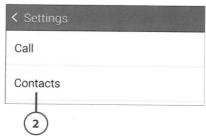

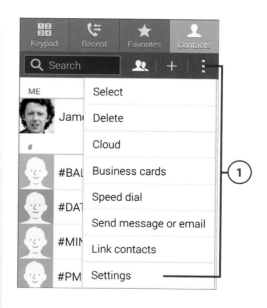

3. Tap Import/Export.

4. Tap Import from SD Card.

5. When the contacts are imported, you must associate them with an account. Select an account from the Save Contact To dialog box.

6. If you've only exported to the memory card once, your contacts are immediately imported. On the other hand, if you've created multiple SD Card backups, the Select vCard File dialog box appears. Select the file or files that you want to import, and then tap OK.

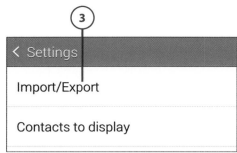

Beware of Duplicates

When restoring a backup from a memory card, the procedure doesn't check for duplicate records. Thus, it's safest to restore to a device that contains no contact records or only new, unique records that you've created on the phone. Remember, too, that if you have any contacts that you previously created or synced with Google Contacts, those contacts will automatically be restored on your first sync. In other words, restoring from the SD card might be unnecessary.

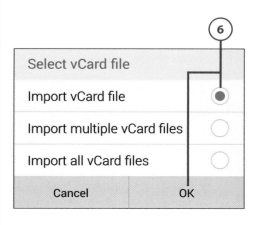

Restoring a USB (Built-In Memory) Backup

If you've stored your Contacts backup in the phone's built-in memory—rather than on an add-in memory card, you can restore it by tapping Import from USB Storage in Step 4. In the Save Contact To dialog box, choose an account to associate with the restored contacts.

If you've only exported to USB once, your contacts are immediately imported. On the other hand, if you've created multiple USB backups, the Select vCard File dialog box appears (see the figure for Step 6). Select the file or files that you want to import, and then tap OK.

It's Not All Good

Problems with Restores

Although the steps required to restore most types of backups are straightforward, the results might not be what you expect. Getting a clean restore that doesn't require hours of deleting duplicates and joining records from multiple sources can be something of a rarity. Perhaps your best bet—and the simplest approach—is to use Google Contacts as the repository of all contact records and just allow it to restore the Contacts database on the first sync.

Importing Contact Data from Other Sources into Google Contacts

Although Google Contacts (Gmail's address book) is the *de facto* source for Android contact data, it's not the place in which many of us have chosen to store our contacts. You may already have years of contacts stored in email clients and address book utilities on your computer. This section explains how to export your existing computer contacts and then import them into Google Contacts.

Exporting Your Computer's Data

Here's how to export your data from your existing contact-management application on your Mac or PC:

- *Address Book or Contacts (Mac).* Select the contacts to export and then choose File, Export, Export vCard (or Export Group vCard). Alternatively, drag the contacts out of the Address Book or Contacts window to your Desktop or a convenient Finder window.

- *Outlook 2010 or 2013 (Windows).* Click the File tab, click Options, and then click Advanced. Click the Export button to launch the Import and Export Wizard, click Export to a File, and click Next. Select the Comma Separated Values (Windows) option and click Next. Select the Contacts folder and click next. Click Browse, select the folder in which to place the exported file, and click Next. Finally, click Finish to export the data.

Import the Exported Data into Google Contacts

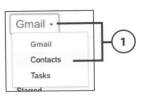

1. In your computer's browser, go to mail.google.com or gmail.com and log into your account. Open the Gmail menu and choose Contacts.

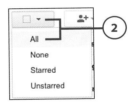

Just in Case...

As a safety measure, you might want to back up the Google Contacts data by opening the More menu and choosing Export. If the import described in this task doesn't go as planned, you can then restore your original Google Contacts data by choosing More, Import or by choosing More, Restore Contacts. The former command restores from your backup file, whereas the latter restores from one of several Google-provided backups.

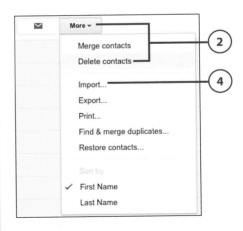

2. To replace all current data in Google Contacts with the new data, you must delete all the records. From the first Contacts menu, choose All to select all visible records. Then from the More menu, choose Delete Contacts.

Caution: Selective Deletions

If Google Contacts contains records that do *not* exist in the imported data, you may want to delete all records *except* those.

3. If still more records exist, repeat Step 2. Continue until all records have been deleted.

4. Choose More, Import.

5. Select the data file to import by clicking the Choose File button in the Import Contacts dialog box.

6. Select the exported data file in the dialog box and click the Choose button.

7. Click the Import button in the Import Contacts dialog box. The exported data appears in Google Contacts.

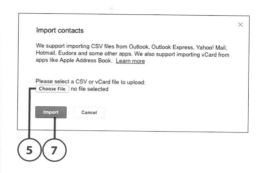

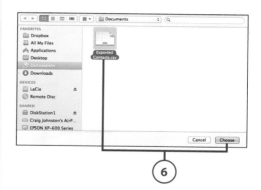

Setting Display Options

With the Contacts tab selected, you can set a variety of useful options that determine which records are displayed and the order in which they appear.

1. Tap the menu icon and choose Settings.

2. Tap Contacts.

3. Tap the Only Contacts with Phones check box to hide contact records that don't include a phone number. (To restore the full contacts list, tap it again to remove the check mark.)

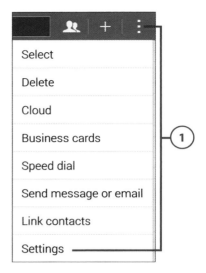

Select

Delete

Cloud

Business cards

Speed dial

Send message or email

Link contacts

Settings

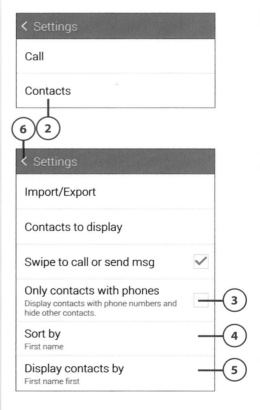

< Settings

Call

Contacts

< Settings

Import/Export

Contacts to display

Swipe to call or send msg ✓

Only contacts with phones
Display contacts with phone numbers and hide other contacts.

Sort by
First name

Display contacts by
First name first

4. You can sort contacts alphabetically by first name or last name. To change the current sort order, tap Sort By and then select an option in the Sort By dialog box.

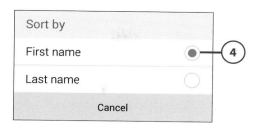

5. Regardless of the Sort By order specified in Step 4, you can display each contact as first name first (Bob Smith) or last name first (Smith, Bob). Tap Display Contacts By, and then select an option in the Display Contacts By dialog box.

6. When you finish making changes, tap the Back icon or press the Back key.

Specifying Contacts to Display

There's also an option to view only those contacts associated with a particular account. For instance, you can view only your Facebook friends or LinkedIn colleagues. On the Settings screen, tap Contacts to Display, and select the account that you want to view. To create a custom view that combines several accounts, tap the Settings icon to the right of the Customized List option.

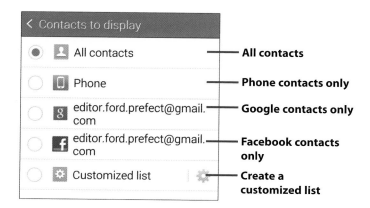

Month and Agenda view

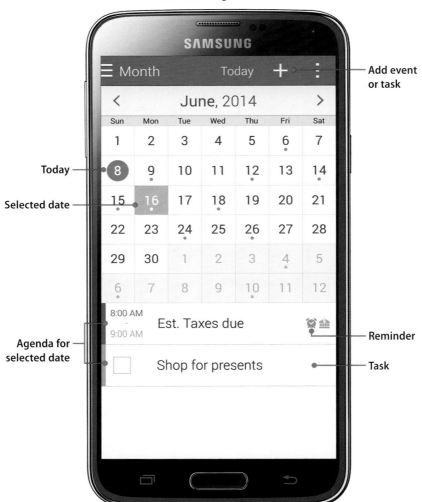

Add event
or task

Today

Selected date

Agenda for
selected date

Reminder

Task

In this chapter, you find out how to use Calendar to create, view, and edit events and tasks. Topics include the following:

→ Adding Calendar accounts to display events and tasks from your Gmail, Microsoft Exchange ActiveSync, and other account calendars

→ Creating events and tasks, viewing the calendar, and managing events and tasks

→ Responding to reminders for upcoming events and tasks

→ Setting Calendar preferences

Using the Calendar

Similar in design to a full-featured calendar application (such as the one in Microsoft Outlook), the Calendar app enables you to record upcoming events, meetings, and tasks and then receive reminders for them. If you already maintain calendars in Google, Facebook, Outlook.com (Microsoft Exchange ActiveSync), or a corporate Exchange Server account, you can synchronize your Calendar app data with that of your other calendars.

Adding Calendar Accounts

If you've used a Google/Gmail account on your phone to access any Google service, Calendar has two calendars that it can immediately associate with new events and tasks: your Google/Gmail Calendar and My Calendar, a phone-specific calendar created by the Calendar app. In addition to these sources, Calendar can use data from and sync with Samsung, Facebook, and Microsoft Exchange Server calendars. Thus, before you experiment extensively with Calendar, decide which external calendar sources you want to use and keep in sync with Calendar (adding other accounts as needed). You can find instructions for automatically and manually synchronizing your calendar data in Chapter 17, "Synchronizing Data."

1. To add a Facebook, Microsoft Exchange ActiveSync, Samsung, or Gmail calendar account (only these account types support calendar syncing with your phone), go to the Home screen and tap Apps, followed by Settings.

2. Tap the Accounts icon.

3. Tap Add Account at the bottom of the My Accounts list.

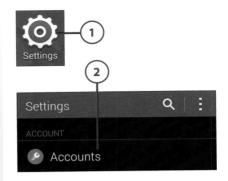

Multiple Accounts of the Same Type

Account types that are marked with a green dot have already been added. You can have multiple Exchange, Email, and Google accounts, but only one instance each of Samsung and Facebook accounts.

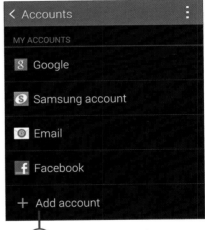

4. Select one of these account types: Facebook, Microsoft Exchange ActiveSync, Google, or Samsung Account. This example uses Microsoft Exchange ActiveSync.

Active accounts

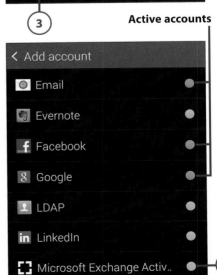

5. Follow the instructions to add the account. At a minimum, you need to supply your username and password (or use the provided option to create an account).

6. Ensure that Sync Calendar is enabled if that option is available on the Sync Settings screen.

7. You can add other accounts by repeating Steps 3–6. When you finish, press the Home key to return to the Home screen.

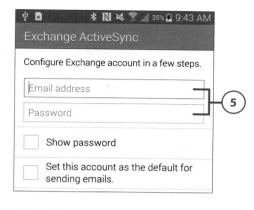

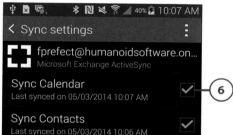

Working in Calendar

Within Calendar, you can create events and tasks, choose a view (Year, Month, Month and Agenda, Week, Day, or Agenda), and edit or delete events and tasks.

Creating Events and Tasks

In addition to events and tasks that are pulled from your Gmail/Google, Facebook, Exchange, and Samsung accounts, you can also create new items within the Calendar app. These new items can be synced with your accounts automatically, manually, or not at all (as explained in Chapter 17).

Every Calendar item is either an *event* (a scheduled item for a specific date, with or without a start time) or a *task* (an unscheduled item with or without a due date). An event can be an all-day occurrence, such as a vacation day or birthday, or have a defined start and end time.

Create an Event

1. Launch the Calendar app by tapping Apps, Calendar or by tapping a Home screen shortcut.

2. *Optional:* On the calendar, select the date or time when you want to schedule the event. (Selecting the start date or time saves you the trouble of specifying this information when you create the event.) To change the Calendar view so that you can pick a start date or time, tap the active view name and choose Month, Week, or Day.

3. Tap the plus (+) icon to create a new event. The scheduling screen displays.

Be General or Specific

The more specific your selection (start date or date/time), the more information is prefilled for the event. On the other hand, regardless of the currently selected date or start time, you can still set a different date or time when you create the event.

Another Plus Icon Option
You can also create a new event or task by tapping the plus icon in a Calendar widget.

Calendar (Mini Today) widget

Create event or task

4. Ensure that Add Event is selected.

5. Select an account to use if you want to associate the event with a different calendar. (My Calendar is the phone-specific calendar.)

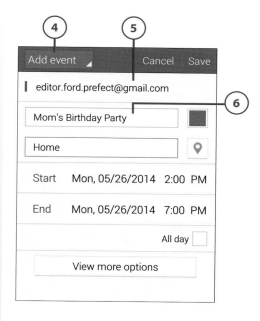

Using Multiple Calendars
The calendar you specify for each new item is very important. When you sync calendars, it's the calendar that records the event. If you choose your Google/Gmail calendar, for example, the event will also be available to you from Google's website using any browser. On the other hand, if you choose My Calendar, the event will be available only on your Galaxy S5. To use other account calendars with Calendar, see "Adding Calendar Accounts" at the beginning of this chapter.

6. Enter a title for the event.

7. *Optional:* Select a color that signifies something about or helps classify the event.

8. *Optional:* Enter the event's location. This can be something simple like "Home" or a real, physical address. Type in the Location box or tap the Location icon, perform a search, and tap Done.

9. Do one of the following:

    *   If this is an all-day event or one with no specific schedule other than the day on which it occurs, tap the All Day check box. The From and To times are removed, as well as the time zone. Go to Step 10.

    *   If the Start or End date or time is incorrect, tap the date or time item and correct it. Tap arrow icons to increment or decrement a component (such as the hour) by one unit. Alternatively, you can select the item you want to change and type the new value. If the other date or time is also incorrect, tap its button at the top of the screen (Start or End) and repeat this process. Tap Set to accept the corrected dates and/or times.

10. Tap View More Options to view more event options including the ability to set a reminder, choose a meeting time zone, and more.

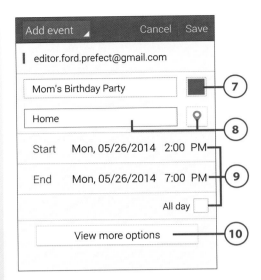

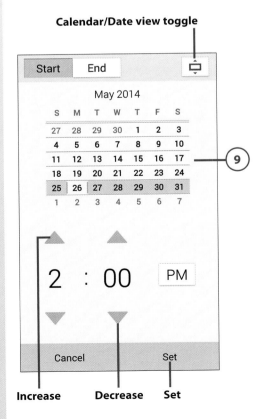

Calendar/Date view toggle

Increase   **Decrease**   **Set**

11. *Optional:* Set a *reminder* (alarm) for the event by tapping the Reminder plus (+) icon. To specify an interval other than the default (15 minutes before), tap the interval box, and select a new one from the scrolling list. Select Customize if none of the intervals is correct.

More About Reminders

You can optionally set *multiple* reminders for an event. Tap the plus (+) icon to add a new reminder. To remove a reminder, tap the minus (–) icon to its right. If the Calendar account with which this event is associated has an email address (such as your Google/Gmail account), you can elect to be notified via email rather than by the usual methods. Tap the box to the right of the reminder interval and choose Email.

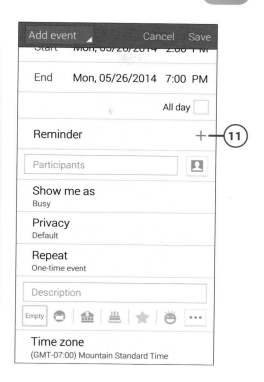

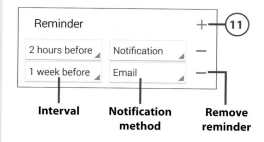

Interval   **Notification method**   **Remove reminder**

12. *Optional:* Specify an interval for repeating this event (such as a weekly staff meeting on Monday at 1:00 p.m.) by tapping Repeat and selecting a repetition interval. Then specify a duration or end date, and tap OK.

13. *Optional:* Enter a detailed description of or notes related to the event in the Description box.

14. *Optional:* Select a sticker to visually identify the event on the calendar and to use as a filtering criterion.

15. *Optional:* Tap the Time Zone entry to specify a different time zone to use for scheduling this event.

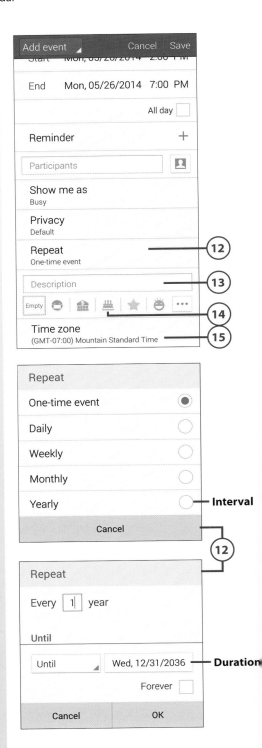

Advanced Calendaring

To maintain compatibility with events created in Google/Gmail and Microsoft Exchange ActiveSync accounts (or created in Calendar and designated as either of these account types), additional fields (Participants, Show Me As, and Privacy) appear when you create, edit, or view such events. The fields are normally used to manage attendance at corporate meetings and can—or should—be skipped when creating standard Calendar events. When you save an item with designated participants, each person is automatically emailed an invitation when you save the event.

Event participants ——— 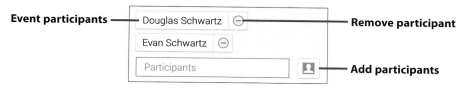 ——— **Remove participant**

Add participants

16. Tap the Save button at the top of the screen to add the event to the calendar or tap Cancel to discard it.

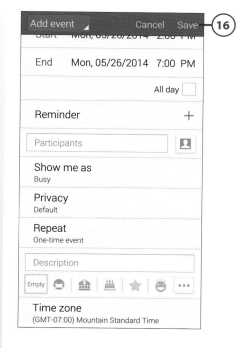

Create a Task

1. Launch the Calendar app by tapping Apps, Calendar or by tapping a Home screen shortcut.

2. *Optional:* Select the due date for the task's completion from the calendar. (Selecting the date saves you the trouble of specifying it when you create the task.) To change the Calendar view so that you can select a due date, tap the active view name and choose Month, Week, or Day.

3. Tap the plus (+) icon. The scheduling screen appears.

4. Ensure that Add Task is selected.

5. Select the account to use if you want to associate the new task with a different account. (My Task is the phone-specific account.)

6. Enter a title for the task.

7. Do one of the following:

    - If there's a particular date on or by which the task must be completed, tap the Due Date entry, specify the date in the Set Date dialog box, and tap the Set button.

    - If the task is open-ended, tap the No Due Date check box.

8. Tap View More Options to see other scheduling options for the task.

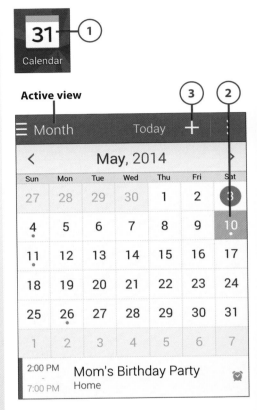

9. *Optional:* Set a *reminder* (alarm) for the task by tapping the plus (+) icon. In the Reminder dialog box, select either On Due Date or Customize (to specify a different date). The selected date and the current time are set as the reminder. To change the time, tap its entry, specify the time in the Set Time dialog box, and tap the Set button.

10. *Optional:* Enter a detailed description of or notes related to the task in the Description text box.

11. *Optional:* Specify a completion priority (high, medium, or low) by tapping Priority.

12. Tap the Save button to add the task to the calendar or tap Cancel to discard it. (When added to a calendar, a task is preceded by a check box.)

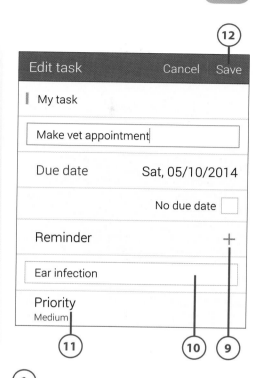

View the Calendar

Calendar has six *views*: Year, Month, Month and Agenda, Week, Day, and Agenda. You interact differently with Calendar in each view.

1. When you launch Calendar, the last displayed view appears. To change views, tap the active view (such as Month) or swipe from the left edge of the screen, and then select a new view.

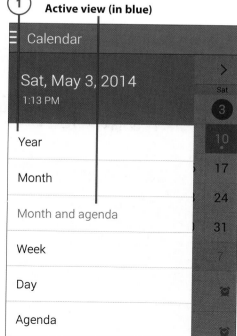

2. *Year view.* You can't view events or tasks in Year view. Its purpose is to enable you to easily select a month for viewing—in this or another year. Scroll to previous or future years by tapping the arrow icons or by swiping the screen horizontally. When the target month and year appear, tap the month to view it in Month view.

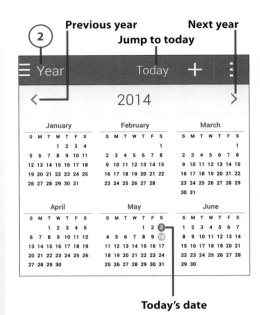

Other Year View Options
To immediately return to the current year, tap the Today button. Today's date is encircled in dark blue.

3. *Month view.* In Month view, event/task text is color-coded to match the calendar account with which the item is associated. For example, bright blue text is used to show My Calendar items, dark blue for Facebook events, purple for Google Calendar items, and green for holidays. Tap a date to display events and tasks for that date in a pop-up window. To move forward or back one month, tap an arrow icon or flick the screen vertically or horizontally.

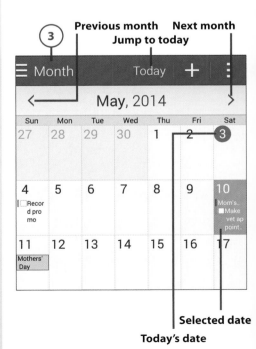

Month and Agenda
If you choose the Month and Agenda view, a reduced version of Month view is presented. Scheduled events and tasks for the selected date appear at the bottom of the screen.

4. *Week view.* In Week view, items are colored-coded to match the calendar with which they're associated. Tap an item to view its details in a pop-up. Tap the pop-up to edit or delete the item. Scroll to the previous or next week by tapping an arrow icon or swiping horizontally.

Changing the Magnification

To make it easier to examine scheduled items in Week or Day view, you can change the magnification by pinching two fingers together (decrease) or spreading them apart (increase).

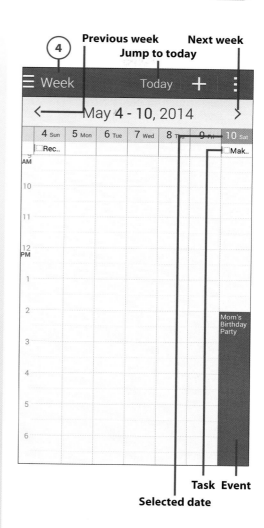

5. *Day view.* Use Day view to see scheduled items and their duration for a selected date. Items are colored-coded to match the calendar with which they're associated. Tap an item to view its details in a pop-up. Tap the pop-up to edit or delete the item. Press and hold a time slot to create a new item with that start time. You can scroll the day's time slots by flicking vertically and switch days by tapping arrow icons or swiping horizontally.

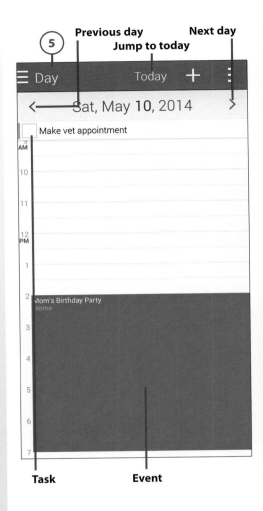

Previous day

Next day

Jump to today

Task

Event

6. *Agenda view.* Select Agenda view to see a chronological list of events and tasks. Items are color-coded to match the calendar with which they're associated. Tap an item to view its details, edit, or delete it. Scroll through the list by flicking vertically.

Filtering the Agenda

Your Agenda is made up of Events, Tasks, and Anniversary items. Normally the filter for the view is set to All, which means that all Events, Tasks, and Anniversaries are shown. You can limit the view by filtering it to only show certain items. For example, if you choose Events, you only see Event items.

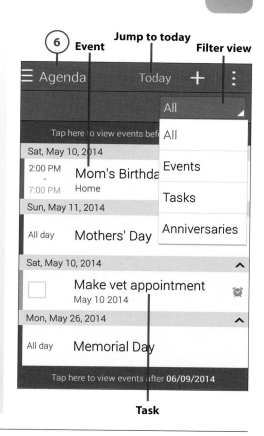

Event — Jump to today — Filter view

Task

Searching in Views

To display the search box, tap the menu icon and choose Search. You can optionally filter a search to display only events to which a particular sticker has been assigned. With the search box displayed, open the menu, choose Filter by Sticker, and select a sticker.

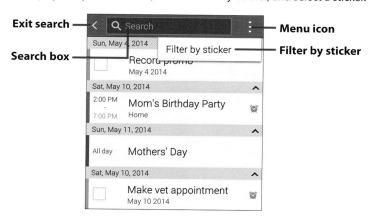

Exit search — Menu icon

Search box — Filter by sticker

7. Go to a specific date by tapping the menu icon and choosing Go To. In the Go To dialog box, specify the target date and tap Done.

8. You can display events and tasks from one or multiple calendar accounts. To select accounts to show, tap the menu icon and choose Calendars. Select the calendar and task accounts to display, and tap the Back icon when done.

Increase 7

Decrease

Back **Select all**

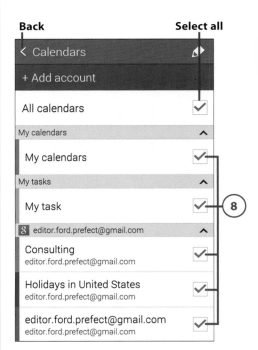

8

>>>*Go Further*

CONSIDER CALENDAR WIDGETS

You can do much of your Calendar viewing on the Home screen by installing Calendar widgets. They draw their data from Calendar and enable you to view upcoming events and tasks, as well as create new ones.

- *Calendar (Mini Today).* This widget displays a day's events and tasks. Tap any item to view, edit, or delete it in Calendar; tap an arrow icon to move one day forward or backward; tap a task's check box to toggle its completion status; and tap the plus (+) icon to create a new event or task.

- *Calendar (Month).* This widget reproduces Calendar in Month view. You can tap an event or task to view, edit, or delete it in Calendar. Select a date and tap the plus icon (or tap the selected date again) to create a new event or task on that date. Tap the arrow icons to scroll to the previous or next month.

For help with adding, moving, and removing widgets, see "Add Widgets" and "Reposition and Remove Home Screen Items" in Chapter 3, "Making the Phone Your Own."

Manage Events and Tasks

After creating an event or task, you can delete it or edit any aspect of it, such as the title, start date, start time, description, reminder interval, or completion status.

1. Open the Calendar app and, in any view, tap the item that you want to delete or edit. If a pop-up appears, tap the item in the pop-up to examine it in Detail view. In certain views (such as Agenda), no pop-up appears; the item is immediately displayed in Detail view.

Faster Editing, Deleting, and Rescheduling

In Week and Day views, you can change the date/time or duration of an event by dragging in the Calendar. To reschedule the event, press and hold the event, and drag it to a new date/time slot. To change its duration, drag the event's top or bottom edge (marked by dots) up or down. Note that only events—not tasks—can be rescheduled this way.

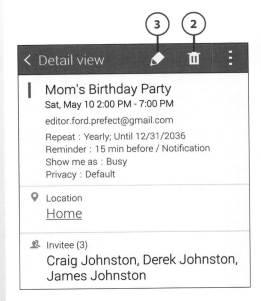

2. Tap the Trash icon to delete the task or event and confirm by tapping OK.

3. Tap the edit icon to edit the task or event, and then tap Save to save your edits.

Task Completion

To mark a task complete, tap its check box on the calendar, in its pop-up, or in a widget.

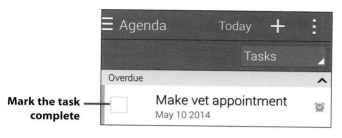

Mark the task complete

Editing or Deleting a Repeating Event

When you edit a repeating event, a dialog box appears that enables you to change only this occurrence or every occurrence. Similarly, when you try to delete a repeating event, a dialog box asks you to confirm whether to delete all or only a specific occurrence of the event.

Edit a repeating event

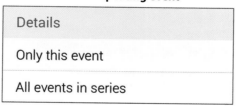

Responding to Reminders

When an event or task reminder is triggered, a message appears briefly in the status bar and is replaced by a number (denoting the number of current alerts) or a separate alert screen appears. A distinctive ringtone may also play. The notification methods used are determined by Event Notification settings, as explained in "Setting Calendar Preferences," later in this chapter. You can respond to a reminder by *snoozing* (requesting that it repeat later), dismissing, or ignoring it.

Simple Alarms

If you just need an alarm to remind you that it's time to wake up or do *some-thing*, you don't need to schedule a Calendar event. You can create alarms in the Clock app.

Clock app

Dismiss ——— Snooze

1. If the Set Alerts and Notifications setting is *Status Bar Notifications*, an icon showing the number of waiting reminders appears in the status bar. Open the Notification panel to view them.

2. Tap Snooze to snooze the alert.

3. Tap the event to open an Event Notifications screen in which you can set a specific snooze duration.

4. Swipe the alert left or right off the screen to dismiss it.

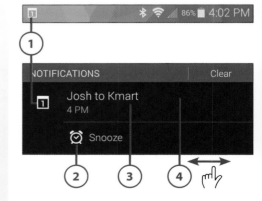

Dismissing a Reminder

Dismissing an event or task's reminder doesn't delete the item from Calendar; it merely eliminates the reminder. To *delete* the event or task, you must perform the procedure described in "Manage Events and Tasks," earlier in this chapter.

Responding to a Lock Screen Reminder

A full-screen notification appears when the screen is dark; that is, when the lock screen is active. To respond, press and drag the Dismiss (X) or Snooze (zZ) icon. If you elect to snooze, the reminder is snoozed for the default duration.

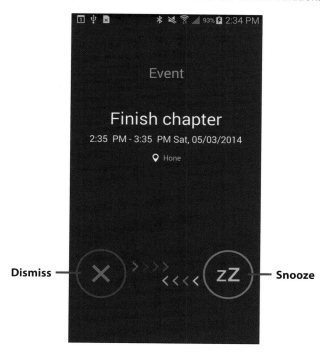

Setting Calendar Preferences

You can set options on Calendar's Settings screen to customize the way the app works.

1. Launch the Calendar app.

2. Tap the menu icon and choose Settings. Review Steps 3–14 for descriptions of each option that you can set.

3. *First Day of Week.* Specify whether calendar weeks should start on Saturday, Sunday, Monday, or match local customs.

4. *Show Week Numbers.* When checked, Week view also displays the week number (1–52).

5. *Hide Declined Events.* When checked, event invitations that you've declined aren't shown in Calendar.

6. *Hide Completed Tasks.* When checked, tasks that have been marked as completed aren't shown in Calendar.

7. *Weather.* When this option is checked and the calendar is in Month view, the weather forecast for the next six days is shown.

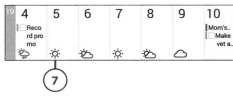

8. *Lock Time Zone.* When Lock Time Zone is disabled (unchecked), all event times reflect the phone's current location. When enabled (checked), event times always reflect the time zone specified in Select Time Zone (see Step 10).

A Lock Time Zone Recommendation

This is one of the most confusing aspects of Calendar. In general, the easiest way to use Lock Time Zone is to leave it disabled. When you're home in California, for example, all event times reflect Pacific time. If you travel to New York, the events display Eastern times. Finally, when you return home, events automatically change to show Pacific times again.

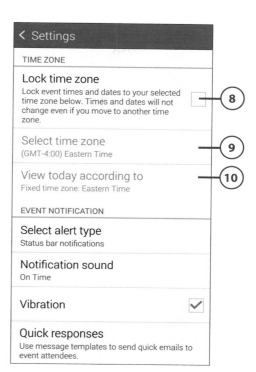

9. *Select Time Zone.* To force all event times to reflect a particular time zone (when you're traveling or if you want events to always reflect the home office's time zone, for example), enable Lock Time Zone (see Step 8) and tap Select Time Zone to choose a time zone.

10. *View Today According To.* If you have chosen to lock the time zone (as described in Step 8), use this option to specify how today's events are displayed. You can elect to use the current local time zone or the one you specified in Step 9.

11. *Select Alert Type.* Specify whether a reminder will display as a status bar icon (Status Bar Notification), as a full screen pop-up (Sound Alerts), or not at all (Off).

12. *Notification Sound.* Select a sound to play with each reminder alert. Select Silent if you want to disable this option.

13. *Vibration.* Enable Vibration if you want Calendar reminders to cause the phone to vibrate. Like other notification settings, you can set Vibration as the sole notification method or use it in combination with other methods.

14. *Quick Responses.* View, edit, add, or delete brief email responses that you can send in response to event invitations.

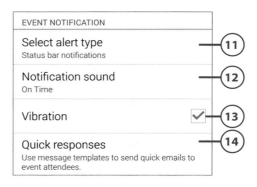

EVENT NOTIFICATION

Select alert type
Status bar notifications

Notification sound
On Time

Vibration ✓

Quick responses
Use message templates to send quick emails to event attendees.

What Are Quick Responses?

Quick Responses are canned messages that you can send to event attendees. For example, if you are running late, there is a Quick Response that reads "I'm running just a couple of minutes late." As your meeting approaches, your Galaxy S5 alerts you. If you are running late, you will be given the option to send one of the Quick Responses.

Synchronizing Calendar Data

To quickly perform a manual Calendar sync based on your current account settings, tap the menu icon and choose Sync. To learn more about synchronizing data, see Chapter 17.

Open in Reader   Windows Menu

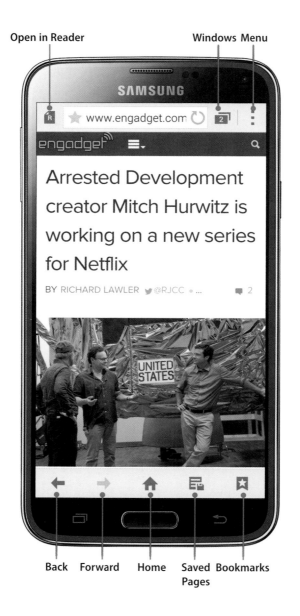

Back Forward Home Saved Bookmarks
                          Pages

In this chapter, you find out how to use the Internet app and Google Chrome to browse the Web. Topics include the following:

→ Launching Internet
→ Visiting web pages
→ Setting options for viewing pages
→ Creating and organizing bookmarks
→ Configuring Internet
→ Using other menu commands
→ Learning about Google Chrome

Browsing the Web

You're probably already familiar with the basics of using a web browser. Making the transition from browsing on a computer to browsing on your phone is relatively easy. As with a desktop browser, you can enter page addresses by typing, tapping links, and selecting bookmarks for your favorite sites.

The Galaxy S5 generally ships with a pair of browsers: Internet and Google Chrome. Although this chapter focuses on using Internet (the default browser for most carriers), you should check out Chrome, too. You can use whichever browser app you prefer, as well as switch between them whenever you like. See "Google Chrome Essentials," at the end of this chapter, for information on getting started with Chrome and how it differs from Internet.

Verizon Users and the Internet App

At its launch, the Verizon Galaxy S5 included Google Chrome as its *only* web browser. Because Chrome is so similar to Internet, Chrome users should review both the Internet and Chrome material in this chapter.

Launching Internet

You can launch the Internet app in several ways. The most common are as follows:

- On the Home screen, tap the Internet icon at the bottom of the screen.

Internet app **Apps**

Phone   Contacts Messages   Internet   Apps

- On the Home screen, tap Apps, followed by Internet.

- Tap a web link in an email message. Links can be blue underlined text, images, or other objects. If the item you tap is indeed a link, the linked page appears in the browser.

Check out my Web site when you get the chance: www.siliconwasteland.com

Sent on a Sprint Samsung Galaxy S® 5

Link in an email message

Complete Action Using

Because there *are* two browser apps installed on the phone (and you may have installed others), whenever you perform an indirect action that requires a browser (such as tapping a link), a Complete Action Using dialog box appears that asks which browser to launch. Select a browser (Internet or Chrome), and then tap Just Once. After familiarizing yourself with both browsers, you can specify a *default browser* to use for all future indirect launches by tapping Always.

If you ever want to reverse your decision, open Settings, scroll to the Applications section, and tap Default Applications. In the Clear Defaults area, find the browser that you previously set as the default and tap its Clear button.

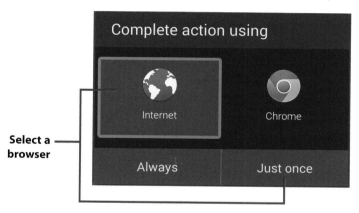

Select a browser

• Tap a blue underlined link in a text or multimedia message. In the dialog box that appears, tap Open Link to open the link in the browser or tap Cancel if you change your mind.

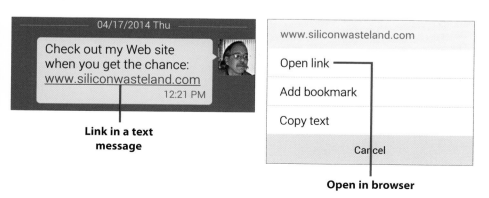

Link in a text message

Open in browser

Unexpected Web Redirections

Apps and certain documents can contain links that automatically redirect you to web pages, causing the browser to launch if it isn't currently running. For example, if you tap text, an icon, or a button in some apps when searching for instructions, a help file or manual might open in the browser.

Visiting Web Pages

You can go to a particular web page (called an *address* or *URL*) using the same methods that you use with Internet Explorer, Safari, Firefox, and other popular desktop web browsers. The most common methods are typing the address, tapping a link on the current page, choosing a bookmarked or recently visited (History) site or page, and searching for a site or page with one of the popular search engines.

Immersion Mode

In this new version of Internet, web pages are normally displayed in a full-screen *immersion* mode, enabling you to see as much of every page as possible without the distraction of the address box. Regardless of where you are in the current page, you can reveal the address box and status bar by dragging down slightly.

Type the Address

1. If the browser isn't currently running, go to the Home screen and tap the Internet icon.

2. Tap the address box. The current page's address is selected.

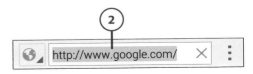

3. Enter the new address and tap Go. (Because the current address is already selected, typing anything immediately replaces the old address.) The web page loads.

Fast Address Selection

As you type, a list of possible addresses appears. If you see the one you want, you can tap it instead of completing the address. You can also select a search suggestion if the site's actual URL isn't in the list.

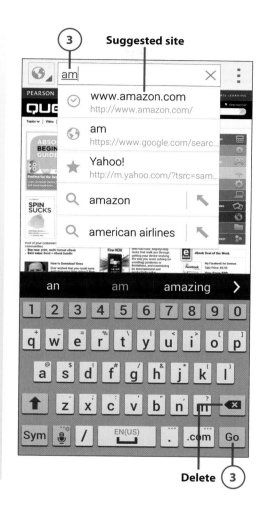

Following a Link

In the browser, if you tap an object, graphic, or text that represents a web link, the link briefly flashes blue and then the linked page loads.

Not Every Link Leads to a Page

Other than special *mobile* versions of web pages (designed for viewing on cell phones), pages displayed in the Internet app are identical to those you see in Internet Explorer, Safari, and other desktop browsers. That means that they also contain links designed to download PC and Mac applications, device drivers, and the like. Of course, such programs and drivers can't be used by your phone, but you might not be prevented from downloading them.

To remove these downloads, go to the Home screen and tap Apps, My Files, Download History. Select any listed item by pressing and holding its entry. Then tap the check box of every additional inappropriate download and tap Delete.

You can also delete files directly from the Download folder. In the Local Storage section of My Files, tap Device Storage or SD Card, and then open the Download folder. Select any listed item by pressing and holding its entry. Tap the check box for every additional inappropriate download, and then tap the Delete icon.

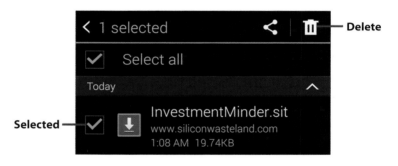

Delete

Selected

Visit a Bookmarked, Recent, or Saved Page

1. Drag or flick down until the Address box appears, and then tap the Bookmarks (star) icon at the bottom of the screen.

Lumen Toolbar handle (Sprint only)

2. To visit a *bookmarked* page (one whose address you stored), tap its thumbnail or name. (For information about creating and managing bookmarks, see "Working with Bookmarks," later in this chapter.)

Back   **Menu**

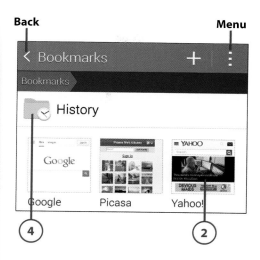

Bookmark Display Options

You can view bookmarks as a thumbnail grid or scrolling list. To switch views, tap the menu icon, and choose List View or Thumbnail View.

You can change the order of your bookmarks by tapping the menu icon and choosing Change Order. (If you've created folders, open the folder whose bookmarks you want to reorganize *before* choosing Change Order.) To move a bookmark, long press the bookmark's dot grid to select it and then drag it to the new position. When you're satisfied with the changes, tap Done—or tap Cancel to ignore the changes.

Rearranging bookmarks

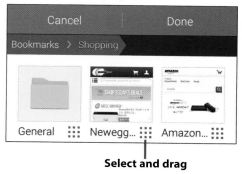

Select and drag

3. To open a *saved* page (one that you saved for later or offline reading), drag or flick down until the Address box appears, and tap the Saved Pages icon on the bar at the bottom of the screen. Locate the page in the scrolling list, and tap its thumbnail.

Saving a Page

To store a copy of the current page in Saved Pages, tap the menu icon and choose Save Page. Use this command for any page that you want to read later or that might not be readily available online, such as a receipt for an online purchase.

4. Internet stores the list of recently viewed pages in History, a folder at the top of the Bookmarks screen. To revisit a recently viewed page, drag or flick down until the Address box appears, and tap the Bookmarks icon on the bar at the bottom of the screen. Open the History folder, scroll to locate the desired page, and tap its name. To make it easier to find the page, you can *expand* (show) or *collapse* (hide) page-view periods (Today, Last 7 Days, and so on) by tapping section heads.

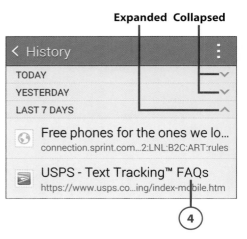

Expanded Collapsed

It's Not All Good

Configuring or Removing the Lumen Toolbar (Sprint)

If you have a Sprint S5, an additional toolbar (called Lumen Toolbar) that presents links to social media, other popular sites, and added favorites can be displayed at the bottom of the current page. To reveal it, tap its handle; to hide it, tap any spot in the current page.

Unfortunately, even when the toolbar is hidden, its handle can make it difficult to tap the Bookmarks icon (see the Step 1 figure). If you find that it interferes, you can reposition the handle or eliminate the toolbar altogether. To remove, restore, or configure the toolbar, go to the Home screen and tap Apps, Lumen Toolbar, Settings.

Lumen Toolbar (Sprint)

Search for a Site or Page

1. The address box doubles as a search box. Enter your search phrase, such as "exercise machines" or "trim a parrot's beak." As you type, the search engine builds a list of possible search topics.

2. You can do any of the following:

   • Tap a suggestion to immediately perform that search in the default search engine.

   • Tap the arrow at the end of a suggestion to transfer the text into the address box—enabling you to add to or edit the search text before performing the search.

   • Tap a direct link in the suggestion list to load that specific page—rather than performing a search.

   • Tap the Go key on the keyboard to perform the search using the text that's in the address box.

Changing Search Engines

The active search engine's icon is shown to the left of the address box. To change search engines, tap the icon and choose a different one.

Current search engine

Google search

Direct links

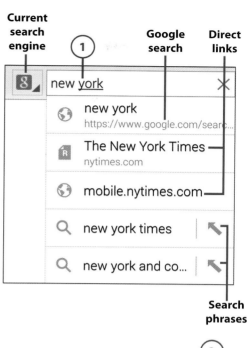

Search phrases

Tap to choose a search engine

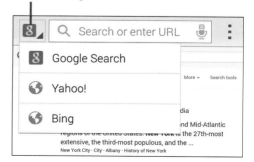

Viewing Pages

Similar to your computer's browser, the Internet app provides several ways for you to view pages, such as viewing in portrait or landscape mode, scrolling the page, changing the magnification, reloading the page, and displaying multiple pages in separate windows.

Portrait or Landscape View

Depending on the direction that you rotate the phone, you can view any page in *portrait* (normal) or *landscape* (sideways) mode. You can change the phone's orientation whenever you want; the page adjusts automatically. (If the orientation doesn't change when you rotate the phone, launch Settings; tap Display, Screen Rotation; and set the Rotate Screen slider to On. By default, there's also a Screen Rotation button in the Quick Setting buttons at the top of the Notification panel.)

Portrait   **Landscape**

Scrolling the Page

Many pages don't fit entirely onscreen. To view parts that are off-screen, flick or drag up, down, right, or left, depending on the direction you want the page's material to scroll. If you want to take advantage of some tricks, you can scroll by tilting your head or the phone up and down (*Smart Scroll*) or by waving your hand up and down over the sensor at the top of the phone (*Air Browse*).

- To activate Smart Scroll, open Settings and tap Accessibility, Dexterity and Interaction, Smart Scroll. Drag the Smart Scroll slider to the On position, and select Tilting Head or Tilting Device.

- To activate Air Browse, open Settings and tap Motions and Gestures, Air Browse. Drag the Air Browse slider to the On position, and ensure that Internet is one of the checked options.

Magnification (Zoom)

You can increase the magnification of the current page to make it easier to read (*zoom in*) or reduce it to get a bird's-eye view of the entire page (*zoom out*).

- To *zoom in* (making everything on the page larger), put your thumb and forefinger on the page and spread them apart.

- To *zoom out* (making everything on the page smaller), put your thumb and forefinger on the page and pinch them together.

Zoomed in

Zoomed out

Other Zoom Options

You can quickly zoom in or out by double-tapping the screen. Repeat to reverse the zoom. If Magnification Gestures (an Accessibility setting) is enabled, you can triple-tap to zoom. To enable or disable Magnification Gestures, open Settings and then tap Accessibility, Vision, Magnification Gestures.

Reader View

To make it easier to read certain pages (such as articles), tap the Reader icon—if it's present—to the left of the address box. When reading an article in Reader view, you can increase or decrease the size of text by tapping an icon. To view the text as white on a black background, tap the menu icon and choose Night Mode. To return to the original web page, tap the Back icon or press the Back key.

Reader icon

Back   **Increase font size**   **Decrease font size**   **Menu**

Original web page   **Page in Reader**

Refreshing the Page

If the current page didn't load correctly or you think the content might have changed while you were viewing it, you can refresh the page by tapping the Reload icon in the address box. If a page is loading slowly, you can stop it by tapping the X icon.

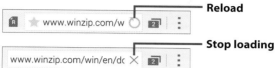

Reload

Stop loading

Working with Windows

The tabbed interface of current desktop browsers enables you to keep several web pages open simultaneously and easily switch among them. The Internet app mimics this feature by enabling you to open multiple *windows*. Each window is the equivalent of a new browser and operates independently of other windows.

Windows icon   Menu

New window

New Window command

Remove this window   Add New Window

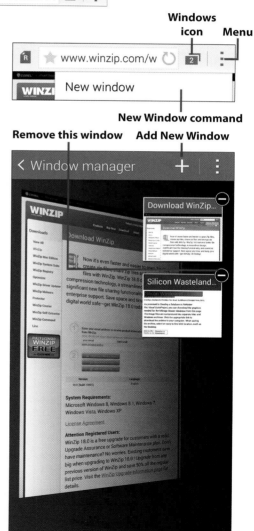

- To create a new window, tap the menu icon and choose New Window. You can also tap the Windows icon to the right of the address box and then tap the plus (+) icon in Window Manager. A new browser window opens.

- To navigate among or manage the open windows, tap the Windows icon to open the Window Manager. To switch to a window, tap its thumbnail. To remove a window that you no longer need, tap its minus (–) icon or swipe its thumbnail horizontally off the screen.

Create a New Window from a Bookmark or History Item

You can press and hold a site's name in Bookmarks or History to select it, and then tap the Add New Window icon in the toolbar. Doing so opens the website or page in a new window.

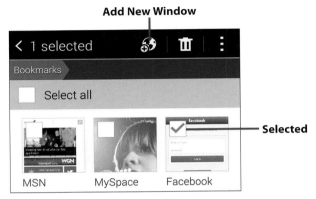

Page Navigation

As you replace the current page with new ones by entering addresses, tapping links, and selecting bookmarks, you can move back or forward through the stack of pages. (Note that each window has its own stack.) To return to the previous page, tap the Back icon at the bottom of the screen or press the Back key. You'll go back one page for each tap or key press. If you've gone back one or more pages, you can move forward through the stack by tapping the Forward icon.

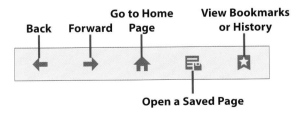

One Too Many

If you use the Back key to move back through the pages in the current window and press it when you're on the *first* page, you'll exit Internet.

Incognito Browsing

The Internet app supports *incognito browsing* in which entries aren't recorded in History, searches aren't recorded, and cookies aren't stored. Rather than make this a general browser setting, Internet enables it only for pages loaded into a designated incognito window.

1. Tap the Windows icon at the top of any browser page.

2. In Window Manager, tap the menu icon and choose New Incognito Window.

3. Review the text in the Incognito Mode dialog box, and tap OK to dismiss it.

4. A new browser window appears. Specify the first page to display by tapping a Quick Access icon, entering an address in the address box, performing a search, selecting from bookmarks or History items, or using another method. Web activities performed in this window are secure; activities performed in *other* Internet windows are recorded normally.

Quickly Switching to Incognito Mode

In addition to creating a new window for Incognito mode, you can apply Incognito mode to the *current* window by tapping the menu icon and choosing Incognito Mode.

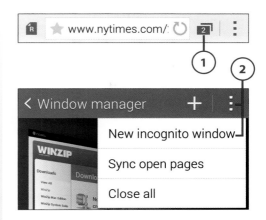

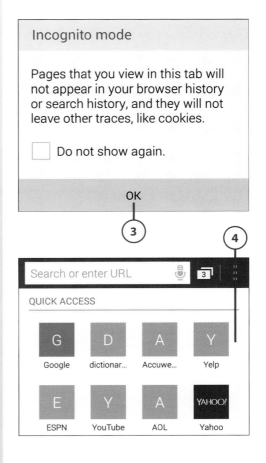

5. To remove an incognito window and its pages, open the Window Manager, find the incognito window, and delete it by tapping the minus (–) icon in its upper-right corner.

Incognito icon

Working with Bookmarks

As explained earlier in this chapter, *bookmarks* are stored addresses of websites and pages that you regularly visit. The purpose of creating a bookmark is to enable you to view the site or page again by simply tapping its entry in the Bookmarks grid or list rather than having to reenter the address.

Create a Bookmark from the Current Page

It's common to decide to bookmark a page while you're viewing it.

1. Do either of the following:

- Tap the star icon at the left end of the address bar.

- Tap the Bookmarks icon at the bottom of the screen and then tap the plus (+) icon on the Bookmarks toolbar.

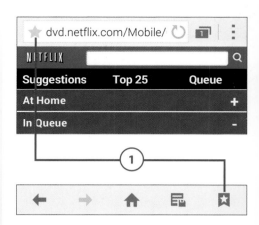

2. Edit the bookmark name, if necessary.

3. By default, new bookmarks are stored in the Bookmarks folder. To select a different folder or subfolder, tap the current folder name and select a destination folder.

4. Tap Save to store the new bookmark.

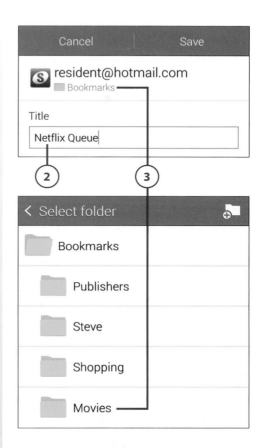

Bookmark   Folder
title

Create a Bookmark from the History List

If you've recently visited a page, the quickest way to add it as a new bookmark is to locate it in the History list.

1. With any web page displayed, tap the Bookmarks icon at the bottom of the screen.

2. Open the History folder at the top of the Bookmarks list or grid by tapping its icon.

3. In the History list, locate the page that you want to bookmark. Press and hold its entry to select it.

4. Tap the menu icon, and choose Add Bookmark.

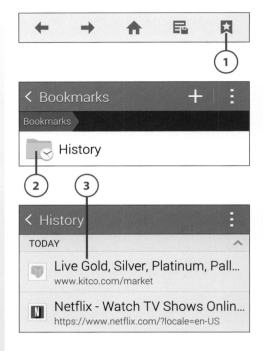

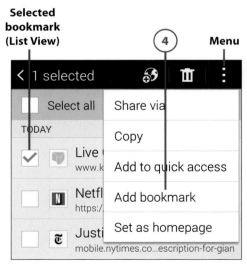

Selected bookmark (List View)

Menu

5. Perform Steps 2–4 from the previous task: editing the name, selecting a storage location, and saving the new bookmark.

Bookmark title   Folder

Edit Bookmarks

You can edit a bookmark's title, its address (setting it for a site's main page or another specific page), or the folder in which it's stored.

1. In the Bookmarks list, find the bookmark that you want to edit—opening folders, if necessary. Press and hold the bookmark to select it.

2. Tap the menu icon and choose Edit.

Other Options
The menu also enables you to set the selected bookmark as your home page, share it with a friend, create a Home screen shortcut to it, or delete it.

Selecting a bookmark (Thumbnail View)

3. Make any desired changes to the title, address, and/or its folder, and then tap Save.

URL (address) Bookmark title Folder

Editing the Address

Although you normally won't want to edit a page's address if it requires a lot of typing, it's relatively simple to change a page-specific address to one that goes to the site's main page. Just delete the extraneous material to the right of the main part of the address, such as http://m.newegg.com/.

Using Bookmark Folders

After amassing more than a handful of bookmarks, you can optionally create folders in which to organize your bookmarks—rather than storing them all in Bookmarks, the main folder. When creating a new bookmark or editing an existing one, you can move it into the most appropriate folder.

Navigating Among Bookmark Folders

When viewing items in a bookmark folder, don't press the Back key or tap the Back icon if you want to move up a level. Either action exits Bookmarks and returns you to the browser screen. If you want to continue working in Bookmarks, tap the appropriate path element (such as Bookmarks or the name of a higher folder in the hierarchy) at the top of the screen.

Back

Path elements

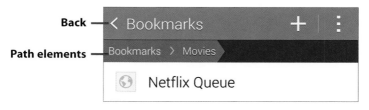

Create a Bookmark Folder

1. With any web page onscreen, tap the Bookmarks icon at the bottom of the screen.

2. Tap the menu icon and choose Create Folder.

3. Name the new folder.

4. Select a *parent* (containing) folder for this new folder.

5. Tap Done. The new folder is created within the selected folder and added to the Bookmarks list.

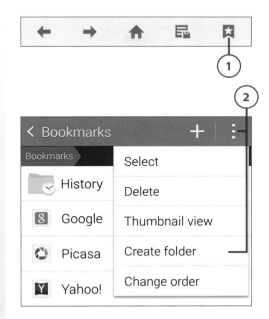

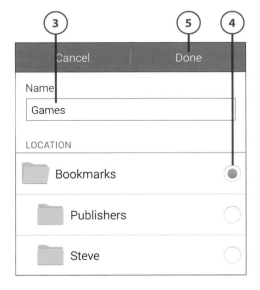

Move Bookmarks into Folders

1. With any web page onscreen, tap the Bookmarks icon at the bottom of the screen.

2. As necessary, open folders to expose the bookmarks that you want to move. (Bookmarks to be moved must all have the same destination folder.) Tap the menu icon and choose Select.

3. Select each bookmark by tapping its check box (in List View) or its thumbnail (in Thumbnail View).

4. Tap the menu icon and choose Move to Folder.

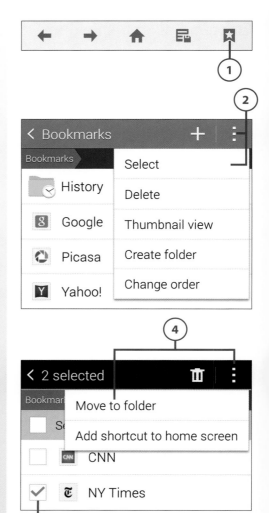

5. Tap the destination folder. The selected bookmarks move into the folder.

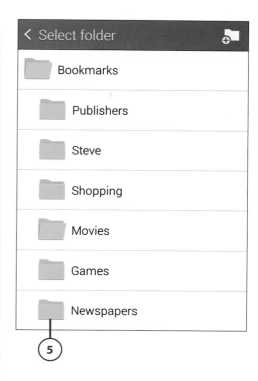

Delete Bookmarks

You can delete bookmarks that you no longer use.

1. With any web page onscreen, tap the Bookmarks icon at the bottom of the screen.

2. Opening folders as necessary, press and hold one of the book-marks that you want to delete. (When deleting more than one, they must all be in the same folder.)

3. *Optional:* Tap the check boxes of additional bookmarks that you want to delete. If desired, you can mark entire bookmark folders—and their contents—for deletion.

4. Tap the Delete toolbar icon. The selected bookmarks are immediately deleted.

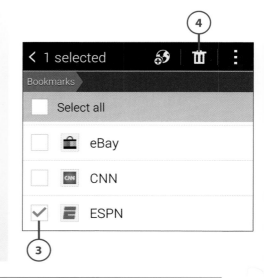

Another Approach

In Bookmarks, display the list of items from which you want to delete, tap the menu icon, and choose Delete. Tap the check box of each bookmark and folder that you want to delete. When you finish selecting, tap Done.

Deletions performed in this manner are also immediate. However, if you realize that you made a mistake, quickly tap the Undo bar that briefly appears near the bottom of the screen.

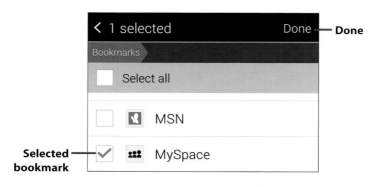

Selected bookmark

Done

More Menu Commands

The main menu contains additional useful commands that haven't been discussed. Here's an explanation of what the remaining commands do.

1. With any web page displayed, tap the menu icon. (To see all the commands, you have to scroll the menu.) Brightness and Settings apply to all pages; the other commands apply only to the current page.

2. *Add to Quick Access.* When you create a new window, your list of Quick Access icons appears. Choose this command to add the current page to the Quick Access roster.

3. *Add Shortcut to Home Screen.* Create a Home screen shortcut for the current page. When you tap the shortcut, the Internet app launches and displays the web page.

4. *Share Via.* Share the page with another person or device using a variety of methods.

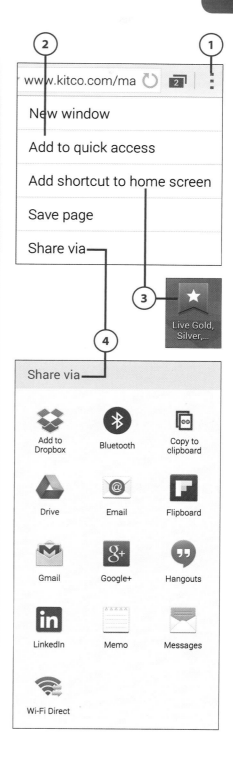

5. *Find on Page.* Search the current page for a text string. Each match (if any) is highlighted. To move between matches, tap an arrow icon. The page scrolls as needed to display each match.

6. *Desktop View.* By default, if a mobile version of a site is available, it is displayed; otherwise, the desktop version is shown. Enable this option to automatically display *all* sites as though they were being viewed in a desktop browser—ignoring a mobile version, if one is available.

7. *Brightness.* Enables you to specify a browser-specific brightness setting.

8. *Print.* Print the current page on a supported Wi-Fi printer.

9. *Settings.* View and modify Internet app preferences (see the next section, "Configuring the Browser").

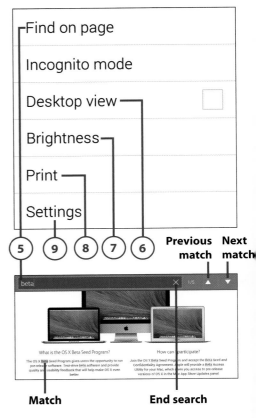

Configuring the Browser

As is the case with a Mac or PC browser, you can configure the Internet app to match your preferred way of working and perform common browser actions, such as clearing the cache and managing cookies.

1. With any web page displayed, tap the menu icon and choose Settings. (You may have to scroll the menu to see the Settings command.)

Another Path to Settings

Regardless of whether Internet is currently running, you can also configure it by opening Settings, scrolling to the Applications section, and tapping the Internet icon. The same screen appears.

2. The Settings screen appears, divided into two sections: Basics and Advanced.

- *Account.* Specify the types of data that you want to sync with your Samsung account.

- *Set Homepage.* Specify a new home page by setting it to the carrier's default, the current page, your Quick Access links, Most Visited Sites, or Other—a URL that you manually enter.

- *Auto Fill Forms.* Enable forms on web pages to be automatically filled in with stored text for your name, address, phone number, and email address.

- *Privacy.* Propose common search terms when performing finds and popular websites when entering addresses; remember form data and site passwords; delete a variety of cached data types.

- *Screen and Text.* Adjust zoom control and full-screen mode; text size and scaling.

- *Content Settings.* Accept cookies; enable/disable location information access and JavaScript; block pop-ups; specify the default storage location (device or memory card); clear all data stored by selected websites; enable or disable website notifications; and reset browser settings to defaults.

- *Bandwidth Management.* Preload pages; disable image downloads.

To view or modify any of these settings, tap a category and make the necessary changes. When you're done, press the Back key or tap the Back icon.

Back   (2)

< Settings

BASICS

Account
Select the type of data you want to sync.

Set homepage
http://mobile.nytimes.com/

Auto fill forms
Manage your text for automatically filling out Web forms.

ADVANCED

Privacy

Screen and text

Content settings

Bandwidth management

Privacy settings

Delete personal data

Browsing history   ☐

Cache   ☐

Cookies and site data   ☐

Passwords   ☐

Auto fill data   ☐

Location access   ☐

Cancel   Done

Google Chrome Essentials

Although most carriers treat the Internet app as the S5's primary browser, you might want to give Chrome a whirl, too. As you experiment with Chrome, you'll note that many of the instructions provided in this chapter for Internet also apply to Chrome. The two apps have similar menu commands, Settings options, and display options, for example. This section contains a rundown of some Chrome features that differ substantially from those of Internet.

Launching Chrome. Go to the Home screen and tap Apps, Chrome. Or tap a Home screen shortcut for Chrome, if you have one.

Specifying a Default Browser. If you tap a web link in an email or text message, a Complete Action Using dialog box appears. If you decide that you prefer Chrome to Internet (or vice versa), select the desired browser and tap Always. From that point forward, the selected browser will automatically launch whenever you open a link. For more information on setting or changing the default browser, see "Launching Internet," at the beginning of this chapter. Note that you aren't *required* to specify a default browser.

Tabs versus windows. Like Internet's windows, Chrome's *tabs* enable you to keep multiple web pages open simultaneously and switch among them as desired.

- To create a new tab, tap the menu icon and choose New Tab, or tap the Tabs icon and tap New Tab. The tabs icon always shows the number of open tabs.

Tabs **Menu**

- To switch among tabs, you can swipe horizontally across the address box area. You can also tap the Tabs icon, and then tap the tab that you want to make active.

- To remove a tab, tap the Tabs icon. Then tap the X in the tab's name or swipe the tab off either side of the screen. To simultaneously remove all tabs, tap the menu icon and choose Close All Tabs.

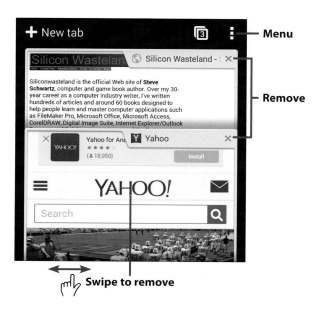

Search engine. Google is Chrome's default search engine. To use a different one, tap the menu icon and choose Settings, Search Engine.

Working with bookmarks. You can create, open, delete, and organize book-marks for frequently visited pages.

- To create a bookmark for the current page, open the menu; tap the star icon; specify the bookmark's name, address, and containing folder; and tap Save.

Creating a bookmark

- To remove a bookmark or edit its details, open the menu and tap the star icon. Then tap Remove or make the desired edits, respectively, and tap Save.

- To open a bookmark, tap the menu icon and choose Bookmarks. Open folders as necessary, and then tap the thumbnail of the bookmark to open.

History. To open the list of recently viewed pages (History), tap the menu icon and choose History. Tap any page name to view it, search History for a particular page, delete an entry by tapping its X, or quickly delete the stored browsing history and other data, such as cookies.

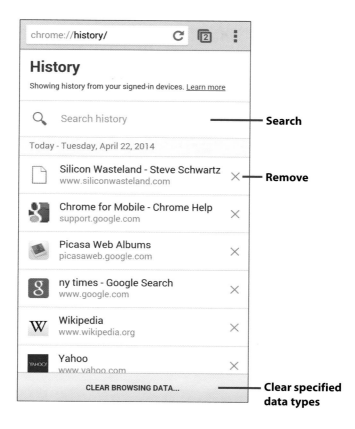

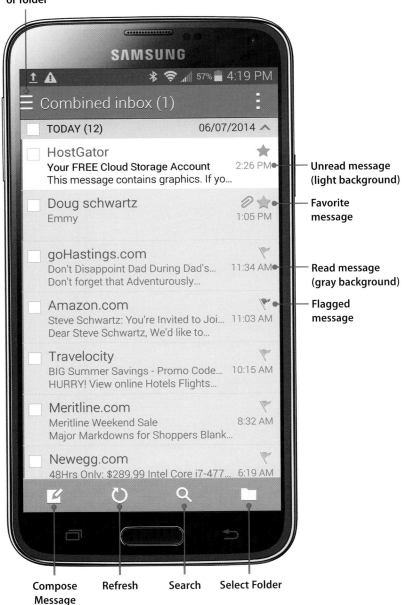

Select account
or folder

Unread message
(light background)

Favorite
message

Read message
(gray background)

Flagged
message

Compose
Message

Refresh

Search

Select Folder

In this chapter, you add your email accounts to the phone so you can send and receive email and attachments. Topics include the following:

→ Adding and configuring email accounts

→ Automatically and manually checking for new email

→ Reading mail, working with attachments, and designating priority senders

→ Composing, replying to, and forwarding messages

→ Adding attachments and inserting material into messages

→ Managing email

→ Using Gmail

Sending and Receiving Email

You can easily configure your phone to send and receive mail for your POP3, IMAP, and Exchange Server email accounts. In addition, the Email app supports many web-based accounts—as long as they also provide POP, IMAP, or Exchange support. If you aren't sure what types of email accounts you can set up, contact your *Internet service provider* (*ISP*), call your information technology (IT) department, or review the Help information for your web-based accounts. (For information on creating and adding Gmail accounts, see Chapter 1, "Galaxy S5 Essentials.")

Adding Email Accounts

You can add accounts to your phone in two ways: automatically or manually.

Corporate Exchange Server Users

If you're adding a corporate Microsoft Exchange Server account, contact your IT department or system administrator for the correct settings and then follow the instructions in "Manually Add an Account," later in this section. Exchange Server accounts cannot be added using the automatic method.

Automatically Add an Account

1. On the Home screen, tap the Email icon. (If the icon isn't present, you can tap Apps, Email.)

Setting Up Your First Email Account

If you haven't already set up an account, when you open the app, the Email Accounts screen automatically appears. Go directly to Step 5.

2. On any message list screen, tap the menu icon and choose Settings.

3. Tap Manage Accounts.

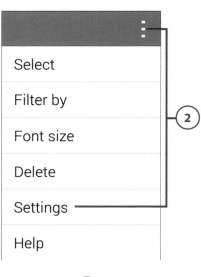

Select

Filter by

Font size

Delete

Settings

Help

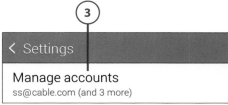

< Settings

Manage accounts
ss@cable.com (and 3 more)

4. Tap the plus (+) icon to add a new account.

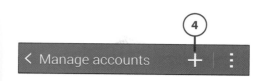

Verizon Users Only

If Verizon is your carrier, you'll see a screen asking you to Choose an Account to Set Up. Tap the icon that represents your email service provider, such as Outlook.com or Verizon.net. Tap Others if your email account type isn't shown.

5. Enter your full email address and account password. If you have difficulty using the onscreen keyboard, tap the Show Password check box to ensure that you enter the password correctly.

6. *Optional:* Tap the Set This Account as the Default for Sending Emails check box if you want the phone to treat this account as your main, default account from which email is normally sent. This check box appears only when you set up a second or subsequent account; when you set up your first email account, Email assumes this account is the default and doesn't give you the choice.

7. Tap the Next button.

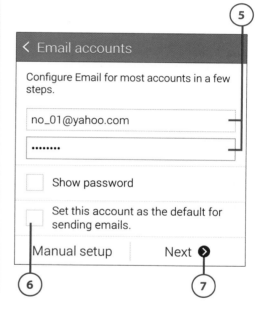

8. Email attempts to verify the account and determine the correct Internet standard protocol to use: POP3, IMAP, or Microsoft Exchange ActiveSync.

- If successful, the Account Options screen appears. Make any desired changes and tap Next. (If this is a Microsoft Exchange ActiveSync account—used by Outlook.com, Hotmail.com, Live.com, and many corporations—additional options are presented, such as Email Retrieval Size and whether you want to sync data other than email.)

Now or Whenever

If you don't understand some of the options, you can just tap Next. You can change the account settings whenever it's convenient by following the instructions in "Edit Individual Account Settings," later in the chapter.

- If there's a problem, an error dialog appears. Automatic setup can fail for a variety of reasons. Check your username, domain name, and password for errors, and then try again. If automatic setup fails *repeatedly*, use the manual setup method described in the next task.

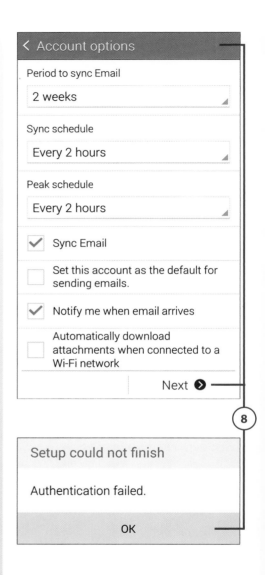

9. You're given an opportunity to name the account and specify the name that displays on outgoing mail from the account. Make any necessary changes and tap Done. (If you're a Verizon customer, tap Next and then tap Done with Accounts.)

No Option to Set the Display Name

Certain account types, such as Hotmail, automatically take the display name from your current account information.

10. The account's Inbox appears and email downloads to the account.

Manually Add an Account

1. Perform Steps 1–6 of the previous task ("Automatically Add an Account") and tap the Manual Setup button.

Continuing from Automatic Setup

If you just performed an automatic setup and it failed with an error, you can also begin a manual setup here.

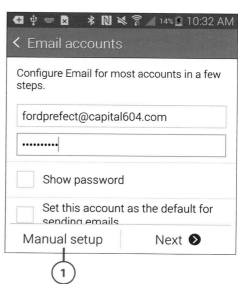

2. Specify the Internet standard protocol for sending and receiving account email by tapping its button. If you aren't sure which protocols are supported, contact your ISP or IT department for the correct option(s). This example uses IMAP.

Multiple Protocols

If your ISP supports multiple protocols (such as POP3 and IMAP), performing a manual setup is sometimes the only way to ensure that your preferred protocol is used.

3. Check the proposed settings on the Incoming Server Settings screen, and make any necessary changes. Tap the Next button to open the Outgoing Server Settings screen.

Entering Your Username

Depending on the account provider, Username may be the part of the name that precedes the @ symbol or it may be the complete email address. If this step fails and an error dialog appears, enter the username the other way and try again.

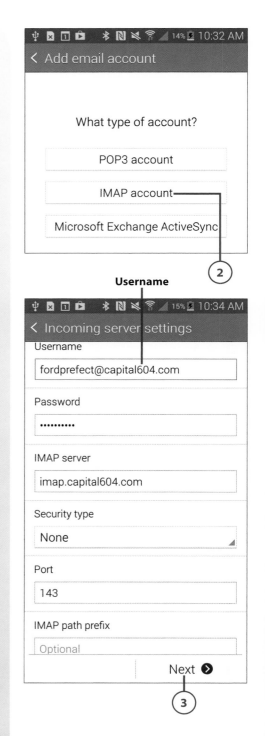

>>>Go Further
DELETE MAIL FROM SERVER (POP3 ONLY)

If you're adding a POP3 account, scroll to the bottom of the Incoming Server
Settings screen and you'll see a Delete Email from Server option. Normally,
POP3 email is deleted from the mail server immediately after it's delivered. If
this account is also on other devices, such as your computer or tablet, leave
this option set to Never to ensure that messages are also delivered to the other
devices. If this is your *only* device, choose When Deleted from Inbox.

This option isn't available for IMAP or Microsoft Exchange ActiveSync accounts.
Because these accounts are designed to synchronize across all your devices, if
you delete an email message on *any* device, it's simultaneously deleted from all
devices. Otherwise, the message remains on the server indefinitely.

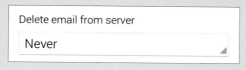

Delete email from server

Never

4. Check the Outgoing Server
Settings screen and make any
necessary changes. Tap Next.

5. Specify settings on the Account Options screen and tap Next.

6. Name the account, specify the name to display on outgoing mail from the account, and tap Done. (If you're a Verizon customer, tap Next and then tap Done with Accounts.)

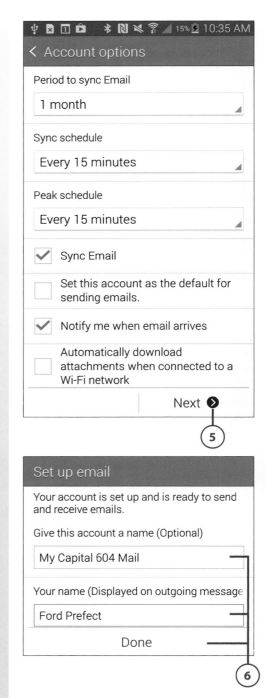

>>>Go Further

TIPS FOR ADDING ACCOUNTS

Although the process of adding an email account has improved considerably with the current version of Android, it doesn't always go smoothly. Here are some actions to take when adding an account fails:

- *Try, try again.* When using automatic setup, if you're certain that the username and password are correct, wait awhile and try again. Because of the vagaries of the Internet and the fact that mail servers aren't available 100 percent of the time, you may simply have been unlucky on the initial attempt—or three.

- *Switch to manual.* When repeated automatic attempts fail, it's time to switch to manual. If you try manual setup immediately after an automatic failure, much of the correct information is already filled in. Leave it as is, but try Username as the full email address and as only the username—with *@domain* stripped off. Some mail servers have specific requirements for the username and will accept it only in one form. (In automatic mode, you *must* use the full email address—even if only the username portion is all that's normally accepted.)

- *Contact your ISP or IT department.* When all else fails, contact your ISP or network administrator, find out the exact settings needed, and—in manual mode—override the proffered settings with the ones you're given. (This is a requirement when configuring a corporate Microsoft Exchange Server account.)

Configuring Email Accounts

With the exception of General Settings (which apply to the Email app and to all registered accounts), settings for each email account can differ. After adding an email account, check its settings to ensure that the default choices are satisfactory.

Go to Settings

You can also view or change your email settings on the phone's Settings screen. Open Settings and tap the Email icon (in the Applications section).

Edit General Settings

1. On any message screen, tap the menu icon and choose Settings.

2. The Settings screen appears. General Settings are presented in the lower half of the screen.

3. *Display.* Tap Display to set the following display-related options:

   - When enabled, Auto Fit Content shrinks messages to fit onscreen. (Although text messages typically wrap to fit, HTML advertisements from online stores frequently require you to scroll horizontally. You can increase the size of such a reduced-size message as necessary.)

   - Tap Message Preview Line to specify the number of lines of text (between 0–3) that are used to preview email in the message lists.

   - Tap Title Line in List to specify whether the Sender or Subject will be displayed on the first line of each message in the message lists.

   - When Hide Checkboxes is disabled, each message in a message list is preceded by a check box. The check boxes simplify the process of issuing commands that affect multiple messages, such as Delete or Move. When Hide Checkboxes is enabled, you must choose the Select menu command or press and hold a message to make the selection check boxes appear.

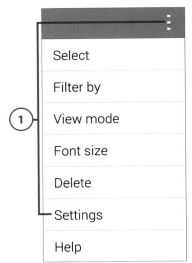

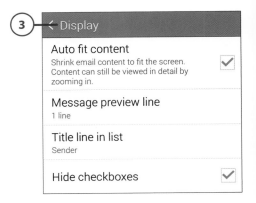

4. *Default Display.* When reading messages, this setting determines what is shown after you move or delete the active message: Next Email, Previous Email, or Email List.

5. *Priority Sender Settings.* Tap this option to modify settings that apply to the people and organizations that you've designated as *priority senders*. Options include Set as Default Folder to automatically display the Priority Senders Inbox whenever you launch Email and notification methods used to announce received mail from priority senders. (For additional information, see "Designate and Work with Priority Senders," later in the chapter.)

6. *Spam Addresses.* Tap Spam Addresses to manually record email addresses that you want to block. You can also block addresses from individual messages as you receive them, which saves you the effort of typing or pasting their addresses into Spam Addresses. For more information, see "Managing the Spam Senders List."

7. *Delay Email Sending.* Although you can't cancel or retrieve a message after tapping Send, enabling this option serves to delay the sending of each message. If you tap the Cancel button before the delay elapses, you can prevent the current message from being sent.

⑤

< Priority sender settings

Set as default folder
Show the priority sender inbox whenever you open Email.

Email notifications
Receive status bar notifications when emails arrive. (When this option is turned off, check the notification settings for each account.) ✓

Notification sound
Tickety-Tock

Vibrate

Edit Individual Account Settings

You can change a variety of settings to ensure that your messages are retrieved on a reasonable schedule, display proper identifying information, and so on. Note that certain account types (such as Microsoft Exchange ActiveSync) may have additional options that aren't shown in this task.

1. On any message screen, tap the menu icon and choose Settings.

2. Tap Manage Accounts.

3. Tap the account whose settings you want to review or change, and set options as described in Steps 4–18.

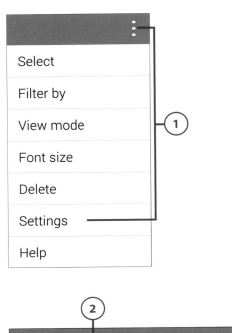

4. *Sync Settings.* Tap Sync Settings to edit synchronization settings including whether to sync the account, set the sync schedule, and specify whether to set a size limit for retrieved messages. For details, see "Configure an Account's Sync Settings" in the next section.

5. *Signature.* To automatically add a personal *signature* (static text) to the end of each outgoing message, set the Signature switch to On. To change the default signature, tap Edit Signature, edit the signature, and tap Done.

6. *Default Account.* If you have multiple email accounts on the phone, you must enable Default Account for one of them. When composing a new email message, Email uses this account automatically as the sending account—although you're always free to choose a different account before sending. (On the other hand, when replying to or forwarding a message, Email uses the account that received the message rather than the default account.)

7. *Password.* If you've changed the account's password, you must also edit the password used by Email so it matches.

8. *Email Notifications.* Enable this option if you want an email icon to appear in the status bar whenever new mail arrives.

9. *Notification Sound.* Change the notification sound that announces the arrival of new email. In the Notification Sound dialog box, tap a sound to hear it. When you've made your selection, tap OK.

No Notification Sound

Select Silent if you don't want an audible notification of new mail.

10. *Vibrate.* Enable Vibrate if you want the phone to vibrate when it receives mail.

11. To view the remaining settings, tap the More Settings button.

12. *Account Name.* To change the name used to label the account in Email's account list, tap Account Name, make the necessary changes, and tap OK.

13. *Your Name.* To change the name used to identify you to recipients of your email messages, tap Your Name, make the necessary changes, and tap OK.

14. *Always Cc/Bcc Myself.* Specify whether outgoing messages automatically include this account in the *CC* (carbon copy) or *BCC* (blind carbon copy) recipient list. The purpose is to ensure that a backup copy of each outgoing message from this account is also delivered to the account's Inbox. If your email account automatically keeps a copy of each outgoing message in a folder called Sent (or a similar name), choose None for this setting.

15. *Show Images.* Check this option to automatically display all linked images that are present in messages. As explained later in the "Show Images Judiciously" sidebar, it's best to leave this option unchecked if you are on a limited data plan or are concerned about receiving junk mail.

16. *Security Options.* If you need to encrypt messages that you send, sign them with a digital signature, or both, tap Security Options. You are more likely to need these options for corporate email than for personal email.

17. *Number of Emails to Load.* Tap to set the number of recent messages to be shown at one time. You can specify from 25 to Total (all).

18. *Auto Download Attachments.* Enable this option to instruct Email to automatically download attachments when your phone is connected to a Wi-Fi network; in other words, *not* over your cellular connection. This is usually a good choice unless you receive many massive attachments. In that case, you may prefer to download them manually as needed—leaving large ones for downloading only to your computer.

19. Tap the Back icon or press the Back key to return to the Settings screen for the email account.

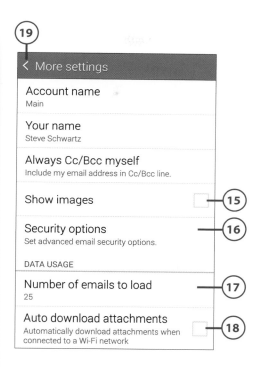

It's Not All Good

Show Images Judiciously

If you shop on the Internet, you probably receive sales fliers from sites such as Amazon.com, Newegg, and JC Penney. To make these messages smaller, they frequently contain *links to images on the Web* rather than the actual images. To automatically see the images, you must enable Show Images in Step 15.

Unfortunately, spammers also include linked images in their emails. If you display them in a spam message, the image is retrieved by Email—simultaneously verifying to the spammer that your email address is a real, active one. *Loads* of spam are liable to follow. The safest approach is to disable Show Images. To view linked images in a trusted, *safe* message, tap the Show Images button that appears directly under the message header. Another option for trusted messages—if the message provides it—is to click a link to view the message in your phone's browser (Internet or Chrome).

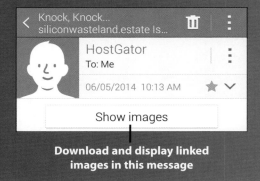

Download and display linked images in this message

Configure an Account's Sync Settings

After adding a new email account, you'll want to configure the account's *sync settings* (specifying the schedule on which email will be retrieved).

1. Perform Steps 1–3 of the "Edit Individual Account Settings" task and then tap Sync Settings.

2. The Sync Settings screen appears. Set options as described in the remaining steps.

3. *Sync Email.* When checked, Email syncs this account using the schedules specified in Sync Schedule.

4. *Sync Schedule.* Tap to display the Sync Schedule screen on which you can specify how often the phone automatically checks for new, incoming mail to this account. Press the Back key or tap the Back icon when you're ready to return to the Sync Settings screen.

   - Tap Set Sync Schedule to display the Set Sync Schedule dialog box and select a frequency with which to sync the account's email. Options include Manual or a specific interval, such as Every 15 Minutes or Once a Day.

   - Tap While Roaming and choose Manual or Use Above Settings to adjust how your phone syncs email when you roam on other networks.

   - To sync email on a different schedule during peak hours, enable Peak Schedule. You can then tap Set Peak Schedule and specify a frequency. Tap Peak Days buttons to indicate the peak days. Tap the Peak Time buttons to set the start and end times for peak days.

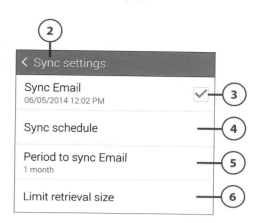

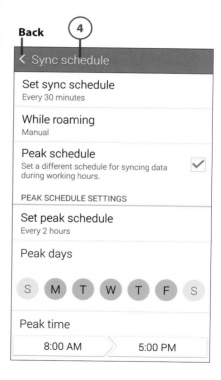

5. *Period to Sync Email.* Specify the period for which the phone will keep email in sync. Although you can select All, it's best to specify a shorter time period such as One Month. Doing so ensures that you have access to your current mail and that the phone isn't bogged down by having to sync a huge volume of older mail.

6. *Limit Retrieval Size.* To avoid data charges when out of range of a Wi-Fi network, you can specify the maximum size message that will automatically be delivered to the phone via a sync. Larger messages—primarily those with attachments—must be manually retrieved by tapping the message header. This option can be set separately for those instances when you're roaming.

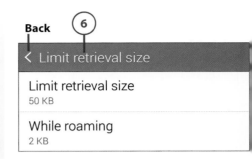

Back ⑥

Message Format

If Sync Settings for your account includes a Message Format setting, tap it to specify whether retrieved messages will be in HTML format (containing fonts, colors, and formatting) or plain text format (all formatting removed).

Delete an Account

You can delete any email account
that you no longer want on your
phone. Deleting an account simultaneously removes the account's
messages and other data from your
phone. (Deleting an account merely
removes it from the phone; it doesn't
cancel the account.)

1. On any message screen, tap the
   menu icon and choose Settings.

2. Tap Manage Accounts.

3. Select the account that you want
   to delete by pressing and holding
   its name, and then tap the Trash
   icon.

4. Confirm the deletion by tapping
   the OK button.

Another Method

You can also delete accounts
by tapping the menu icon and
choosing Delete Account. Select
the account(s) to delete, tap
Done, and confirm by tapping OK.

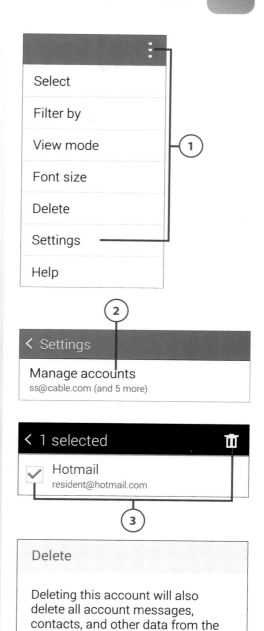

Retrieving Mail

Email can be delivered to your phone in two ways. First, the Email app performs a check for new mail automatically for each account according to the account's Sync Schedule settings—every 15 minutes or once per hour, for example. (For information on setting a retrieval schedule for an account, see "Configure an Account's Sync Settings.") Second, you can manually check for new mail whenever you want—regardless of an account's schedule—by tapping the Refresh icon.

1. Launch Email by tapping its Home screen icon or by tapping Apps, Email.

2. *Optional:* To change the displayed Inbox or folder, tap the menu icon above the left edge. In the Accounts drawer, do one of the following:

   - Tap Combined Inbox to simultaneously view all accounts' Inboxes in a single message list.

   - Tap Priority Senders to view only received email from designated priority senders—regardless of the accounts in which their messages were received. (To learn about priority senders, see "Designate and Work with Priority Senders," later in the chapter.)

   - Tap a specific account's Inbox or Sent folder to view only that account's received or sent mail.

   - To view a folder other than Inbox or Sent (such as Trash or Junk, for example), tap the account or entry's Show All Folders icon and then select the folder you want to view. (You can also tap the Select Folder icon at the bottom of the current account's message list.)

Number of unread messages

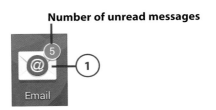

Menu icon ② **Unread messages**

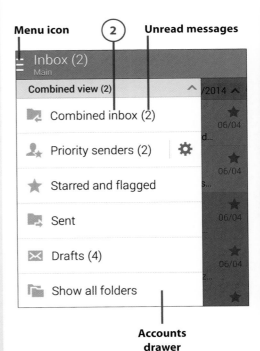

Accounts drawer

Interpreting the Accounts Information

If present, the number to the right of an account in the list indicates the number of unread messages it contains. By scanning the list, you can quickly determine which accounts have new messages.

---

3. *Optional:* Tap the Refresh button at the bottom of the screen to manually check for new messages.

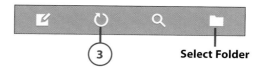

3   **Select Folder**

>>>*Go Further*

OTHER WAYS TO LAUNCH EMAIL

You can also open Email by responding to a received mail notification or tapping a message header in the Email widget:

- Open the Notification panel by dragging downward. Tap the Email notification.

New email notification

NOTIFICATIONS	Clear
2 new emails 5:32 PM	
Steve Schwartz: FW: Today's Shell Shock...	
University of Minnesota Alumni Associati...	

- If you've installed the Email widget on a Home screen page, tap a message header to view that message in Email.

Reading Mail

When new mail arrives or you want to review older messages, you can read the email on your phone. You can read messages in portrait or—by rotating the phone—in landscape mode.

1. Perform Steps 1–2 of the "Retrieving Mail" task.

2. *Optional:* You can filter the message list to make it easier to find the messages you want to read. Open the menu, choose Filter By, and select a filtering option. Only those messages in the current list that match the Filter By setting are displayed, and the Filter By setting is shown at the top of the screen. When you're ready to return to the full message list, press the Back key or tap the Back icon.

Setting a View

You can also switch between standard and conversation view, presenting message headers as a continuous list sorted by date (standard) or grouped by Subject (conversation). To learn about views, see the "Standard Versus Conversation View" sidebar at the end of this section.

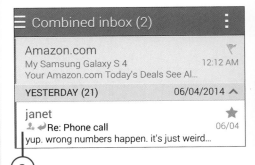

3. Tap the header of the message that you want to read. Headers with light backgrounds are unread messages; headers with gray backgrounds are previously read messages.

4. The message appears. You can change the magnification by pinching your fingers together or spreading them apart. Drag to see any parts of the message that are off-screen. You can rotate the phone to view the message in landscape mode.

5. To read another message in the current message list, do one of the following:

   • Tap the Back icon or press the Back key to return to the message list. Tap the header of the next message that you want to read.

   • Swipe the screen to the left or right to view the next or previous consecutive message in the list.

   • Tap the Previous or Next icon at the bottom of the screen to view the next or previous consecutive message in the list.

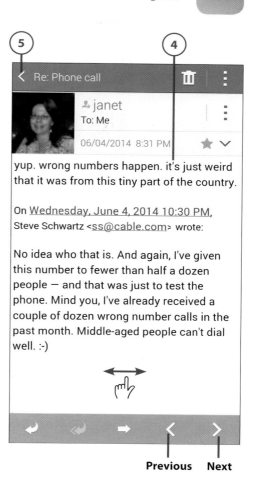

Previous   Next

>>>Go Further
STANDARD VERSUS CONVERSATION VIEW

You can configure the message list in either of two views: standard or conversation. To specify a view, tap the menu icon, choose View Mode, and select Standard View or Conversation View.

In *standard view*, each message, reply, and forwarded message is shown with a separate message header and messages are grouped by date. You can collapse or expand messages for any date or period by tapping the date designator, such as Today, Yesterday, or Last Week.

Standard view

Date and number of messages

Collapsed

Expanded

In *conversation view*, messages are grouped by conversation, according to their Subject. For example, suppose that you and a co-worker exchange several messages with the subject Budget Proposal. In the Inbox, all received messages with the subject Budget Proposal and RE: Budget Proposal are grouped under a single expandable message header. The number of messages in each conversation is indicated beside the message header. Note that multiple people can be involved in a conversation.

When you select a conversation in a message list, all messages from the conversation are shown in a list that's arranged from oldest (top) to most recent (bottom). To read a message in the conversation, tap its header. Similarly, to collapse a message in the conversation, tap its header again. Only one message can be expanded at a time.

Conversation view

Number of messages in conversation

Conversation view (expanded)

Oldest message

Newest message

View and Save Attachments

Some email messages contain *attachments* (accompanying files), such as photos and documents. If you want, you can download the attachments and—if you have compatible app(s)—view the files on your phone.

1. In a message list, files with attachments are denoted by a paper clip icon. Tap the message header to open the message.

2. The Attachments line shows the number of attached files. Tap it to view or download the files.

3. Tap an attachment's Preview button to see a preview of the file. Your phone downloads the file and, if a compatible app is installed, displays or plays the file's contents. To return to the Attachments screen, press the Back key.

4. *Optional*: Tap an attachment's Download button to save a copy of the file on your phone. To save *all* of the attachments, tap the Download All button. Downloaded files are stored in the Download folder of the phone's built-in memory (Device Storage).

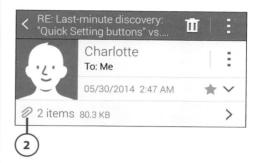

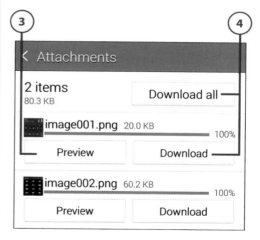

Revisiting Downloaded Attachments

There are several methods you can use to view a downloaded attachment. First, launch My Files, tap Download History, and then tap the file. Second, in My Files, open the Download folder in Device Storage and select the file. Finally, if it's an image file, you can also open it by launching Gallery, opening the Download folder, and tapping the file's thumbnail.

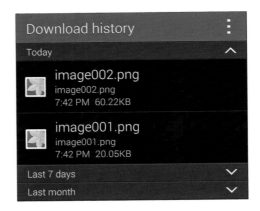

Designate and Work with Priority Senders

By using the new Priority Senders feature, you can ensure that you never miss an email from an important person in your business or personal life. You can see all messages from priority senders in a single message list (similar to the Combined Inbox) or use it to filter your list so you can see only the messages from a specific person or company. Priority Senders is also available in Messages, enabling you to quickly find your favorite conversations.

Add Priority Senders

1. Open the Accounts drawer and tap Priority Senders.

Menu icon

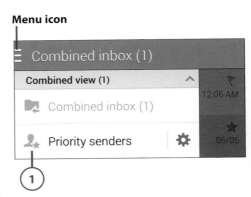

2. Tap the + (plus) icon to add one or more priority senders.

3. The Add Priority Senders screen appears. Do any of the following:

   - Tap the + (plus) icon of any-one in the Recommended list. If they have multiple email addresses, each address is a separate entry. Tap each person or address that you want to designate as a priority sender.

   - Tap Enter Email to search for someone with whom you've exchanged mail or who has a record in Contacts. Enter their name or email address. As you type, matches are presented in a scrolling list. When you see the correct one, select it and then tap OK.

   - Tap Contacts to select people to add from your Contacts records. Select one or more records, and then tap Done. (If a person has multiple email addresses, you must specify the address to use.)

4. Press the Back key when you're done. The scrolling Priority Senders list is displayed at the top of the screen.

Adding More Priority Senders

Some Step 3 actions *automatically* dismiss the Add Priority Senders screen and display the current Priority Senders list. If you want to add other people or addresses, scroll to the end of the list, tap the + (plus) icon, and repeat Step 3.

Use the Priority Senders List

1. Open the Accounts drawer and select Priority Senders.

2. The message list for Priority Senders appears. At the top of the screen are icons for your priority senders.

3. By default, all messages from all priority senders are displayed in the message list. You can do any of the following:

   • Tap an icon to view only messages from that person or organization. If you've added more priority senders than will fit onscreen, you can scroll the list by swiping horizontally.

   • Tap the All icon to view all messages from all priority senders.

4. Filter, read, and manage messages as described elsewhere in this chapter.

Manage Priority Senders

1. Perform Steps 1–2 of the "Use the Priority Senders List" task.

2. Press and hold any priority sender's icon and select Edit List of Priority Senders.

3. Each priority sender's icon is shown with a – (minus) symbol in the corner. Do any of the following:

   • Change a priority sender's position in the scrolling list by pressing and holding its icon and then dragging to the left or right.

   • Remove an individual or organization from the list by tapping its – (minus) symbol.

4. When you're finished making changes, tap Done to save or Cancel to ignore the changes.

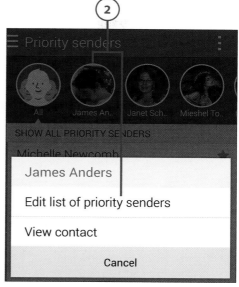

Composing and Sending Mail

You can create new email messages, as well as reply to or forward received messages.

Create a New Email Message

1. Display the message list for Combined Inbox or a specific account, and then tap the Create Message icon at the bottom of the screen.

2. A new message screen appears, addressed from the current account. (If you're viewing the Combined Inbox or Priority Senders message list, your default email account is used instead.)

3. *Optional:* To send the message from a different account, tap the expand/collapse icon and select the account name in the From box. In the Select Email Address dialog, select the account from which the message will be sent.

4. *Optional:* To add Carbon Copy (Cc) or Blind Carbon Copy (Bcc) fields, tap the expand/collapse icon to make them visible.

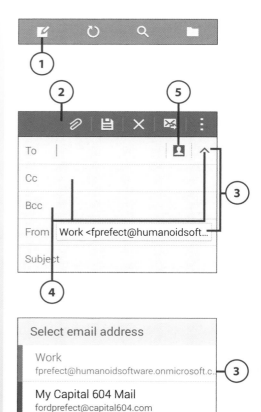

5. Tap the To, Cc, or Bcc box, and add one or more recipients by doing the following:

   - Tap the Contacts icon to the right of the To, Cc, or Bcc box to select recipients that you have stored in Contacts. (See Chapter 5, "Managing Contacts," for more information about the Contacts app.) Select each person that you want to add and tap Done. (If there are multiple email addresses for a person and you haven't specified a default address for him or her, a dialog appears in which you can choose the correct address.)

Select from Contacts

Select by Typing

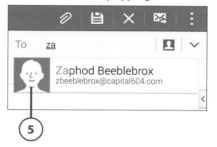

Filter the Contacts

In addition to selecting people from the normal Contacts list, you can pick people from Groups or Favorites by tapping the appropriate tab at the top of the screen.

   - Select the To, Cc, or Bcc box. Begin typing part of the recipient's name, email address, or other information that's stored in the person's or company's contact record. Select the recipient from the match list that appears.

Removing Recipients

Prior to sending, you can remove a recipient if you change your mind. Tap the box that contains the recipient (To, Cc, or Bcc) and then tap the minus (–) icon beside the recipient's name.

6. Enter the message subject in the Subject box.

7. Type or use voice input to enter the message text.

8. Tap the Send icon to transmit the message.

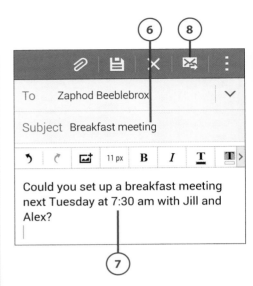

Attachments and Inserts

An email message can optionally include embedded material or be accompanied by attached files. For instructions, see "Add Attachments and Inserts," later in this section.

>>>Go Further
BEGONE PLAIN TEXT!

While composing a message, you can use the toolbar to format selected text, insert material, and assist in editing or making corrections. (If the toolbar isn't visible, tap the arrow icon at the right edge of the message box.) The toolbar icons' functions are similar to those found in a typical word-processing application. You can use Undo and Redo to correct errors and typos, insert images and other material into the message body, and format currently selected text by changing its size, color, highlighting, or font. In portrait mode, swipe the toolbar left and right to see all its icons. Read "Entering Text" and "Editing Text" in Chapter 2, "Understanding the Android/TouchWiz Interface" for additional helpful information.

Note that when you select text for editing, the pop-up editing toolbar contains a new command: Dictionary. Tap Dictionary and download a dictionary to the S5. From that point forward, you can look up the definition of any selected word and assure yourself that you're using it correctly.

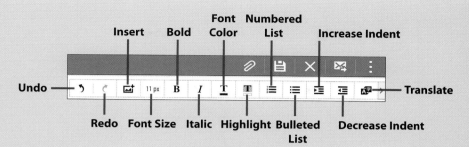

Undo — Redo Font Size Insert Bold Font Color Italic Highlight Numbered List Bulleted List Increase Indent Decrease Indent Translate

Definition of "galaxy"

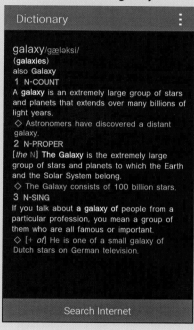

Dictionary

galaxy /ˈɡæləksi/
(galaxies)
also Galaxy
1 N-COUNT
A galaxy is an extremely large group of stars and planets that extends over many billions of light years.
◇ Astronomers have discovered a distant galaxy.
2 N-PROPER
[the N] The Galaxy is the extremely large group of stars and planets to which the Earth and the Solar System belong.
◇ The Galaxy consists of 100 billion stars.
3 N-SING
If you talk about a galaxy of people from a particular profession, you mean a group of them who are all famous or important.
◇ [+ of] He is one of a small galaxy of Dutch stars on German television.

Search Internet

Reply to Mail

1. When reading a received message, tap the Reply icon. (To address your reply to all recipients of the original message, tap the Reply All icon.)

2. A message appears, formatted as a reply (RE: *original subject*). The text insertion mark is positioned for your reply. The original message text is displayed at the bottom of the window.

3. Enter your reply text in the top section of the message window.

4. *Optional:* You can edit the original message text (to eliminate extraneous material, for example) by tapping the Edit button or remove the original message text by clearing the check box in the Original Message bar.

5. Tap the Send icon to send the message.

① **Reply All**

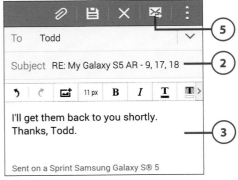

Forward Mail

1. When reading a received message, tap the Forward icon.

2. A message formatted for forwarding appears. Specify recipients in the To, Cc, and/or Bcc boxes, as described in "Create a New Email Message."

3. *Optional:* You can add your own text to a forwarded message in the top section of the message window.

4. *Optional:* You can edit the original message text (to eliminate extraneous material, for example) by tapping the Edit button or remove the original message text by clearing the check box in the Original Message bar.

5. Tap the Send icon to send the message.

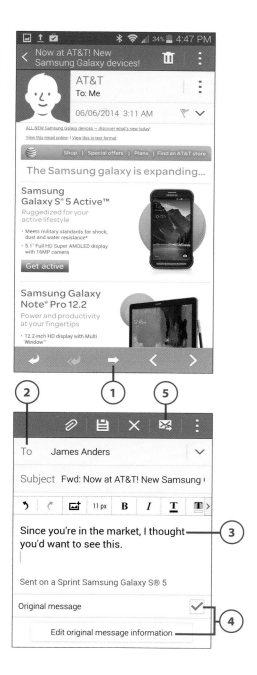

Original Message Attachments

By default, attachments received in the original message are forwarded. To prevent them from being forwarded, tap the – (minus) icon to the right of each attachment's filename.

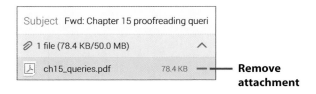

Remove attachment

Add Attachments and Inserts

Any message sent from Email—whether a new message, reply, or forward—can optionally include one or more file attachments, such as photos, PDFs, and Office documents. The recipient uses a compatible program or app to open and view the attachments.

In addition to sending file attachments with a message, you can insert any of the following directly into the body of a message: an image file from Gallery, selected data from a Contacts record, a memo, an S Note, a location, or a Calendar event.

Message Size Limits

The maximum size for a message and attachments created in Email is 50MB. Note, however, that the recipient's email account may have a size limit for incoming messages that is smaller than this, causing the message to be rejected. Check with the recipient before emailing massive attachments.

Add Attachments

1. Create a new message, reply, or forward, as described earlier in this section.

2. Tap the Attach icon at any point during the message-creation process.

3. Choose the type of item that you want to attach. (Choose My Files to select any file that's stored on your phone.) This example uses a picture attachment.

Create an Attachment On-the-Fly

You can choose Take Picture, Record Video, or Record Audio to use the phone to create a photo, video, or audio recording to send as an attachment.

4. Select the specific file to attach to the message, and respond to any dialog boxes or menus that appear. When sending a picture, for example, you can specify a resizing percentage or keep the original size.

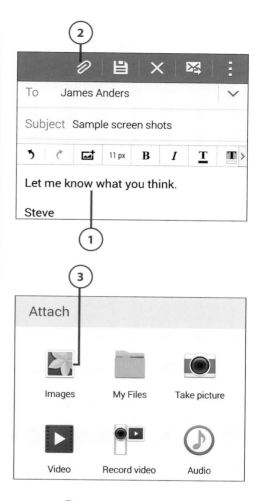

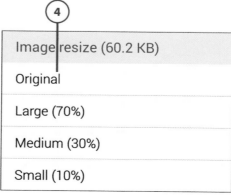

Expand/collapse Attachments list

5. Repeat Steps 2–4 to add other attachments. To remove an attachment, expand the Attachments list and tap the red minus (–) icon to the right of the item.

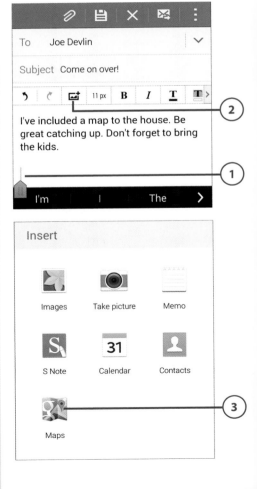

Add Inserts

1. In the message you're composing, position the text insertion mark at the spot in the message body where you want to insert the item.

2. Tap the Insert toolbar icon.

3. Choose an item type to insert. For instance, you can insert an image from Gallery, memo, Calendar event, or selected elements of a Contacts record (such as an email address).

4. The image and/or text appear in the message body at the text insertion mark.

Resizing Inserted Objects

You can change the size of an inserted object (such as a photo or map) by tapping it and then dragging handles that appear around the edges. Drag a corner handle to resize proportionally.

Managing the Mail

Although the Email app has fewer message-management options than a typical PC or Mac email client, you can manage message-list clutter by deleting unwanted messages, moving messages to different folders, changing the status of messages from read to unread (and vice versa), and marking important messages.

Deleting Messages

You can delete messages while you're viewing a message list or reading a particular message. All message deletions are immediate; there's no confirmation dialog box. If you realize you've made a mistake, quickly tap the Undo button that appears briefly at the bottom of the screen.

Undo button

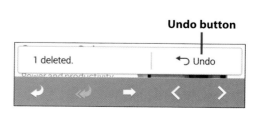

• While reading a message, tap the Delete icon at the top of the screen.

- While viewing a message list, you can quickly delete any individual message by swiping it off-screen to the left or right—the same way you clear individual notifications in the Notification panel. If you change your mind, tap the Undo button that appears. Otherwise, complete the deletion by flicking up or down over the buttons or in the message list.

- You can simultaneously delete multiple messages while viewing a message list. The method depends on the Display, Hide Checkboxes setting (see "Edit General Settings," earlier in the chapter).

  When Hide Checkboxes is enabled, tap the menu icon and choose Delete. Tap the check box to the left of each message that you want to delete, and then tap the Delete icon at the bottom of the screen. When Hide Checkboxes is disabled, tap the check box to the left of each message that you want to delete, and then tap the Delete icon at the bottom of the screen.

Delete

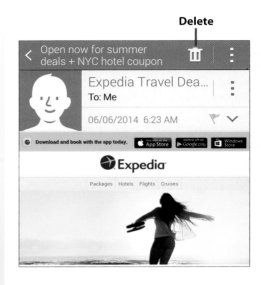

Hide Checkboxes enabled

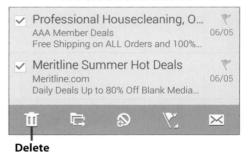

Delete

Hide Checkboxes disabled

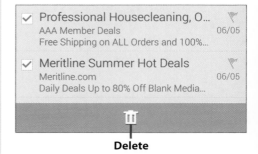

Delete

>>>Go Further

DELETIONS IN STANDARD AND CONVERSATION VIEWS

In *standard view*, you can select an entire group of messages for deletion (that is, messages for a particular day or period) by tapping the blue group header's check box above the messages. Tap the Delete icon to delete the selected messages.

Number of messages

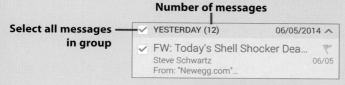

Select all messages → ✓ YESTERDAY (12)   06/05/2014 ⌃
in group   ✓ FW: Today's Shell Shocker Dea...   ✈
                    Steve Schwartz   06/05
                    From: "Newegg.com"...

Standard view

In *conversation view*, any deletion you make in an Inbox deletes the entire conversation. The number of messages in the conversation is shown following the Subject. When reading messages, only the active message is deleted—regardless of the number of messages in the conversation.

Moving Messages

You can move an email message to a different folder in the current account, as well as to a folder in another account. For example, you may be able to move a message from the Trash back into the Inbox or a project-related message into a project folder. You can move messages while you're viewing a message list or reading the message.

While Reading a Message

When reading a message, it can be moved to any account's folder.

1. Tap the message's menu icon and choose Move.

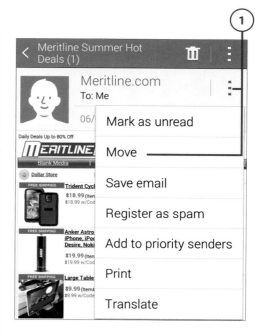

(1)

< Meritline Summer Hot Deals (1)   🗑   ⋮

Meritline.com   ⋮
To: Me

06/   Mark as unread

Daily Deals Up to 80% Off

MERITLINE   Move ─────
Blank Media
Dollar Store

FREE SHIPPING Trident Cycl   Save email
$18.99 (Iten
$18.99 w/Cod

Anker Astro   Register as spam
iPhone, iPod
Desire, Noki
$19.99 (Iten   Add to priority senders
$19.99 w/Cod

FREE SHIPPING Large Table   Print
$9.99 (Item4
$9.99 w/Code
            Translate

2. Select a destination folder in the current account or a different account. Tap Cancel if you've changed your mind.

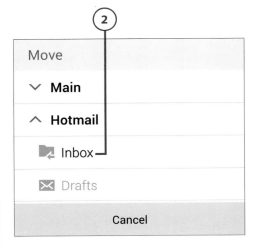

While Viewing a Message List

When moving messages from a message list, the destination folder *must* be in the current account—and the same destination folder must be used for all selected messages.

1. If each message in the message list is preceded by a check box, go to Step 2; otherwise, tap the menu icon and choose Select.

2. Select each message that you want to move to a particular destination folder.

3. Tap the Move icon beneath the message list. (Note that the position of the icon may vary.)

4. In the Move dialog box, select a destination folder in the current account. Tap Cancel if you've changed your mind.

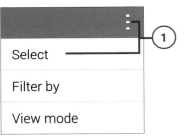

Creating Account Subfolders

Although custom account folders are typically created in your Mac/PC email program or—for web-based clients such as Outlook.com—using your browser, you can also create them in Email. Open the Accounts drawer and tap Show All Folders for the account in which you want to create the folder. (Don't tap Show All Folders in the Combined View—you can't create folders from there.) Tap the plus (+) icon at the top of the screen, select a *parent folder* in which to create the new folder, name the folder, and tap OK.

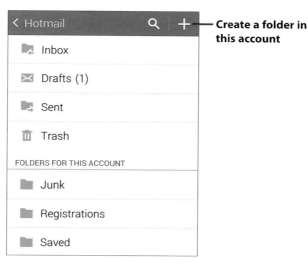

Create a folder in this account

Changing the Message Read Status

Sometimes it's useful to change a previously read message's status to unread or a new message to read. For instance, if you've fallen behind in reading incoming messages from an account, you can mark the unimportant ones as already read.

- While reading a message, you can mark it as unread by choosing Mark as Unread from the message menu. When you return to the message list, the message shows that it hasn't been read.

Message menu

Change status to unread

- While viewing the message list, you can toggle the read status of multiple messages by selecting each message of the same kind (read or unread) and then tapping the Toggle Read Status icon. (If check boxes don't precede the messages, start by choosing Select from the menu.)

- If you select a *mixed* group of messages in a message list—some read and others unread—a pop-up menu appears when you tap the Toggle Read Status icon. Choose Mark as Read or Mark as Unread to set all selected messages to the same read status.

Selected

Toggle Read Status

Marking Important Messages

If you'd like to mark certain messages as important, you can designate them as *favorites* (POP3 and IMAP accounts) or *flag* them (Microsoft Exchange ActiveSync accounts).

Favorite

Flagged

- *Favorite messages.* In a message list or while reading the message, tap the star icon. To remove the star from a previously marked favorite, tap the star icon again.

Marking Multiple POP3 or IMAP Messages

When viewing a message list, you can simultaneously change the favorite status of multiple messages by selecting each header, tapping the star icon at the bottom of the screen, and choosing Add Star or Remove from the menu that appears. (All selected messages will be marked the same.)

- *Flagged messages.* In a Microsoft Exchange ActiveSync message list or when viewing one of its messages, tap the flag icon to the right of the message header. The icon works as a toggle. Tap it to cycle between flagged (red flag), completed (blue check mark), and cleared (blank).

Flagging Multiple Exchange ActiveSync Messages

When viewing a message list, you can simultaneously change the flag status of multiple messages by selecting each header, tapping the Flag icon at the bottom of the screen, and choosing Flag, Unflag, or Mark as Complete from the menu that appears. (All selected messages will be marked the same.)

Managing the Spam Senders List

To prevent your account Inboxes from being cluttered with *spam* (junk mail), you can add email addresses to the Spam Senders List by doing any of the following:

- When reading a message, open the message menu and choose Register as Spam.

- When viewing a specific account's Inbox message list, select the message header by tapping its check box (if messages are preceded by check boxes) or by pressing and holding the message header. Then tap the Register as Spam icon at the bottom of the page.

Message menu

Add to Spam Addresses list

Register as Spam

- To manually add an email address to Spam Senders, open the menu and choose Settings, Spam Addresses. Tap the + (plus) icon, enter the email address or only its *domain* (the part of the address that follows the @ symbol), and tap OK. If you later want to remove an address from the list, return to this screen, tap the Trash icon, select the address(es) to remove, and tap Done.

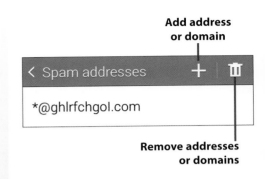

Add address or domain

Remove addresses or domains

Using the Gmail App

In addition to the Email app, your phone includes a dedicated Gmail app—designed to access Google's Gmail service. The app shares many similarities with Email, but also has some key differences. (For the sake of convenience, you might prefer to simply add your Gmail account to the Email app.)

When you first set up your phone, the setup wizard walks you through the process of adding your Gmail account—so the Gmail app is ready to run. To launch Gmail, go to the Home screen and tap Apps, Gmail. Following are some general and account-specific settings that you'll want to review when configuring and using the app:

- *Add another Gmail account.* If you have multiple Gmail accounts, you can add the others and switch among them as needed by opening the drawer and choosing the account you want to make active. To register another Gmail account on your phone, follow the directions in "Register Your Gmail Account" in Chapter 1.

Menu/drawer icon

Active account

Account drawer

• *Configure general settings for your accounts.* Gmail works well with the default settings, but you can get better results by spending a few minutes choosing settings that suit your needs. Open the drawer on the left, choose Settings, and then tap General Settings. You'll typically want to ensure that Reply All remains unchecked and that Confirm Before Deleting is checked.

Gmail General Settings

< ✉ General settings   ⋮

Archive & delete actions
Show archive & delete

Swipe to archive   ☑
In conversation list

Sender image   ☑
Show beside name in conversation list

Reply all   ☐
Use as default for message replies

Auto-fit messages   ☑
Shrink messages to fit the screen

Auto-advance
Show conversation list after you archive or delete

Message actions
Always show message actions at the top of the screen

ACTION CONFIRMATIONS

Confirm before deleting   ☐

Confirm before archiving   ☐

Confirm before sending   ☐

- *Configure account-specific settings.* After choosing Settings, select an account name. You can configure sound and vibration notifications, specify a signature, and set the number of days of mail to sync.

Account Settings

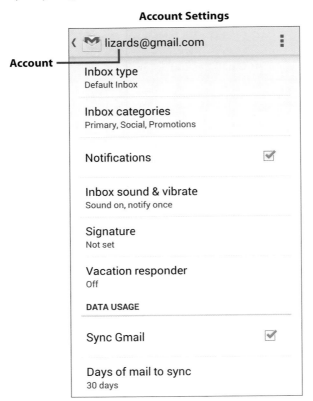

Account ——

- *Organize your messages with labels.* Whereas most email services use folders to store messages, Gmail uses a system of *labels*—tags that you can apply to messages to categorize them. To apply a label to an open message, open the menu in the upper-right corner, choose Change Labels, select the label(s) you want to apply, and tap OK.

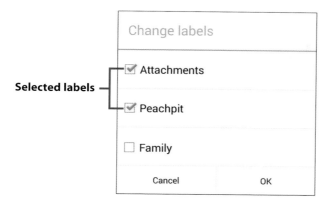

Selected labels

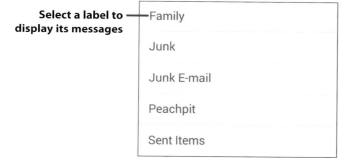

- *View your messages by labels.* Tap the drawer icon to display the list of Inboxes and labels—or carefully swipe the list in from the left edge of the screen. Then tap the label for the messages you want to view.

Select a label to display its messages

In this chapter, you explore the fine points of texting with the Messages app. Topics include the following:

→ Using Messages to send and receive text and multimedia messages
→ Managing conversations
→ Configuring Messages
→ Using alternative apps for messaging and chat

Messaging

After mastering the calling features of the Galaxy S5, many users want to explore the world of *texting*—the exchange of short text and multimedia messages. Compared to a phone call, texting is equally immediate but considerably briefer and less intrusive. To help you learn about messaging, this chapter explains the ins and outs of using and configuring Messages, the default messaging app on most Samsung Galaxy S5s.

About Text and Multimedia Messaging

Phone calls can be time-consuming and, depending on the caller's timing, intrusive. To get a quick message to a friend or colleague, you can text that person by sending a text or multimedia message. A message exchange between you and another person is called a *conversation* or *thread*. The messaging process is similar to what you're probably familiar with from chat programs, such as Yahoo! Messenger. Either party can start a conversation. After the conversation is initiated, it can progress in a back-and-forth manner with each person's contributions shown in colored balloons.

Two types of messages can be exchanged: *Short Message Service* (SMS) text messages and *Multimedia Messaging Service* (MMS) messages to which you've attached a photo, video or audio clip, or similar item. Although text messages are normally exchanged between mobile phones, some carriers also allow you to text to an email account or landline.

Texting is strikingly similar to emailing. You specify recipients, compose the message text, and—optionally—add attachments. The main differences are that texting generally occurs between mobile phones, the messages must be short (160 characters or less), and a subject is optional rather than the norm.

Some Differences Among Carriers

Different carriers have slightly different messaging features, determined by their implementation of text and multimedia messaging. Settings options depend on your carrier, too. As a result, not all of the information in this section will apply to every carrier.

Composing a Text Message (SMS)

A text message can contain only text and is limited to 160 characters. If a message is longer, it is transmitted as multiple messages but typically recombined on the recipient's screen.

1. Tap the Messages icon at the bottom of any Home screen page. (If you've removed the Messages shortcut, tap Apps, Messages.)

2. A screen showing all ongoing conversations appears. Do one of the following:

   - To continue a conversation, tap its entry in the conversations list, and then go to Step 9.

   - To start a conversation with someone who isn't in the conversations list, tap the Compose Message icon. Each message can have one or more recipients. Use any of the methods described in Steps 3–5 to specify recipients.

3. The New Message screen appears.

4. *Manually enter a mobile number.* If you know that the recipient doesn't have a Contacts record, type the person's mobile phone number in the Enter Recipients box and then tap the plus (+) icon.

5. *Enter partial contact info.* Type any *part* of the person's contact information (such as a first name, area code, or email domain) in the Enter Recipients box and select the person from the match list that appears.

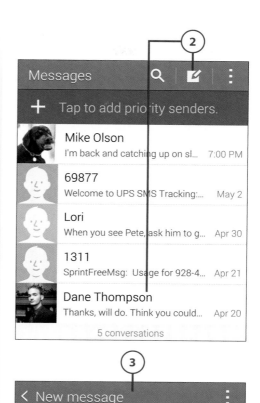

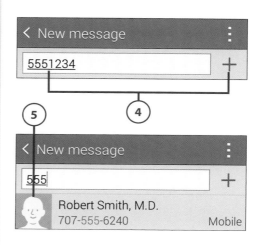

6. *Select recipients from Contacts.* Tap the Contacts icon. Select one or more recipients from the list by tapping each person's check box and then tap Done.

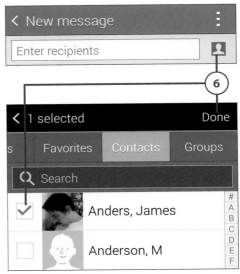

Finding Recipients in Contacts

To find someone in Contacts, you can scroll through the list by flicking up or down, go directly to an alphabetical section of the list by tapping an index letter, or drag down or up in the index letters and release your finger when the first letter of the person's name displays.

You can also filter the list to show only certain people. To view people with whom you've recently spoken, tap the Logs tab. Tap the Favorites tab to restrict the list to contacts you've marked as *favorites*. To search for a person, select the Contacts tab and type part of the name, email address, or phone number in the Search box; press the Back key to view the results; tap the person's check box; and tap Done.

7. If a recipient selected from Contacts has only one phone number or you've set a default number for him, that number is automatically used. Otherwise, a screen appears that lists the person's contact details. Tap the phone number—normally a *mobile* number—to which you want to send the message.

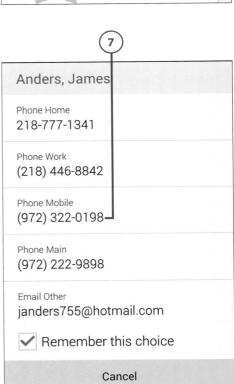

8. *Optional:* Remove a recipient by tapping the minus (–) icon following the person's name. Similarly, you can change or edit a person's phone number by tapping her name and selecting Edit in the dialog box that appears. (If recipients are listed as "Joan Duran and 1 more," tap this text to list them separately and display the minus (–) icon.)

9. Enter your message in the Enter Message box. You can type the message or tap the microphone key to dictate your message. (If the microphone isn't shown on the key, press and hold the key, and *then* select the microphone.) As you type or dictate, the number of remaining characters is shown beneath the Send button.

10. Tap the Send button to transmit the message.

Voice input   Remaining characters

Group Conversations

When you specify multiple individuals or a contact group (see "Working with Contact Groups" in Chapter 5, "Managing Contacts") as recipients, Messages considers it a *group conversation*. Each message is treated as a multimedia (MMS) message (even if it contains only text), is transmitted only once to the message server, and then is delivered to all recipients.

To treat this as a normal conversation, remove the check mark from Group Conversation. Each text message is transmitted repeatedly to the message server (once per recipient), but retains its normal text message (SMS) form.

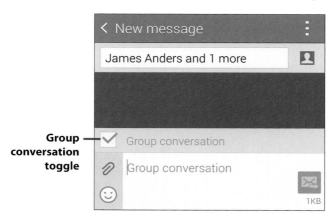

Group conversation toggle

Saving a Message as a Draft

If you aren't ready to send the message, you can save it as a draft by pressing the Back key. To later open the message, select it in the conversations list. You can then edit, send, or delete it. (To delete a draft message that you're viewing, open the menu and choose Discard.)

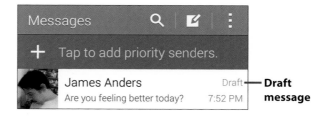

Draft message

>>>Go Further
LAZY MESSAGING

If you text frequently, many of your messages are short, simple phrases that you use regularly, such as "When will you be home?", "Where are you?", or "Can't talk now. I'm in a meeting." Rather than laboriously typing such messages when-ever one's needed, you can pick it from a list. Open the menu, choose Quick Responses, and select the phrase that you want to send.

Quick Responses

Quick responses
Can't talk right now. Send me a message.
Call me.
Where are you?

Note that many phrases aren't complete; they're the beginnings of messages that you must finish, such as "Don't forget to…", "Meet me at…", and "I'll be there at…" In addition, Quick Responses don't have to be the sole message content. When you select one, it's inserted at the text insertion mark—so it can be added to the beginning, middle, or end of a message.

To modify the Quick Responses phrases, go to the main Messages screen and tap the menu icon. Choose Quick Responses or Settings, Quick Responses—depend-ing on your carrier. You can do any of the following:

- To delete unwanted phrases, tap the Trash icon, select phrases to delete, and tap Done.

- To add a new phrase, tap the plus (+) icon, enter the phrase, and tap Save.

- To edit an existing phrase, tap the phrase to open it for editing, make the necessary changes, and tap Save.

Quick Responses (in Messages Settings)

< Quick responses 🗑 ——— **Delete phrases**

Add + ——— **Create a new phrase**

Can't talk right now. Send me a message.

Call me. ——————————— **Tap to edit this phrase**

>>>Go Further
MORE WAYS TO START A CONVERSATION

Choosing a contact record is only one of the ways to start a texting conversation. Others include these:

- Immediately after completing a call, you can begin a conversation with the person by tapping the Message icon.

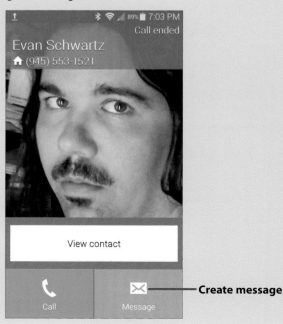

Evan Schwartz
🏠 (945) 553-1521

Call ended

View contact

Call   Message ——— **Create message**

- To text someone to whom you've recently spoken, launch Phone and then tap the Logs tab. Find the person in any log and then swipe his entry to the left. You can use this swipe technique on the Contacts and Favorites tabs, too—as long as items are displayed in List View rather than Grid View.

- Open the person's record in Contacts and tap the envelope icon.

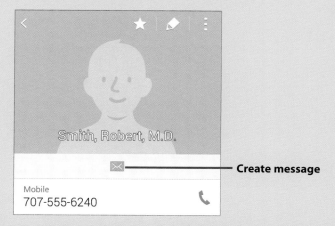

Create message

- You can also send a message to a *group* you've defined (see "Working with Contact Groups" in Chapter 5). Tap the Contacts icon, the Groups tab, and the group's name. Select the specific members whom you want to message and then tap Done.

>>>Go Further
MORE MESSAGE-COMPOSITION OPTIONS

Although somewhat unusual, the following composition options can sometimes be very useful:

- *Adding a Subject.* Unlike email messages, text messages generally don't have a Subject. If you'd like to add one, tap the menu icon and choose Add Subject.

- *Inserting Smileys.* If you want to insert a *smiley* (also called an *emoticon*) into a message you're creating, tap the menu icon, choose Insert Smiley, and select the smiley to insert. It appears at the text insertion mark. To insert more elaborately drawn emoticons, switch to Emoticons input. Tap the emoticon icon to the left of the Enter Message box or long-press the multi-mode key and select Emoticons.

Emoticons

Multi-mode key

- *Embedded links in messages.* If a message contains a web address, email address, or phone number shown as underlined text, you can tap the embedded text and choose Open Link, Send Email, or Call to visit the page using the phone's browser, address a new email message to the person, or dial the phone number, respectively.

- *Texting to email or a landline.* If a recipient doesn't have a mobile phone, you can send text messages to an email address. Some carriers, such as Sprint, even allow you to send texts to a landline phone. Create the message as you normally would, but specify an email address or landline number in the Enter Recipients box. As appropriate, the text message is emailed, or the service calls the landline and a computer voice reads the text when the phone is answered. (Emoticons are read, too!)

- *Schedule a message.* Rather than send a message immediately, you can set a date and time at which it will be delivered. (The scheduled time must be at least 6 minutes in the future.) Prior to tapping the Send button, tap the menu icon and choose Schedule Message. Set a date and time for delivery, tap Done, and tap the Send button. A copy of the message (in gray) with the scheduled delivery time appears in the conversation. When finally sent, the message color changes to match that of your normal outgoing messages.

Specifying a delivery date and time   **Scheduled message**

Cancel	Done
SCHEDULE MESSAGE	
Time and date	
05/04/2014	11 : 07 PM

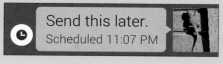

Send this later.
Scheduled 11:07 PM

Composing a Multimedia Message (MMS)

A *multimedia message* (*MMS*) is any message that has one or more attachments, such as a picture, video, audio recording, Contacts record, or Calendar item.

Some Attachments Are Just Text
Material that you add to a message from Maps, My Location, or Memo is text and does not result in a text message becoming a multimedia message.

1. Perform Steps 1–9 of the "Composing a Text Message (SMS)" task—that is, every step other than tapping Send.

2. Tap the paper clip icon at any time during the message-creation process.

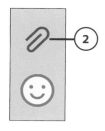

3. Select the item type that you want to attach to the message. If you're attaching a file that's already on your phone, continue with Step 4. If you want to create a *new* file, skip to Step 5.

4. *Attach an existing file.* Select the item(s) to attach, opening enclosing folders if necessary. For most item types, you complete the attachment process by making the selection or by tapping Done. Go to Step 6.

Size Matters

Existing video clips and audio recordings such as songs may be too large to transmit as part of an MMS message. Depending on the file type, Messages may either reject the item as an attachment, ask you to trim the item, or compress it for you. Photos, on the other hand, are automatically compressed to meet MMS size limits.

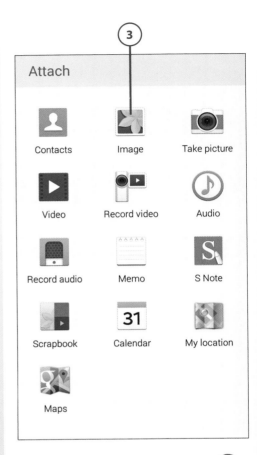

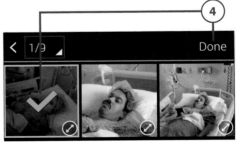

5. *Create an attachment (Take Picture, Record Video, or Record Audio).* Take a new picture or capture a video. Tap Save to add it to the message or tap Discard to try again. When you finish recording an audio clip, tap the Stop button to save it, listen to the clip, and tap Done.

Shooting a photo

Recording an audio clip

Discard

6. A thumbnail representing the media is inserted into the message or the item is shown as a file attachment. As you add items, the total size of the message and attachments updates.

7. If you want to view/play, replace, or remove a multimedia item, press and hold its thumbnail and then select the appropriate option. (If you remove *all* attachments from a message, it reverts to a text message.)

Another Removal Option
You can also remove a multimedia item by selecting it and tapping the Delete key.

8. Tap Send when the message is complete.

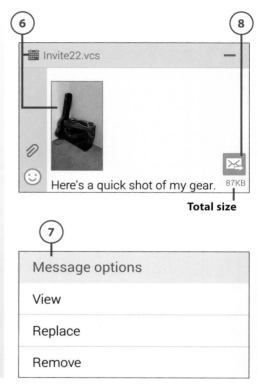

Here's a quick shot of my gear. 87KB

Total size

Message options
View
Replace
Remove

It's Not All Good

Your Mileage May Vary

When it works, nothing is cooler than having a photo, video, or other MMS attachment appear on your screen during a texting session. Unfortunately, MMS transmissions aren't 100 percent reliable. Each message must pass through multiple servers and conversions. As a result, multimedia messages sometimes arrive late, vanish altogether, or are dramatically compressed. The moral? MMS messages are more appropriate for fun than for mission-critical transmissions. When sending important data (especially when it needs to be delivered quickly and uncompressed), stick with computer-to-computer email. For lengthy back-and-forth text conversations, you might also consider trying one of the many chat apps, such as the ones mentioned at the end of this chapter.

Managing Conversations

There's more to participating in a conversation than just creating messages. The following tasks explain how to respond to new message notifications; continue, review, and delete conversations; and search for messages.

Responding to a New Message Notification

If you're in Messages and a message for the current conversation arrives, it simply appears onscreen as a new message balloon. If you're doing something else with the phone, the phone is resting quietly on your desk, or you're viewing a different conversation, a new message notification appears.

Depending on your Messages settings (see "Configuring Messages Settings," later in this chapter) and what you're currently doing, you may be notified of a new message in one of several ways:

- The message text appears briefly in the status bar and is replaced by an envelope icon. The Messages shortcut on the Home screen shows the number of new messages.

- A pop-up notification with options may appear. Tap Call to initiate a phone call to the person, tap Reply to type your reply in the pop-up— without leaving the current screen, tap View to open the message and its conversation in Messages, or tap the X to dismiss the pop-up window.

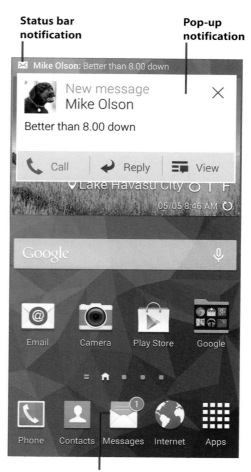

Status bar notification

Pop-up notification

1 new message

- You can view a preview of the new message in the Notification panel. Tap the message notification to view the complete message or respond to it in Messages.

- You can launch Messages (if it isn't currently running) and open the conversation that contains the new message.

- Finally, if the screen is dark when a message arrives, press the Power button to see a preview of the message on your lock screen. To remove the message from the lock screen, tap Clear.

Notification panel

New message

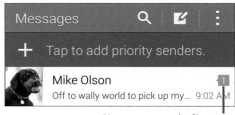

New message indicator

Lock screen

New message   **Clear the notification**

Continue a Conversation

The default length for a conversation on your phone is 200 text or 20 multimedia messages—whichever occurs first. As long as the length limit hasn't been exceeded, a conversation can be continued immediately or whenever either participant wishes—days, weeks, or even months after it was begun.

Creating a New Message

Don't worry if you mistakenly create a new message to someone already in the conversations list. Messages automatically treats the message as a continuation of the existing conversation rather than generating a second conversation with the person.

1. If Messages isn't running, launch it by tapping its Home screen shortcut or by tapping Apps, Messages.

2. On the Messages main screen, select the conversation that you want to continue. The conversation appears.

3. Tap in the Enter Message box to display the onscreen keyboard.

4. Create a text or multimedia message as described in "Composing a Text Message (SMS)" or "Composing a Multimedia Message (MMS)," earlier in this chapter.

5. Tap the Send button to transmit the message. It is appended to the end of the conversation.

Reviewing a Conversation

As long as you haven't deleted a conversation, you can reread it whenever you like. This is especially useful when a conversation contains important information, such as the time of an upcoming meeting, a phone number, a web address (URL), or driving directions. To review a conversation, select it from the conversations list on the Messages main screen (as described in the previous task) and scroll through the messages by flicking or dragging up and down.

Reviewing a conversation

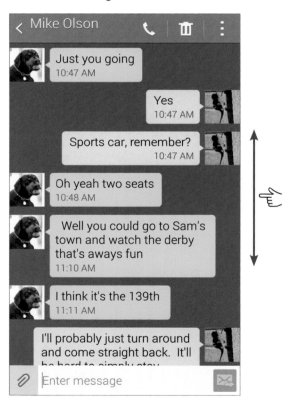

Delete Conversations

For the sake of privacy, saving storage space, or eliminating clutter in the conversations list, you can delete entire conversations.

1. Launch Messages by tapping its Home screen shortcut. (If you're currently in a conversation, press the Back key until the conversations list appears.)

2. Tap the menu icon and choose Delete.

3. Select the conversations that you want to delete, or tap Select All to select all conversations.

4. Tap Done.

5. Confirm the conversation deletion(s) by tapping OK.

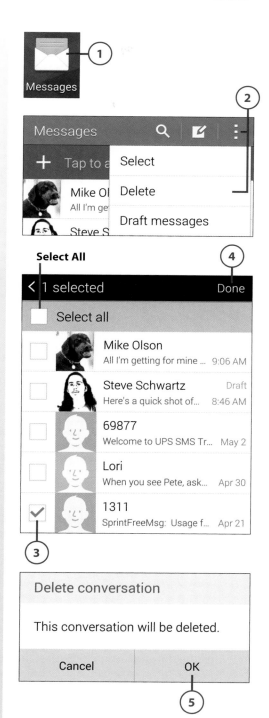

Delete Messages

In addition to deleting entire conversations, you can selectively delete individual messages from a conversation.

1. In Messages, open the conversation from which you want to delete messages.

2. Tap the Delete icon.

3. Scroll through the conversation, and select each message that you want to delete.

4. Tap the Delete button.

5. Tap OK to confirm the deletion(s).

Deleting a Single Message

To delete a *single* message in a conversation, you can press and hold the message, tap Delete in the Message Options dialog box, and confirm the deletion by tapping OK.

Other Options for Individual Messages

In addition to deleting individual messages, you can copy message text to the Clipboard for pasting elsewhere, lock a message to prevent it from being deleted, save the multimedia elements in an MMS message, forward a message to others, or view a message's properties.

SMS (text) message	**MMS (multimedia) message**

Message options
Delete
Copy text
Forward
Lock
Share
View message details
Translate

Message options
Delete
View slideshow
Copy text
Forward
Lock
Save attachment
Share
View message details
Translate

1. Within a conversation, press and hold a message for which you want to display options. The Message Options dialog box appears. SMS and MMS messages offer slightly different options, as explained in Step 2.

2. Tap an option to perform one of the following actions:

    - *Delete.* Delete the current message.

    - *View Slideshow (MMS messages only).* Display message text and certain types of attachments (such as photos) as a slideshow.

    - *Copy Text.* Copy the message text to the Clipboard, making it eligible for pasting into another message or app, such as an email message.

    - *Forward.* Send the message to another recipient—passing along a picture, phone number, address, or driving directions, for example.

    - *Lock.* Prevent an important message from being inadvertently deleted—even if you delete the conversation that contains the message. After a message has been locked, the Lock command is replaced by Unlock. You can optionally override the lock while attempting to delete the message or its conversation.

    - *Share.* Share the message by posting it to a social networking site, emailing it, transferring it to a computer or another phone, and so on.

    - *Save Attachment (MMS messages only).* Save an attached item, such as a picture or video, to the Download folder.

    - *View Message Details.* Examine the message properties, such as who sent it and when, the date and time it was received, and its total size including attachments.

    - *Translate.* Translate the message text from its current language to another.

Search for Messages

You can search all conversations for specific text.

1. On the Messages main screen, tap the Search icon. A Search text box appears.

2. Enter the search text; matches appear as you type. Continue typing until the desired message is shown.

3. Do one of the following:

   • Tap a message to display the match. The conversation appears and displays the selected message. The matching text is shown in blue anywhere that it appears in the conversation.

   • Tap the search key on the keyboard to display a list of *all* matches. The matches are shown in blue. Tap a match to display the message in the context of its conversation.

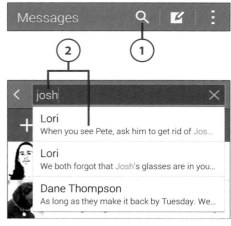

Match in context

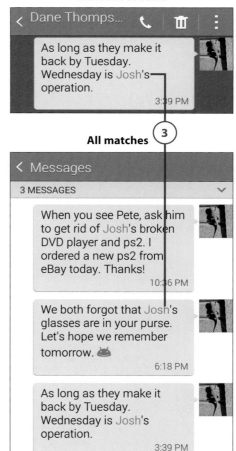

All matches

Designating Priority Senders

After you get into the swing of messaging, a set of people whom you frequently message will develop. To make it easier to message them, you can designate those individuals as *priority senders*—creating icons for them that appear above the conversations list.

Priority Senders for the Home Screen

You can also initiate messages to favorite recipients from the Home screen by adding a Direct Message widget for each person. To see the widget (see "Add Widgets" in Chapter 3, "Making the Phone Your Own," for instructions), tap Widgets, Contacts, Direct Message.

Add Priority Senders

1. On the Messages main screen, tap the Tap to Add Priority Senders text. (If you don't see this text or the plus (+) icon at the end of an existing priority senders list, tap the menu icon, choose Settings, and ensure that Priority Senders is enabled.)

2. The Add Priority Senders screen appears.

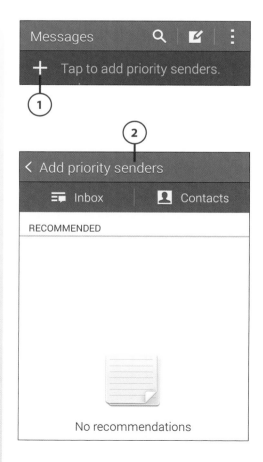

3. *Current conversations.* Tap Inbox to select senders from those in the conversations list. Select senders by tapping check boxes and then tap Done.

4. *Contacts.* Tap Contacts to select senders from Contacts. Select a tab that makes it easy to find the senders, tap their check boxes, and then tap Done.

Recommended Senders
If Messages displays individuals in the Recommended section, you can select them there.

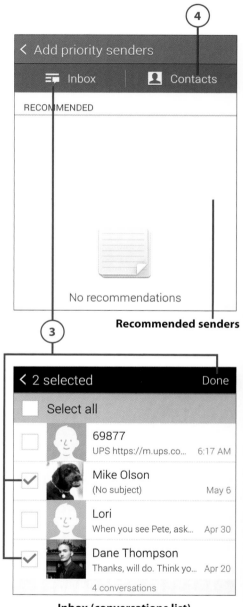

Recommended senders

Inbox (conversations list)

5. Icons for the selected individuals are added to the scrolling Priority Senders list (above the conversations list).

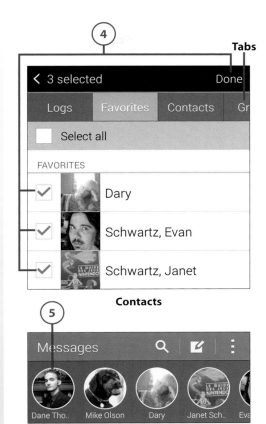

Manage Priority Senders

You can add new people to the priority senders list, remove senders, rearrange their icons, and disable the feature.

1. Navigate to the main Messages screen. Priority sender icons are shown above the conversations list.

2. Press and hold any priority sender's icon and choose Manage Priority Senders from the pop-up menu that appears.

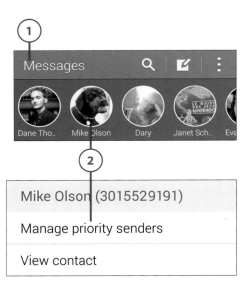

3. *Remove priority senders.* Tap the icon of each sender that you want to remove and then tap Done. (Tap Cancel if you remove some-one by mistake.)

4. *Rearrange priority senders.* Perform Step 2. Then press and hold the icon of the sender that you want to move, drag it to the left or right, and release it in the desired position. When you're finished rearranging icons, tap Done. (Tap Cancel if you remove someone by mistake.)

5. *Add senders.* If necessary, scroll the list to display the plus (+) icon on its right. Tap the icon and perform Steps 2–5 from the "Add Priority Senders" task.

6. *Disable or enable priority senders.* To disable the priority senders feature, display the conversations list, tap the menu icon, choose Settings, and remove the check mark from Priority Senders. To enable this feature (or re-enable it and restore a priority senders ros-ter that you previously created), ensure that the box is checked.

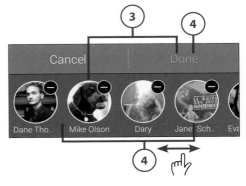

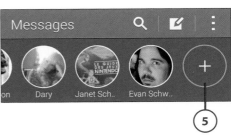

Configuring Messages Settings

You can customize the way Messages works by changing its settings. All changes take effect immediately. Note that Settings options differ among carriers, depending on the features that each supports. The most common settings are discussed in this section in the approximate order in which they appear.

1. Launch Messages. If you're already in or viewing a conversation, press the Back key until the conversations list appears.

2. Tap the menu icon and choose Settings. The Settings screen appears. Scroll as necessary to view the entire menu. The following steps explain the most important settings.

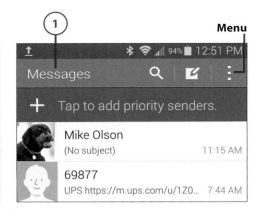

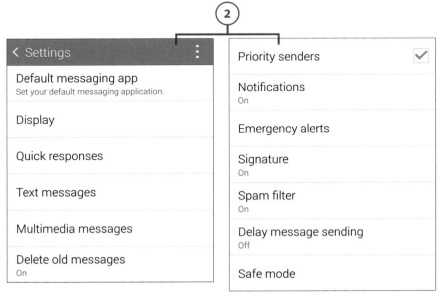

3. **Default Messaging App.** Tap Default Messaging App, Default Messaging App to specify your preferred app for text and multimedia messaging. When you respond to an incoming message notification or tap the messaging icon on a Phone or Contacts screen, the default messaging app launches. (You can also set or change the default messaging app by opening Settings and tapping Default Applications, Messages.) If you set a new default messaging app, you might also want to replace the Messages primary shortcut on the Home screen with that of the replacement messaging app. See the "Rearranging and Replacing the Primary Shortcuts" sidebar in Chapter 3 for instructions.

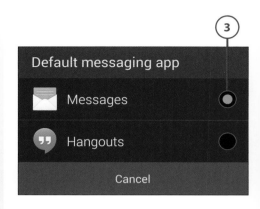

4. **Display.** The following settings determine the appearance of conversations:

   • *Bubble Style.* Enables you to vary the color and/or style of message bubbles. The top bubble is used to display your messages and the bottom one is used for messages received from others. Select a style pair from the scrolling list and tap Save.

   • *Background Style.* Enables you to specify a different color background or pick a photo on which to display conversations. Select a style from the scrolling list and tap Save. (Select the first thumbnail to use an existing image or take a photo to use as the background.)

   • *Change Font Size.* When enabled, makes it possible for you to use the hardware volume control on the left side of the phone to increase or decrease the size of message text.

5. **Quick Responses.** These are text snippets you can use to quickly create messages or responses to incoming calls. Examples include "What's up?" and "Please call me." See the "Lazy Messaging" sidebar earlier in this chapter for an explanation of how to add, edit, and delete Quick Responses.

6. **Text Messages.** These settings govern the creation and handling of text (SMS) messages.

    *   *Auto Combination.* When enabled, text messages that exceed the maximum length limit are automatically combined into single messages. In general, enabled is the preferred setting.

    *   *Delivery Reports.* When enabled, you're notified when your sent messages are successfully delivered.

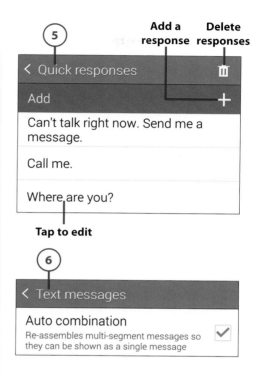

Add a response   Delete responses

5

< Quick responses   🗑

Add   +

Can't talk right now. Send me a message.

Call me.

Where are you?

Tap to edit

6

< Text messages

Auto combination
Re-assembles multi-segment messages so they can be shown as a single message   ✓

7. **Multimedia Messages.** These
   settings govern the creation and
   handling of multimedia messages.

   - *Group Conversation.* When
     enabled, you can create a
     single message for delivery
     to multiple recipients. When
     disabled, the carrier sends a
     separate copy of the message
     for each specified recipient.

   - *Auto Retrieve.* When enabled,
     the entire content of each
     multimedia message is
     automatically retrieved—the
     message header, body, and
     attachments. Otherwise,
     only the message header
     is retrieved. (If you're on a
     limited data plan and have
     friends who constantly attach
     material to their messages
     or you find that auto retrieve
     uses too much of your battery
     charge, you can disable this
     setting.)

   - *Roaming Auto Retrieve.* When
     enabled, MMS messages
     and their contents are auto-
     matically downloaded—even
     when you're roaming.

   - *MMS Alert.* Enable this setting
     if you want to be notified that
     the message you're creating is
     a multimedia message rather
     than a text message. If data
     charges are a concern for you,
     enabling this setting can be
     useful.

⑦

< Multimedia messages

Group conversation ✓
Send messages as group conversations by
default.

Auto retrieve ✓
Automatically retrieve messages.

Roaming auto retrieve ☐
Automatically retrieve messages while
roaming.

MMS alert ☐
Receive alerts when the mode changes to a
multimedia message.

8. **Delete Old Messages.** Enable this setting to automatically delete the oldest messages in any conversation that exceed either the text or multimedia message limit. Tap Text Message Limit or Multimedia Message Limit to change the maximum number of messages of that type that are allowed in a conversation.

Manual Deletions

When Delete Old Messages is *disabled*, the maximum text and multimedia messages per conversation are ignored. However, you can manually delete old conversations or specific messages if you're short on space, as explained in "Reviewing a Conversation," earlier in this chapter.

9. **Priority Senders.** When this setting is checked, you can display, add, remove, and rearrange icons for people whom you regularly message—simplifying the process of sending them new messages or continuing a conversation. For more information, see "Designating Priority Senders," earlier in the chapter.

10. **Push Messages.** When Push Messages (not shown) is enabled (default setting) and new messages are received by the network, they are *pushed* to your phone. That is, you don't have to perform an action to receive the messages—they are simply transmitted to you.

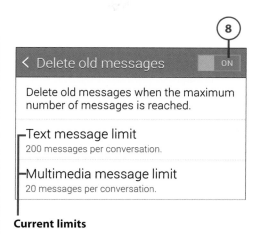

Current limits

11. **Notifications.** The following settings determine whether you receive notifications of newly received messages, as well as the manner in which the notifications are presented. At a minimum, all carriers support status bar notifications.

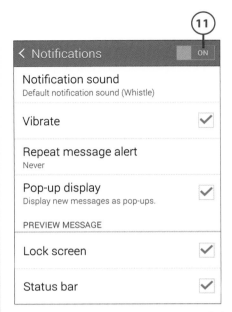

- Enable Notifications if you want to receive one or more notifications when a new message is received. To specify the types of notification methods to use, you must first enable this setting.

- Tap Notification Sound to pick a sound snippet to announce new messages. Select a sound from the scrolling list and tap OK.

- With Vibrate enabled, the phone vibrates whenever a new message is received.

- Tap Repeat Message Alert to specify how frequently you will be notified of the receipt of each new message.

- When Pop-up Display is enabled, notifications automatically appear on the Home screen or the app in which you're working. In the pop-up, you can call the person, write a reply, or open the message in Messages, as explained earlier in "Responding to a New Message Notification."

- When Lock Screen is enabled, new message notifications automatically appear on the lock screen.

- When Status Bar is enabled, notifications appear in the status bar—as a message preview and a new message icon.

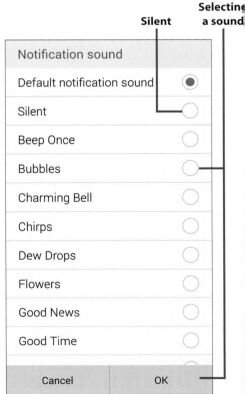

Silent

Selecting a sound

Sound Options

When you tap a sound on the Notification Sound screen, it plays—enabling you to sample sounds before committing to one. If you'd rather *not* hear a sound when a message arrives, select Silent.

Preview Message (Verizon)

Verizon users have a Preview Message setting that combines the Lock Screen and Status Bar settings. They're always both enabled or both disabled.

12. Emergency Alerts. These settings are used to specify the types of emergency alert messages that you want to receive and special notification options that will be applied.

Verizon Users Only

Verizon users can view and modify their Emergency Alert settings by running the Emergency Alerts app.

- Tap Emergency Alerts to enable/disable different types of alerts. By default, the important alert types are enabled. You can disable any type of alert except Presidential.

- Tap Emergency Notification Preview to hear a sample of the emergency alert sound.

- Enable Vibrate to cause the phone to vibrate whenever an emergency alert is received.

- Tap Alert Reminder to specify how often or the number of times you want to be reminded of an active alert.

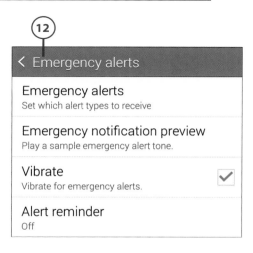

Emergency alert types

13. **Signature.** This setting enables you to append a text signature to each outgoing message—in the same fashion as you can with email messages. Signature must be On in order to create or edit the signature text.

14. **Spam Filter.** These settings enable you to reduce or avoid unwanted (*spam*) messages. Spam Filter is the master control—that is, it must be On to modify any of the spam options.

- Tap Add to Spam Numbers to manually add numbers of people and companies whose messages you want automatically blocked.

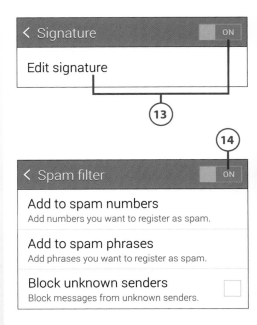

Add a Spam Number Without Typing

When you receive a spam message, press and hold its entry in the conversations list, tap the Add to Spam Numbers toolbar icon, and confirm by tapping OK.

Add to Spam Numbers

Selected message

- Similar to creating a junk mail rule in an email program, you can specify a key phrase or words (such as Viagra, credit, or mortgage) that are frequently found in received spam messages. Tap Add to Spam Phrases and enter phrases that—if found in an incoming message—will result in blocking the delivery of future messages that contain these phrases.

- Enable Block Unknown Senders to block messages from people and companies who have no record in Contacts.

Examine Spam Messages

If you want to review messages that have been marked as spam, go to the Messages main screen, tap the menu icon, and choose Spam Messages.

15. **Delay Message Sending.** If you regularly message the wrong people, your messages occasionally contain embarrassing typos, or you tend to tap Send before you think, enable Delay Message Sending and pick a delay interval (3–30 seconds). When you send a new message, it is shown onscreen but isn't actually sent until the delay interval has elapsed. If you see a mistake in a message, you can quickly tap its message balloon and edit the message.

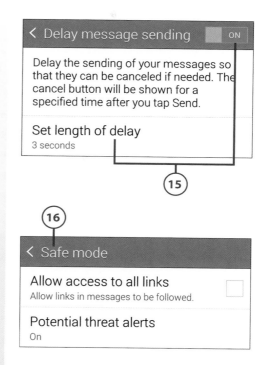

16. **Safe Mode.** Tap Safe Mode to review Messages security options. When Allow Access to All Links is disabled, an additional dialog box appears that warns of the danger of following links in messages. When Potential Threat Alerts is enabled, a notification appears if you install any app that has the ability to send and receive messages.

17. When you finish reviewing and changing settings, press the Back key. Changes take effect immediately.

Restore the Default Settings

When examining these settings, you can revert to the defaults by tapping the menu icon and choosing Restore Default Settings.

>>>*Go Further*

MESSAGING CONSIDERATIONS

Here are a few practical and etiquette considerations for texting:

- *Know your service plan*. Although your Galaxy S5 can create and receive text and multimedia messages, your plan determines how you're charged—whether messages are unlimited, limited to a certain number per month, or there's a per-message charge. Received messages generally count, too—including unsolicited ones. Review your plan before you leap into texting.

- *Check with the recipient before texting*. Whether you *should* text someone depends on many factors, such as the recipient's phone (not all phones can display multimedia messages and many older phones can't even accept text messages) and the recipient's data plan. Unless someone has texted you first, it's a good idea to ask before initiating a conversation.

- *You can refuse all incoming messages*. If your plan doesn't allow for texting or it's expensive and you have no interest in receiving messages, contact your plan provider to see if there's a way to block incoming messages. Incoming messages typically cost the same as those you initiate, so you might prefer to refuse them.

>>>*Go Further*

OTHER MESSAGING APPS AND ALTERNATIVES

One of the great things about messaging is that it's platform- and device-independent. That is, you can exchange text messages with anyone who has a mobile phone and a messaging plan—regardless of the manufacturer and model of phone or their carrier. Apps you use can be different, too. (Note, however, that some *features* aren't universal, such as the availability of certain emoticons and the ability to exchange some types of multimedia data.) Most carriers ship their Galaxy S5 with *multiple* messaging apps: Messages, Hangouts, and Messaging+, for example. After you get your feet wet with Messages, you should check out the others to see if their approach and feature sets better suit your needs. When you decide on a favorite, you can set it as your default messaging app.

Before texting became popular, people relied on dedicated chat programs to conduct online conversations. Many of those same programs are now available as Android apps. Unlike texting, chat messages carry no per-message surcharge, and there's no limit to the number of messages that can be exchanged in a billing cycle. In addition, some go further than chat, enabling you to exchange files—considerably larger ones than those allowed in multimedia messages. Some social networking apps—Facebook, for example—also have a chat feature, in addition to enabling you to post updates and share items.

Many chat programs only allow you to chat with other users of the program (although the app may be available on multiple devices and platforms). In some cases, you must be using the same type of device; that is, Galaxy S5 owners may not be able to chat with iPhone owners. If you already have chat friends who use many different chat programs, you have a few options:

- Install a dedicated app for each chat program and hop among them as you attempt to find friends who are online and available to chat. Most of the major chat services, such as Yahoo! Messenger, AIM, and ICQ, have a free Android app that you can download from Google Play.

- Convince your friends to switch to a specific chat service to chat with you. For example, previous Galaxy S phones shipped with ChatON, a Samsung chat app/service. Note, however, that not all chat services are platform-independent or device-independent.

- Search Google Play for an app that can aggregate your chats and chat buddies from multiple services.

The logical step up from text chat is audio or video chat. Rather than type, you can say—or say and show. Note that audio and video chat apps are good options in two situations: when you're at home using Wi-Fi (avoids hits to your data plan and assures you of a high-speed connection) or when you have an unlimited data plan and are in a 4G/LTE area with a solid cellular connection. Some popular apps for video and voice chat are Skype, ooVoo Video Call, and Yahoo! Messenger with plug-in for voice and video calls. Another is SnapChat, which combines text and video chatting with photo sharing.

Search

Share

This chapter covers the essentials of downloading, installing, running, and maintaining applications on your phone. Topics include the following:

→ Launching and using apps

→ Downloading and installing apps from Google Play and Amazon Appstore

→ Enabling app downloads from other sources

→ Adding Home screen shortcuts to apps

→ Uninstalling, disabling, and hiding unwanted apps

→ Installing app updates

→ Moving apps to your memory card and setting default apps

→ Using the Toolbox to quickly access favorite apps

→ Other preinstalled and downloadable apps to consider

Installing and Using Applications

Applications (or *apps*, as they're called when referring to smartphone software) are programs that run on your phone. They add new functionality to the phone, such as enabling you to stream video, manipulate databases, play video games, and do almost anything else you can imagine.

The Galaxy S5 comes with dozens of apps preinstalled, ready for you to use. In addition, you can download and install other apps from Google Play, the Amazon Appstore, Samsung Apps, and developers' websites.

Using Apps

In this section, you learn the fundamentals of running apps: launching an app, using the hardware keys (Recent Apps, Home, and Back) with apps, switching among running apps, and exiting from an app. The information presented here applies to any app you encounter.

Launching an App

As with programs on a computer, you can launch a phone app *directly* (by tapping its icon or a Home screen shortcut) or *indirectly* (by performing an action that requires the app to be running).

Directly Launching an App

To launch a specific app, you can do any of the following:

- On any Home screen page, tap the app's shortcut. (In addition to the app shortcuts that are preinstalled on the Home screen pages, you may have added shortcuts to some of your favorite apps to make them more readily accessible.)

App shortcuts

Apps icon

Primary apps

- Tap Apps at the bottom of any Home screen page, and then tap the icon of the app that you want to run.

Navigation

Because you probably have several pages of apps, you can move from page to page by swiping the screen to the right or left or by tapping a navigation dot below the app icons. To show only apps that you've downloaded, tap the menu icon and choose Downloaded Apps.

Installed apps   **Menu icon**

**Navigation dots
(page indicators)**

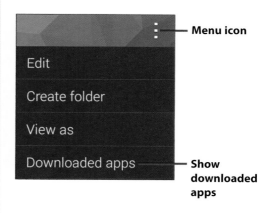

Menu icon

Show downloaded apps

- On almost any screen, you can press the Recent Apps key to display a list of recently run apps, as well as ones that are currently running. Scroll vertically until you see the app that you want to launch or to which you want to switch, and then tap its thumbnail.

Recent and running apps

Indirectly Launching an App

In addition to tapping an app's icon, many actions that you perform on the phone can cause an app to launch. Consider these common examples:

- In any program or widget, tapping a link to material stored on the Web, to an *HTML* (web) file stored on the phone, or to a particular web page or site causes the Internet or Chrome app to launch to display the page. App help files are sometimes handled this way.

Social networking site links

- Tapping a *mailto:* (email address) link on a web page or in an app opens a dialog box that enables you to create a new message to that address in Email.

- Tapping a file icon (such as a music, video, or photo file) in My Files, in Downloads, on the Home screen, or in a folder you created causes an appropriate app to launch and display the file's contents. Tapping a document icon, such as a PDF or Microsoft Office document, may also cause an app to launch and open the file. Both depend on having an app installed that is capable of reading and displaying the file, such as Polaris Office 5.

- Performing certain actions in an app can cause a related app to launch. For example, tapping the Contacts icon to select message recipients in Email or Messages launches Contacts.

- Tapping certain entries in the Notification panel, such as a new email, message, or screen capture notification, causes the appropriate app to launch.

Email (mailto:) link

If you have a comment about CNN Wireless services, please send an e-mail to mobile@cnn.com.

Dialog box

mobile@cnn.com

Send email

Send message

Add to contacts

Copy

Select text

PDF file

9780789753...

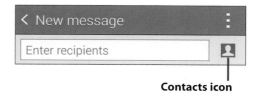

< New message

Enter recipients

Contacts icon

Using the Hardware Keys

The three hardware keys at the bottom of the phone (Recent Apps, Home, and Back) can be useful—and occasionally *essential*—when running apps.

Light 'em Up!

When the keys aren't in use, only the Home key—a physical button—is visible. Until you tap one of the three keys or the touchscreen, the Recent Apps and Back keys are hidden. Whether you can see the keys, however, is irrelevant. If you tap the hidden Recent Apps or Back key, the key still performs its function.

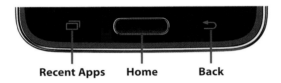

Recent Apps   Home   Back

Opening Menus

In current Android apps, a menu is denoted by an icon consisting of three large, vertically stacked dots. Although it's commonplace to place a menu icon in the upper-right corner of the screen, some apps—including Google's—don't adhere to this convention; that is, you sometimes have to hunt for them. To open a menu, tap its icon.

The Recent App key (described previously) has a secondary purpose. In apps that contain menus, you can press and hold the Recent Apps key to open a menu if one is associated with the current screen. Note that menus are often context-sensitive—that is, they may change depending on what you're currently doing or the app screen you're viewing.

Contacts app

Other Menus, Drawers, and Trays

In addition to these standard menus, apps may contain other menus. Some automatically appear onscreen (such as the Select menu in Gallery), whereas others are contextual menus that pop up when you press and hold an item (such as an image on a web page). Some apps, such as Calendar and Gallery, include a secondary menu called a *drawer* or *tray*. Denoted by a stack of three bars or lines, you tap it to reveal a pop-out panel of commands.

Web image contextual menu (Google Chrome)

Drawer icon (Calendar)

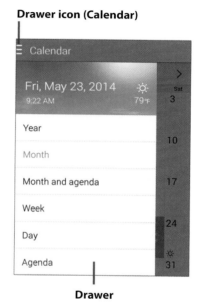

Drawer

Returning to the Home Screen

To immediately exit the current app, press the Home key. The most recently accessed Home screen page appears.

Home screen page indicator

Google, Voice Search, and Google Now Launcher

If you press and hold the Home key, the interconnected Google, Google Now, and Voice Search launches. To learn more about these apps and how they work together, see "Using Google/Voice Search" in Chapter 15, "Using Voice Services."

Navigating within an App

Within most apps, forward navigation options are obvious. You tap entries, icons, thumbnails, or buttons to go to the next screen or to perform an action. However, the method of *returning* to the previous section or screen isn't always as obvious. When it doesn't happen automatically, you can usually press the Back key. Some app screens also have a Back icon—a "less than" symbol (<)—in the upper-left corner that you can tap.

In addition to moving you back through screens (when using Internet or Chrome to view web pages or when modifying layered Settings, for example), the Back key functions similarly to a computer's Esc (Escape) key. You can press the Back key to avoid making a selection in a dialog box or menu, leave the Notification panel, or dismiss the onscreen keyboard.

It's Not All Good

One Too Many Presses

Using the Back key has one drawback. If you press it one too many times, you'll find that you've inadvertently exited the current program and are now staring at the Home screen. When this happens, launch the app again or press the Recent Apps key and tap the app's thumbnail.

Using Multi Window™ to Run Two Apps

With the Multi Window feature enabled, you can split the screen to run two apps at the same time. Note, however, that only certain apps can currently operate in Multi Window, such as Email, Gallery, Internet, and Messages. To enable or disable Multi Window, tap its Quick Setting button. (If the button isn't visible, tap the Grid View icon.) You can also enable or disable Multi Window by navigating to the Sound and Display section of Settings.

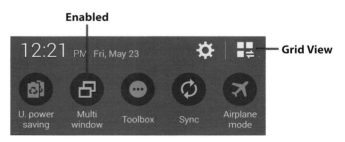

Enabled but Hidden

If you only occasionally use Multi Window or find its ever-present tab annoying, you don't have to keep opening Settings or the Notification panel to enable and disable it. When Multi Window is running, just press and hold the Back key to instantly hide or reveal the Multi Window tab.

Work with Multi Window

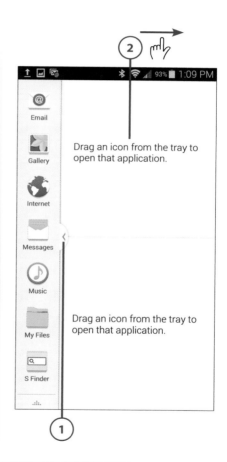

1. Open the vertically scrolling Multi Window bar by tapping its exposed tab.

2. To launch a Multi Window app, do any of the following:

   • To launch an app, press and hold its icon on the bar and then drag it into the top or bottom half of the screen.

   • To replace an app running in Multi Window, press and hold an icon, and then drag it onto the app in the top or bottom half of the screen.

   When two apps are running in Multi Window, they are separated by a divider line that's marked with a large white dot called the *Border button*. The active app is surrounded by a white border.

Drag an icon from the tray to open that application.

Drag an icon from the tray to open that application.

Enabling Multi Window When a Compatible App Is Active

If you enable Multi Window when a Multi Window–compatible app is already onscreen, the original app immediately switches to split-screen mode when you drag the first app from the Multi Window bar. The newly added app can be placed in the top or bottom half of the screen. The original, full-screen app automatically occupies the other half.

3. To modify the display, you can do either of the following:

- Resize the two windows by pressing and holding the Border button, and then dragging up or down.

- Tap the Border button to reveal a three-icon menu. From left to right, tap the first icon to swap the apps' onscreen positions, tap the second icon to drag-and-drop text or an image from the active app's window into the other window, or tap the third icon to close the active app.

Gallery (active app)

Resizing the windows

Messages app

Multi Window tab

3

3

Gallery (active app)

Multi Window tab   **Messages**

>>>*Go Further*

MULTI WINDOW NOTES

Note the following when using Multi Window:

- If you return to the Home screen and launch an app, the Multi Window apps are cleared.
- Opening Settings doesn't interfere with Multi Window. When you're done making changes in Settings, press the Back key to resume using the open Multi Window app(s).
- If you launch a series of Multi Window apps (each one replacing another), you can frequently step backward through them by pressing the Back key or by repeatedly deleting each one by tapping the X icon in the Border button menu.
- If audio apps (such as Music and Videos) occupy both windows and you play one, the other automatically pauses.

Customizing the Multi Window Display

You can do any of the following to customize the Multi Window display:

- *Reposition the tab.* With only the tab exposed, press and hold the tab, and then drag up or down to a new position.

- *Change the location of the Multi Window bar.* The Multi Window bar can be on the left or right side of the screen (in both standard and landscape rotation). With Multi Window open, press and hold the tab until Multi Window undocks, and then drag it to the opposite side of the screen.

Repositioned tab (top of screen)

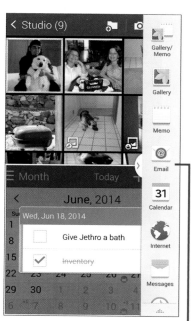

Repositioned Multi Window bar

- *Edit the Multi Window bar.* With Multi Window bar open, tap the arrow icon at its bottom to reveal the Create and Edit icons, and then tap Edit. You can drag apps off the bar into the open window (removing them from the bar), drag them from the window onto the bar, or rearrange the apps on the bar. (Press and hold an icon, and then drag it to a new position on the bar.) When you finish editing the Multi Window bar, tap Done.

- *Create Multi Window groups.* You can create Multi Window *groups* based on pairs of apps that you frequently run together. Open the two apps in Multi Window, scroll to the bottom of the Multi Window bar, tap the menu icon, tap Create, and name the group. An icon for the new group appears at the top of the bar.

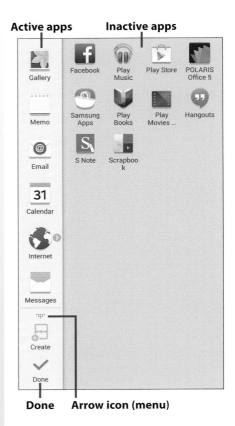

Active apps   **Inactive apps**

Done   **Arrow icon (menu)**

Create window group

Gallery/Memo

Cancel   OK

Exit/Quit an App

If you're new to smartphones, you've probably noticed a major difference between phone apps and computer programs: *Most apps have no Quit or Exit command.* The few that do are typically those that, if left running, would run up data-related charges or rapidly drain the battery.

Whenever you perform an action that leaves the current app (such as pressing the Back or Home key), the Android operating system decides whether to quit, suspend, or allow the app to continue running. Similarly, if app activities are causing the phone to run low on memory, Android performs these same functions as needed. However, if you want to quit an app *manually* to ensure that it's no longer running, draining the battery, using memory, or running up data charges, you can use the Task Manager.

1. Press the Recent Apps key and tap the Task Manager icon.

2. To quit a specific app, tap its End button. To simultaneously quit all listed apps, tap End All.

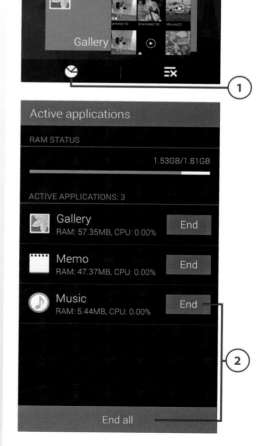

Clearing Doesn't Exit

Clearing an app from the Recent Apps list isn't the same as quitting the app.

Downloading and Installing Apps from Google Play

Google Play (or Play Store) is the most common place for you to find apps for your phone. In addition to apps, you can download ebooks, movies, and music from Google Play.

1. Launch Google Play by tapping its Home screen icon (Play Store) or by tapping Apps and then Play Store.

2. Tap Apps, Music, Games, or another item on the main screen to specify the type of material that you're seeking or want to browse.

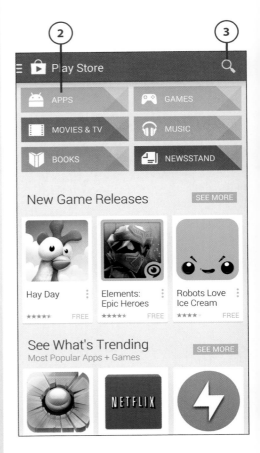

3. Do one of the following:

- Browse for apps by continuing to tap items to focus your search.

- Tap the search icon at the top of the screen and begin typing to find an app by specific name or type. A dropdown list of matches appears as you type. Tap an app name or search suggestion in the list or continue typing to further narrow the search.

4. Tap an app's name to view it.

5. Review the description and user ratings for the app. You can also do the following:

- Tap the sample screen shots or videos. If multiple screen shots are available, you can view them by swiping left and right.

- Learn more about the app by reading the What's New and Description sections. If provided, you can also tap the link to the developer's website.

6. If you want the app, tap the green icon. If the app is free, the icon is labeled Install; otherwise, it's labeled with the app's price. (See the "Paid Apps" sidebar at the end of this task for information about purchasing apps from Google Play and applying for a refund, if necessary.)

7. Before starting the download, the App Permissions screen appears, detailing how the app interacts with the operating system and uses your personal information. If the permissions are acceptable to you, tap the Accept button. The app is downloaded, installed on your phone, and its icon is added to the Apps pages. Many apps automatically place a shortcut on a Home screen page, too.

8. *Optional:* When the installation finishes, you can immediately launch the new app by tapping the Open button. Otherwise, you can launch it at your leisure by tapping its icon in Apps or its Home screen shortcut (if one was created).

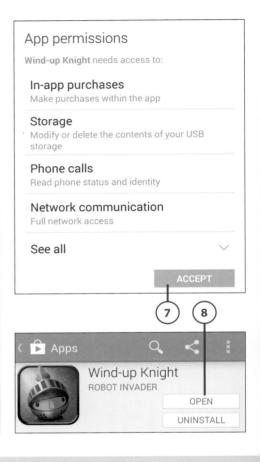

App permissions

Wind-up Knight needs access to:

In-app purchases
Make purchases within the app

Storage
Modify or delete the contents of your USB storage

Phone calls
Read phone status and identity

Network communication
Full network access

See all

ACCEPT

⑦ ⑧

‹ ▶ Apps 🔍 ⤴ ⋮

Wind-up Knight
ROBOT INVADER

OPEN

UNINSTALL

>>>Go Further

PAID APPS

If an app isn't free, you can charge it to a credit or debit card that you've registered with Google Play or, in some cases, add the charge to your monthly carrier bill. Specify a payment method or add a new one, and follow the instructions to complete the purchase.

The first time you accept the permissions for a paid app, you'll be asked to add a payment method, creating a Google Wallet account. To learn about Google Wallet, visit www.google.com/wallet/.

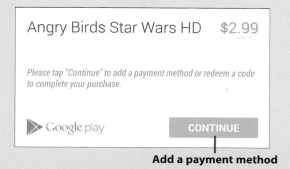

Add a payment method

Whenever you purchase an app from Google Play, you have 15 minutes to try it and decide whether you want to keep it. If not, do the following:

1. Launch Google Play, open the drawer (on the left) by tapping its icon, and choose My Apps.

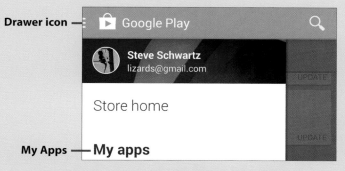

2. The My Apps list of Google Play–installed apps appears. Tap the app that you just purchased and want to return.

3. If you're within the 15-minute window, you'll see a Refund button in the app's description window. Tap it to proceed.

4. The Refund button changes to Uninstall. Tap it to remove the app from your phone and initiate the refund.

Customize Google Play

Google Play has its own Settings screen that enables you to customize the way app updates are handled. It also provides an option to create a PIN that you can use to authenticate purchases.

1. Open Google Play's drawer and tap Settings.

2. Following are the options that you can change on the Settings screen.

3. *Notifications.* When checked, an item appears in the Notification panel when updates are available for apps that you've downloaded from Google Play. You can download and install the updates by tapping the notification.

4. *Auto-Update Apps.* This setting determines whether updates for apps are automatically downloaded and installed from Google Play as they become available. To specify how and when automatic updates occur, tap Auto-Update Apps.

5. *Add Icon to Home Screen.* When enabled and you download a new app, a shortcut to the app is automatically added to your Home screen.

6. *Clear Search History.* Delete all previous searches that you've performed in Google Play.

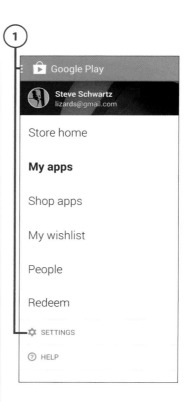

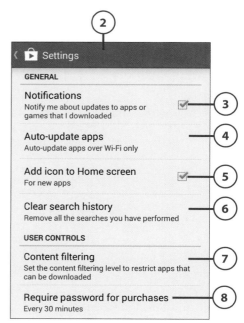

Manually Check for Updates

To manually check for updates, launch Google Play, open the drawer, and choose My Apps to display the list of your downloaded apps. All apps for which updates are available are listed in the Updates section. Tap Update All to update all of the listed apps; tap an app's Update text to update only that app.

Update all apps in Updates section

Update this app only

7. *Content Filtering.* To prevent certain types of apps from being downloaded, tap Content Filtering, enter or remove check marks on the Allow Apps Rated For screen, and tap OK.

8. *Require Password for Purchase.* Depending upon the option selected, Google Play requests your Google/Gmail password whenever you purchase content, every 30 minutes the app is running, or never.

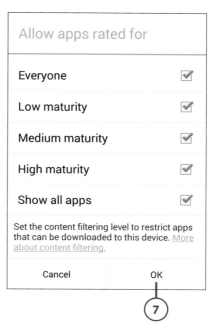

Enabling App Downloads from Other Sources

Google Play is the *official* source of Android apps. However, if you'd like to download and install apps from unofficial sources, such as developer websites or the Amazon Appstore, you must change one of your phone's settings.

1. On the Home screen, tap Apps, followed by Settings.

2. Tap the Security icon (in the System section).

3. Scroll to the Device Administration section and enable Unknown Sources. When checked, you can download apps from any source that you choose.

4. Confirm by tapping OK in the confirmation dialog box.

Verify Apps

Regardless of the sources from which you acquire your apps, you should ensure that Settings, Security, Verify Apps is checked. It enables Google to warn you or block the installation of known harmful apps.

Using the Amazon Appstore for Android

The popular online retailer Amazon.com is another major source of free and paid Android apps. If you already have an Amazon account, you can use it to purchase apps for your phone, too. (If you haven't already done so, you must allow downloading of apps from Unknown Sources, as explained previously in "Enabling App Downloads from Other Sources.")

Install the Amazon Appstore App

1. Launch Internet or Chrome, and enter www.amazon.com/getappstore in the address box.

2. Read the instructions and tap the Download the Amazon Appstore button.

3. When the download finishes, open the Notification panel and tap the AmazonApps-release.apk entry.

Instructions

4. Review the Privacy and Device Access information, and then tap Install. Tap Open on the following screen.

5. The opening screen appears. To link your Amazon.com account to the Appstore app, enter your Amazon email address and Amazon password, and tap Sign In with My Amazon Account. (If you don't have an Amazon account, you can create one by tapping the Create Account button.)

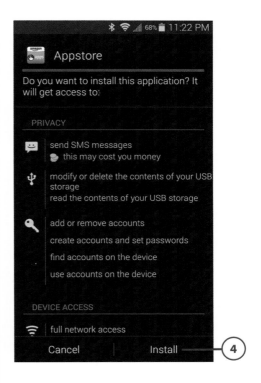

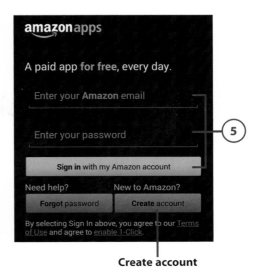

Create account

Download Apps from the Amazon Appstore

1. Launch Appstore by tapping Apps, Appstore.

2. The Appstore opening screen presents general categories that you can use to begin your browsing. Apps within a category scroll horizontally. You can tap app thumbnails or, if you don't see something that catches your eye, tap See All to view all apps of that type.

3. Alternatively, you can browse by category. Tap the menu icon, choose Browse Categories, and select a category of interest. You can further focus your browsing in larger categories by selecting a subcategory from the All Category icon and/or applying a sorting or filtering option from the Refine icon, such as Price or Avg. Customer Review.

Better Browsing

If you're at a loss concerning where to start, return to the main screen by opening the menu and choosing Store Home. Check out the Recommended for You lists—apps that Amazon thinks might interest you, based on your previous downloads.

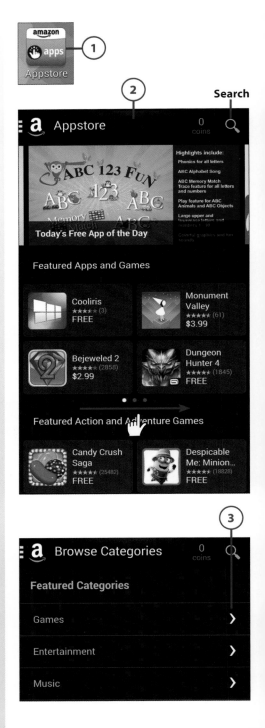

Search

4. If you know the name or type of app that you want, you can perform a search. Tap the search icon at the top of any page and enter the search text. When sufficient characters have been typed, a list of matches appears. Matching apps are preceded by the app's icon. Suggestions preceded by a magnifying glass are completed search phrases that you can use to perform your search. Select a suggested app, perform one of the suggested searches, or continue typing to further refine the suggestions. To clear the current search and start over, tap the X.

5. Tap an entry that interests you and review the product description, screenshots, and reviews. Tap any screenshot to see it at full size.

6. If you decide to download the app, tap its Free or Buy App button.

1-Click

Until you enable Amazon's 1-Click ordering and specify a preferred payment method, you can't download apps. If you haven't already completed this process, Appstore walks you through the process of completing your Amazon account setup the first time you attempt a download. To add a payment method to your account, use your computer's browser to visit www.amazon.com, log into your account, and go to Add a Credit or Debit Card.

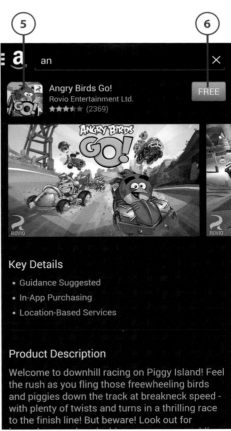

Key Details

- Guidance Suggested
- In-App Purchasing
- Location-Based Services

Product Description

Welcome to downhill racing on Piggy Island! Feel the rush as you fling those freewheeling birds and piggies down the track at breakneck speed - with plenty of twists and turns in a thrilling race to the finish line! But beware! Look out for

7. One of the following happens:

   - *Free apps.* The button's label changes to Get App. Tap the button to begin the download.

   - *Paid apps.* A dialog box shows the amount you'll be charged if you complete the purchase. Tap Confirm to continue or Cancel if you've changed your mind.

8. Read the Key Details and tap OK.

Free app

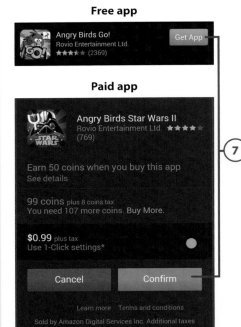

Paid app

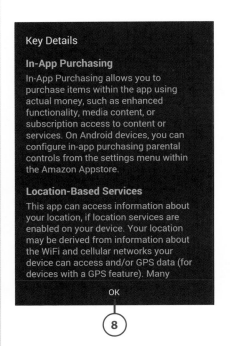

9. Review the permissions. Tap Next to install the app or Cancel if you've changed your mind.

10. The app is installed on your phone and its icon is added to Apps. If you'd like to run it now, tap Open; otherwise, tap Done to return to the Appstore. Check your email for a receipt from Amazon.

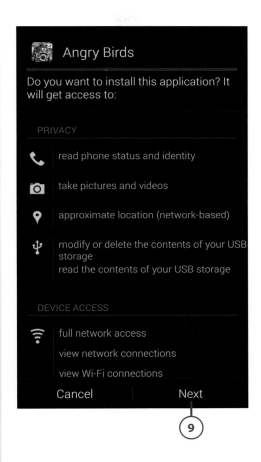

Customize the Amazon Appstore

1. Open the menu and tap Settings (in the About section).

2. The Settings screen appears, enabling you to change important Appstore options. Altering some settings requires that you supply your Amazon.com user password.

3. *Wi-Fi Settings.* To avoid using your data connection to download large apps, tap this option to require that apps larger than the specified size should be downloaded only using Wi-Fi. (Apps smaller than that size can be downloaded using 3G/4G if you don't currently have Wi-Fi access.)

4. *In-App Purchasing.* When this option is enabled, you can buy app add-ons or subscriptions from within any app that offers them. (This option is enabled by default.)

5. *Parental Controls.* Tap Parental Controls to change the settings. When Enable Parental Controls is checked and anyone attempts to purchase in-app material such as subscriptions or game add-ons, your Amazon.com password or a PIN is requested.

   If Use PIN isn't checked, your Amazon.com password is requested for in-app purchases. If Use PIN is checked, you must enter a numeric PIN instead of the password.

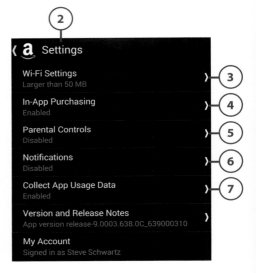

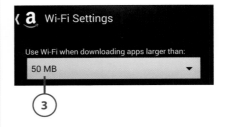

6. *Notifications.* Enable the various Notifications options to allow the Amazon Appstore to transmit notifications to the phone whenever something important occurs. (To enable *any* notification options, you must enable the first one.)

7. *Collect App Usage Data.* When enabled, Amazon collects usage data concerning the frequency and duration that you use the apps you've downloaded from the Appstore.

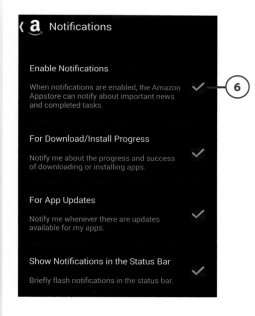

>>>Go Further

MORE AMAZON APPSTORE COMMANDS

You might find the following additional Appstore commands helpful:

- Open the menu and choose My Apps to view the list of apps you've downloaded from the Appstore. Tap a category at the top of the screen to view apps you've previous downloaded for this or another device (Cloud), installed apps on the current phone (Device), or only those apps for which an update is available (Updates). Tap a button to open, download, or update a listed app.

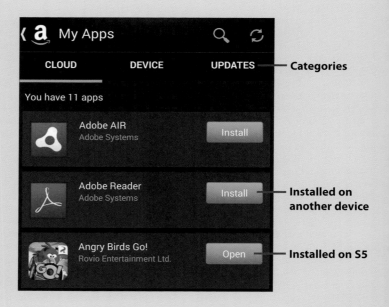

- When browsing for apps, note that every app page has a Share This App button at the bottom of the screen. Tap it to forward information about the app to others via an email, text message, or social networking post.

- If you have an Amazon gift card or a promotional code, open the menu and tap Gift Cards & Promos to add the item to your account (enabling you to apply the amount to app purchases). Enter the gift card or claim code and then tap Redeem.

Managing Apps

You can manage your installed apps by creating Home screen shortcuts to your favorites and uninstalling, disabling, or hiding apps you no longer want.

Create Home Screen Shortcuts

To simplify the process of accessing your favorite apps, you can add Home screen shortcuts to them. You can accomplish this by manually dragging icons from Apps. In addition, a shortcut is often created automatically when you install a new app. (To learn more about moving and removing shortcuts, see "Customizing the Home Screen" in Chapter 3, "Making the Phone Your Own.")

1. Navigate to the Home screen page where you want to add the app shortcut, and then tap the Apps icon.

2. Press and hold the icon of the app for which you want to create a shortcut.

3. Drag it into position on the previously selected Home screen page (or to another page, if you like) and release the icon when it's in the desired spot.

Uninstall, Disable, and Hide Apps

If you're unhappy with an app or no longer need it, you can uninstall it, removing it from your phone and reclaiming the space it was using. Generally, however, only apps you've downloaded can be uninstalled; you can't remove most of the built-in, core apps—but you might be allowed to *disable* some of them and *hide* others using methods described in this section.

It's Not All Good

Trolls in the Basement

When you bought your Samsung Galaxy S5, you were probably impressed by the number of preinstalled apps. As is the case with any smartphone, the initial app set is determined by Google, the manufacturer (Samsung, in this case), and your carrier. Unfortunately, after using the phone, you might find you have little use for some preinstalled apps—because they perform no compelling function, interfere with your use of the phone, serve only to sell you something, or could be replaced by better alternatives. Depending on how critical these apps are to the phone's proper functioning (or the importance that Google, Samsung, or your carrier places on them), you can *hide* any app, *disable* others (stop them from functioning but not remove them), and *uninstall* noncritical apps (remove them from the phone). However, many of the preinstalled apps simply can't be removed.

Imagine that you just bought a house. Upon moving in, you discover there are trolls living in the basement! You complain to the seller because they smell bad, scare the kids, keep you awake at night, and steal your food. But when you ask how to get rid of them, he explains, "They're a permanent feature of the house. You can throw a blanket over them to hide them or give them a sleeping potion to disable them, but you're *not* allowed to remove them. The fact that you don't want them is irrelevant." So, yes…your S5 comes with trolls. Be comforted by the fact that all other smartphones do, too.

Uninstall Using the Application Manager

1. Open Settings and tap Application Manager (in the Applications section).

2. Select the Downloaded category, scroll to find the app that you want to uninstall, and tap its entry.

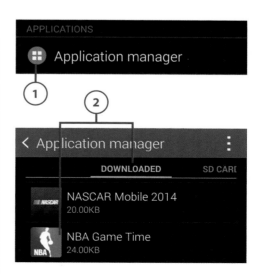

3. Tap the Uninstall button on the App Info screen. (Only apps that you're permitted to remove have an active Uninstall button.)

4. Tap Uninstall in the confirmation dialog box.

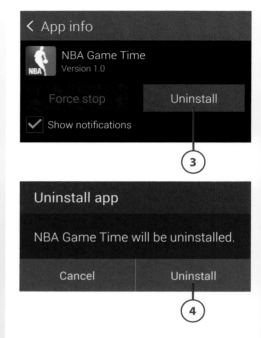

Uninstall Using Google Play

1. Tap the Play Store shortcut on your Home screen or tap Apps, Play Store.

2. Open the drawer by tapping its icon and choose My Apps.

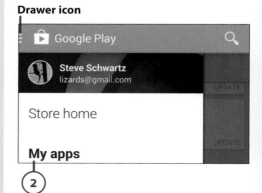

Drawer icon

3. Select the Installed category and tap the app that you want to uninstall.

4. Tap the Uninstall button. (Although this button is available for most apps, it isn't presented for system apps.)

5. Confirm the app's removal by tapping OK.

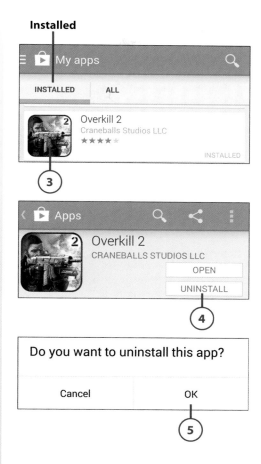

Apps Menu: Uninstall Downloaded Apps

This method restricts you to removing downloaded apps. In addition to the apps that you personally downloaded, this subset includes apps that your carrier downloaded to the phone during setup.

1. On the Home screen, tap the Apps icon.

2. Open the menu and choose Downloaded Apps.

3. Open the menu again and choose Uninstall.

4. Navigate to the page that contains the app you want to uninstall and tap its icon.

Navigation dots

5. Tap the Uninstall button in the confirmation dialog box.

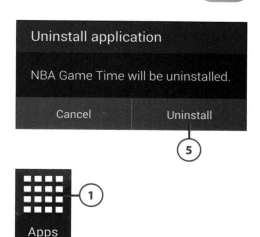

Apps Menu: Uninstall or Disable Apps

This method presents *all* installed apps—not merely those that you or your carrier downloaded to the phone. Whether you can uninstall, *disable* (stop an app from functioning but leave it on the phone), or do neither depends on the app.

Disable at Your Own Risk

As the figure for Step 5 on the next page states, disabling an app deletes all data for the app. In addition, if other apps rely on the disabled app for some functionality, they may no longer work properly.

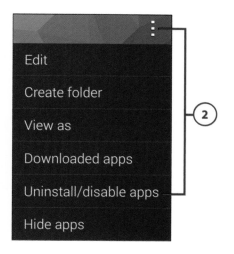

1. Tap the Apps icon on the Home screen.

2. Open the menu and choose Uninstall/Disable Apps.

3. Apps that can either be uninstalled or disabled are displayed with a minus (–) icon. The remaining apps can neither be uninstalled nor disabled.

4. Tap the app that you want to uninstall or disable.

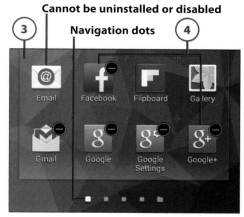

5. If the app can be uninstalled, an Uninstall Application dialog box appears; otherwise, a Disable and Reset dialog box appears. To proceed, tap Uninstall or OK, respectively.

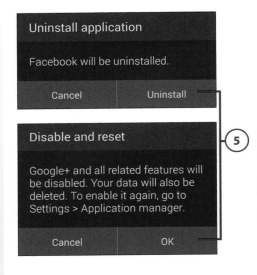

Disable—Then Uninstall

When you elect to disable certain apps by tapping OK, the Disable and Reset dialog box may be followed by an Uninstall Application dialog box. Tap Reset to continue or Cancel if you've changed your mind.

Apps Menu: Hide Apps

Hiding an app is mainly useful when you want to reduce clutter on your Apps pages by hiding icons of apps you never use. Unlike uninstalling or disabling, the apps remain installed and continue to function if required to do so by the operating system and other apps.

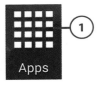

1. Tap the Apps icon on the Home screen.

2. Open the menu and choose Hide Apps.

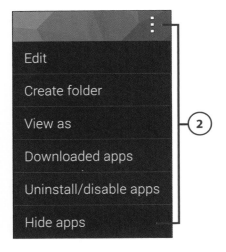

3. Tap the check box of each app that you want to hide. Use the navigation dots or swipe horizontally to select apps on other pages.

4. Tap Done.

Navigation dots

Restore Uninstalled, Disabled, and Hidden Apps

Sometimes we change our minds, discovering that an app that we removed, disabled, or hid is important after all. These situations can be reversed.

- To restore an uninstalled app, go to the original source of the app (such as Google Play, Amazon Appstore, or the developer's website), and download and install the app again.

- To restore a disabled app, tap the Apps icon on any Home screen page, open the menu, and choose Show Disabled Apps. Select the apps that you want to enable and tap Done.

- To restore a hidden app, tap the Apps icon on any Home screen page, open the menu, and choose Show Hidden Apps. Select the apps that you want to unhide and tap Done.

Restore these
hidden apps

Update Apps

Google, Samsung, carriers, and developers occasionally release app updates. When an update of an installed app becomes available at Google Play, a notification appears in the Notification panel.

On the other hand, if Auto-Update is enabled for a Google Play app, updates are handled automatically rather than manually. Notification of an auto-update appears in the Notification panel *after* the update occurs. To determine if an app has Auto-Update enabled, go to its page in Google Play and open the menu. To switch the app to manual updates, choose the Auto-Update command. For more about updating Google Play apps, see the "Customize Google Play" task earlier in the chapter.

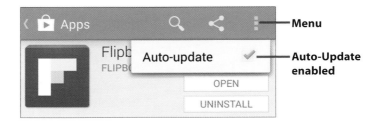

Menu

Auto-Update
enabled

Yet Another Update or Uninstall Option

You can also update or uninstall an app by going to its page in Google Play and tapping the appropriate button.

Google Play app page

>>>*Go Further*

MORE ABOUT UPDATES

Here's some additional information about updating that you may find helpful:

- Updating apps from the Amazon Appstore works in much the same way as in Google Play. When you tap an update notification, Amazon Appstore launches and takes you to the My Apps section. Select the App Updates tab to view the list of new updates and then install one or all.

- You can manually check for Amazon Appstore updates by launching the Appstore app, opening the menu, and choosing My Apps.

- If you've downloaded an app directly from a developer's website, you should periodically revisit the site to check for newer versions.

Move Apps to Your Memory Card

Another way that you can manage apps is to move some of them from built-in memory to an add-in memory card—enabling you to reclaim the device memory used by large apps.

1. Open Settings and tap Application Manager (in the Applications section).

2. Swipe horizontally to display the SD Card app list.

3. Tap the check box of a listed app that you want to move to your memory card.

4. Check the Total figure on the App Info screen. This is the amount of device memory that you'll reclaim by moving the app. To continue, tap Move to SD Card. Otherwise, press the Back key to exit.

Undo a Move

If you later want to move an app back to the phone's built-in memory, repeat Steps 1–3 for the app and then tap the Move to Device Storage button.

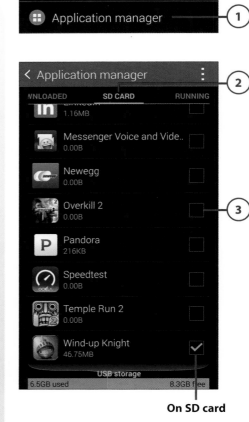

On SD card

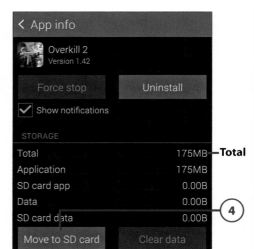

Total

Designating Default Apps

New in the box, your Galaxy S5 includes several sets of apps that are designed to perform the same function. For example, if you open Apps, you may see Internet and Chrome web browsers; Music and Play Music for playing songs; and Messages, Messaging+, and Hangouts for texting. In addition to app pairs provided by Google and Samsung (or Google versus Samsung), your carrier may offer its own competing apps.

There's no confusion when you *directly* launch an app by tapping its icon in Apps or its Home screen shortcut; the S5 knows exactly which app to run. However, when a request to *indirectly* launch an app occurs (by tapping a photo in My Files or a web page link in a received email or text message, for example), the S5 may not know which app to use. In such instances, a Complete Action Using dialog box appears, asking you to specify the app to use. To avoid seeing this dialog box in the future, you can select an app and tap Always. In the future, the S5 will assume that you want to use the selected app—your designated *default app* for performing that function.

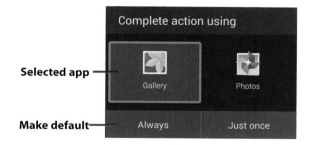

Selected app ———— Gallery / Photos

Complete action using

Make default ———— Always / Just once

You can also set a few default apps in the Default Applications section of Settings. But Default Applications is more useful for *clearing* existing defaults if you've changed your mind. Just tap the app's Clear button. The next time the Complete Action Using dialog box appears, you can specify a new default or decide that you'd prefer not to have a default for that type of app.

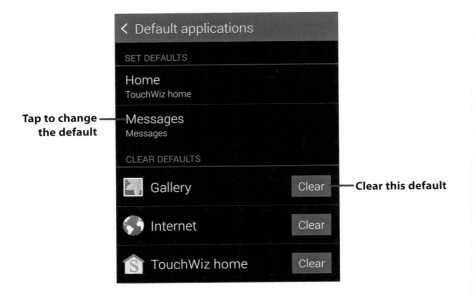

Tap to change the default

Clear this default

You can also clear a default app in the Application Manager section of Settings. Select the All category at the top of the screen and tap the app that you want to remove as a default. Scroll to the Launch by Default section and tap the Clear Defaults button.

Internet app

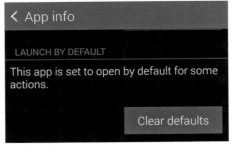

Enable the Toolbox App Launcher

The Toolbox is a new utility that provides immediate access to up to five of your most frequently used apps.

1. Open Settings and tap the Toolbox icon (in the Sound and Display section).

2. Toolbox must be enabled in order to configure it. Drag its slider to the On position. The Toolbox icon appears onscreen.

Use the Quick Setting Buttons

Toolbox also has a Quick Setting button with which you can quickly enable or disable it. Drag down the Notification panel and tap the Toolbox button. To go directly to its Settings screen, press and hold the Toolbox button.

3. Tap the Edit button to add or remove apps. Select up to five apps and tap the Save button.

Toolbox icon
Current toolbox apps

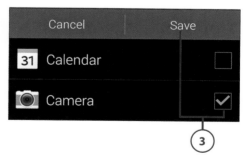

4. Position the Toolbox icon by pressing and dragging. To launch one of its apps, tap the Toolbox icon and then tap the app you want to run.

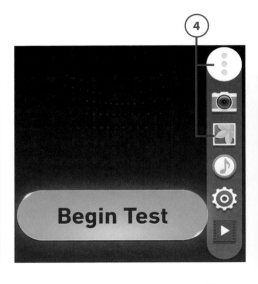

An Edit or Disable Shortcut

In addition to the options specified in this task, you can quickly access Toolbox's Edit screen or disable Toolbox. Long-press its icon and drag it onto the Edit or Remove icon at the top of the screen.

It's Not All Good

Toolbox Shortcomings

I love the idea of a handy program launcher, but Toolbox could be improved in several ways. First (and most important), no matter where you put Toolbox, it's bound to be in the way, intrusive, and somewhat distracting—similar to the Multi Window tab. It doesn't *need* to be onscreen at all times. I'd prefer to be able to summon it via a keypress, such as long-pressing Home or Back. (Yes, I know that long-pressing Home launches Google Now, but I find Toolbox—or, at least, the *idea* of Toolbox—more useful.)

Second, why limit Toolbox to favorite *apps*? There are some Settings categories and items that I'd like to be able to access quickly, too.

Third, it should be possible to specify the *order* of the apps.

Finally, I'd like to be able to add more than five apps. Because the Toolbox icon automatically repositions itself upward (when dictated by its onscreen position) to display the app icons beneath it, it should be possible to easily expand the roster to at least ten. In summary, Toolbox is potentially a useful feature, but it needs more work.

Special and Noteworthy Apps

Given the current length of this book, it's not possible to provide in-depth, step-by-step instructions for every built-in app. So here's a quick rundown of some of the more noteworthy and special-purpose apps you should consider checking out.

Calculator. Use this basic calculator to perform calculations involving addition, subtraction, multiplication, and division. Tap the bar above the keypad to review recent calculation results.

Clock. Use Clock to create alarms (for those occasions when creating a Calendar event is overkill), activate the stopwatch to time an event, set the countdown timer to let you know when your pizza is done cooking, and check the time in other time zones.

Cloud (Drive, Dropbox). As you learned when you ran the setup wizard, your Samsung account is used to back up key phone data to Samsung's remote servers (in the *cloud*). The S5 also includes an app (or two, depending on your carrier) that enables you to upload and back up important files to the cloud. You can access your files with the S5, other devices, or any computer with a web browser, as well as share them with others. A major advantage to having certain files in the cloud is that you can work with them while they're on the servers, make changes and edits as required, and then save—without downloading copies to your current device.

Flipboard (My Magazine). My Magazine is the front end to Flipboard, a highly customizable news, business, infotainment, and social networking aggregator. You can use Flipboard to read articles, watch videos, and follow posts made by Facebook, Twitter, and LinkedIn friends and colleagues. You can launch Flipboard by tapping its Apps icon or by swiping to the left of the first Home screen page (the navigation dot marked with an equal (=) sign).

Flipboard (Engadget article)

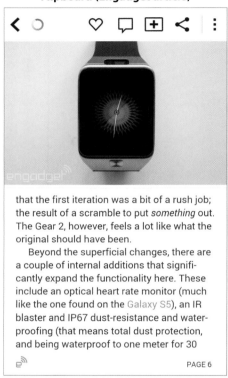

that the first iteration was a bit of a rush job; the result of a scramble to put *something* out. The Gear 2, however, feels a lot like what the original should have been.

Beyond the superficial changes, there are a couple of internal additions that significantly expand the functionality here. These include an optical heart rate monitor (much like the one found on the Galaxy S5), an IR blaster and IP67 dust-resistance and waterproofing (that means total dust protection, and being waterproof to one meter for 30

PAGE 6

Google +. Access the Google+ social networking site.

Google Now. Presents up-to-the-minute information in the form of cards customized to meet your daily needs. Card topics include weather, sports, stocks, transportation information, and nearby events and attractions. To dismiss a card, simply swipe it off-screen. Google Now is integrated with Google Search and is enabled or disabled in the latter's settings (see "Use Google Search" in Chapter 2, "Understanding the Android/TouchWiz Interface"). When enabled and you press and hold the Home key, Google Now appears; otherwise, Google Search opens.

Google Now

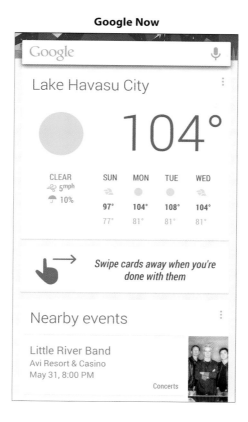

Google Settings. Configure the preinstalled Google apps. You can also view and launch these apps by opening the Google folder on the first Home screen page.

Hangouts. Google Hangouts wants to be your default messaging app. (But you can still use it even if you don't make it the default.) Hangouts is a multi-platform—including iPhones and iPads—app for conducting one-on-one and group conversations using text messages, voice, and video.

Memo. Create, edit, and categorize notes that can optionally include photos and audio.

Optical Reader. Use the S5 camera to capture text or QR codes and convert the image into editable text. Options include voice control, using the flash for illumination, reading the translation aloud, and sharing the resulting text via email. Although it does an excellent job with QR codes, the text capture would be more useful if you could select the text to include.

Polaris Office 5. View and edit Microsoft Office documents (Word, Excel, and PowerPoint) and view PDFs.

Polaris Office 5

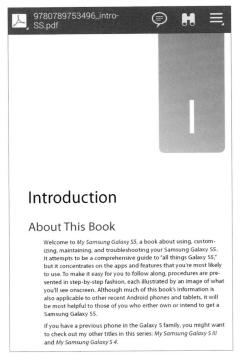

S Health. If you'd like some assistance with a fitness regimen and goals, S Health can be coupled with the Gear 2, Gear Neo, or Gear Fit watches, enabling you to automatically record your pulse as you work out and perform routine activities throughout your day. Even without added gear, S Health can track your physical activity (running, walking, hiking, and cycling), diet (caloric intake, calories burned, and weight), sleep patterns, and stress level. You can use its pedometer to record the number of steps taken in a day and the heart rate sensor to take your pulse. (In S Health, tap the Heart Rate icon and rest your fingertip lightly on the flash/heart rate sensor on the back of the phone.)

S Health

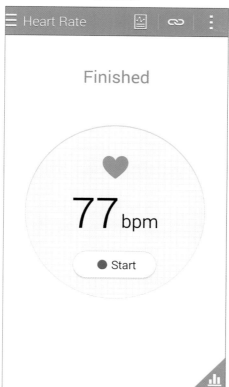

Will You Love Me Forever?

If you activate S Health to try it out and decide it's not for you, there is no simple way to exit and stop its processes from running continuously in the background. The only way I've found to halt S Health is to disable it (see the "Apps Menu: Uninstall or Disable Apps" task) and then restart the phone. Return to Apps, open the menu and choose Show Disabled Apps, select S Health, and tap Done. The S Health app will then be available should you elect to set it up again. You'll have to redownload any updates on the first run.

S Note. Use this note-taking app in conjunction with provided templates to create to-do lists, appointment calendars, and freeform notes. You can input text via typing, audio recording, or handwriting using your fingertip or a stylus. Notes can include maps, illustrations, charts, photos, videos, and voice memos.

S Translator. Translate typed or spoken text into another language and view or hear the translation. Higher-quality versions of some languages are offered as free downloads.

Samsung Apps. This is Samsung's app store. Many of the important prein-stalled Samsung apps are updated through this online store. When you tap the Galaxy Gifts and Galaxy Essentials widgets (see the following sidebar) or choose Galaxy Essentials from the Apps menu, you're taken to Samsung Apps.

YouTube. View YouTube videos over your Wi-Fi or cellular connection.

>>>Go Further
GALAXY ESSENTIALS AND GALAXY GIFTS

Samsung includes two sets of downloadable apps with the S5 that it thinks will interest you: Galaxy Essentials and Galaxy Gifts. When you're ready to start cus-tomizing your phone with new apps, open the Apps menu and choose Galaxy Essentials. Samsung Apps launches and displays a scrolling list of free, special-purpose Samsung apps. Be sure to check out Milk Radio, a free streaming music app that employs a unique dial to select stations by music genre. When a song is playing, you can tap anywhere onscreen to make the dial materialize. If S Note and S Translator (described in the previous section) aren't installed on your S5, you can download them from this list. Currently installed apps have a blue right-arrow icon.

You can access the Galaxy Gifts section of Samsung Apps by tapping the Galaxy Gifts widget. If the widget isn't installed, launch Samsung Apps, select the Category tab, and tap Galaxy Gifts. Among the 18 free apps are utilities, fit-ness programs, and games. You can also begin trial subscriptions to *Bloomberg Businessweek, LinkedIn Premium, The Wall Street Journal*, and *The New York Times*. Be sure to read the descriptions and reviews before installing any of the subscrip-tions.

Milk Radio (Galaxy Essentials)

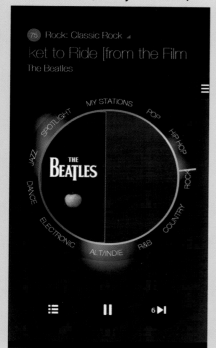

Galaxy Gifts

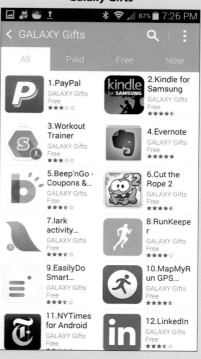

In this chapter, you learn how to use the phone's GPS chip in conjunction with Google Maps, the preinstalled location-based app for viewing maps and getting directions between any pair of points. Topics include the following:

→ Enabling and disabling GPS

→ Using Voice Search and S Voice to request directions to a destination

→ Exploring direction and navigation options in Google Maps

→ Configuring Location Settings

Using the GPS

The Galaxy S5 has an embedded *GPS* (Global Positioning System) chip that enables the network to determine your phone's current location. When the GPS is active, the phone can use E911 emergency location services to transmit your location (see "Emergency Calling" in Chapter 4, "Placing and Receiving Calls"). Some apps can use the GPS to provide information relevant to your current location, such as notifying you of nearby friends and businesses. The most common use of the GPS, however, is to run apps that display maps of your surroundings, provide turn-by-turn driving and walking directions, determine the distance to locations, and show you where you are in relation to your friends.

If you previously owned a Galaxy S III or S 4, you'll note that the confusing array of GPS apps with overlapping functions has—for the most part—been eliminated from the S5. Unless your carrier has preinstalled similar or complementary apps, Google Maps is the primary GPS-driven app for navigation on your phone.

Enabling/Disabling GPS

As with Bluetooth and Wi-Fi, you can enable and disable the phone's GPS as needed. Because the regular polling of GPS drains the battery and consumes data, you can disable the feature when you aren't using it. Use any of the following methods to enable or disable GPS (Location):

- Pull down the Notification panel and tap the Location button to toggle its current state. Enabled Quick Setting buttons are bright green.

Notification panel

Enable/disable GPS — Settings — Quick Setting buttons

- Open Settings (switch to the Home screen and tap Apps, Settings or tap the Settings icon in the Notification panel). In the Network Connections section, tap Location. Tap the Location slider to toggle its state.

Enable/disable GPS

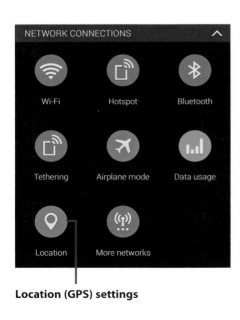

Location (GPS) settings

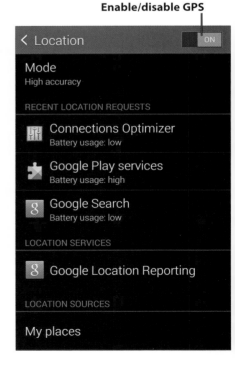

The Direct Route to Location Settings

The fastest way to go to the Location screen in Settings is to press and hold the Location Quick Setting button.

- If you perform an action in an app that requires GPS (such as requesting navigation instructions or tapping the AccuWeather widget for the detailed forecast) but GPS isn't enabled, you are usually asked to enable it in Location Services. Enable GPS by toggling the Location slider to On.

Current location

Location services is disabled. Go to Settings > Location services to enable Location services.

Cancel   Settings ———— **Open Location Services Settings**

Getting Directions from Google Maps

The most common use of GPS is to get turn-by-turn driving, bicycling, or walking directions from your current location (determined by the GPS) to a destination. Turn-by-turn directions and detailed maps are provided by Google Maps. There are two ways to use Maps. First, if you know your destination, are in a hurry (already driving, for example), and don't care to set options, you can use a voice command to go directly to Maps' turn-by-turn voice navigation. Second, if you don't have a specific destination in mind (you might be searching for a gas station or pizza restaurant, for example), want to view a map, or want to set options, you can launch Maps and *then* specify the details.

Voice Search: Direct to Navigation

1. If the Google Search widget is installed on a Home screen page, navigate to the page, and say "OK, Google" or tap the microphone icon. Alternatively, you can tap Apps, followed by Voice Search.

2. Voice Search launches. Request directions by saying "Go to *destination*," "Drive to *destination*," or "Navigate to *destination*," where *destination* is a business name, street address, landmark, or city, for example.

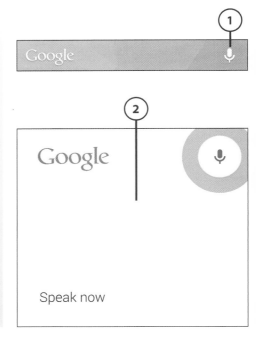

Complete Action Using

If an app that provides similar functions to Google Maps is installed (such as Sprint's Scout) and you haven't specified a default app to automatically use, a Complete Action Using dialog box appears. Tap Maps and the Just Once button. To prevent this dialog box from interrupting *future* navigation requests, make Maps the default by selecting it and tapping the Always button.

Indicate which app you want to use

3. Assuming that Voice Search can identify an unambiguous destination, Maps launches, displays a route map beginning from your current location, and speaks the first direction. At each location change, Maps provides a new instruction.

Use S Voice to Fetch Navigation Instructions

You can also request navigation instructions using Samsung's S Voice. Quickly press the Home key twice to activate S Voice, or go to the Home screen and tap Apps, S Voice. When S Voice launches, follow Steps 2–3 from this task.

Launch Google Maps

Navigation and maps are provided by the Google Maps app. You can launch Maps using any method that's convenient, such as the following:

- On the Home screen, tap Apps, followed by Maps.

- If there's a Google folder on your Home screen, it contains shortcuts for every preinstalled Google app. Open the folder and tap Maps.

- If the Google Search widget is installed on a Home screen page, navigate to the page and activate it by saying "OK, Google." Then say "Open Maps."

- Quickly press the Home key twice to activate S Voice. When S Voice launches, say "Open Maps."

Maps app

Google folder contents

Set a Trip within Google Maps

Google Maps provides maps, text directions, and voice-guided navigation between any two points. When you want more control over options for your point-to-point trip, launch Maps (see "Launch Google Maps") and specify options within it.

The Order Is Up to You

The following task is presented in a *general* (rather than a specific) order. You'll find that you can perform most of the steps in any order that's convenient. In many instances, you can also step back to make changes by pressing the Back key.

1. Ensure that GPS (Location) is enabled (see "Enabling/Disabling GPS," earlier in the chapter) and launch Maps using any of the methods outlined in the previous section.

2. *Optional:* If your current location (represented by a blue dot) isn't visible on the map, tap the My Location button.

3. Tap the Directions icon to specify your starting point and destination.

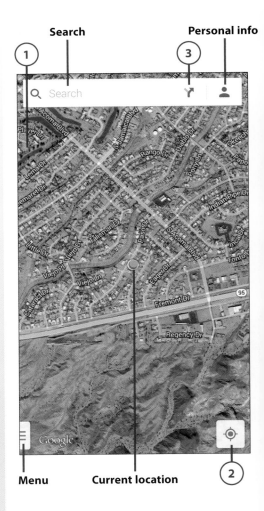

Search   Personal info

Menu   Current location

4. Indicate your mode of travel (Driving, Public Transit, Bicycling, or Walking) by tapping an icon at the top of the screen.

5. *Optional:* To begin from somewhere other than your current location (as determined by the phone), tap My Location. Perform a search for the starting point or select it from the recently visited and searched locations.

6. Tap Choose Destination. Indicate your destination by typing, tapping the microphone icon and speaking, or tapping a history entry.

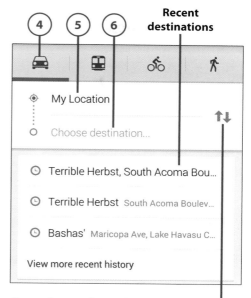

Swap the starting point and destination

Try a General Search

In addition to searching for a particular business, you can search for a type of business by entering a search phrase, such as *gas station* or *dentist*.

7. Do one of the following:

- If the starting point is a location other than your current one, a list of routes appears. Tap a route to view it. (If desired, you can change routes when the map is shown.)

- If the starting point *is* your current location, tap a route to view it or tap Start Navigation to accept the proposed route in the miniature map and immediately begin navigation.

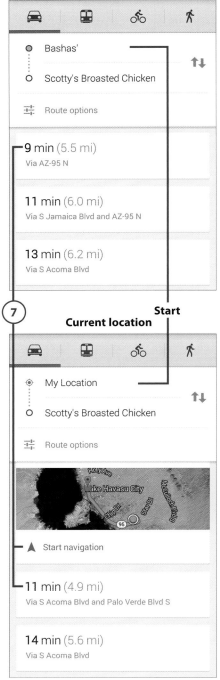

Different starting location

Current location

Start

8. A route map appears. Prior to beginning navigation, you can optionally do any of the following:

- Alternate routes are gray. To switch routes, tap one of the alternates.

- To view text-based directions for the selected route, tap the route description at the bottom of the screen or swipe it upward. When you're finished, press the Back key or swipe the text directions downward.

- To change the display, tap the menu icon and choose options, such as displaying a satellite view or a normal map view.

- To change the origin or destination, tap the box at the top of the screen. To *clear* the current trip, tap the X.

9. Do one of the following:

- Tap the Start icon to begin turn-by-turn voice instructions. This option is only available if the trip begins from your current location.

- If you're starting from a different location, a Preview icon appears rather than a Start icon. Tap it to view the trip.

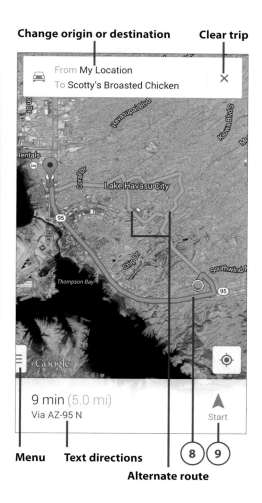

Change origin or destination   **Clear trip**

Menu   **Text directions**

Alternate route

Changing the Magnification

While viewing the map or navigating, you can change the magnifcation by double-tapping, spreading your thumb and forefinger apart, or pinching your thumb and forefinger together.

Configuring Location (GPS) Settings

There are several ways that your phone can determine your location. You can vary the Location mode, depending on your data plan and whether you're within Wi-Fi range.

1. Open Settings and tap the Location icon. (Alternatively, you can open the Navigation panel and then press and hold the Location button.)

2. Tap Mode.

3. Select a Locating Method: High Accuracy, Power Saving, or GPS Only.

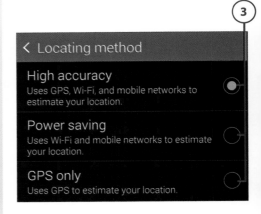

It's Not All Good

My Places

By tapping My Places at the bottom of the Location Settings screen, you can record some important locations (such as Home and Work) and add others, as well as specify a non-GPS method for determining these locations: Wi-Fi, Maps, or Bluetooth. Apps that require location information are supposed to be able to use entries in My Places in lieu of constantly pinging your GPS.

Unfortunately, *how* one gets the apps to use My Places is beyond me. For example, the Weather widget insists that Location be enabled to determine my current location—even though my Home entry clearly indicates my town. Even Maps doesn't appear to provide a way to set a Places entry as a trip origin or destination—other than Home, that is.

Album cover   Volume   Menu

Track name ———— Knockin' on Heaven's Door

Artist ———— Bob Dylan

Album ———— The Essential Bob Dylan

Controls ————

0:59   2:30

In this chapter, you learn to play your favorite music on the phone. Topics include the following:

→ Using the Music app to play songs stored on the phone
→ Creating, using, and managing playlists
→ Deleting unwanted songs

Playing and Managing Music

If you're in the mood for musical entertainment, your Galaxy S5 is up to the task. In this chapter, you find out how to use the built-in Music app to play songs and other tracks stored on your phone.

Playing Stored Songs with the Music App

You might have amassed a collection of your favorite tracks in iTunes, Windows Media Player, or another PC or Mac media organizer. By following the techniques described in Chapter 16, "Transferring and Sharing Files," you can use USB, Wi-Fi, or Bluetooth to copy those songs to your phone. Using Music, you can play these songs whenever you want.

Some Songs Can't Be Played

Most tracks stored on your PC or Mac will play in Music. Copy-protected songs, such as those encoded with Apple's *AAC* (*protected*) codec, can be copied to the phone, but they will not play.

Select and Play Songs

The first step in playing music is to select the song you'd like to hear. You can select a track to play from any of Music's tabs (at the top of the screen).

1. From the Home screen, tap Apps, and then tap Music.

Another Music Player

A second music player app is preinstalled on the Galaxy S5. Play Music is a general music player that works much like Music. In addition to playing content stored on your phone, Play Music links directly to Google Play, enabling you to preview and buy new songs.

2. To find the first song you'd like to hear, tap the Tracks, Albums, or Artists tab to view an alphabetical list of your songs, albums, or artists/groups. Alternatively, tap Playlists to view *playlists* (groups of songs) you've created, as well as your favorite, most played, recently played, and recently added tracks. See "Working with Playlists," later in this chapter, for additional information. You can customize the tabs, as explained in "More Fun with Music."

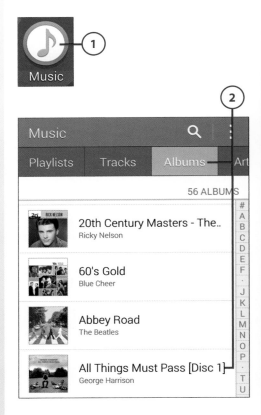

I Can't Find the Tab I Want

If you don't see the tab you're looking for at the top of the main Music screen, scroll horizontally until it comes into view.

Song Selection Affects Playback

The song you initially select determines what other songs automatically play after the selected song ends, as well as what additional songs are available to you without returning to the main screen. For instance, if you select a song from an album, all later songs from the album will play until the last track is completed.

3. If the song you want isn't visible, continue tapping icons to narrow the results. For instance, when viewing the Artists list, tap an artist, tap an album, and then tap the song you want to play.

Searching for a Song

You can *search* for music, too. Tap the Search icon to search for the song, album, or artist you want to hear.

Back Album   Search

4. The song begins to play.

5. You can display the album cover or the current track list by tapping the music or album icon in the lower-left corner. Switch to Track List view if you want to select a different track from the album, playlist, or selection.

6. Tap the Play/Pause button to pause or continue playback.

7. To go forward or backward in the song, drag the playback slider or tap the spot on the line that is approximately where you'd like to be in the song.

8. Press and hold the Previous or Next button to rewind or fast forward through the track. Tap the Previous or Next button to play the previous or next track in the album, playlist, or current selection, respectively. (In Album Cover view, you can also switch tracks by swiping the cover to the right or left.)

Returning to Music

If you leave Music to run another app, you can return to Music by launching it again or by tapping the album icon in the Notification panel or the Music widget (if it's installed). Note that you can also control playback in the Notification panel, in the widget, or on the lock screen.

Album Cover View

9. *Optional:* Tap the star icon to mark or unmark the track as a *favorite.* (Favorite tracks are denoted by a filled gold star.) Your favorites can be found in the Favorite Tracks playlist (see "Working with Playlists," later in the chapter).

10. Adjust the volume by pressing the Volume control or by tapping the Volume icon and adjusting the slider that appears.

What Happens Next?

When the song ends, the remaining songs in the album, playlist, or track list play until the final song ends. You can select a different song to play by tapping the Previous or Next button to move backward or forward through the current track list, switching to Track List view and tapping a track title, or pressing the Back key repeatedly. When you reach the main Music screen, you can repeat this process starting with Step 2.

Track List View

SoundAlive equalizer

>>>Go Further

SHUFFLE AND REPEAT

The order in which the songs in the selection play is determined by the state of the Shuffle icon. When there's a slash through it, songs play in listed order. If you tap the icon to remove the slash, the songs play in random (shuffled) order.

You can instruct Music to repeat the current track or track list. Repeatedly tap the icon above the right end of the playback line to choose a repetition option.

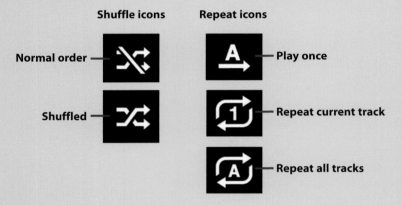

Shuffle icons

Normal order

Shuffled

Repeat icons

Play once

Repeat current track

Repeat all tracks

Use the Equalizer

SoundAlive is Music's equalizer. While a song is playing, you can use SoundAlive to adjust levels to suit the music and adapt to current acoustics. SoundAlive settings affect the playback of *all* songs and remain in effect until you change settings again. (Note that SoundAlive settings aren't song-specific and aren't saved with each song.)

1. Tap the *SoundAlive* icon on the volume slider or tap the menu icon, Settings, SoundAlive to change the equalizer settings. You can alter settings on the Basic and/or Advanced tabs.

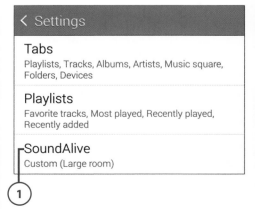

< Settings

Tabs
Playlists, Tracks, Albums, Artists, Music square, Folders, Devices

Playlists
Favorite tracks, Most played, Recently played, Recently added

SoundAlive
Custom (Large room)

2. Use the Basic tab to do any of the following:

 - Tap a square that best represents the tonal qualities of the music to which you're listening. Higher squares boost the treble, whereas lower ones boost the bass. Squares to the right emphasize vocals, and ones to the left emphasize instruments.

Let SoundAlive Do the Work

Tap the Auto check box to allow SoundAlive to analyze the current song and select a square for you.

 - Select an effect from the horizontally scrolling Effect list. Note that certain effects can be selected only when you're using earphones. (To remove an applied effect, tap None.)

3. Use the Advanced tab to fine-tune the Basic settings. You can drag level sliders; emphasize bass, emphasize clarity, and/or simulate 3D sound; and apply an effect from the horizontally scrolling list. Note that 3D sound and certain effects can be selected only when you're using earphones.

4. Tap Done to apply the SoundAlive settings, Cancel to ignore all changes, or Reset to reapply the default settings.

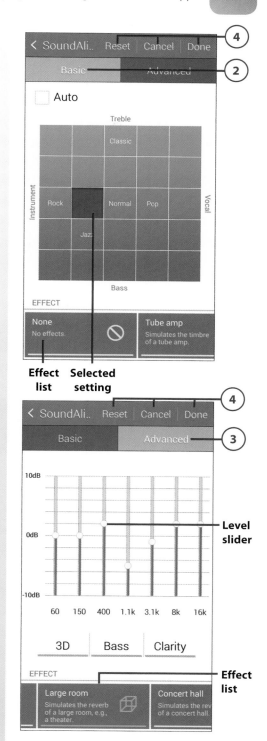

Effect list

Selected setting

Level slider

Effect list

Working with Playlists

Playing a specific song or album isn't always what you want to do. For those occasions, you can create special song groupings called playlists. A *playlist* is any combination of tracks that you want to play together. For instance, you might create a playlist that includes all albums by a favorite group or songs from a genre, such as electric blues, techno, or classical.

Create a Playlist

You can create a new playlist in several ways, but the simplest—and the one you're most likely to remember—is to start from the Playlists tab.

1. Press the Back key as many times as necessary to reach the main Music screen, and select the Playlists tab.

2. Tap Create Playlist in the My Playlists section.

3. Name the new playlist, and tap OK.

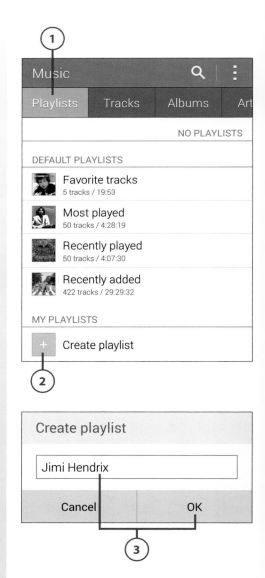

4. The new, empty playlist appears. Its name is added to the My Playlists section.

Playlist name

No tracks

④

Add Songs to a Playlist

There are several ways that you can add songs to any user-created playlist—whether it's a new, empty one or a playlist that already contains tracks:

Done

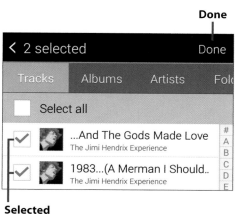

Selected songs

- To select from an alphabetical list of all songs on your phone, select the Playlists tab and then open the playlist by tapping its name. Tap the plus (+) toolbar icon. The Tracks tab is automatically displayed. Select songs/tracks by tapping their check boxes, and then tap Done.

- Add entire albums or all material by a given artist to a playlist by tapping a view tab (such as Albums or Artists) to help you find the material to include in the playlist. Press and hold the artist or album name to select it. You can select additional artists or albums, if desired. Tap the Add to Playlist toolbar icon, and then select the playlist to which you want to add the material.

- While browsing songs from an album or by an artist, you can add multiple songs by tapping the menu icon, choosing Select, selecting songs you want to add, tapping the Add to Playlist toolbar icon, and selecting the target playlist.

- Add a song that's currently playing to a playlist by tapping the Add to Playlist icon (beneath the playback line) and selecting the destination playlist.

- When playing a song in Track List view, press and hold its title (or the title of any other listed song) to reveal the Add to Playlist command in a pop-up menu.

That's a Big Oops

When adding songs to a playlist, Music won't warn you if you inadvertently select songs that are already in the playlist nor will it prevent you from adding them again—and again.

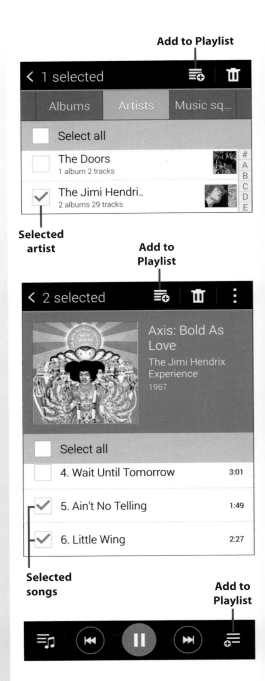

Add to Playlist

Selected artist

Add to Playlist

Selected songs

Add to Playlist

Play Songs from a Playlist

To play songs from a playlist, follow these steps.

1. Return to the main Music screen by pressing the Back key as many times as necessary. Tap the Playlists tab to view the defined playlists, and tap the playlist that you want to hear. Your created playlists (My Playlists) appear below the built-in ones (Default Playlists).

2. Tap the song that you want to hear first. (If you select the first song, the entire playlist plays.)

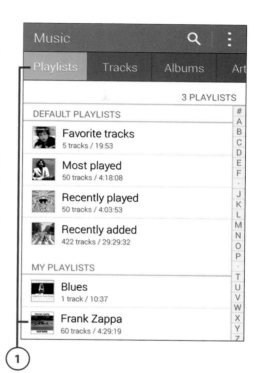

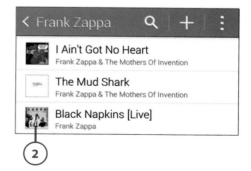

3. The selected song begins to play. When it's done, other songs from the playlist play until Music reaches the last song in the playlist or you halt playback.

What's Next?

To view the playlist and see the songs ahead, switch to Track List view (see Step 5 of "Select and Play Songs"). In this view, it's also easy to pick a different song to play next—rather than accept the one that's next in the queue.

4. *Optional*: Tap the Shuffle icon to toggle between playing the songs in order (slashed) and playing them in random order (no slash).

Manage Playlists

You can modify your custom playlists in several ways, such as removing songs, changing the playback order, and editing a playlist's title. You can also delete any playlists that you no longer want. To learn how to add songs to a playlist, see "Add Songs to a Playlist," earlier in this chapter.

Switch Between List and Grid View

1. Select the Playlists tab on the main Music screen.

2. Tap the menu icon. Choose List View or Grid View to specify the manner in which playlists are displayed on the Playlists tab.

Switch to Track List view

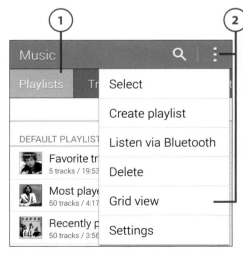

Change a Playlist's Title

1. Select the Playlists tab on the main Music screen and open the custom playlist that you want to rename.

2. Tap the menu icon, and choose Edit Title.

3. Edit the title, and tap OK.

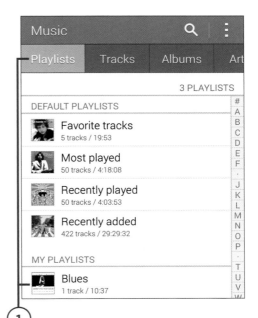

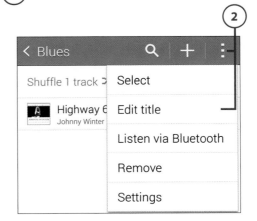

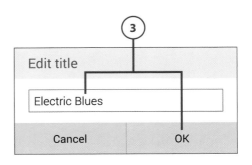

Delete Playlists

1. Select the Playlists tab on the main Music screen.

2. Tap the menu icon, and choose Delete.

3. In the My Playlists section, select the custom playlist(s) that you want to delete and tap Done.

4. Tap OK to confirm the deletion(s).

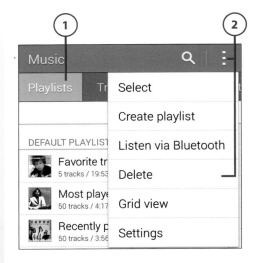

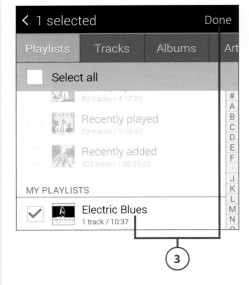

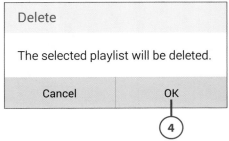

Remove Songs

1. Select the Playlists tab on the main Music screen and open the custom playlist from which you want to remove songs. (Note that removing a song doesn't *delete* it from your phone; it only removes the song from the playlist.)

2. Tap the menu icon, and choose Remove.

3. Select the songs you want to remove, and tap Done. The selected songs are immediately removed from the playlist.

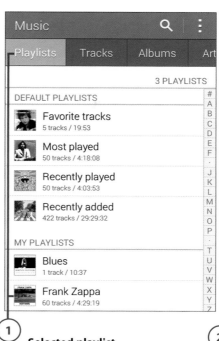

Selected playlist

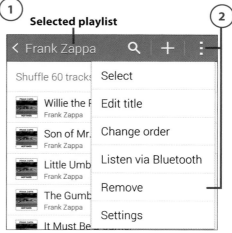

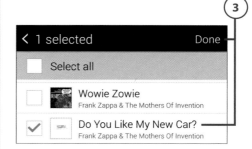

Change the Track Order

1. Select the Playlists tab on the main Music screen and open the custom playlist for which you want to change the track order.

2. Tap the menu icon, and choose Change Order.

3. Use the dot pattern to drag a song up or down to change the song's position in the playlist. When you finish, press the Back key or tap the Back icon.

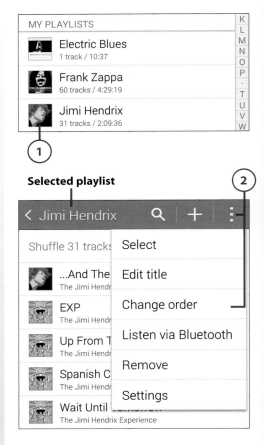

MY PLAYLISTS

Electric Blues
1 track / 10:37

Frank Zappa
60 tracks / 4:29:19

Jimi Hendrix
31 tracks / 2:09:36

K L M N O P · T U V W

(1)

Selected playlist

(2)

< Jimi Hendrix   🔍 + ⋮

Shuffle 31 track│ Select

...And The │ Edit title
The Jimi Hendr│

EXP │ Change order
The Jimi Hendr│

Up From T │ Listen via Bluetooth
The Jimi Hendr│

Spanish C │ Remove
The Jimi Hendr│

Wait Until │ Settings
The Jimi Hendrix Experience

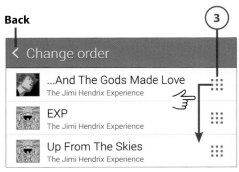

Back

(3)

< Change order

...And The Gods Made Love
The Jimi Hendrix Experience   ⠿

EXP
The Jimi Hendrix Experience   ⠿

Up From The Skies
The Jimi Hendrix Experience   ⠿

>>>*Go Further*
BUILT-IN PLAYLISTS AND FAVORITES

In addition to the custom playlists you create, Music provides several playlists that it automatically maintains: Most Played, Recently Played, and Recently Added. An additional playlist called Favorite Tracks contains all songs you've marked as favorites. To mark a playing song as a favorite, tap the star icon above the playback indicator. To simultaneously mark *multiple* songs as favorites, open any track list (an album or playlist, for example), tap the menu icon, and choose Select. Tap the check box for each track that you want to mark as a favorite, open the menu again, and choose Add to Favorites.

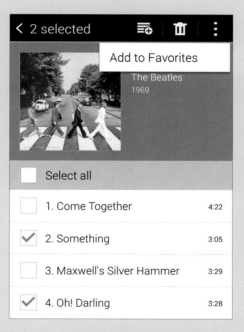

To remove a playing song from the Favorite Tracks playlist, tap its star icon again. To remove *multiple* favorites, open the Favorite Tracks playlist, tap the menu icon, and choose Select. Select each favorite that you want to remove, open the menu again, and choose Remove from Favorites.

It's Not All Good

iTunes Issues

When copying songs from computer to phone, you'll quickly note two major iTunes-related shortcomings. First, because iTunes supports synchronizing only with Apple hardware, such as the iPhone, iPod, and iPad, there's no built-in, painless way to copy tracks from your computer's iTunes library to the Galaxy S5. You have two options:

- Manually select songs on your computer and copy them to the phone using any of the methods discussed in Chapter 16. Like most Android apps, Music doesn't care where on your phone your tracks are stored, so you can copy them into any folder (or folders) that you like—either to system memory or an installed memory card. To locate the music files on your Mac, check the /Users/*username*/Music/iTunes/iTunes Music folder. You can find iTunes for Windows music in the \Users*username*\ Music\iTunes\iTunes Media\Music folder. If you have other songs stored on your PC, you need to know the folders in which they're stored.

- Install a music-management app that simplifies the process of downloading and, optionally, syncing music with that of your iTunes-based PC or Mac song library. One option is DoubleTwist (www.doubletwist.com), a desktop application and companion Android app. You can also hunt for other software solutions in Google Play using **iTunes sync** as the search text.

Second, although most of your albums have cover art in iTunes, many of those images will be missing in Music. The easiest way to fill in the blanks is to install an Android app that can tap into online music databases. Three of the most popular are Cover Art Downloader, Album Art Grabber, and Cover Art Grabber—all free.

Deleting Unwanted Songs

You can delete songs that you're tired of hearing or if you want to reclaim their storage space for more important material. If you know where on the phone they're stored, you can delete them in My Files. The simplest method, however, is to find and delete them within Music. There are several ways to delete single or multiple songs.

Delete a Track While Playing a Song

1. When the song is playing, tap the icon to switch to Track List view.

2. Press and hold the name of the track that you want to delete. It can be the song that's playing or any other song in the current track list.

3. Choose Delete from the pop-up menu.

4. Tap OK to confirm the deletion.

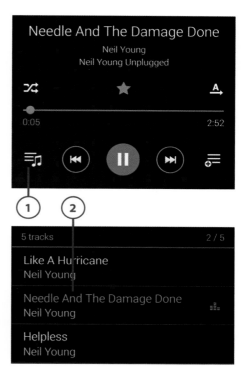

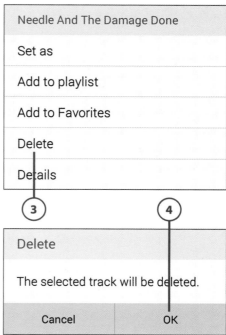

Delete Tracks While Browsing

1. Select the Tracks, Albums, or Artists tab. As necessary, drill down to display the track list from which you want to delete songs.

2. Tap the menu icon and choose Delete.

3. Select each song that you want to delete and tap Done.

4. Tap OK to confirm the deletion(s). All selected songs are deleted from the phone.

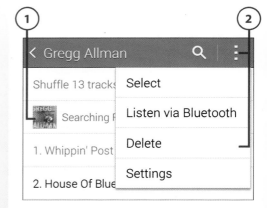

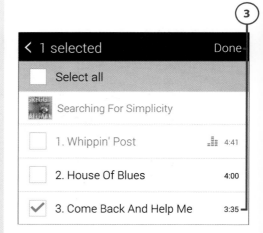

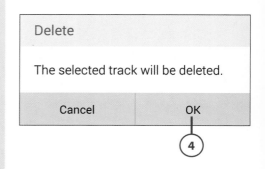

Delete an Album or Artist

1. On the main Music screen, tap the Albums or Artists tab (depending on what you want to delete), tap the menu icon, and choose Delete.

2. Select each album or artist that you want to delete, and tap Done.

3. Tap OK to confirm the deletion(s). All songs by the selected artists or in the selected albums are deleted from the phone.

Selected tab

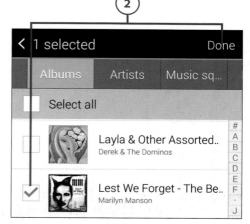

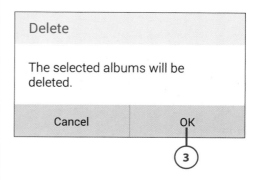

>>>*Go Further*

MORE FUN WITH MUSIC

To get the most from Music, here are some additional tips:

- The Galaxy S5's external speaker has similar fidelity to that of the inexpensive transistor radios that were commonplace in the early 1960s. For better sound, place the phone on a solid surface, such as a desk or table. For *much* better sound, connect earphones. As mentioned previously, several SoundAlive effects are available only when you use earphones.

- Music can also be run with the phone rotated. A subset of playback controls is presented, similar to those available to you in the Notification panel, on the lock screen, and on the Music widget (if it's installed).

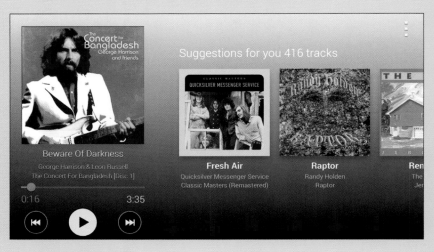

Simplified controls

- If you select a song and choose Set As from the menu, you can use it as a phone ringtone, caller ringtone, or alarm tone. See the "Create Ringtones from Songs" sidebar in Chapter 3, "Making the Phone Your Own," for instructions.

- Although it's far from a core function, you can use the Group Play app to share music with nearby friends—enabling the members' phones to act as stereo speakers.

- Be sure to explore Settings—tap the menu icon and choose Settings. For example, Tabs enables you to control the tabs that appear above the Music lists; Music Auto Off ends playback after a time interval (like a sleep timer); and Smart Volume automatically adjusts all songs to use the same playback volume. If your hearing is subpar or differs between ears, you can enable Adapt Sound to improve music playback when you're listening with earphones or a Bluetooth headset. To set up Adapt Sound, see the "Personalize Call Sound" sidebar in Chapter 4, "Placing and Receiving Calls."

>>>Go Further
STREAMING MUSIC FROM PANDORA AND SPOTIFY

In addition to playing songs that are stored on your phone, some apps can *stream* music to the phone from the Internet or your computer. (Streamed music resides on a distant server, not on your phone.) With the appropriate Android apps, you can listen to music transmitted to your phone over 4G, Wi-Fi, or Bluetooth.

Pandora Internet Radio is a popular Internet-based music streaming service. You define favorite *stations* by selecting from presets (such as Blues or Southern Rock), or you can create more specific stations based on artists, groups, or particular songs. Pandora sets the content for each station according to your specifications, and adds songs and groups that it considers similar—based on user ratings. To download Pandora, launch Play Store, tap the search icon, and type **Pandora**. Select the *Pandora Internet Radio* entry.

Another streaming service called Spotify does an exceptional job of helping satisfy more specific listening requirements. For instance, you can instruct it to play only tracks from a particular album, artist, or playlist—albeit in shuffle mode only. That is, you can't dictate the order in which the songs play or pick a particular song. Still, if your interest is in hearing *specific* albums or artists (rather than expanding your musical horizons with *similar* songs and artists), Spotify will fill the bill.

Spotify

Pandora

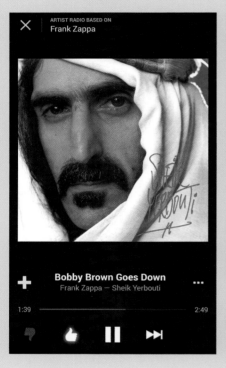

In this chapter, you learn to use the phone's cameras to shoot, edit, share, and manage photos of yourself and other subjects. Topics include the following:

→ Using the front and rear cameras to shoot self-portraits and photos of other subjects

→ Viewing, managing, and sharing the current photo

→ Viewing stored photos in Gallery

→ Using Photo Studio to edit your shots

→ Generating a slideshow from selected folders or photos

Shooting, Editing, and Sharing Photos

If you keep your phone handy, there's no excuse for missing an unexpected photo opportunity. Using the built-in cameras on your Galaxy S5, you can easily shoot posed and candid high-resolution photos of friends, family, yourself, and anything else that catches your eye.

Setting a Storage Location for Photos and Videos

If you've added a memory card to the phone, be sure to set the Storage setting to Memory Card (as explained in "Using the Settings Palette," later in this chapter).

Shooting Photos

You can shoot photos of subjects in front of you using the 16MP (*megapixel*) rear camera or take self-portraits with the 2MP front camera.

Shoot Self-Portraits with the Front Camera

Use the front camera to take pictures of yourself—or yourself and a friend or two. Note that you can't use the flash or zoom in this mode.

1. From the Home screen, launch Camera by tapping its shortcut (if you haven't removed it) or by tapping Apps, Camera.

Other Launch Options

You can launch Camera from the lock screen by sliding the Camera icon upward (if it's present). Of course, launch speed is more critical when photographing others than when taking a self-portrait. For instructions on configuring the lock screen in this manner, see "Setting Lock Screen Options" in Chapter 18, "Securing the Phone."

You can also launch Camera from within Gallery by tapping the Camera toolbar icon.

Lock screen icon

2. Determine whether the rear or front camera is active. If the rear camera is active, change to the front camera by tapping the Switch Camera icon.

3. *Optional:* Review or adjust the camera settings that will be used for the shot by tapping the Settings icon. Make any desired changes in the vertically scrolling palette, and then dismiss it by tapping the Settings icon again, tapping elsewhere on the screen, or pressing the Back key. For additional information about Settings, see "Changing the Camera Settings," later in this section.

Shortcut Icons

As described later in "Changing the Camera Settings," you can customize the Camera toolbar by adding shortcuts to frequently used settings. You can tap a shortcut icon rather than opening Settings.

4. *Optional:* Tap the Mode button to set a shooting mode, such as Beauty Face. The default setting is Auto. The current mode is displayed near the top of the viewfinder screen. To learn more about modes, see "Selecting a Shooting Mode" later in this chapter.

Adjust the Mode

Some modes, such as Beauty Face, can be adjusted prior to taking the shot.

5. When you're ready to take the picture, tap the Camera button. (The Volume key can also be used as a shutter button.)

Shortcuts   Adjust the mode

Beauty face

Most recent photo   Video

Where's the Photo?

To review all photos taken with the cameras, launch the Gallery app, select Album view, and open the Camera folder. (If you have an add-in memory card, there may be *two* Camera folders.) To go straight from the Camera app to the most recent photo you've taken, tap its thumbnail in the lower-left corner of the viewfinder screen.

Shoot Photos with the Rear Camera

Of course, most of the photos you'll shoot with the Galaxy S5 will be of other people and subjects. Shooting photos of others is similar to shooting self-portraits, but it uses the higher-resolution rear camera and has many additional options. Note that virtually every step in the following task is optional, and you can perform Steps 2–5 in any order that's convenient.

1. Launch the Camera app and determine whether the rear or front camera is active. If the front camera is active, switch to the rear camera by tapping the Switch Camera icon.

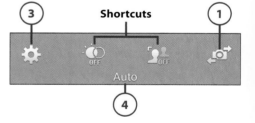

Shortcuts

Portrait or Landscape

Whether you use the front or rear camera, you can take any photo in *portrait* (right-side up) or *land-scape* (sideways) mode. To shoot in landscape mode, turn the phone sideways.

2. *Optional:* Frame your subject by zooming in or out. (The Galaxy S5 has a digital zoom.) Touch the view-finder screen with two fingers and spread them apart to zoom in or pinch them together to zoom out.

3. *Optional:* To review or adjust the camera settings that will be used for the shot, tap the Settings icon. Make any desired changes in the vertically scrolling palette, and then dismiss it by tapping the Settings icon again, tapping elsewhere on the screen, or pressing the Back key. For additional information about Settings, see "Changing the Camera Settings" later in this chapter.

Shortcut Icons

As described later in "Changing the Camera Settings," you can customize the Camera toolbar by adding shortcuts to frequently used settings. You can tap a shortcut icon rather than opening Settings.

4. *Optional:* Tap the Mode button at the bottom of the screen to set a shooting mode, such as Beauty Face, Panorama, or Shot & More. The default setting is Auto. The currently selected mode is displayed near the top of the viewfinder screen. To learn more about modes, see "Selecting a Shooting Mode," later in this chapter.

5. *Optional:* To set the focus to a particular area, tap that spot on the viewfinder screen. The focus rectangle turns green when the lighting and focus are sufficient to snap the photo.

6. When you're ready to take the picture, tap the Camera button. (The Volume key can also be used as a shutter button.)

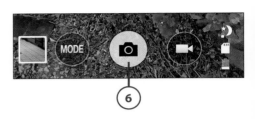

Avoid Odd Angles for Faces

When shooting portraits, you can avoid misshapen faces by holding the camera at the same angle as that of your subject. If your results are subpar, try another shot while ensuring that the phone isn't tilted—even a little.

Changing the Camera Settings

Before taking a photo, you can apply optional settings to enable or disable the flash and adjust the exposure, resolution, ISO, and so on. Note that some settings are available only for the rear-facing camera, others only for self-portraits, and still others apply only to video recordings. Also, certain automated settings can interact with and prevent you from altering manual settings. For example, when Picture Stabilization is enabled, you cannot set ISO.

You can change settings in three places: the shortcuts, the Settings palette, and by selecting a shooting mode.

Configure and Use the Shortcuts

The *shortcuts* are user-selected icons that appear at the top of the viewfinder screen between the ever-present Settings and Switch Camera icons. You can tap them to make the settings adjustments that they represent without opening the Settings palette. You can replace the default shortcuts (HDR and Selective Focus) with up to three shortcuts of your choosing.

1. Tap the Settings icon to open the Settings palette.

2. In the Settings palette, press and hold the icon that you want to use as a shortcut, and drag it into the shortcuts. If you currently have fewer than three shortcuts, you can drag it into any position. If you already have three short-cuts, drag it onto the shortcut that you want to replace.

Removing Shortcuts

You can remove a shortcut by long-pressing it, and—when the Settings palette appears—drag-ging the shortcut into the palette.

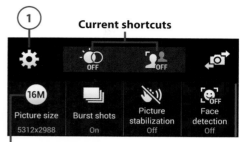

Current shortcuts

Settings palette (top row)

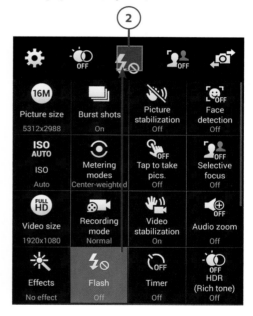

Display-Only Icons

In the lower-right corner of the screen, one or more settings icons may be dis-played, such as the current Flash setting and a Storage icon (indicating that the shot will be saved to an installed memory card). Settings icons in this area are for informational purposes only; you can't interact with them.

Current settings

Using the Settings Palette

To modify most settings, you must first open the Settings palette by tapping the Settings icon. Here's what the photo-related settings do (see "Recording Videos with the Phone" in Chapter 14, "Watching and Creating Videos," for information about the video-related settings):

Settings icon ———

- *Picture Size.* To shoot at the camera's highest resolution, select 16M: 5312×2988 (16:9). If you're running out of storage space or intend to share the photo on the Web or in email, you can select a lower resolution.

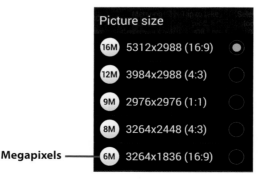

Alter the Resolution After the Shot
Using almost any image-editing program, you can reduce the resolution *after* shooting the photo.

- *Burst Shots.* When enabled, you can quickly take up to 30 shots by hold-ing down the Camera button or Volume key. Burst Shot photos are stored in Device memory, regardless of your Storage setting.

- *Picture Stabilization.* This anti-shake setting adjusts shots for unintended blur caused by camera movement.

- *Face Detection.* Enable Face Detection when you want the camera to search for a face in the shot and optimize the focus for the face.

- *ISO.* The ISO setting is for film speed or sensitivity to light. You can use a lower ISO for shots taken on a bright, sunny day and use a higher ISO for dimly lit shots or ones taken in dark settings. Options include Auto (allows the camera to set the ISO), 100, 200, 400, and 800.

- *Metering Modes.* Specify the method used to perform light metering: Center-Weighted, Matrix, or Spot.

- *Tap to Take Pics.* When enabled, you can tap anywhere on the screen to take a picture.

- *Selective Focus.* In general, everything is in sharp focus in photos taken with a fixed-lens digital phone or camera. When Selective Focus is enabled, Camera simulates an effect similar to that of focusing a 35mm camera lens. That is, a nearby object on which you're focusing (less than 1.5 feet away) is in sharp focus, and background objects are out of focus or blurred.

- *Effects.* Select an effect that will be applied as you frame and take the photo. Tap Manage Effects to specify the effects that will be included in the scrolling list. Tap the Download icon to acquire additional effects from Samsung Apps. Select No Effect to cancel the selected effect. (You can't apply an effect when shooting in HDR mode.)

Oil Pastel effect

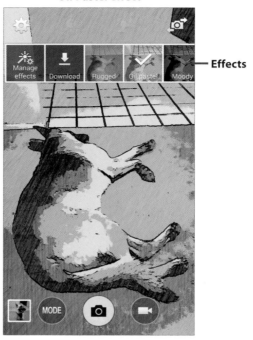

—— **Effects**

- *Flash*. Tap Flash repeatedly to cycle through its three states: On, Off, and Auto. When set to Auto, the camera fires the flash when current lighting dictates that it's needed. To avoid blinding you, Flash is automatically disabled when you're taking self-portraits.

- *Timer*. To instruct the camera to snap the upcoming picture after a preset delay, select a 2-, 5-, or 10-second delay.

Timer Shots

With a 35mm camera, you'd use its timer to give yourself a few seconds to dash into a photo. With your Galaxy S5, however, using the timer assumes that you have some way to make the phone stand on its own. Prop it up or mount it in a tripod designed for smartphones.

- *HDR (Rich Tone)*. Takes photos in *High Dynamic Range (HDR)* mode, increasing the amount of detail. When shooting in HDR mode, some other settings—Effects, for example—cannot be enabled.

- *Location Tags.* When enabled, the photo file's metadata contains information that shows where the shot was taken, based on the GPS.

- *Save as Flipped.* This setting is available only when shooting a self-portrait with the front-facing camera. Enable it to automatically flip each shot horizontally.

- *Storage.* Specify where photos are stored as they're shot: *Device* (internal memory) or *Memory Card* (add-in memory card). If Camera detects a need for speedier storage (when shooting Burst Shots, for example), Device is automatically used.

- *Review Pics/Videos.* When set to On, each new photo immediately opens in Gallery, enabling you to examine, delete, or edit it. (To *manually* review the most recent camera pic, tap the thumbnail in the lower-left corner of the screen.)

- *Remote Viewfinder.* When enabled, you can use the viewfinder of a compatible device that's connected via Wi-Fi Direct to take pictures.

- *White Balance.* To adjust shots for current lighting "temperature" and how white will be displayed, select Auto (allow the camera to determine the best setting), Daylight, Cloudy, Incandescent, or Fluorescent.

- *Exposure Value.* Drag the Exposure value slider to the right to adjust for a dark scene or to the left for an overly bright scene.

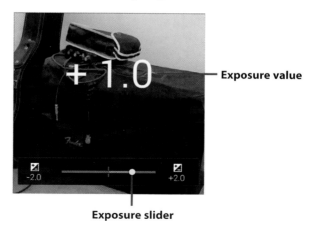

Exposure value

Exposure slider

- *Guide Lines.* When enabled, white guidelines divide the screen into a 3×3 grid to make it easier to center and frame the subject matter.

- *Voice Control.* When enabled, you can optionally use voice commands (Smile, Cheese, Capture, or Shoot) to snap photos.

- *Help.* View elementary Help information about using Camera to take pictures and record videos.

- *Reset.* Select this option and tap OK to reset all settings in the Settings palette to their default values. Remove the check mark if you want to leave modified shortcuts intact.

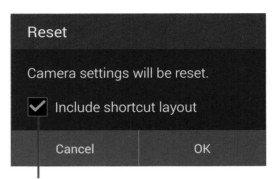

Restore default shortcuts

Selecting a Shooting Mode

When you're in a rush—but not *that* much of a rush—you can select a shooting mode that automatically specifies a combination of camera settings or enables a special feature to use for the upcoming shot(s). Tap the Mode button and select one of these options:

Shooting modes

- *Auto.* This default mode snaps a single normal photo.

- *Beauty Face.* Smooths the subject's facial features, reducing simple wrinkles, hiding pores and small blemishes, and so on. (People might accuse you of having these shots professionally retouched.) Tap the Beauty Face icon on the right edge of the screen to specify the amount of smoothing.

- *Shot & More.* The camera rapidly takes eight shots in portrait or landscape orientation. (Zooming isn't allowed.) After taking the photo, you can immediately apply one of five modes or do so when it's opened for editing. See the "Using Shot & More" sidebar for an explanation of its modes.

- *Panorama.* Takes multiple shots as you pan across a scene and stitches them together into a single photo. Tap the Camera button to start the shot, slowly pan the camera, and then tap the Stop button to conclude the process. When viewed in Gallery, you can optionally tap the Play icon to pan slowly across the entire scene.

Panorama

Play

- *Virtual Tour.* By automatically taking multiple pictures as you walk around and follow the onscreen turn directions (left, straight, right), this mode creates a "virtual tour" video that's similar to what you see in online advertisements for homes.

- *Dual Camera.* Simultaneously activates both cameras when shooting photos or videos, enabling you to achieve a picture-in-picture effect. To select an effect for the inset picture, such as Cubism, Instant Pic, or Heart Shape, tap the greater than (>) symbol on the viewfinder's left edge. Either the rear or front camera can be dominant when using this mode.

- *Download.* Links to a Samsung Apps page where you can download additional Camera modes—including some that came with the Galaxy S 4, such as Animated Photo and Sound & Shot.

Downloadable modes

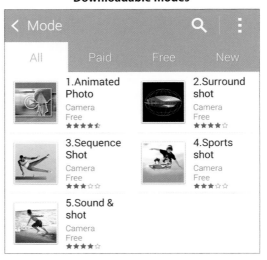

Reset the Shooting Mode

Be sure to always check the onscreen mode indicator before you take the next shot. The most recent shooting mode is sometimes retained. Other settings may also be retained and should be reset as needed.

>>>Go Further
USING SHOT & MORE

Immediately after taking a photo in Shot & More mode, a mode-selection arc appears. Modes appropriate to the shot are highlighted; ineligible ones are grayed out. Select a mode by tapping its button, or you can wait until you're reviewing the photo in Gallery. Shot & More images are identified in Gallery by a star icon in the upper-left corner. To apply a mode to the shot, tap the Edit icon.

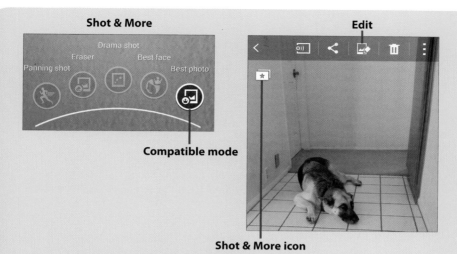

Shot & More

Edit

Compatible mode

Shot & More icon

The following modes are supported:

- *Panning Shot*. Enables you to simulate action by selecting the subject and blurring the background.

- *Eraser*. Creates a composite photo that eliminates any person, animal, or object that wandered into the shot.

- *Drama Shot*. Combines multiple shots of a moving person or object into a single photo. Tap thumbnails of the images that you want to include, and tap the disk icon to store the composite photo in the Studio folder. Drama Shot works best when the subject moves *through* the shot—from one side of the frame to the other—rather than toward or away from you.

- *Best Face*. Enables you to pick the best expression for each person in a group and then merge them into a single shot. When editing the shot, the camera identifies each face by surrounding it with a rectangle. One person at a time, tap the individual's selection rectangle, review their facial expression thumbnails, and tap the one you like best. Repeat this process for each additional person in the photo, and then tap the disk icon to save the composite photo.

- *Best Photo*. Asks you to pick the shots you want to keep. The photo judged by Camera to be the best is marked with a crown. Review the shots, tap thumbnails of photos you want to save, and tap the disk icon. Selected photos are stored in the Studio folder, while the editable original remains in the Camera folder.

Reviewing Photos

After taking a photograph, you can immediately examine and perform various actions on it, such as sharing, deleting, or renaming the shot. Read about additional options when viewing *any* stored photo or video in "Using Gallery to View and Edit Photos," later in this chapter.

Automatic Review

If you find that you typically review each photo before taking the next one, you can automate the switch to Gallery. In Camera, tap the Settings icon and enable Review Pics/Videos.

1. To review the most recent shot in Gallery, tap the photo's thumbnail on the viewfinder screen.

2. In Gallery, if the toolbar isn't visible across the top of the screen, you can make it appear by tapping anywhere onscreen. From left to right, tapping icons enables you to do the following:

   - Select a different folder to open.

   - Use screen mirroring to share the image with a compatible device.

   - Share the image using a variety of methods, such as sending by Email, enclosing in a multimedia message, or posting to Facebook.

   - Edit the photo with Photo Studio.

   - Delete the photo.

   - Open Gallery's menu.

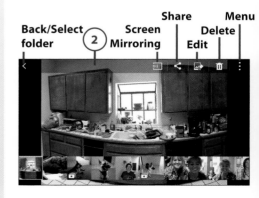

3. While examining the photo, you can also do the following:

- Review the photo in portrait or landscape orientation by rotating the phone.

- Zoom in or out by double-tapping the photo, spreading your fingers apart, or pinching your fingers together.

- View a different image by tapping a thumbnail at the bottom of the screen or swiping horizontally across the screen.

- Tap the menu icon and choose commands to perform other operations on the photo, such as rename, rotate, crop, or use it as wallpaper (Set As).

4. When you're ready to return to Camera, press the Back key. (If you're on a Gallery screen that has a camera icon in the toolbar, you can tap the icon to return to Camera.)

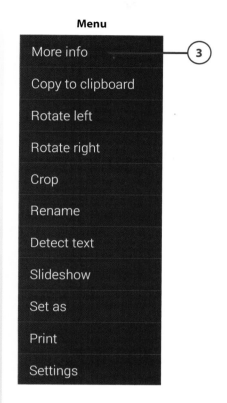

Menu

More info ————(3)

Copy to clipboard

Rotate left

Rotate right

Crop

Rename

Detect text

Slideshow

Set as

Print

Settings

Using Gallery to View and Edit Photos

All photos and videos stored on your phone—regardless of whether you took them with Camera—can be viewed, edited, and managed in the Gallery app.

1. From the Home screen, launch Gallery by tapping Apps, Gallery.

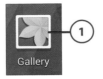

2. *Optional:* Tap the icon in the upper-left corner and choose a view that makes it easy for you to find the images you want to examine, edit, share, or delete. By default, your most recent view is used. Choose Album to work with images arranged in folders or choose Time to see them organized by when the images were taken or created. This example uses Album view. (To learn more about views, see the "Choosing a Gallery View" sidebar later in this chapter.)

A Time View Trick

You can change the size of thumbnails in Time view by spreading your fingers apart or pinching them together.

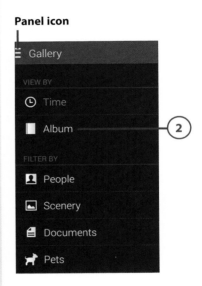

3. On the main Album view screen, tap the album/folder that holds the pictures you want to view. The Camera folder, for example, contains photos you've taken with the phone's cameras. (Note that *all* folders that contain photos or videos are automatically listed in Gallery, regardless of the files' sources or whether they're in device memory or on an add-in memory card.)

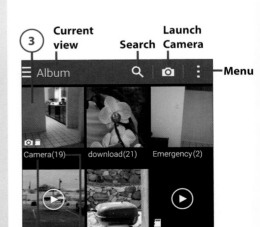

4. Thumbnails of the photos or videos contained in the folder appear. Tap a thumbnail to view its photo.

Pop-Out Folder List

To enable you to quickly change folders without having to tap the Back icon or press the Back key, a pop-out scrolling list of image folders can optionally be displayed on the left side of the screen. Swipe in from the left edge to reveal the folder list; swipe back to the left to dismiss it.

Back

4

Selected folder

4

Pop-out folder list

5. You can view photos in portrait or landscape mode by rotating the phone. (Note that you must have Settings, Display, Screen Rotation enabled.)

Portrait

Landscape

6. You can change the magnification by doing any of the following:

- Double-tap the image to double the current magnification. Repeat to shrink it to its previous size.

- Touch the screen and pinch your fingers together (zoom out) or spread them apart (zoom in).

7. To share the current photo via Email, Messaging, Facebook, or another means, tap the Share Via icon and choose a sharing method from the scrolling palette. Options vary according to your installed apps, registered accounts, and carrier, but typically include the following:

Open other folders

Selected thumbnail

- *Add to Dropbox, Drive.* Upload the photo to one of your cloud accounts.

- *Bluetooth.* To transmit the photo to a Bluetooth-paired device (such as an iMac or a Bluetooth-equipped laptop), tap the Bluetooth icon and then tap the destination in the list of paired devices. See "Transferring Files Using Bluetooth" in Chapter 16, "Transferring and Sharing Files," for instructions.

- *Email, Gmail.* Send the image file as an email attachment using one of your email accounts or Gmail. See "Emailing Files" in Chapter 16 for instructions.

- *Flipboard.* Post the photo as a status update to your Facebook, Twitter, or similar account using the Flipboard app (see Chapter 10, "Installing and Using Applications").

- *Google+, Twitter, Facebook.* Post the photo as a status update to your account.

- *Memo.* Create a new memo that includes the photo.

- *Messages, Messaging+, Hangouts.* Transmit the photo as part of a multimedia message. See "Composing a Multimedia Message (MMS)" in Chapter 9, "Messaging," for instructions.

- *Picasa.* Upload the photo to Picasa Web Albums (associated with your Google account). To view the uploaded photo, visit https://picasaweb.google.com.

- *Wi-Fi Direct.* Send the photo to another cell phone within range of yours that supports Wi-Fi Direct. See "Transferring Files Between Phones" in Chapter 16 for information on using Wi-Fi Direct.

8. To delete the photo, tap the Delete icon. Tap OK in the confirmation dialog box.

9. To launch the Camera app to shoot a photo or video, tap the Camera icon.

10. Tap the menu icon to see the following additional options:

   - *Edit.* Open the image for editing in Photo Studio, an image editor that's integrated with Gallery. See "Image-Editing with Photo Studio," later in this chapter, for instructions.

   - *More Info.* Tap the Edit icon to change or set categories and tags. Tap Details to view the image's title, dimensions, file size, storage location, and other properties.

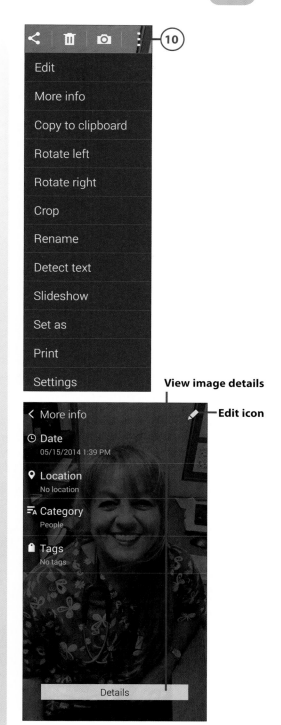

View image details

Edit icon

- *Copy to Clipboard.* Copy the image so you can paste it elsewhere—into an email message, for instance.

- *Rotate Left, Rotate Right.* Rotate the image 90° in the specified direction.

- *Crop.* By dragging the selection rectangle and its handles, specify the portion of the image that you want to retain and tap Done. The cropped image is saved *in addition* to the original image—not as a replacement for it.

- *Rename.* Change the default name assigned to the photo to something meaningful. In the Rename dialog box, enter a new filename and tap OK.

- *Detect Text.* If the photo contains a clear shot of some text, this command attempts to extract the text. Although there's no option to save the text, you can use various sharing methods (such as Email or Gmail) to send the text to yourself or others.

- *Slideshow.* Generate a slideshow from all images in the current folder, selected folders, or selected images. See "Running a Slideshow," later in this chapter, for instructions.

- *Set As.* Use the photo as a person's Contacts image, the Home screen wallpaper, the Lock screen wallpaper, or both types of wallpaper.

- *Print.* Print the photo on a compatible wireless printer.

- *Settings.* Open Google/Gmail Settings in which you can enable/disable tagging in your photos and select Filter options.

Crop selection

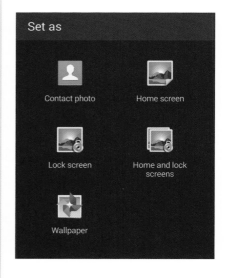

11. To view additional images, do one of the following:

- *Images in the current folder.* Swipe the screen to the left or right. As an alternative, you can tap the thumbnail of the specific image that you want to view. (If the thumbnails aren't visible, tap the current image once to reveal them.)

- *Images in a different folder.* Press the Back key or tap the Back icon repeatedly until the main screen appears, and then go to Step 3.

Back

Selected thumbnail

>>>*Go Further*
CHOOSING A GALLERY VIEW

Time and Album are the main Gallery views. Choose Time to arrange images by date. Album organizes images by folder, based on the images' source or use. For instance, Camera contains photos taken with the phone, Download holds images that you've transferred to the phone, and Studio has photos that you've edited with Studio. The number in parentheses shows the number of files in the folder.

Finally, you can choose a Filter By option to restrict images to those of a type, such as pets or people. Note, however, that image classification is based on assigned *categories*. Although I have dozens of dog photos on my S5, only a small number—those downloaded from my Picasa and Facebook accounts—appear when filtering by Pets. To assign categories to a selected photo, tap the menu icon and choose More Info, tap the Edit icon, tap the + (plus) icon to the right of Category, select one or more categories and tap OK, and then tap Done.

>>>*Go Further*
FOLDER AND IMAGE SELECTION

In addition to operating on one folder or photo at a time, you can apply some commands to multiple selected folders or images.

- *Folder-selection screen (Album view)*. You can delete an entire folder or transmit all of its files with a single command. Firmly press the folder and release; a green check mark appears on the folder to show it's selected. Then tap the Share Via or Delete icon. If you want to transmit or delete multiple folders, tap to select the additional folders before tapping a command icon. (To simultaneously select all folders, tap the Selection menu and choose Select All.) The Share Via or Delete command is performed on all selected folders. You can also tap the menu icon and choose Slideshow to create a slideshow based on only images in the selected folder(s)—or choose Studio, Collage Studio to create a collage from the photos.

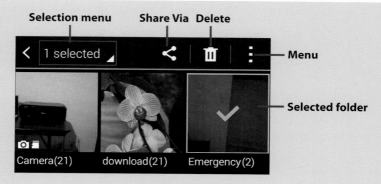

Selection menu   Share Via Delete

Menu

Selected folder

Camera(21)   download(21)   Emergency(2)

Folder-selection screen (Album view)

- *Image-selection screen.* Similarly, after opening a folder (or with Time view selected), you can select one or more files on which to perform a command. Firmly press and release an image thumbnail to select it; a green check mark appears on the image to show it's selected. To select additional images, tap their thumbnails or choose Select All from the Selection menu. Then tap the Share Via or Delete icon.

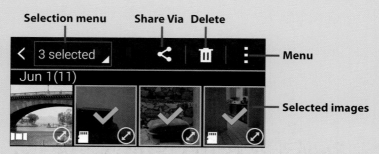

Selection menu   Share Via Delete

Menu

Jun 1(11)

Selected images

Image-selection screen (Time view)

Different Options for Different Image Sources

Not all actions can be performed on every folder. For example, Picasa and Facebook images can be shared, downloaded, or used to generate slideshows, but you can't delete them.

Image-Editing with Photo Studio

If you don't need the feature set of a dedicated Mac or PC image-editing program, you can use Photo Studio (a Samsung tool that's integrated with Gallery) to perform essential edits on any image stored on your phone. Note the following important tidbits while using Photo Studio:

- You can reverse the most recent edit by tapping Undo or tap Undo repeatedly to step backward through multiple edits. To reverse an Undo, tap Redo.

- If you tap Cancel while applying an edit, changes made with the current editing tool are removed.

- You complete most edits by tapping Done. Before you tap Done, you can compare the edit's effect to the image prior to the edit by pressing and holding anywhere onscreen.

- If you tap Discard (*X*), *all* edits are discarded.

1. From within Gallery, do one of the following to open an image for editing:

   - Edit the photo you're currently viewing by opening the menu and choosing Edit.

   - Edit a photo that you've selected on an image-selection screen by opening the menu and choosing Studio, followed by Photo Studio.

Make a Photo Collage

If you select *multiple* images and then choose the Studio command, you can select Collage Studio to create a collage from the photos.

2. Tool icons are displayed above and below the photo and are explained in the following steps. If the tools aren't visible, tap anywhere onscreen to reveal them.

3. *Enhance.* Enhance is similar to Photoshop's Auto Levels command, automatically adjusting tonal values in the photo. In some instances, tapping the Enhance button will be the only adjustment you'll need to make.

2   Undo   Redo   Discard   Save   Menu

Enhance

Adjustment   Tone   Effect   Portrait   Decoration

4   **5**   **6**   **7**   **8**   **3**

4. *Adjustment.* Tap the Adjustment button to open the adjustment palette, enabling you to rotate, crop, or resize the image.

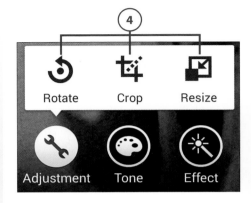

- Tap Rotate to rotate or flip the image. From left to right, the Rotate buttons enable you to rotate the image left or right in 90° increments, flip the image horizontally (left-to-right) or vertically (top-to-bottom), or split the image vertically to create a mirror image effect.

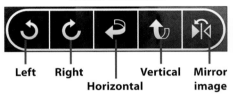

Rotate commands

Left Right Horizontal Vertical Mirror image

- Use a Crop tool to retain only a selected portion of the image, while discarding the rest. Tap the Free-form button if you don't want any restrictions on the cropping dimensions. To constrain the dimensions to a ratio, tap the 1:1, 4:3, or 16:9 button. To set the cropping area, drag the rectangle's edge and corner handles to change the size of the selection, and drag the center of the rectangle to reposition it. To create an irregular selection, select Lasso and use your fingertip to trace around the area you want to crop. In all cases, the bright area of the image will be retained; the dark areas will be discarded.

Handle Selection

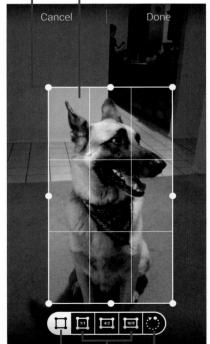

Free-form Ratios Lasso

- Tap Resize to reduce the image size. You can tap a percentage button or resize manually by dragging a corner handle. The resulting size (in pixels) is shown above the image.

5. *Tone.* Tap the Tone button to adjust the contrast, brightness, saturation, temperature, and color attributes of the image. You can apply tone adjustments to the entire image or to a selected area. After selecting a Tone option in the scrolling list, do one of the following:

   - To apply the Tone option to the entire image, drag your finger horizontally across the screen to increase or decrease the setting value.

   - To apply a Tone option to a selection, tap the Marquee button, select a Marquee tool (Free-form, Rectangle, or Oval), use your fingertip to select the area that you want to affect, and tap Done. Then drag your finger horizontally across the screen to increase or decrease the setting value.

Before and After

To determine the impact of the new setting, press and hold anywhere onscreen to see the Before image. Release to see what it will look like if you tap Done.

Drag to resize   Percentage Handle Reduced
Marquee   reduction   size

Making Multiple Adjustments

If you want to make several tone adjustments, you must tap Done after each one. Otherwise, only the last adjustment is applied to the image. (Tapping a different icon is treated the same as if you tapped Cancel.)

6. *Effect.* Tap the Effect button and select a special effect to apply from the scrolling list. To change the intensity of the effect, drag your finger horizontally across the screen. To compare the image with and without the effect, press and hold anywhere onscreen. Note that effects aren't cumulative; each one you apply replaces the current effect.

Selectively Applying an Effect

Like applying tone adjustments, effects can optionally be restricted to a selected area. Select any effect, tap the Marquee button that appears, use a Marquee tool to select the desired area, and tap Done. Then select the effect that you want to apply and, if you're satisfied, tap Done.

7. *Portrait.* Tap the Portrait button to apply facial corrections (ideally to a head shot). To use the Remove Red-Eye tool, tap each eye that you want Studio to automatically correct. Out-of-Focus enables you to blur the background, making the person stand out. You can set the intensity of the active tool by dragging your finger horizontally across the screen.

No Zooming Allowed

You can't change the magnification when applying facial corrections. If you intend to crop the photo, do so *before* using the Portrait tools.

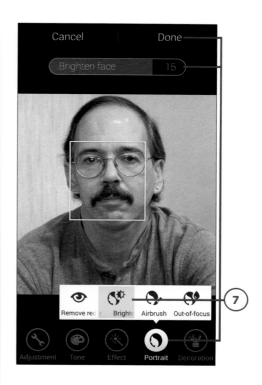

8. *Decoration.* Select options from the Decoration button to apply decorative embellishments to a photo—adding a sticker, text label, frame, or freehand drawing. Note that many of these items can be resized, moved, and rotated.

Drawing with the Pen and Eraser

Use the Pen and Eraser tools together to do freehand drawing or write on the image. If you want to correct part of the Pen's drawing, you can remove it using the Eraser.

9. When you finish editing, you can save your work. Tap Save, select a quality setting in the Save As dialog, and tap OK. The image is saved to a separate file in the Studio folder—not to the original file, which remains unaltered. The edited file is named with today's date and time. To rename the image, open it in Gallery, tap the menu icon, and choose Rename.

Running a Slideshow

You can create a slideshow with transition effects and music using all or selected images from one or multiple folders. The show plays in portrait or landscape mode, depending on the phone's orientation.

1. In Gallery, select the folder(s) or images that you want to include in the show. (If you're reviewing a photo that you just took with Camera and request a slideshow, the Camera folder is automatically used as the basis for the show.) You can use any of the following file and folder selection techniques:

-   On the main screen (in any view), select nothing to include all stored photos in the show, or select one or more folders in Album view to include all of their photos.

-   If a folder is open, make no selection to use all of its photos or select the particular photos that you want to use.

2. Tap the menu icon and choose Slideshow.

3. Set options for the show in the dialog that appears:

   • Select a transition effect to use when transitioning between slides.

   • Select a filter to apply to each slide.

   • Select a music track to accompany the show. To change the current track, tap its name. To run the show without music, set the track selection to None. Select a song in the Slideshow Music dialog box or—to use a track other than the listed ones— tap Add Music, select a song, and tap Done.

4. Tap the Start button to begin the show. To end the show, tap the screen or press the Back key.

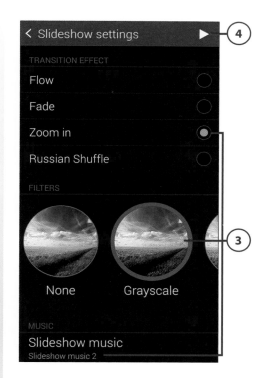

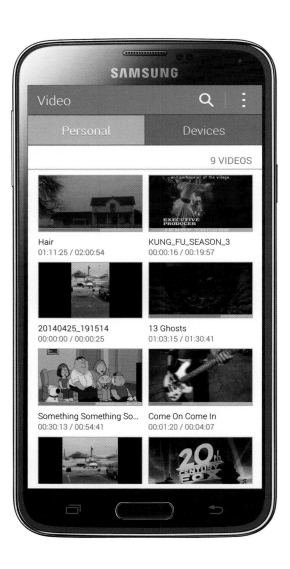

In this chapter, you find out how to use your phone to view videos from a variety of sources, as well as to shoot and share your own videos. Topics include the following:

→ Streaming video over the Internet to your phone
→ Using the Video app to play videos
→ Converting DVD videos for playback on your phone
→ Recording videos with the rear and front cameras
→ Using dedicated video chat apps

Watching and Creating Videos

With the pair of cameras on the Galaxy S5, you can record videos of yourself, others, or anything that moves. The phone's high-resolution screen makes it ideal for viewing those videos, as well as movies and TV shows that you've extracted from DVDs, rented or purchased online, or streamed to the phone.

Streaming Video to the Phone

Streaming video is sent to your phone as a stream of data that plays as it's transmitted. Unlike material that you download, streaming requires an active Internet connection and doesn't result in a file that's permanently stored on your phone. If you want to watch the same video again, you need to stream it again. You can access streaming video through dedicated apps such as YouTube or by clicking web page links.

Streaming with a Dedicated App

The two common classes of streaming video apps are subscription-based and free. Examples of subscription-based apps include Netflix, HBO Go, and Max Go (for Cinemax). To access Netflix movies, you must be a Netflix streaming subscriber. To access HBO or Cinemax, you must currently receive HBO or Cinemax through a supported satellite or cable TV provider.

After installing and launching one of these apps, you sign in with the username and password that you use to log on to www.netflix.com, www.hbogo.com, or www.maxgo.com. (In the case of subscription TV services, your username and password are generally the ones you use for your cable or satellite provider's website.) The apps are designed to remember this login information, so future launches won't require you to reenter it.

Many other apps for streaming video don't require a subscription for basic access. Examples include YouTube, MTV News, and Adult Swim.

Adult Swim app

Depending on how the streaming app was designed, when you select a video to view, it plays in a dedicated player or in Video, an app that's prein-stalled on the Galaxy S5. The controls most players provide are similar to the ones in Video. The most recent implementation of the Adult Swim player, on the other hand, has a spartan controller that focuses on the progress bar (also called a *scrubber bar*). You can tap the screen at any time to display the bar, and then tap the approximate spot on it that indicates where you want the video to continue playing. To dismiss the bar, tap the video.

Exit video

Adult Swim player

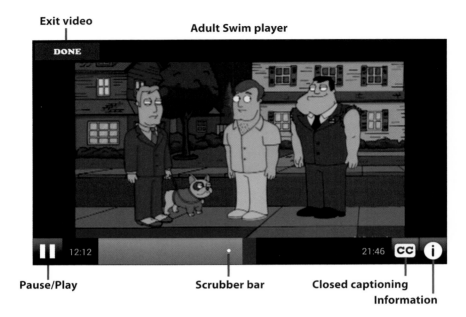

Pause/Play

Scrubber bar

Closed captioning

Information

You can also do the following:

- To exit the current video, press the Back key or tap the Done button when the scrubber bar is onscreen.

- Press and hold the Recent Apps key to assist in your search for videos, clips, games, and scheduling information.

Streaming from Web Pages

Video clips are embedded in many web pages. When viewed in the Internet or Chrome app, these clips play in a similar manner to what you'd see in a computer browser—although the controls might be different. For example, some embedded clips display only a progress bar. However, if you search carefully, you might find a Full Screen icon or a similarly worded link that enlarges the video and adds normal playback controls.

Full Screen

>>>Go Further
IT'S GONE!

The advantages of streaming are that the videos can be viewed on virtually any popular device (computer, tablet, phone, or iPod touch) that has Internet access. However, there's a downside to streaming. What happens if you want to watch a particular video or clip, but you don't have Internet access, don't want to rack up connection charges with your cellular service, or—if the unthinkable happens— the video is removed from the website or streaming provider's servers? The solution is to get a video capture application that can record a streamed video and convert it to a compatible format for playback on your computer, phone, or other device. You can start your search with Jaksta Media Recorder (available for both Mac and Windows from www.jaksta.com).

Playing Videos with the Video App

Regardless of whether a video was shot by you, downloaded, bundled with or converted from a DVD, sent by a friend, or rented or purchased online, all compatible videos stored on your phone play using the Video app.

Technically Speaking

The Video app is *not* the app that actually plays your videos; it's Video Player— a linked app, *but one that has no icon in Apps*. When you want to return from the Home screen or another app to continue viewing a paused video, press the Recent Apps key to see the list of active and recently run apps. You'll see that both Video and Video Player are listed. If you tap Video Player, playback resumes. Tapping Video takes you to the Video app launch screen rather than to your video.

1. From the Home screen, tap Apps, followed by Video.

2. To play a video that's stored on your phone, select the video by tapping its title or thumbnail.

Video Selection Assistance

To make it easier to find the video that you want to watch, your video collection can be displayed as live thumbnails, as a list, or organized by the folders in which videos are stored. Tap the menu icon, choose View As, and select an option. If you have many videos, you can specify a different sort order for the thumbnails or list by tapping the menu icon and choosing Sort By.

You can also open a video in Gallery, My Files, or another app. Doing this launches Video Player, enabling you to skip Steps 1 and 2. Tap the Play icon to play the selected movie or clip.

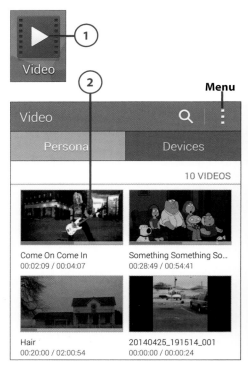

3. The controller appears and the video begins to play. Rotate the screen to the desired orientation: landscape or portrait.

4. You can tap the screen while the video is playing to display the controller and then do any of the following:

- Start/restart or pause playback by tapping the Play/Pause button.

- Tap the Video Size icon to change the way the video is sized to fit the screen. Depending on how the video was encoded and the display type for which it was intended, some sizes may stretch the image in one direction, and others may clip the image horizontally or vertically to fit. Tap the icon repeatedly to see all display options.

- Jump forward or backward in the current video by dragging the position marker to the approximate spot.

- Tap the Rewind button to jump to the beginning of the current video or, if you're at the beginning, to the previous video in the list. Press and hold the Rewind button to scroll backward through the current video; the longer you hold the button, the faster it scrolls.

- Tap the Fast Forward button to jump to the next video. Press and hold the Fast Forward button to scroll forward through the current video; the longer you hold the button, the faster it scrolls.

- Adjust playback volume by tapping the Volume icon and dragging the slider that appears. (You can also change the volume by pressing the Volume control on the left side of the phone.)

- Leave the current video by pressing the Back key twice. To exit Video, press the Home key.

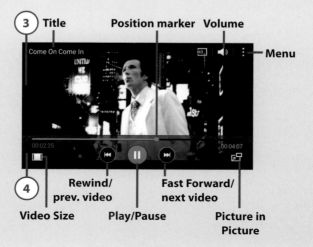

>>>*Go Further*
SMART PAUSE

If the Smart Pause system setting is enabled, you can pause the current video by turning your eyes away from the screen. When you're ready to resume, face the screen again. To enable or disable Smart Pause, open Settings and tap Motions and Gestures, Mute/Pause. Ensure that Mute/Pause is On, and then tap the Smart Pause check box. Smart Pause works best when you're not wearing glasses.

You might also want to enable the other Mute/Pause options, so you can pause a video by turning the phone over or covering the screen with your palm.

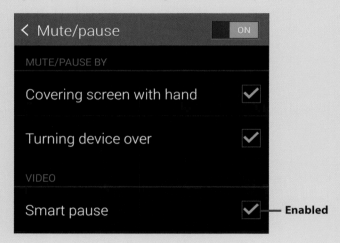

>>>*Go Further*

PICTURE IN PICTURE (POP-UP PLAY)

If you want to continue viewing a video while doing other things on your phone (reading email, for instance), tap the Picture in Picture icon. A miniature, movable version of the playing video appears on your Home screen. Use your fingertip to move the video to any part of the screen. If you switch to a different Home screen page or launch an app, the Picture in Picture video moves, too. (Note that this feature is only available for unprotected videos.)

To pause playback, tap the Picture in Picture video. Tap it again to continue, or tap the X icon to end playback. To resume playback in Video, double-tap the Picture in Picture video.

Picture in Picture —

Using the Video Menus

On Video's main screen, you can tap the menu icon and choose from these commands:

Main screen menu

Select
Delete
View as
Sort by
Auto play next

- *Select, Delete.* Delete unwanted videos that are stored on the phone. Tap the check box of each video that you want to delete, tap the Delete icon or Done, respectively, and tap OK in the confirmation dialog box that appears.

- *View As, Sort By.* See "Video Selection Assistance," earlier in this section.

- *Auto Play Next.* When enabled, this option causes Video to automatically play the next video in sequence when the current one finishes.

While a video is playing, you can press and hold the Recent Apps key (or pause the video and tap the menu icon), and then choose from these menu commands:

Playback menu

Edit
Share via
Delete
Chapter preview
Listen via Bluetooth
Subtitles (CC)
Settings
Details

- *Edit*. Launch Video Trimmer to remove extraneous material from the beginning or end of the video, or launch Video Editor to create a video by combining photos and videos. You can add themes, music, voiceovers, and special effects. (If Video Editor isn't installed, choosing this command launches Samsung Apps so you can download and install the app.)

- *Share Via*. Transmit the video to others (Messaging, Email, and Gmail) or another device (Bluetooth and Wi-Fi Direct), or post it on a social networking or chat site (YouTube, ChatON, Google+, and Facebook). Note that many videos are too large to be shared via text messaging, email, or Gmail.

- *Delete*. Delete the current video, removing it from your phone. Tap OK in the confirmation dialog box.

- *Chapter Preview*. Displays thumbnails representing breakpoints in the video. When you tap a thumbnail, the video resumes at that point.

Chapter Preview thumbnails

- *Listen Via Bluetooth*. Transmit the audio to a paired Bluetooth headset.

- *Subtitles (CC)*. If subtitles/close captioning are stored as part of the video file, you can elect to display them.

- *Settings*. Change playback settings for all videos, such as setting the brightness, switching to a mini controller, and adding an onscreen capture button to simplify the process of taking screenshots of favorite scenes.

- *Details*. Display information about the video, such as its file format, resolution, size, and storage location.

Converting DVD Videos for Playback on the Phone

You can use many programs to extract video content from DVDs for playback on the Galaxy S5 and other devices. The following task shows how to extract video using DVDFab/DVD Ripper, a DVD-to-mobile conversion utility for

Windows and Mac OS X from www.dvdfab.cn. Each extracted movie or TV show results in a single MPEG-4 (.mp4) file that you can view with the Video app.

Which Version Should I Use?

Currently, there are two versions of the DVDFab line of products: the older DVDFab 8 QT and the new DVDFab 9. Both are available as free 30-day trials. If you decide to purchase a license for DVDFab, you are entitled to use both versions. As an example of converting DVD videos for playback on your phone, the following task employs DVDFab 9.

1. Launch DVDFab on your computer.

2. Select the Ripper tab. Ensure that the correct profile to convert the video is selected. If so, go to Step 4.

Advanced Settings

3. To change profiles, click the current profile icon. In the dialog box that appears, select the Device tab, select Samsung in the scrolling list, and select the Galaxy S5 profile (or a comparable one, such as the Galaxy S 4).

4.   Insert the DVD that contains the material you want to extract. Wait for the program to scan and analyze the DVD's file structure.

5.   Select the material that you want to convert to videos for the phone by doing one of the following:

   • If this is a movie DVD, the movie is automatically selected. (Generally, the movie will have the longest Runtime of the items on the DVD.)

- If this is an *episodic* DVD (containing multiple episodes of a television show, for example), click the check box of each episode that you want to convert. The application analyzes each checked episode; each results in a separate video.

If the individual episodes aren't visible, click the Other Titles icon to view them. You can usually tell the episodes from extraneous material (such as recaps and previews) by their runtimes. In the figure, the last three entries are the episodes.

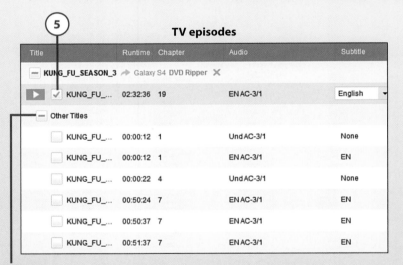

View/hide other titles

All Episodes

In the TV episodes example, the first entry combines all episodes into a single video—note its long runtime. Some DVDs provide this option; others don't. You can either convert this lengthy video or individual episodes.

Using the Preview Window

Regardless of a DVD's contents, you can preview each movie, episode, and other material (such as bloopers and deleted scenes) in the Preview window. Previewing can ensure that you've selected the correct video(s) and appropriate audio. Preview a video by moving the cursor over its entry and then clicking the green play button that appears (as shown in the previous figure, for example).

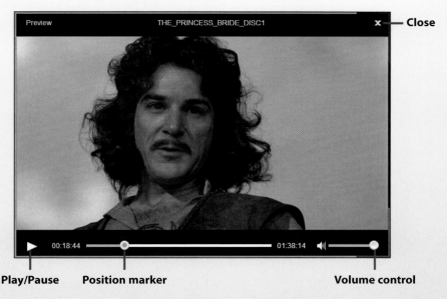

Play/Pause   **Position marker**   **Volume control**

6. For each checked item, select an audio option. Normally, the recommended option will be correct. You can preview the material in the Preview window to ensure that you've chosen normal dialogue rather than the director's commentary or a foreign language version.

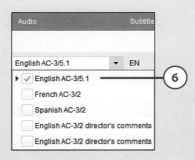

7. For each checked item, you can enable or disable subtitles (if the disk includes them). Select a subtitle language, and do one of the following:

   • To disable normal subtitles, ensure that Display Only Forced Subtitle is checked. Subtitles will appear only when an actor is momentarily speaking in a foreign language.

   • To display subtitles throughout the video, remove the check mark from Display Only Forced Subtitle.

8. Select a movie, episode, or another checked item and review the proposed conversion settings displayed under the Advanced Settings button. If they're satisfactory, skip to Step 14; otherwise, continue with Step 9.

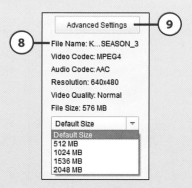

9. You can review or change the settings for resolution and other options for each item you're extracting. Select the checked video that you want to modify. Then click the Advanced Settings button (beneath the device profile) to review its settings in the window that appears.

Changes you make in Advanced Settings can apply to only the selected video or to all checked videos. This is determined by the state of the Apply to All check box. When converting TV episodes, you'll generally want to apply the same settings to all episodes.

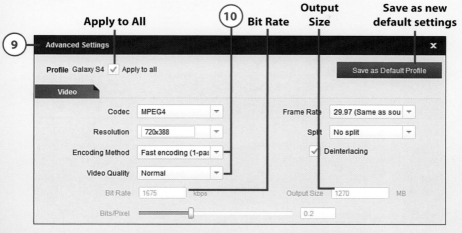

Apply to All   (10) **Bit Rate**   **Output Size**   **Save as new default settings**

9

Advanced Settings				x
Profile Galaxy S4 ✓ Apply to all			Save as Default Profile	
Video				
Codec	MPEG4 ▼	Frame Rate	29.97 (Same as sou ▼	
Resolution	720x388 ▼	Split	No split ▼	
Encoding Method	Fast encoding (1-pas ▼	✓ Deinterlacing		
Video Quality	Normal ▼			
Bit Rate	1675 kbps	Output Size	1270 MB	
Bits/Pixel	▬▬▬◯▬▬▬	0.2		

10. *Video.* You can change Encoding Method and/or Video Quality to improve the visual quality of the video or reduce the size of the video output file.

   - Encoding Method can be 1- or 2-pass. The latter improves the quality but increases the time required to perform the encoding because it makes two passes through the source video.

   - Changes in Video Quality (Low, Normal, and High Quality) are reflected in Bit Rate and Output Size. The higher the Video Quality setting, the higher the bit rate (quality) and the larger the file size. To manually set Bit Rate and Output Size, choose Customized.

Can You Tell the Difference?

As an experiment, you might try encoding the same movie at the three Video Quality settings and see if you can detect the difference. If you can't or you're willing to accept a small sacrifice in quality, smaller is better because you can fit more videos on your S5. For example, when encoding the movie shown in this example, the High Quality file size is almost twice that of the Low Quality file.

Volume

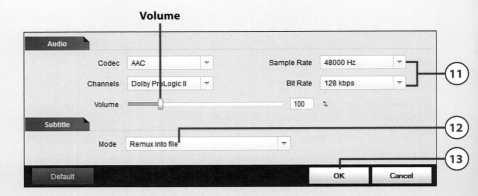

11. *Audio.* Set audio quality/clarity by choosing a Sample Rate and Bit Rate. Higher numbers yield higher-quality audio. (Bit Rate options are profile-dependent.) After conversion, if you notice that the playback audio is unusually loud or quiet, you can repeat the conversion after making an appropriate change in the Volume setting.

12. *Subtitle.* If you want the video to include subtitles, choose Direct Render to Video. This setting embeds subtitle text *into* the video rather than generating a separate subtitle file. As a result, subtitles will *always* display when the video is played. (If you disabled subtitles in Step 7, this setting is irrelevant.)

13. Click OK when you've finished reviewing the settings and are ready to close the Advanced Settings window.

14. The Save To box at the bottom of the window shows the *path* (disk\folder) where the resulting video file will be saved on your computer. To pick a different location, click the down arrow to specify a location you've previously used or click the folder icon to browse for a new location.

Previous locations

15. Convert the selected video(s) by clicking the Start button (refer to the Step 2 figure). When you finish extracting videos, transfer them to your phone using any of the file-transfer techniques described in Chapter 16, "Transferring and Sharing Files." (You'll find the video files in a Samsung folder in the location specified in Step 14.) After transferring the new files to the phone, they'll appear in the Video file list.

>>>Go Further
MORE VIDEO SOURCES

In addition to extracting videos from your personal DVD collection, there are other sources of ready-to-play videos for your Galaxy S5. You can rent or pur-chase videos in the Play Store, Play Movies and TV, Amazon Appstore, and carrier-provided online stores; some recent DVDs include a version for phones and other multimedia devices; and you can install software that can convert streaming video to MPEG-4 videos that you can play on the phone.

Recording Videos with the Phone

Using your phone's cameras, you can create movies that are suitable for posting on websites, emailing to friends, and playing on your phone or a flat-screen TV.

1. Launch Camera by doing one of the following:

   • Tap a Camera shortcut on the Home screen.

   • On the Home screen, tap Apps and then Camera.

   • On the lock screen, slide the Camera icon up (if present).

2. Decide whether to shoot the video in portrait or landscape. Rotate the phone to the proper orientation.

3. *Optional:* Switch between the rear-facing and front-facing cameras by tapping the Switch Camera icon. (Yes, you can make "selfie" videos.)

Settings shortcuts

Storage setting

Settings Shortcuts

You can change the Settings shortcuts that appear at the top of the screen to ones that you use more often, as explained in "Configure and Use the Shortcuts" in Chapter 13, "Shooting, Editing, and Sharing Photos."

When You're in a Rush

You won't always have time to leisurely set options before you begin recording. If you're in a hurry to capture something that's happening right now, you can often make do by simply launching Camera, rotating the phone to the appropriate orientation, and tapping the Video button.

4. Tap the Settings icon to check the current settings in the scrolling Settings palette. Note that most settings are for photos and have no effect when shooting a video. However, you should pay close attention to these settings:

- *Video Size.* Select a Video Size that's appropriate for the device on which the video will be played. Each set-ting specifies the horizontal by vertical dimensions (in pixels). For playback on a flat-screen TV in letterbox format (16:9), select any of the first three resolutions: 3840×2160, 1920×1080, or 1280×720, depending on whether the set or video monitor is capable of display-ing UHD/4K videos (2160), full HD (1080), or only HD (720). Select 640×480 (4:3) for playback on the Web or for video that you intend to email. Note that the Galaxy S5 can play videos at any of these resolutions.

- *Recording Mode.* Tap the Recording Mode icon and select a setting. Use Normal for a standard recording and Limit for MMS for a video that you intend to attach to a multimedia (MMS) mes-sage. For a description of the other settings, tap the *i* (Information) button.

(4)   **Settings palette**

OFF	OFF	
Picture size	Burst shots	Picture stabilization	Face detection
5312x2988	On	On	Off
ISO	Metering modes	Tap to take pics.	Selective focus
Auto	Center-weighted	Off	Off
Video size	Recording mode	Video stabilization	Audio zoom
1920x1080	Normal	On	Off
Effects	Flash	Timer	HDR (Rich tone)
No effect	Off	Off	Off
Location tags	Storage	Review pics/videos	Remote viewfinder
Off	Memory card	Off	Off
AWB White balance	Exposure value	Guide lines	Voice control
Auto	0	Off	Off
Help	Reset		

- *Video Stabilization.* Compensate for camera shake while recording. (Picture Stabilization, on the other hand, must be disabled while recording.)

- *Audio Zoom.* When enabled, zooming in on a person or object amplifies sound coming from that source.

- *Storage.* The video can be stored in the phone's internal memory (Device) or on a memory card, if one's installed.

- *White Balance, Exposure Value.* Adjust one or both of these settings to accommodate difficult lighting conditions.

When you finish making changes, dismiss the menu by tapping anywhere else onscreen, tapping the Settings icon, or pressing the Back key.

5. Set the zoom level by placing two fingers on the screen and spreading them apart or squeezing them together. Note that you can change the zoom level as you record.

6. Set the focal point for the recording by tapping the approximate spot or subject on the viewfinder screen.

7. Tap the Video button to begin recording.

Information

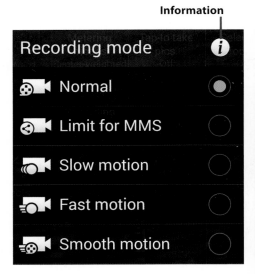

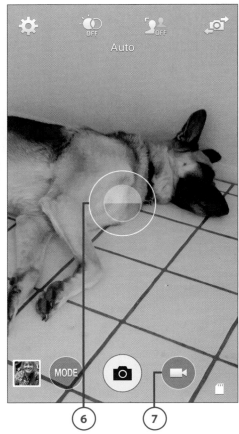

8. Temporarily pause during recording by tapping the Pause button. To resume recording, tap the button again. When you finish recording, tap the Stop button. The MPEG-4 video is automatically stored in the DCIM/Camera folder in the phone's built-in memory or on the memory card, depending on the Storage setting in Step 4.

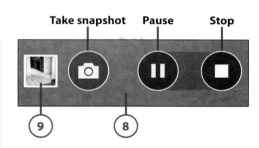

Take snapshot   Pause   Stop

Take a Quick Snapshot

While recording, you can also take photos by tapping the Camera button.

9. If you want to view the resulting video immediately, tap the thumbnail icon in the lower-left corner of the screen.

>>>Go Further

OTHER SETTINGS

Although you won't commonly use the following settings for recordings, there are situations when they can come in handy:

- With varying degrees of success, you can shoot in dim or even pitch black settings when Flash is forced On. Repeatedly tap the Flash icon to change its setting.

- You can apply an Effect (such as Grayscale or Moody) as you record. To download additional free or inexpensive camera and recording effects, tap the Download icon near the beginning of the Effects list. To remove a selected effect, tap the No Effects icon.

Selected effect

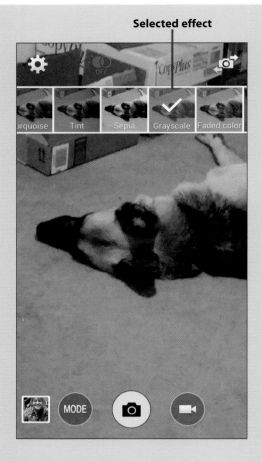

- Enable Guidelines if you have trouble framing your subject.
- When Voice Control is active, you can begin recording by saying "Record video."

Participating in Video Chats

A final video-related use for your front (and, occasionally, rear) camera is participating in *video chats*—Internet-based conversations that combine voice and video. Not only can you hear each other, but you can also *see* the other person's expressions as he/she talks, as well as what's happening nearby. Because of the large amount of data exchanged during video chats, they're best conducted over Wi-Fi or between users who have steady, high-speed connections and unlimited data plans.

To get started with one-on-one or group video chats, launch Google Play (Play Store) and search for *video chat*. As you read the app descriptions, you'll note that many require you and your friends to use the same app and be on the same platform; that is, Android, not Apple's iOS. Some apps also let you chat with people who have a desktop or tablet version of the app. Regardless, to test any of the apps (other than those that permit uninvited chat requests from strangers), you need someone willing to download and try them with you.

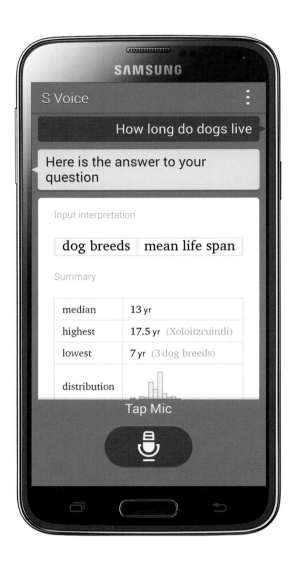

In this chapter, you learn about controlling your Galaxy S5 using voice commands. Topics include the following:

→ Using and configuring S Voice
→ Using and configuring Google/Voice Search

15

Using Voice Services

The Galaxy S5 ships with a pair of competing voice-command apps: S Voice (a Samsung app) and Google/Voice Search. Both operate in a similar fashion, enabling you to speak English-like commands and queries to control the phone and its apps, perform Web searches, and find answers to your questions.

Using S Voice

S Voice is a voice app that enables you to ask questions in natural language ("Where can I find pizza?") and command the phone ("Open Calculator"). The result may be a direct answer, a Web search, launching an app, or performing a specific command within an app.

1. Launch S Voice by tapping Apps, S Voice or by double-tapping the Home key.

Using the Home Key

If double-tapping the Home key doesn't launch S Voice, tap Apps, S Voice; tap the menu icon and choose Settings; and then enable Open Via the Home Key. On subsequent uses, double-tapping the Home key will work properly. To learn more about S Voice settings, see the "Configure S Voice" task later in this chapter.

2. The S Voice screen appears. Say your first question or command. For example, you might ask, "What's the weather like today?" to see the weather forecast for your city. S Voice displays the information it finds.

3. To ask S Voice the next question or give it a new command, tap the microphone button or say the wake-up phrase. ("Hi, Galaxy" is the default phrase.)

Help with S Voice Commands

If you want assistance with question and command phrasing, say "Help," or tap the menu icon and choose Example Commands.

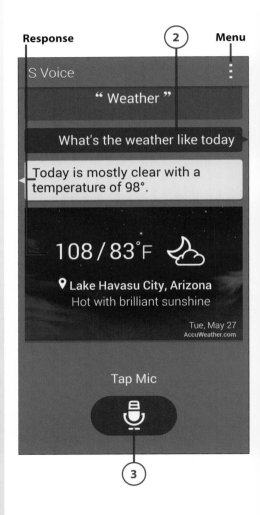

Commanding the Phone

When using S Voice to control the phone or specific apps, there are some important commands you need to know and S Voice limitations of which you should be aware. In addition to the ones presented in this section, you'll discover other general and app-specific commands and limitations as you experiment.

First, if you leave the S Voice screen, you typically lose the ability to issue further commands—until you return to S Voice. This happens, for example, when you issue an Open app command. If you need to perform specific func-tions within the app, you have to do so manually or figure out if there's a way to issue a more complex command from S Voice. Instead of saying "Open Music," you might say "Play Black Oak Arkansas" (a group) or "Play Maxwell's Silver Hammer" (a song), for instance.

Second, in some circumstances, S Voice prompts you for missing details in order to complete a command or clarify what you want. For example, if you say "Create new event Shop for trombone," S Voice asks for a time (because you've requested a new event rather than a task) and then asks whether you want to save it to Calendar.

Third, when buttons are displayed (such as Cancel and Save), you can tap or speak the button name to indicate how the current item should be handled. Alternatives, such as saying "Yes" or "No," are often acceptable, too.

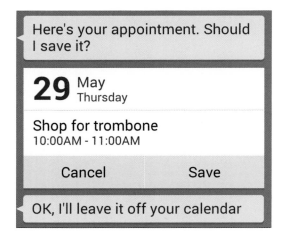

Fourth, you can back out of or halt many commands by saying "Cancel."

To get you started, review some of S Voice's supported commands by opening the menu and choosing Example Commands. Here are some others you can use:

- *Launching apps.* To open an app, you can say "run," "open," "launch," or "start," followed by the app's name. After you finish using the app, you can frequently return to S Voice by pressing the Back key repeatedly until you exit the app.

- *Controlling settings.* Sadly, there are only a few system settings that you can command. You can enable or disable Wi-Fi or Bluetooth by saying "Turn on (or off) Bluetooth," "Enable (or disable) Wi-Fi." Because Settings is an app, you can open it by saying "Open Settings." You can also change the current volume by saying "Volume up (or down)" or "Raise (lower) volume."

I Can't Find a Network Connection

If Mobile Data (in Data Usage Settings) isn't enabled when you turn off Wi-Fi, you won't be able to turn it back on with a voice command. In fact, you won't be able to use S Voice at all because it requires an active Wi-Fi or cellular connection. To resume using S Voice, manually enable Wi-Fi by tapping its Quick Setting button or open Settings, tap Data Usage, and enable Mobile Data.

- *Safer navigation.* Open the Notification panel and enable Car mode by tapping its Quick Setting button. A version of S Voice with huge text and icons launches.

- *Calculations.* Rather than launch Calculator, speak the calculation that you want to perform. Examples include "472.43 divided by 17.6," "Multiply 6 by 17.5," "Square root of 87.5," "Minus 6.5 times 8," "What is three-fourths of 17.65?," and "Calculate 15% of $84.35."

Calculation Difficulties

It can be difficult discovering acceptable phrasing for calculation commands, and many such commands can't be answered—even when S Voice shows that it understands the numbers and operators. For example, I couldn't find a way to multiply by a number less than one (such as 18 * 0.12) other than to state the decimal number as a fraction: "18 times 12 divided by 100."

- *Units of measure and currency conversions.* Examples include "How many pints in a liter?" "How many millimeters in a yard?" "How many British pounds can I get for $14?" and "Convert dollars to yen."

- *Just-for-fun commands and queries.* Try asking/saying the following: "How much wood could a woodchuck chuck if a woodchuck could chuck wood?" "Sing," "Where is Carmen Sandiego?" "What's the ultimate answer to life, the universe, and everything?" and "Tell me a joke."

What About Web Searches?

Like Voice Search (discussed later in this chapter), S Voice can perform Web searches. In fact, when it doesn't hear you clearly or can't determine what you want, it *offers* to search the Web. Interestingly, when you *do* request a search, the request is often handed off to Google Search.

Commanding Apps: Calendar

In addition to merely launching apps, you can use S Voice to issue commands to some of them. As an extended example, here are some ways that you can control Calendar.

You can give voice commands to schedule new appointments (events) or tasks. Examples of creating new tasks include: "Create new task give Jethro a bath next Sunday," "New task install vertical blinds" (when no date is provided, S Voice assumes the task's due date is today), and "Create task wash car on Saturday reminder on Friday" (adding "reminder on…" instructs Calendar to present a reminder notification on the specified day). Another way to add a reminder is to include a time in the command, such as "New task take out garbage tonight at 10:00 p.m." Although tasks don't have scheduled times (only events do), the mention of 10:00 p.m. is interpreted to mean that you want to be reminded at that time.

Scheduling appointments works in much the same way, but events contain additional components. You might say, for example, "Schedule operation at hospital for 7:00 a.m. Wednesday for 4 hours." Because it includes all essential details for a new appointment, S Voice offers to save it as-is. If it's lacking an important element (such as the time), S Voice prompts for it. When asked, you can specify *both* the time *and* date, such as "Saturday at 11:30 a.m."

To view a list of your upcoming tasks or events, you can say "Show my tasks" or "Show my appointments." Each command results in a list, but appointments are read aloud.

Deleting and Editing Tasks and Events

To delete upcoming or recent tasks and events without launching Calendar, you can say "Delete task (or appointment)." S Voice presents a list of tasks or events, asks you to specify the one to delete, and then asks you to confirm the deletion.

You can also be more specific, such as "Delete wash car." If there are multiple instances of a wash car task, S Voice lists them and asks which one to delete. You can select an item by position by saying "the second one," for example.

If you notice an error in a saved appointment or event, say "Edit appointment (or task)." S Voice asks you to select the appointment or task to edit and then prompts for the change(s).

Configure S Voice

Like other apps, you can customize the way that S Voice works.

1. In S Voice, tap the menu icon and choose Settings.

2. The Settings screen appears. Following are some of the most important S Voice settings.

3. *Open Via the Home Key.* When enabled, you can launch S Voice by double-pressing the Home key from almost anywhere on the phone.

4. *Voice Wake-up.* When Voice Wake-up is enabled and S Voice is onscreen, you can speak a phrase (such as "Hi, Galaxy") to get the app's attention; otherwise, you must tap the microphone icon. Tap this item to enable, disable, or change the wake-up command.

5. *Auto Start Speakerphone.* When this option is checked and you instruct the Phone app to place a call, Speakerphone mode is automatically enabled.

Menu

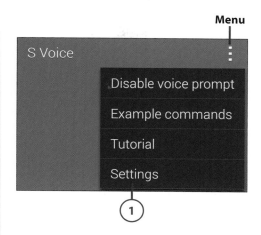

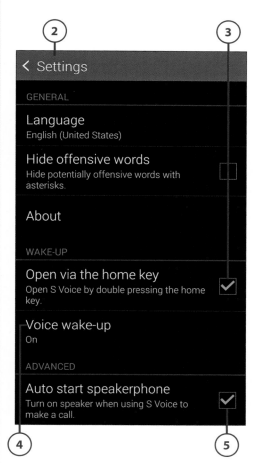

6. *Show Body of Message.* When a text message arrives, S Voice can display the message body (checked) or only the sender's name (unchecked). If the latter option is chosen, you can ask S Voice to read the hidden message text aloud.

7. *Check Missed Events, Personal Briefing.* When enabled, missed events and/or your schedule are displayed when you first launch S Voice.

8. *Home Address.* Tap this setting to record your home address, enabling S Voice to use it to generate responses to you.

9. *Log In to Facebook, Sign In to Twitter.* If you want to use S Voice to post to a Facebook or Twitter account, you must log into your account(s)—enabling S Voice to do so in later sessions. When enabled, you can say commands such as "Facebook update Has anyone seen the new Godzilla movie?" If the appropriate app isn't already installed, you'll be taken to the appropriate Google Play page to download and install it.

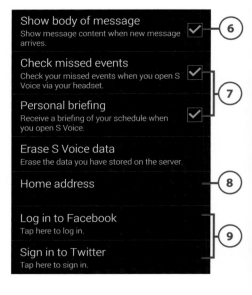

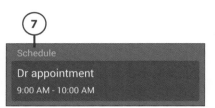

It's Not All Good

It's Only a Start

There are several immediately apparent problems with S Voice. (Many of these criticisms apply equally to Google/Voice Search.) First, commands and queries can only be issued from the voice app's screen. You can control music playback, set or check your schedule, create text messages and memos, and perform calculations, but you can't issue any commands from *within* an app—even if S Voice opens the app for you.

Second, because S Voice is designed to recognize English-like commands, there's no simple way to determine what commands will work without experimentation. You never can tell whether certain commands are impossible or you're simply phrasing them in a way that S Voice doesn't understand. For instance, if I request the song "Happy Together," S Voice ignores the song with that name that's stored on my S5 and instead attempts to play a song that it thinks is a *happy* one. (In point of fact, it failed badly, playing the saddest song I had.)

Third, S Voice is inconsistent. When I'm asked which of two appointments to delete and I say "the second one," it dutifully deletes the correct appointment. But when I ask it to play a song that's available on three albums, regardless of whether I tap one or say "the third one," it ignores me and plays the first.

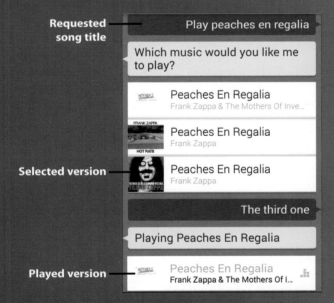

Like many compelling S5 features, I'm torn between marveling at the fact that S Voice works at all and being annoyed that it doesn't work well enough. For now, I consider it something fun to play with that will undoubtedly get better with each update—much like the improvements I've seen in the accuracy of converting voice input into text.

Using Google/Voice Search

Google, Voice Search, and Google Now are interrelated apps. As a result, you can perform several different launch actions to end up in the same place; that is, ready to issue voice commands and requests.

1. Launch Google/Voice Search by doing one of the following:

   - Tap Apps, Google or Apps, Voice Search.

   - With the Google Search widget displayed on the current Home screen, tap the widget or say "OK, Google."

2. The opening screen that appears depends on whether Google Now is enabled (see "Configuring Google/Voice Search," later in the chapter) and the launch method used in Step 1.

3. If the screen doesn't automatically request your voice input, tap the microphone icon or say the wake-up phrase ("OK, Google").

4. Speak a voice command or search request.

5. Depending on the nature of your voice input, an app, web page, or Settings screen opens (taking you to a different screen) or the result is displayed on the Google screen. If you want to issue more commands or requests, do the following:

   • If you're still on the Google screen, tap the microphone icon or say "OK, Google," and then issue your new command or request.

   • If a different app or a Settings screen is onscreen, press the Back key until you reach the Google screen, or press the Home key and start over again at Step 1.

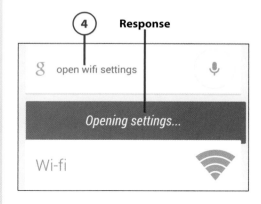

>>>*Go Further*

GOOGLE/VOICE SEARCH VERSUS S VOICE

As you experiment with Google/Voice Search, you'll see that it's *very* much like S Voice. You can issue similar commands in similar language and get similar results. Both require that you have an active Internet connection in order to function. Here are some of the ways in which the Google and Samsung utilities differ:

- In addition to being able to launch apps by saying "run, open, launch, or start *app name*," Google can open many Settings screens. Say "Open *settings name*," such as "Open Display Settings." S Voice, on the other hand, is limited to opening the Settings app.

- Google excels at opening websites when compared to S Voice's ability to do so only with very common sites. Say "Go to" or "Open," followed by the website name, such as "Open kitco dot com." (This advanced capability shouldn't come as a surprise. After all, this *is* Google's business.)

- You can dictate and send email using Google ("Email Evan Wonderful dinner tonight. Good job!"). S Voice doesn't support email.

- S Voice does a better job of handling in-app commands—primarily in Music. You can issue additional commands while a song is playing—as long as you do so from the S Voice screen. If you return to Google while a song is playing (in Google Play Music rather than Music) and issue a music-related command, Google responds with "Controlling media is not supported on this device." Google appears to be unable to issue additional commands of any sort once a target app launches.

- Google doesn't have some calculation restrictions from which S Voice suffers. In addition, an appropriate calculator frequently appears onscreen, enabling you to try similar calculations and variations. (Note that it's *essential* that you speak slowly and clearly.)

- Although Google can schedule appointments (events), it doesn't understand tasks. When you state the essential elements of an appointment (such as "Meet with Jeremy on Sunday"), Calendar launches and displays a new event containing the information that you spoke. You must manually com-plete the item by providing the remaining details and then tapping Save. Thus, although it's far from perfect, S Voice is the better choice for creating, editing, and deleting events—and the *only* choice for creating tasks.

Tip calculation assistance

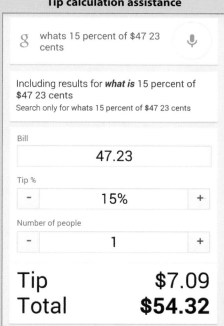

Configuring Google/Voice Search

After familiarizing yourself with the Google/Voice Search capabilities, you should review its settings.

1. On the Google, Voice Search, or Google Now screen, open the menu in the lower-right corner and choose Settings. (If you can't see the menu, you can also open it by long-pressing the Recent Apps key.)

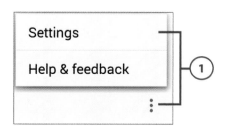

2. The Settings screen appears. Following are some of the most important Google/Voice Search settings.

3. *Google Now.* You can enable or disable Google Now by changing the position of the switch. (This setting has no bearing on the manner in which voice commands and search requests are performed.)

4. *Phone Search.* Checked items specify the types of information on your phone that will be examined when performing voice searches and commands. Generally, you'll want to leave all of these content areas checked.

5. *Voice.* These settings enable you to change the input language, specify whether Google responds audibly (Speech Output enabled) or only in text, whether it activates in response to the wake-up phrase ("OK, Google"), and whether it recognizes input from a Bluetooth headset.

6. *Accounts & Privacy.* The only setting that has a significant effect on voice commands and searches is Contact Recognition. When checked, Google uses your Contacts records to determine who you're trying to reach when calling people or creating text messages and email, for example.

7. When you're done viewing and changing settings, press the Back key or tap the Back icon.

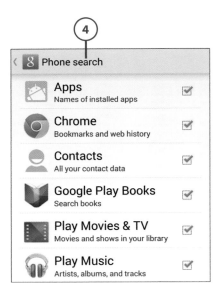

Bluetooth file sharing

This chapter explains how to transfer selected files between your phone, a computer, and other phones. Topics include the following:

→ Using Samsung Kies 3 to transfer files between phone and computer
→ Manually transferring files over a USB cable
→ Transferring files using Bluetooth
→ Emailing files to yourself
→ Using Wi-Fi Direct, S Beam, and Android Beam to transfer files between compatible phones

Transferring and Sharing Files

Although certain types of data, such as Calendar items and Contact records, can be automatically synchronized between the phone and a computer, most other file types—such as photos, videos, music, and various documents—must be manually copied from one device to another or must rely on software that isn't included with the phone. Using the techniques and tools discussed in this chapter, you'll discover many of the ways that you can transfer files between your phone and your computer, as well as between a pair of phones.

You can find instructions for synchronizing Calendar and Contacts data in Chapter 17, "Synchronizing Data."

Transferring Files over USB with Samsung Kies 3

This section shows you how to accomplish program-guided file transfers using Samsung Kies 3 (free Windows and Mac computer applications) and the USB cable, as well as perform manual USB transfers without any special software.

An Important Note for Macintosh Users

Kies 3 and Android File Transfer (the Mac utility discussed in "Manually Transferring Files over USB" in the next section) are incompatible. If you want to try manual USB transfers using Android File Transfer, you must first uninstall Kies 3.

Setup and Basic Operation

1. *First use only.* Download and install the Windows or Mac version of Samsung Kies 3 from http://www.samsung.com/us/kies/. Be sure that you download version 3 rather than an earlier version. After you complete the installation, launch the program.

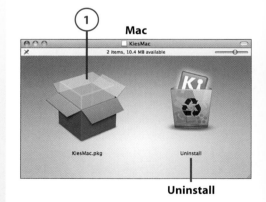

Mac

Uninstall

Uninstalling Kies 3

When you download Kies 3 for Macintosh, be sure to save the file. If it later becomes necessary to uninstall Kies 3, run the installation program again and double-click the Uninstall icon. To uninstall Kies 3 for Windows, use the appropriate control panel, such as Programs and Features (Windows 7).

2. *First run, Kies 3 for Mac:* Kies offers to scan your computer for multimedia files. Select an option and click OK. (On the Windows version, you must manually select files to add or folders to scan for media.)

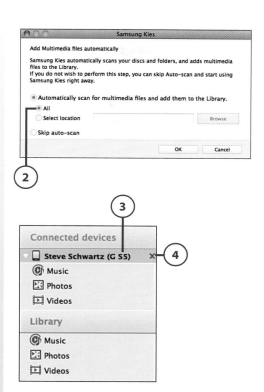

Scan Now or Selectively Add Folders

The Automatically, All option adds every trivial image, song, and video that Kies finds embedded within the operating system, applications, and games to your Kies Library—creating a lot of clutter and a hassle if you want to remove them from the Library. You might prefer to pick Select Location (to direct the scan to examine only a particular folder) or Skip Auto-Scan (to manually add important folders at your leisure with the File, Add to Library command).

3. The control panel on the left edge shows there are no connected devices. Connect the phone's USB cable to the phone and to an empty USB port on your computer. The phone should appear in the Connected Devices pane.

4. When you finish using Kies 3, click the **x** beside the phone's name in the control panel. Then quit the computer program by choosing File, Exit (Windows) or Kies, Exit (Mac). Disconnect the cable from the phone and computer.

About the Control Panel

The control panel has two main sections. The top section (displaying your phone's model name or model number) lists the various content categories that are on the phone. The Library section lists content that's stored on your computer. If you select a category (such as Music or Photos) in either section, a list of these items appears in the window's main area.

If There's No X on Your Mac…

…the control panel is currently too narrow to display it. You can adjust the panel's width by dragging its right edge to the right or left.

Copy Files

1. In the Kies 3 control panel, select the source and category of material to copy as follows:

   - Copy from phone to computer by selecting a category (Music, Photos, or Videos) in the phone's section.

   - Copy from computer to phone by selecting a category (Music, Photos, or Videos) in the Library section.

2. Select files to copy by clicking their check boxes (in List view) or thumbnails (in Thumbnail view). To select multiple thumbnails, you can Shift-click, Ctrl-click (Windows), or Command-click (Mac) items. If items are grouped in Thumbnail View, you can select entire groups by clicking grouping check boxes.

3. To perform the copy, do one of the following:

   - *Copying from phone to computer*. Click the Save to PC button above the list. In the dialog box that appears on the computer, select the computer folder into which the files will be copied, and then click the Save (Mac) or Select Folder (Windows) button.

   - *Copying from computer to phone*. Click the Transfer to Device button. (If a memory card is installed, you must choose Internal Memory or External Memory. The latter represents the memory card.)

- Select Thumbnail view and the By Folder tab when you want to quickly copy an entire folder (such as Camera) to the computer.

- *Mac only:* When you double-click a photo that's on the phone in order to view it, you can immediately save it to your computer by clicking the Save to PC button that appears.

Kies 3 (Mac)　　　　　　　　　　　　　　　**Close**

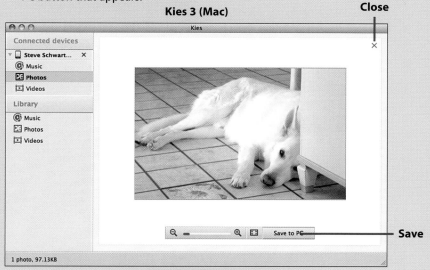

Save

Manually Transferring Files over USB

Using the USB cable provided with your phone, you can connect the phone to a PC or Mac and freely copy files in either direction. The following task temporarily turns your phone into the equivalent of a flash drive.

Mac Users and USB

If you're a Mac user, you must first download and install Android File Transfer, a free application from www.android.com/filetransfer. Note that if you've previously installed Samsung Kies 3 (see "Transferring Files over USB with Samsung Kies 3"), you *must* uninstall Kies 3. It prevents Android File Transfer from functioning properly.

Windows Users and USB

To use *any* USB file transfer method with a Windows PC, you must first install the Samsung USB drivers, as explained in "Tethering the Phone and a Computer" in Chapter 19, "Powering Other Devices."

Transfer to and from a Mac

1. Using the phone's USB cable, connect the phone and the Mac.

2. Open the Notification panel on the phone. In the Ongoing section, it should say Connected as a Media Device. If it says Connected as a Camera, tap the entry and select Media Device (MTP) in the screen that appears.

3. *First run only.* Launch the Android File Transfer program. (It should launch automatically in subsequent sessions.)

4. A window appears that lists all files on your phone. Transfer copies of files from the phone by dragging them onto the Mac's Desktop or into a folder. Transfer copies of files from the Mac by dragging them into an appropriate folder in the window.

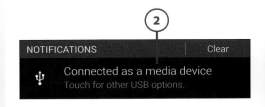

Android File Transfer

Built-in memory | **Memory card** | **Phone name**

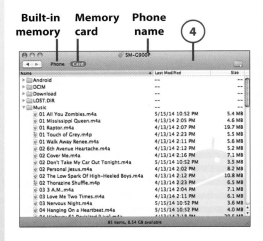

Phone or Card?

If you've installed a memory card in the phone, you can access both the built-in memory and the add-in memory card by selecting Phone or Card, respectively.

5. When you finish, disconnect the USB cable from the phone and the Mac. Android File Transfer should quit automatically.

Transferring Photos from iPhoto

When transferring photos from iPhoto (Mac) to the phone, you may find it easier if you first launch iPhoto and drag the image thumbnails onto the Desktop. Transfer *those* images to the phone, and then delete the Desktop copies when you finish.

Other Quit Options

If necessary, you can manually quit by pressing Command+Q or by choosing Android File Transfer, Quit Android File Transfer. If that fails, right-click the Android File Transfer icon in the Dock and choose Force Quit.

Transfer to and from a PC

1. If you haven't already done so, visit the Support section of Samsung's website (http://www.samsung.com/us/support/) and download the Windows USB driver for your carrier's phone. See "Tethering the Phone and a Computer" in Chapter 19 for instructions. On most phones, you can find your model number by launching Settings and tapping About Device. Note that installing this driver is a one-time process.

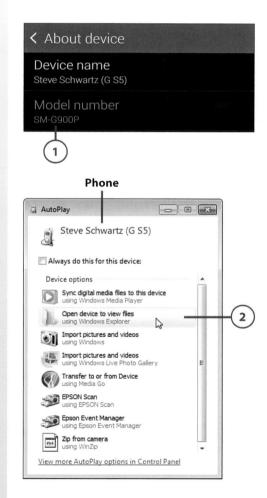

2. Using the phone's USB cable, connect the phone and the PC. After the PC recognizes the connected phone and installs the driver software (if necessary), an AutoPlay dialog box appears. Click the option to Open Device to View Files.

Connect as a Media Device or as a Camera?

Samsung recommends connecting the phone as a Media Device when transferring most types of files and as a Camera to transfer photos from phone to PC. However, my experience with Windows 7 is that it doesn't make a difference. Both AutoPlay dialog boxes offer the option to Open Device to View Files, for example.

3. A file window opens, displaying Phone and Card as "drives"
   (if you've installed a memory
   card) or only Phone (if there's no
   installed memory card). Open
   Phone to view the folders and
   files in the phone's internal memory, or open Card to see the folders and files on the memory card.

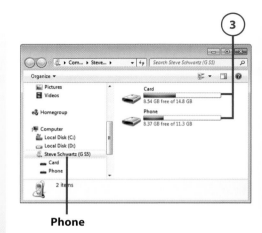

Phone

Where Are My Files?

The hardest part of performing
manual USB file transfers from
a computer to a phone is that
you're expected to know where
those files are stored on your
computer. If you have no idea,
check the Documents folder and
its subfolders first. You may find it
helpful to explore your hard drive
beforehand, making a note of the
names and locations of music,
photo, and video folders.

4. Transfer files from the phone by
   dragging them onto the Desktop
   or into a folder. Transfer files from
   the PC by dragging them into an
   appropriate folder on the phone
   or its memory card.

5. When you finish, disconnect the
   USB cable from the phone and
   the PC.

It's Not All Good

File Handling

To perform these USB transfers, you have to understand the Android filing system; that is, you need to learn where the photos, songs, and movies are stored on your phone. If you find this task unpleasant, you might prefer to use a dedicated file-transfer program that can handle the file- and folder-management chores for you.

In addition to the options discussed in this chapter, you should investigate doubleTwist, a free application available from http://doubletwist.com/ that enables you to selectively transfer or synchronize files between your Galaxy S5 and a PC or Mac. Samsung Kies 3 also provides sync capabilities.

Transferring Files Using Bluetooth

The Samsung Galaxy S5 is a Bluetooth device and can use Bluetooth to wirelessly exchange data with any Bluetooth-equipped computer, such as a Mac or some current Windows laptops.

To use Bluetooth for data transfers, the phone and computer must first be linked (known as *pairing*), as explained in the "Pairing the Phone with a Mac" sidebar at the end of this chapter.

Send Files from Computer to Phone

When the phone is paired with the computer, you can easily transmit selected files in either direction. The following tasks show how to transfer files over Bluetooth from or to a Mac.

1. From the Mac's Bluetooth menu, choose Send File from the *phone name* submenu.

Bluetooth

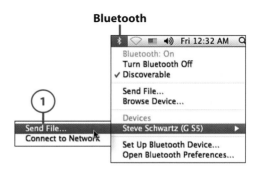

2. Select a file in the Select File to Send dialog box. (To select more than one file, hold down the Command key as you click file-names.) Click the Send button.

3. The phone receives a File Transfer request. Tap Accept to receive the file(s) on your phone.

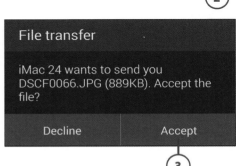

Filing the Files

Files transmitted to the phone via Bluetooth are received in the Download folder in built-in memory (Device Storage). To see the files, go to the Home screen and tap the Apps icon, followed by My Files. Then tap Device Storage, Download.

It isn't necessary to move these files from the Download folder into their normal folders. Music, Gallery, and other apps can find new files without any heroic measures on your part—regardless of where they're stored.

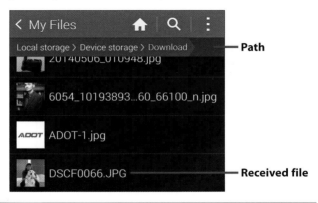

Send Files from Phone to Computer

Similarly, you can transmit files from your phone to a paired Bluetooth-equipped computer. For example, photos created with the phone's camera are convenient to send using Bluetooth. The following task shows how to send photo files from your phone to a Mac.

1. On the Home screen, tap Apps, followed by Gallery.

2. Tap the pop-out panel icon to set the view to the one in which it's easiest to find and select the pictures you want to transmit.

About Album and Time Views

In Album view, images are organized by the names of folders in which they're stored. All image folders are shown, regardless of where on the phone they're stored. The number following each folder name is the number of pictures in the folder. Album view has the advantage of enabling you to transmit an entire folder at once. In Time view, images are listed by date. It's best used for immediately selecting individual images—especially recent ones.

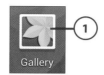

Open pop-out panel

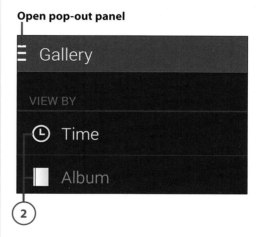

3. *Album view.* To select images, do one of the following:

   - Transmit an entire album by pressing and holding the album's thumbnail to select it. A green check mark appears. To select additional albums, tap their thumbnails.

   - Transmit only selected images within an album by first opening the album that contains the pictures you want to send to the computer. To select an image to transmit, press and hold its thumbnail. Tap the thumbnails of any additional images you want to select.

Entire album selected

Individual images selected

Using Select All

If an album contains many images and you want to transmit all or most of them, select any thumbnail, open the Selection menu, and tap Select All. Then tap the thumbnails of the photos that you *don't* want to send to remove their check marks.

Selection menu

4. *Time view.* Select the first image to transmit by pressing and holding its thumbnail. Tap the thumbnails of any additional images you want to select.

5. Tap the Share Via toolbar icon.

6. Tap Bluetooth to select it as the sharing method.

7. Tap the name of your paired computer on the Select Device screen. That device will receive the transmitted files.

8. An Incoming File Transfer dialog box appears on the Mac.

9. If only one file is being transmitted, click the Accept button. If multiple files are being transmitted, click the Accept All check box and then click Accept. The file(s) are transmitted to the Mac and stored in the default folder.

10. When the transmission finishes, close the Incoming File Transfer dialog box by clicking the red button.

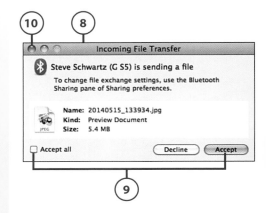

>>>Go Further

PICK YOUR OWN DESTINATION FOLDER AND ACTION

When files are sent via Bluetooth to a Mac, the folder where they're stored on the Mac is specified in Bluetooth preferences (the default is Documents). If you'd rather use a different folder, click the System Preferences icon in the Dock, and then click the Bluetooth icon. In Bluetooth preferences, click the Sharing Setup button. Select Bluetooth Sharing in the Service list, and choose Other from the Folder for Accepted Items drop-down menu. Select a new destination folder, and click the Open button. I created a folder on the Desktop called Screen Captures for this purpose.

In addition, if you get tired of responding to the Incoming File Transfer dialog box, you can specify that all incoming files are *automatically* transferred. From the When Receiving Items menu, choose Accept and Save or Accept and Open.

Emailing Files

You can also use email to move files from your phone to your computer. As long as the final size of the attachment(s) doesn't exceed the maximum allowable message size for your email account, your phone and most email systems will allow the message to be transmitted. This means that if you restrict yourself to sending photos taken with the phone's camera or songs purchased on the phone, you can deliver them to your computer by emailing them to yourself. Of course, you can also use these techniques to email your photos to friends and relatives.

Email Photos from Gallery

The most direct way to email one or more photos from your phone is to use the Gallery app. The images can be sent from any email account that you've added to the Email app.

Work Directly in Email

You can also send photos by composing a new message in Email, tapping the Attach button (the paper clip), and selecting the photo(s) you want to send.

---

1. On the Home screen, tap Apps, followed by Gallery. To select the file(s) you want to send, perform Steps 2–5 of the "Send Files from Phone to Computer" task, earlier in this chapter.

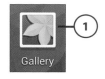

2. In the Share Via dialog box, select Email or Gmail. (If the Share Via icon isn't visible, tap the image once to reveal the toolbar.)

3. Images can optionally be resized prior to sending. Select a scaling percentage or Original (*unaltered*).

4. The file(s) are added as attachments to a new email message. Specify your own email address in the To box.

A Second Email Address

If you have another email address—one that isn't registered on your phone, enter it in the To box. If you email it from and to the *same* address, Email also receives a copy of the email in the account's Inbox—doubling the amount of data that must pass through the phone.

5. *Optional:* Add a subject and message text.

6. Tap the Send icon.

7. When your PC or Mac email program receives the message, save the photo files to any convenient location or drag them onto the Desktop.

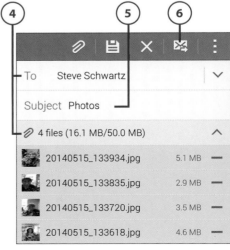

It's Not All Good

Potential Problems

Emailing photos doesn't always go as planned. Emailed photos are occasionally destroyed in the conversion process; others are sometimes delayed for hours or days, and some are never delivered. If emailing a particular photo doesn't pan out, try one of the other phone-to-computer transfer methods described in this chapter.

Email Songs from My Files

If you've purchased a song using your phone, you can listen to it on your computer, too. You can email songs as attachments using the Email app or do so directly from My Files, as described here. In either case, you need to know the folder in which the song is stored.

1. On the Home screen, tap Apps, followed by My Files.

2. Navigate to the folder in which the song is stored.

3. Press and hold the song title to select it, and then tap the Share Via icon.

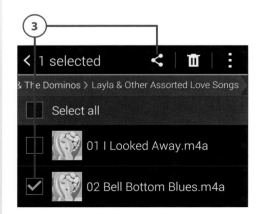

4. Select Email or Gmail as the sharing method.

5. The song file is added as an attachment to a new email message. Finish by performing Steps 4–7 of the "Email Photos from Gallery" task, earlier in this chapter. Then add or import the song(s) into the music organizer program on your computer, such as iTunes or Windows Media Player.

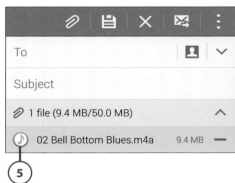

Some Help, Please

The Android filing system automatically stores files as they're received by the phone. When files are transferred, they're sometimes stored in folders named for the transfer method, such as ShareViaWifi for Wi-Fi Direct transfers. For the most part, an app doesn't care where its files are stored. This information is generally invisible—and irrelevant—to you...until, of course, you must know it.

To find your song files, start with the Music folder. Next, see if there's a folder named for the transfer method you used to receive the song on your phone. Finally, check other likely folders in Device Storage (built-in memory). If you've added a memory card, be sure to check its folders, too.

Transferring Files Between Phones

By taking advantage of the Wi-Fi Direct support on your Galaxy S5, there are several methods you can use to exchange files with other Wi-Fi Direct–enabled phones, as well as view material on each other's phones.

Use Wi-Fi Direct

If two phones support Wi-Fi Direct, they can exchange files wirelessly—without the need for a common wireless access point or router. Because of its speed, Wi-Fi Direct is ideal for transferring very large files or large quantities of files. This task shows how to use Wi-Fi Direct with two Galaxy S series phones, although it can be accomplished with any pair of phones that both support Wi-Fi Direct. Both users should activate Wi-Fi Direct by performing Steps 1–4.

1. Open the Notification panel, and press and hold the Wi-Fi Quick Setting button. (You can also reach the Wi-Fi screen by opening Settings and tapping the Wi-Fi icon in the Quick Settings or Network Connections section.)

Other Wi-Fi Direct– Capable Phones

Other phones that also support Wi-Fi Direct may have different procedures for enabling the feature.

2. If Wi-Fi isn't currently enabled, move its slider to the On position.

3. Enable Wi-Fi Direct by opening the menu and choosing Wi-Fi Direct.

4. The Wi-Fi Direct screen appears, and the phone scans for nearby Wi-Fi Direct-enabled devices. When your phone displays the name of the phone to which you want to connect, tap its name. (Only one user needs to do this to establish the two-way connection.)

Naming Your Phone

To give your phone a friendlier name, open Settings, tap About Device, and tap Device Name. Enter a new name in the Device Name dialog box and tap OK.

Rename the phone

5. An Invitation to Connect dialog box appears on the other phone. To allow the connection, the person taps Connect.

6. Each phone lists the other as a connected device.

7. To send a file such as a photo, song, or video from one phone to the other, select the item(s) in My Files, Gallery, or an appropriate app, and issue a Share or Share Via command, followed by Wi-Fi Direct. (You may have to scroll to see the Wi-Fi Direct icon.) Select the device to which you want to send the file(s) and tap Done.

8. To finish the Wi-Fi Direct session, either person can return to the Wi-Fi Direct screen, tap the End Connection button at the bottom of the screen, and then tap OK in the End Connection dialog box that appears.

File Sharing Notes

Consider the following when using Wi-Fi Direct to transmit files between devices:

- Files can be transmitted in either direction between connected devices.

- Wi-Fi Direct file transmissions—both successes and failures—are listed in the Notification panel.

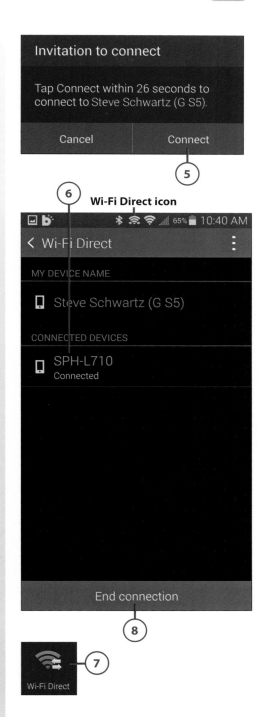

Use S Beam

Using a combination of *Near Field Communication* (*NFC*) and Wi-Fi Direct, S Beam enables you to exchange files and other materials (such as photos, videos, contact records, websites, maps, and YouTube videos) with a Galaxy S III, 4, or 5 phone, as well as other devices that support S Beam. NFC must be enabled on both phones; only the sending phone is required to have S Beam enabled.

1. Open Settings and tap the NFC icon (in the Connect and Share section).

Sending, Receiving, or Both

If *both* people intend to send files, each must enable S Beam by performing Steps 1 and 2. Otherwise, only the sender must enable S Beam, whereas the recipient must enable NFC (at a minimum).

2. Enable NFC by dragging its slider to the On position. If S Beam is off, tap its text and then drag the S Beam slider to the On position.

3. On the sending phone, launch the app that contains the material you want to transmit and then display the material, such as a photo or song. Press the phones back to back, ensuring that neither is displaying the lock screen. Within 10 seconds, a connection is made between the phones and Touch to Beam appears on the sending phone's screen. Tap the thumbnail to initiate the file transfer. You can separate the two phones while the data transmits.

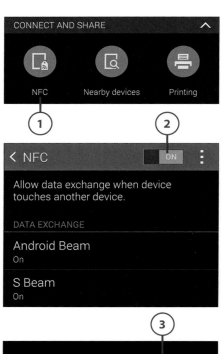

4. The material is transmitted. When the transmission ends, the material displays on the receiving phone in the appropriate app, such as Gallery or Video, and is saved in the Download folder.

Sending Multiple Gallery Items

You can simultaneously send multiple photos in Gallery. Open the folder that contains the photos, select the thumbnails, and then press the phones together.

5. When you finish transmitting material, the phone(s) can disable NFC and/or S Beam by dragging their sliders to the Off position.

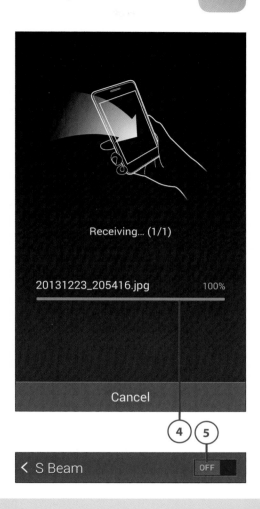

>>>*Go Further*
THE ANDROID BEAM ALTERNATIVE

Think of Android Beam as S Beam's smaller sibling. It works like S Beam but is designed to share smaller bits of information (such as the web page you're currently browsing or a map view in Maps) over shorter distances. To enable Android Beam, open Settings, enable NFC, tap Android Beam, and then drag the Android Beam slider to the On position. Display the information that you want to transfer, and—ensuring that the lock screen isn't displayed on either phone—touch the phones back to back. Tap the Touch to Beam thumbnail that appears. The material is transmitted to the recipient's phone. If the file is too large to send using Android Beam, enable S Beam and try the transfer again.

It's Not All Good

Are Phone-to-Phone Features Worth the Bother?

Like other marginal features you'll find on the Galaxy S5 (and most other Android phones), phone-to-phone transmission and sharing features are seldom simple to set up and use. As this section illustrates, you don't just tap the phones together or press a button or two. Each process requires that you both perform multiple actions on your phone to set up the connection, authorize the data transmission or sharing, accept incoming data, and then disable the feature. The processes are neither simple nor convenient—*and they're only available between compatible devices.* Unless you and a friend or family member regularly use a phone-to-phone feature, you'll struggle to remember and perform the required steps without printed instructions in hand. In fact, if you suggest that a friend use one of these features to exchange photos, a song, or a video, the most likely response will be, "Why don't you just email it to me?"

It's Not All Good

More Data Transmission Features That You're Unlikely to Use

While exploring Settings, you'll find a couple that—based on their names—sound like something you might need or would like to use. To avoid confusion, here's what they do and why you're unlikely to need them.

- *Nearby Devices.* Found in the Connect and Share section of Settings, enable and configure Nearby Devices to allow the S5 to stream photos, music, and/or videos to DNLA (Digital Network Living Alliance) appliances, such as televisions, over your Wi-Fi network. It is *not* for phone-to-phone or phone-to-computer streaming. Unless you have a DNLA-capable device, you can safely ignore this area of Settings.

- *Tap and Pay.* In combination with an installed payment service app (not included), this NFC option allows you to use your phone to make purchases at point-of-purchase registers in stores, coffee shops, and the like.

- *Pay with PayPal.* When enabled, this Finger Scanner option links your fingerprint scan with your PayPal account. A finger or thumb swipe is all it takes to authorize payment for a purchase. Similar to Tap and Pay, Pay with PayPal links your phone to your bank account and/or a credit card. Convenient or not, however, I'm perfectly happy that my phone does *not* have immediate, easy access to my money.

>>>Go Further

PAIRING THE PHONE WITH A MAC

To use Bluetooth for data transfers, the phone and computer must be paired. The following steps show how to accomplish this one-time procedure on a Mac with built-in Bluetooth support. If you have a different computer, refer to its Help for instructions on Bluetooth pairing.

1. On the Home screen, tap Apps, followed by Settings.

2. Tap the Bluetooth icon.

3. Ensure that the Bluetooth slider is On and that your phone is checked, making it visible to other devices such as your Mac.

4. On the Mac's Dock, click the System Preferences icon.

5. In System Preferences, click the Bluetooth icon.

6. The pairing procedure depends on the version of Mac OS X installed on your Mac. To find your version, go to the Finder and choose About This Mac from the Apple menu.

7. *OS X 10.9.x (Mavericks)*

   • If Bluetooth isn't active, click the Turn Bluetooth On button.

   • Select the Galaxy S5 entry in the Devices list and click its Pair button.

   • An attempt is made to pair the phone with the Mac. In the Bluetooth Pairing Request that appears on your phone, tap OK if the number matches the one on the Mac's screen. Go to Step 9.

8. *OS X 10.6.x (Snow Leopard)*

   • Ensure that On and Discoverable are checked.

   • Click the plus (+) button at the bottom of the screen to add a new Bluetooth device—your Galaxy S5—or, if this is your Mac's first Bluetooth device, click the Set Up New Device button.

   • The Bluetooth Setup Assistant launches. The phone should be listed as a visible Bluetooth device. Select it in the Devices list and click Continue.

- The Bluetooth Setup Assistant attempts to pair the phone with the Mac. In the Bluetooth Pairing Request that appears on your phone, tap OK if the number matches the one on the Mac's screen.

- Click Continue in the Bluetooth Setup Assistant. Click Quit to exit the Bluetooth Setup Assistant. Close the Bluetooth preferences dialog box.

9. A phone-specific hierarchical menu is added to the Mac's Bluetooth menu. An entry also appears on the phone's Bluetooth settings screen showing that the phone is paired to the Mac. Whenever you perform a Bluetooth operation on the phone, you'll see this pairing information.

Google/Gmail sync components

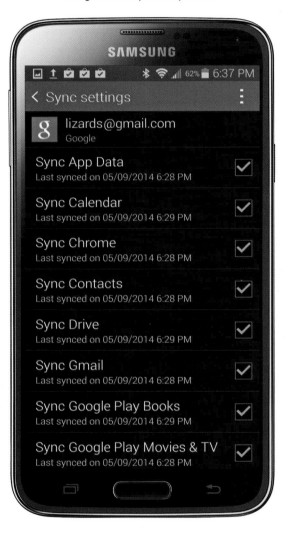

In this chapter, you learn how to synchronize calendar events, contacts, and other data on your phone with data stored elsewhere, such as web-based accounts, Exchange Server accounts, and other devices. Topics include the following:

→ Developing a synchronization strategy
→ Configuring the phone for automatic, scheduled syncs
→ Performing manual syncs

Synchronizing Data

When you got your phone, you probably already had important data such as contact records and calendar events stored somewhere else: in one or several computer applications, on websites, or in an Exchange Server account. Instead of keeping that information separate from the data in your phone's apps, you might want to keep all your data sources synchronized. That is, no matter where you edit or create new data, you can automatically or manually synchronize the other data sources to match.

Developing a Sync Strategy

If you want to keep your phone's important data (such as Calendar events and Contacts records) synchronized with data stored on your PC or Mac, on a Microsoft Exchange Server, or in web-based applications, there are currently only two seamless solutions. *Seamless* means that you can accomplish this automatically (or manually with a simple tap) over a cellular or wireless connection. You don't have to hook up a USB cable or launch a separate application on your Mac or PC to perform a sync.

Although adding software and jumping through hoops are unnecessary, the seamless solutions do require that you accept either a Google/Gmail, Samsung, or Exchange Server account as the repository for your contact and calendar data.

Microsoft Exchange Server

If you work for a company or institution that employs Exchange Server to manage email, contacts, calendar, and other business data, your situation is the easiest. If you've added your Exchange email account to the phone, you have instant access on the phone to much of your important data—regardless of whether you create it on the phone or on one of several computers that you use. Each time you edit a contact or create a new calendar event, the server is responsible for synchronizing that data with every computer, phone, and tablet on which your Exchange account is registered. Unfortunately, most non-business users *don't* have an Exchange Server account. Internet service providers (ISPs) don't provide them.

Exceptions: Hotmail, Outlook.com, and Live Accounts

All email accounts with the web-based Microsoft Outlook.com, Hotmail.com, and Live.com are now handled as Microsoft Exchange ActiveSync accounts—not as POP3 accounts, as was the case in the past. If you have one or more of these accounts, you can sync their Calendar, Contacts, Email, and Tasks entries with data on your phone.

Google/Gmail

Because the Galaxy S5 is an Android-based phone, Android is Google software, and you've probably added a Google/Gmail account to the phone, you can use this account to keep your calendar and contact data in sync. Several approaches facilitate this, but all except the first require concessions:

- If you already use Google and Gmail to manage your contacts and calendar events, you're all set.

- If you're willing to *switch* to Google/Gmail for managing your contacts and calendar events, you probably can export your data from the applications you currently use and import the data into Google Calendar and Contacts.

- Even if you aren't willing to switch to these Google web apps, you can perform the export/import as a one-time procedure. As long as you're willing to manually maintain the Contacts list on your phone and record all new Calendar events on the phone, you can disable the sync process. Everything important to you will already be on your phone, so there's no reason to sync.

- Finally, if you can live with the notion that chunks of your data will be out of sync much of the time and correct only on your computer, you can use Google/Gmail as an *occasional* data receptacle. Periodically delete your Gmail Contacts data on the Web, import your computer's contact data into Gmail Contacts, and then perform a single sync to transfer the up-to-date contact roster to your phone. (For help with importing Microsoft Outlook, Apple contacts, or Address Book contacts into Gmail Contacts, see Chapter 5, "Managing Contacts.")

Using a Samsung, Outlook, Hotmail, or Live Account

The Samsung account that you created during the phone's setup (see "Creating a Samsung Account" in Chapter 1, "Galaxy S5 Essentials") enables you to use certain Samsung apps, such as ChatON. Like a Gmail/Google account, you also can use it to sync your calendar and contact data. Similarly, if you've added an Outlook, Hotmail, or Live account to the phone, you can elect to use it to sync the same data.

Samsung account sync components

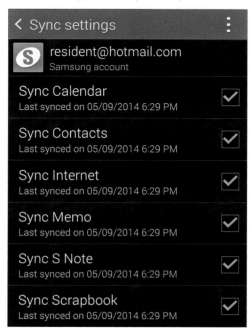

Alternative Software

If you prefer to enter important data on your computer using programs such as Microsoft Outlook (PC or Mac), Contacts or Address Book (Mac), or iCal (Mac), another option is to search Google Play for an app solution that enables you to continue using those programs. An Android app and a companion application installed on your computer generally manage the sync process.

The Missing Sync for Android

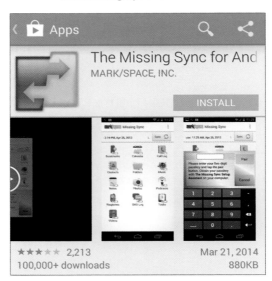

★★★☆☆ 2,213   Mar 21, 2014
100,000+ downloads   880KB

Test with Care

In reading about the Android/computer solutions, you might see a warning from the software company or in user comments concerning potential data loss. Before experimenting with any of these solutions, be sure to back up your data.

The Sneakernet (Manual) Approach

Before the wide acceptance of networking, if a co-worker needed a copy of a Word document, you'd use *Sneakernet*. That is, you'd copy the file to a floppy disk, walk down the hall, and hand it to whoever needed it. (A flash drive is the modern equivalent of a floppy disk.) *Moral*: Sometimes a manual approach is good enough.

This also applies to synchronizing data between your phone and computer. If you don't live in Google/Gmail and don't have an Exchange Server account, you might decide to ignore synchronizing. Create new events and contact records on the device you use most, create them on whatever device happens to be handy, or standardize on using your phone or a computer application for adding all the new data. If you decide that a particular record or event is crucial and needs to be in *both* places, re-create the data on the second device when you have time.

Setting Sync Options and Schedules

Data from each account can be synced manually or on a *schedule* (automatically in the background). Most accounts enable you to specify which data types to sync and which to ignore. Sync *schedules*, on the other hand, can only be set for email accounts. You can allow any account to sync automatically or disable automatic syncs, syncing manually on selected accounts as needed (whenever your data has significantly changed).

1. On the Home screen, tap Apps, Settings.

2. In the User and Backup section, tap Accounts.

3. The Accounts screen lists your account classes (such as Email or Microsoft Exchange ActiveSync) and specific accounts (such as Facebook or LinkedIn) that can be synchronized. Tap the account class name or the specific account whose settings you want to examine or change.

4. *Account classes only:* If you select an account class (such as Email) in Step 3, all accounts of that type are shown. Tap the account whose schedule or settings you want to view or change. The Sync Settings screen appears.

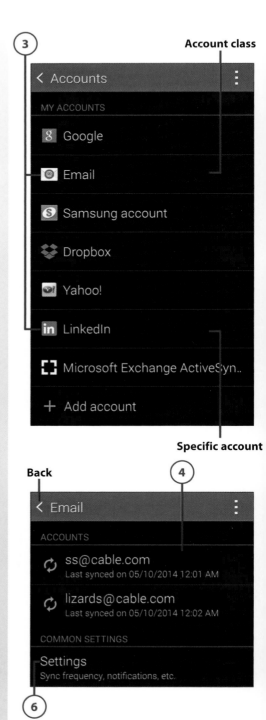

Account class

③

‹ Accounts

MY ACCOUNTS

8 Google

@ Email

S Samsung account

❖ Dropbox

▣ Yahoo!

in LinkedIn

⬚ Microsoft Exchange ActiveSyn..

+ Add account

Specific account

Back ④

‹ Email

ACCOUNTS

↻ ss@cable.com
Last synced on 05/10/2014 12:01 AM

↻ lizards@cable.com
Last synced on 05/10/2014 12:02 AM

COMMON SETTINGS

Settings
Sync frequency, notifications, etc.

⑥

5. Synchronization will be performed only for those data elements that are checked. Make any desired changes by tapping check boxes. When you finish, press the Back key or tap the Back icon.

Stop Here

The remaining steps apply only to email accounts. If you are configuring a *specific* account (as explained in Step 3), you can stop here.

6. To set a schedule for an email or Microsoft Exchange ActiveSync account, tap Email or Microsoft Exchange ActiveSync in the My Accounts list (see Step 3), and then tap Settings in the Common Settings section of the screen.

7. Tap the name of the specific email account whose schedule you want to view or change.

8. Tap Sync Settings.

9. On the Sync Settings screen, ensure that Sync Email is checked and then tap Sync Schedule.

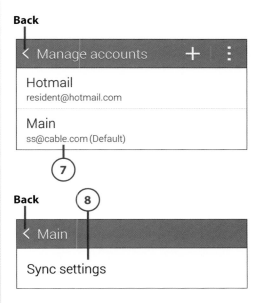

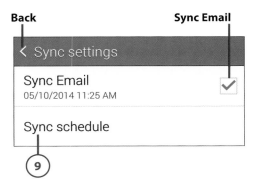

10. Tap Set Sync Schedule.

11. Select a sync interval.

The Manual Interval

Select Manual for accounts that you never want to update or sync with other devices, as well as for those accounts that you intend to sync manually.

12. Review the other scheduling settings on the Sync Schedule screen and then press the Back key or tap the Back icon until your email account list reappears. Repeat Steps 7–12 for each additional email account whose sync schedule you want to view or modify. See Chapter 8, "Sending and Receiving Email," for additional information about scheduling checks for new email.

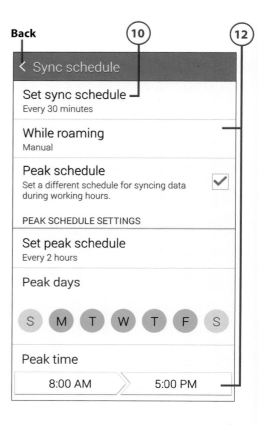

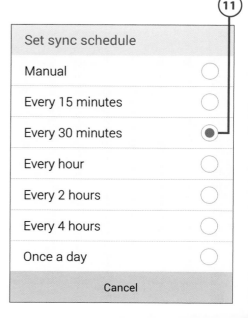

Performing Manual Syncs

You can perform manual syncs whenever you want—on an entire account or selected data elements within an account—regardless of whether an automatic schedule has been set.

1. On the Home screen, tap Apps, followed by Settings.

2. In the User and Backup section, tap Accounts.

3. Tap the account class (such as Email) or the specific account (such as LinkedIn) that you want to sync.

4. *If multiple accounts are listed* (as might be the case if you selected Email or Microsoft Exchange ActiveSync in Step 3), you can do the following:

    -   To simultaneously sync all currently checked components for all listed accounts, tap the menu icon and choose Sync All.

    -   To selectively sync the components of one account, tap the account name. On the Sync Settings screen, tap the menu icon and choose Sync Now to sync all checked components. To sync only a single component, double-tap the component. (It's necessary to double-tap to retain the component's original sync setting.)

5. *If a single account is listed and no components are displayed* (such as a Google or Samsung Account), you can do the following:

    -   To simultaneously sync all currently checked components for the account, tap the menu icon and choose Sync All.

    -   Tap the account name. On the Sync Settings screen, tap the menu key and choose Sync Now to sync all checked components. To sync only a single component, double-tap the component. (It's necessary to double-tap to retain the component's original sync setting.)

Sync all listed accounts

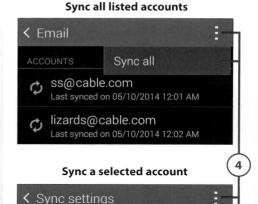

Sync a selected account

④

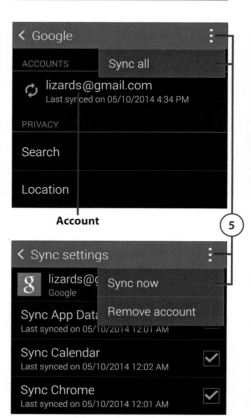

Account

⑤

6. *If a single account is listed and components are displayed* (such as LinkedIn, Facebook, or Twitter), you can do the following:

   - To simultaneously sync all checked components for the account, tap the menu icon and choose Sync Now.

   - To sync only a single component, double-tap the component. (It's necessary to double-tap to retain the component's original sync setting.)

7. When you finish performing manual syncs, exit by pressing the Home key, repeatedly pressing the Back key, or repeatedly tapping the Back icon in the top-left corner of the screen.

It's Not All Good

Think Before You Sync

Although syncing ensures convenient access to your data from anywhere and with any device, think carefully about the accounts you add to the phone and the types of data you elect to sync. Syncing puts your synced material (such as memos, notes, contacts, and calendar events) on Google, Samsung, and other external servers. If there's a security breach, others can potentially view your data. Thus, if you don't want certain personal or business information to be made public, you might not want to sync those items. If you're a corporate or government employee, check with your information technology (IT) department before adding non-business accounts to your phone and enabling syncing. There may be prohibitions against doing so.

>>>*Go Further*

ADDING ACCOUNTS

Whenever you create a new email account or launch and register an app with at least one sync component (such as email, calendar, or contacts), an account of that type is automatically added to the My Accounts list. To see if there are other accounts you can add, open Settings, tap the Accounts icon (in the User and Backup section), and then tap Add Account.

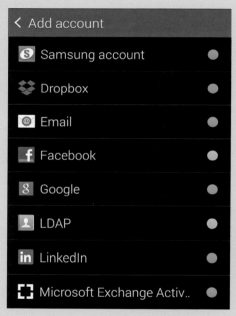

The Add Account screen lists all eligible accounts and account types. Those followed by a green dot currently have at least one registered account on the phone. To add an account, tap an entry and follow the instructions to create or sign in to an account. Note that you can have multiples of some account types, such as Email and Microsoft Exchange ActiveSync. Only a single instance of other accounts, such as Facebook and LinkedIn, is supported.

Time

Date

Owner
information

Unlock
pattern

Launch
Camera

Make an
emergency call

In this chapter, you learn simple methods for securing your phone from prying eyes and unauthorized use. Topics include the following:

→ Securing the lock screen
→ Setting options for the current locking method
→ Unlocking the phone
→ Using Private mode to hide sensitive files

18

Securing the Phone

Do you occasionally leave your phone unattended? If you don't like the idea that someone might use your phone and see everything you've stored on it, you can secure it using lock screen and other security settings.

Securing the Lock Screen

Whenever you turn on the phone or restore it from a darkened state, you normally see the *lock screen*. Its purpose is twofold. First, when the phone is idle, the lock screen appears, providing a bit of privacy from casual observers. Second, you can secure the phone by requiring that a pattern, PIN, password, or fingerprint scan be supplied to clear the lock screen—rather than simply swiping it away.

As with the Home screen wallpaper, you can customize the lock screen wallpaper by choosing a different image to display (see Chapter 3, "Making the Phone Your Own").

Change the Screen Locking Method

Use the following general steps whenever you want to review or change the locking method or its settings. Details for setting specific screen locking methods are presented later in this chapter.

1. On the Home screen, tap Apps, followed by Settings.

2. In the Sound and Display or Quick Settings section, tap the Lock Screen icon.

3. Do either of the following:

   - To change the current screen locking method, tap Screen Lock.

   - To set options for the current screen locking method, tap settings in the lower part of this screen. See "Setting Lock Screen Options" for instructions.

Current Locking Method

You can always view the current lock setting in the Screen Security section. It's displayed in the Screen Lock item.

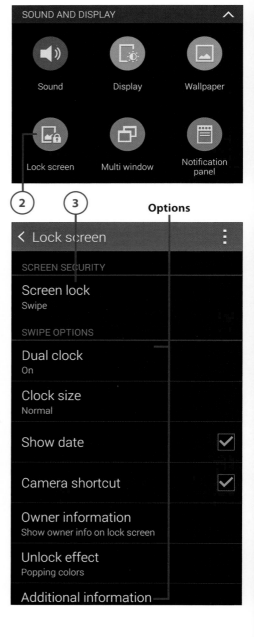

Set a Lock Pattern

A *pattern* consists of four or more connected dots that you trace on a 3×3 grid.

1. Open Settings, tap the Lock Screen icon, and tap Screen Lock.

2. If a secure locking method is in use, you'll be asked to perform the unlock procedure. Otherwise, go to Step 3.

3. Tap Pattern.

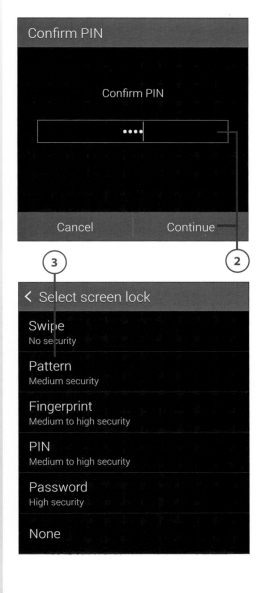

4. In a continuous motion, trace an unlock pattern that connects at least four dots, and then tap Continue. To confirm that you know the pattern, trace it again and tap Confirm.

5. Enter a backup PIN containing at least four digits (to use if you forget the pattern) and tap Continue. To confirm that you know the PIN, reenter it and tap OK.

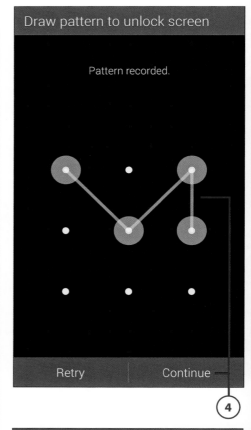

6. The Lock Screen reappears, displaying your new security method. Review the options in the Secured with Pattern section of the screen (see "Setting Lock Screen Options" for instructions).

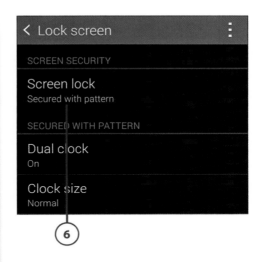

Enable Fingerprint Scan

The Home key on the Galaxy S5 doubles as a *fingerprint scanner*. After teaching the phone to recognize your thumbprint or fingerprint, you can use it as a quick unlocking technique. In addition to using fingerprint recognition as your lock screen method, it can optionally be used to access your Samsung account and as a fast payment verification technique.

1. Open Settings, tap the Lock Screen icon, and tap Screen Lock.

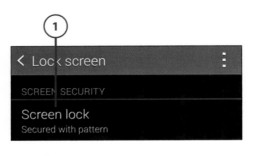

Current Lock Method
If a secure screen lock method is currently in use, you'll be asked to perform the unlock procedure before continuing.

2. Tap Fingerprint.

3. Read and dismiss the Disclaimer screen, and then register your first fingerprint by repeatedly swiping your thumb or a finger over the Home key in the manner shown. Be sure to keep your thumb or finger flat and centered over the Home key while swiping. You can continue when sufficient successes have been registered.

4. Enter a backup password containing at least four characters and tap Continue. Confirm the password by reentering it and tap OK.

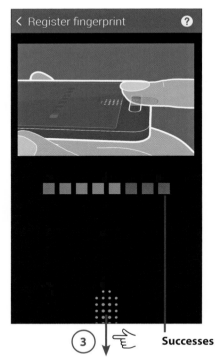

Successes

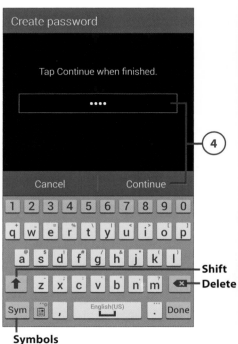

Symbols

Shift
Delete

5. The Lock Screen reappears, displaying your new security method. Review the options in the Secured with Fingerprint Lock section of the screen (see "Setting Lock Screen Options" for instructions).

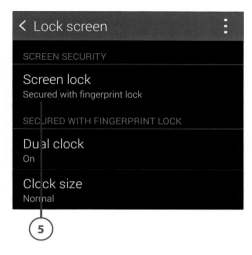

Set a Lock PIN

A *PIN* is a number of four or more digits that you enter on the onscreen keyboard to unlock the phone.

1. Open Settings, tap the Lock Screen icon, and tap Screen Lock.

Current Lock Method

If a secure screen lock method is currently in use, you'll be asked to perform the unlock procedure before continuing.

2. Tap PIN.

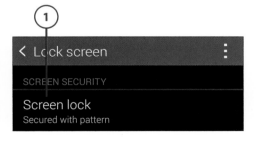

3. Use the keyboard to enter a PIN of four or more digits, and then tap Continue. To confirm that you know the PIN, reenter it and tap OK.

Oops!

If you make a mistake while entering your PIN, you can tap the Delete key to backspace over the incorrect character(s).

4. The Lock Screen reappears, displaying your new security method. Review the options in the Secured with PIN section of the screen (see "Setting Lock Screen Options" for instructions).

Delete

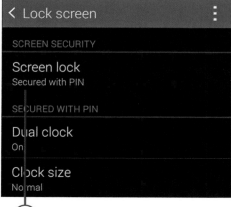

Set a Lock Password

A *password* is a combination of upper- and lowercase letters, numbers, and special characters that you enter on the onscreen keyboard to unlock the phone.

1. Open Settings, tap the Lock Screen icon, and tap Screen Lock.

Current Lock Method
If a secure screen lock method is currently in use, you'll be asked to perform the unlock procedure before continuing.

2. Tap Password.

3. Use the keyboard to enter a password containing at least four characters and tap Continue. Confirm the password by reentering it and tap OK.

Letter Case Counts
If your password contains letters, be aware that letter case counts. *Knot*, *knot*, and *KNOT* are different passwords.

Oops!
If you make a mistake while entering your password, you can tap the Delete key to backspace over the incorrect character(s).

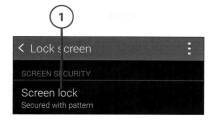

①

< Lock screen

SCREEN SECURITY

Screen lock
Secured with pattern

②

Password
High security

③

Select password

Tap Continue when finished.

● ● ● ● ● ●

Cancel   Continue

1 2 3 4 5 6 7 8 9 0
q w e r t y u i o p
a s d f g h j k l
⬆ z x c v b n m ⌫ —**Shift** / **Delete**
Sym ▤ , English(US) . Done

Symbols

4. The Lock Screen reappears, displaying your new security method. Review the options in the Secured with Password section of the screen (see "Setting Lock Screen Options" for instructions).

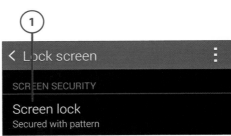

Set a Non-Secure Unlock Method

If security isn't an issue for you, you can select Swipe to simply *hide* the screen or None to dispense with the lock screen altogether.

1. Open Settings, tap the Lock Screen icon, and tap Screen Lock.

Current Lock Method
If a secure screen lock method is currently in use, you'll be asked to perform the unlock procedure before continuing.

2. Select one of these screen lock methods:

- *Swipe*. This is the default screen locking method. When restoring from a dark display, the lock screen wallpaper appears. Dismiss it by swiping in any direction.

- *None.* Select None to make the screen turn black following a screen timeout. When restored, the most recent screen immediately displays.

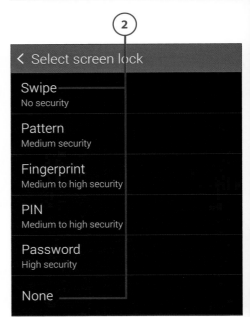

3. The Lock Screen reappears, displaying your new lock screen method. If you selected Swipe, review the options in the Swipe Options section of the screen (see "Setting Lock Screen Options" for instructions). Because None presents a black lock screen, it has no options.

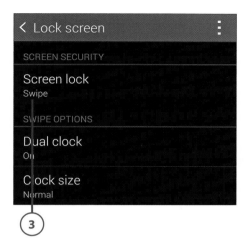

Setting Lock Screen Options

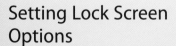

With the exception of None, each screen locking method has options that you can set. To view or change these options, open Settings and tap the Lock Screen icon.

In alphabetical order, these are the options and the locking method(s) to which each option applies:

- *Additional Information (all)*. When this option is enabled, the lock screen can show local weather information and the number of steps you've taken—when S Health's pedometer is enabled.

Options   Lock method

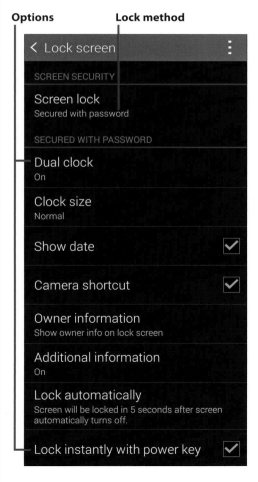

- *Camera Shortcut (all).* When this option is enabled, a Camera shortcut is displayed in the lower-right corner of the lock screen. Drag it up to go directly from the lock screen to the Camera app.

- *Clock Size (all).* Tap Clock Size to set the time display to Small, Normal, or Large.

- *Dual Clock (all).* When this option is enabled and you're traveling, two clocks are displayed; one shows the local time and the other shows your home time. To specify your home time zone, tap Dual Clock, Set Home City. (When you're in your Home City time zone, only a single clock with the local time is shown.)

- *Help Text (Swipe).* When this option is enabled, text is displayed on the lock screen that explains how to dismiss the lock screen.

- *Lock Automatically (Password, Pattern, Fingerprint, PIN).* This option is what makes it practical to apply a secure locking method. Instead of being asked to perform an unlock *every* time the lock screen appears, Lock Automatically enables you to specify the length of inactivity (in seconds or minutes) before you're required to perform your unlocking procedure. If less time has passed, the screen immediately reappears when you wake up the phone—as though None is the screen lock method.

Enabled

Disabled

Help text

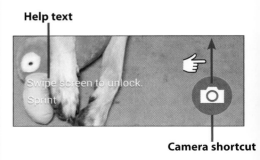

Camera shortcut

Instant Override

If you've also enabled Lock Instantly with Power Key, the Lock Automatically interval is ignored whenever you press the Power key to darken the display.

Lock automatically
Immediately
5 seconds
15 seconds
30 seconds
1 minute
2 minutes
5 minutes
10 minutes
30 minutes
Cancel

- *Lock Instantly with Power Key (Password, Pattern, Fingerprint, PIN).* Rather than waiting for a screen timeout to occur, this option enables you to instantly lock the phone by pressing the Power key.

- *Make Pattern Visible (Pattern).* When this option is enabled, the traced pattern displays. When disabled, the traced pattern is hidden to prevent others from seeing it.

- *Owner Information (all).* Add your name or another text string to the lock screen display.

- *Pattern Type (Pattern).* Set the lock screen dots and drawing colors to Classic (default), Halftone, or Multicolor.

- *Show Date (all).* Display today's day and date.

- *Unlock Effect (Swipe).* Specify the visual effect that occurs whenever your finger approaches or touches the lock screen.

- *Vibration Feedback (Pattern).* When this option is enabled, the phone vibrates if an incorrect pattern is entered.

Show Date

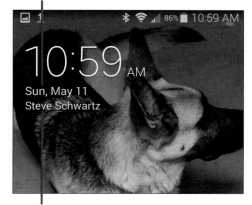

Owner Information

Customize Fingerprint Options

In addition to using a fingerprint scan to unlock the phone, you can set options and enable other related capabilities for finger scanning.

1. Open Settings and tap Finger Scanner (in the Personalization section).

2. Tap Fingerprint Manager to register additional fingers or thumbs (up to the maximum of three) or deregister existing ones. Log in by swiping a registered finger or by entering the alternate password, and then do any of the following:

   - Tap the + (plus) icon to register an additional fingerprint.

   - To remove one or more registered fingerprints, tap the menu icon and choose Deregister. Select a fingerprint, tap the Trash icon, and confirm the deletion by tapping OK.

   - To rename a fingerprint (indicating which digit it is, for example), tap Fingerprint Manager, press and hold the entry you want to rename, and tap the Edit (pencil) icon.

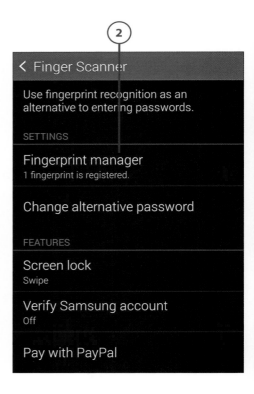

Any Finger Will Do

Whenever a fingerprint scan is requested, you can use any of your registered fingers or thumbs.

3. Tap Change Alternative Password to replace the backup password with a different one. You must enter the *current* backup password before you can create a new one.

4. Enable logging into your Samsung account via a fingerprint scan (when making purchases, for example) by tapping Verify Samsung Account and dragging the slider to the On position.

5. If you have or are willing to create a PayPal account (www.paypal. com), you can designate fingerprint scanning as a PayPal purchase authorization method. Tap Pay with PayPal and follow the onscreen instructions.

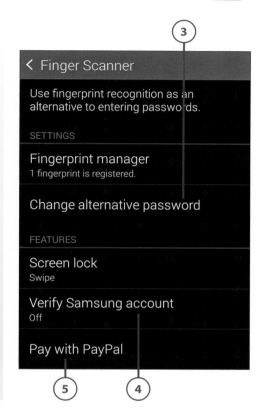

Showing/Hiding Passwords and PINs

If you're concerned that people might peek as you enter passwords or PINs, you can disable Make Passwords Visible to obscure the characters as you type. Conversely, when enabled, this setting briefly shows each typed character and then quickly replaces it with a bullet (•).

To change this system setting, open Settings, tap the Security icon (found in the System section), and enable or disable Make Passwords Visible.

Unlocking the Lock Screen

The manner of clearing the lock screen depends on whether you've set a secure (PIN, Password, Fingerprint Scan, or Pattern) or an unsecure (Swipe or None) lock method. When the lock screen is cleared, it reveals the Home screen or whatever you were doing when the screen darkened—reading messages in Email, for example.

- *Swipe.* Use your finger to swipe the lock screen in any direction.

- *Pattern.* Trace your unlock pattern, connecting dots in the correct sequence. Don't lift your finger from the screen until you complete the pattern.

Lock screen (Swipe)

Lock screen (Pattern)

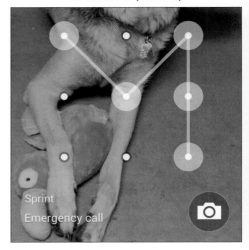

- *Fingerprint Scan.* Smoothly drag any registered finger or thumb downward over the Home key. If you prefer, you can tap Alternative Password and enter the backup password.

- *PIN.* Using the keyboard, enter your PIN and tap OK. If you make a mistake while entering the PIN, tap the Delete key to backspace over the incorrect character(s).

- *Password.* Using the keyboard, enter your password and tap Done. (You can tap the tiny keyboard icon to switch input methods, selecting Samsung Keyboard or Swype.) As previously noted, if the password contains letters, make sure that you use the correct letter case for each one. If you make a mistake while entering the password, tap the Delete key to backspace over the incorrect character(s).

Lock screen (Fingerprint Scan)

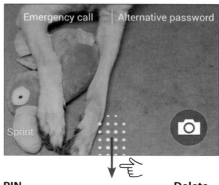

Lock screen (PIN)

PIN   Delete

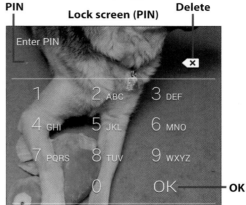

OK

Lock screen (Password)

Password   Change input method

Delete   Done

>>>*Go Further*

IF AT FIRST YOU DON'T SUCCEED...

You're allowed five tries to correctly enter your unlock pattern, PIN, or password. If you fail, an alert appears, explaining that the phone will remain locked for the next 30 seconds. Tap the OK button. A countdown timer shows the seconds remaining until you can try again.

After five unsuccessful fingerprint scans, you're asked for the backup password. However, even if the scan fails repeatedly *and* you can't recall your backup password, all is not lost. Tap Unlock Via Google and log into your Google/Gmail account. If successful, the Screen Unlock Settings screen appears, enabling you to set a different lock method.

Invalid unlock attempts

You have incorrectly drawn your unlock pattern 5 times.

Try again in 30 seconds.

OK

Enabling Private Mode

If your phone contains sensitive or personal material, you can use the new Private mode to make selected files in Gallery, Video, Music, Voice Recorder, and My Files invisible to others. When you first enable Private mode, a folder named Private is created. The folder is visible only when Private mode is active. You can hide files by choosing the Move to Private menu command in any supported app or by launching My Files and manually moving documents into the Private folder.

1. Open Settings and tap the Private Mode icon (in the Personalization section).

2. Review the instruction screens and set a Private mode unlock method, such as a password.

3. Enable Private mode in later sessions by tapping its icon in Settings, tapping the Private Mode slider, and performing the unlock procedure you established in Step 2. The slider is moved to the On position. Whenever Private mode is active, its icon (keyhole) appears in the status bar and a Private Mode item is added to the Notification panel.

Changing the Unlock Method

To change the unlock method, tap Unlock Method on the Private Mode screen, perform the current unlocking procedure, and select a new method.

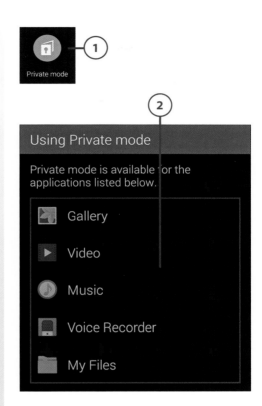

Using Private mode

Private mode is available for the applications listed below.

- Gallery
- Video
- Music
- Voice Recorder
- My Files

Private Mode icon

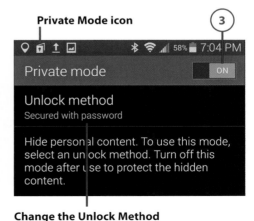

Change the Unlock Method

Gallery

4. Whenever Private mode is active, you can add or remove items from Private mode, as well as see all items that you previously marked as private.

   • To make an item private, open Gallery, Video, Music, or Voice Recorder; select one or more items; and tap the menu icon and choose Move to Private. In My Files, you can select *any* file, open the menu, choose Move, and specify the Private folder as the destination.

Private Designation

Different apps have different methods of designating items as private. In Gallery and My Files, they're shown in the Private folder. In Video, they're marked with the tiny keyhole icon.

   • To remove an item's Private designation, select the item, tap the menu icon, and choose Remove from Private.

   • To view or otherwise use a Private item, open it as you normally do. (Any files that you manually moved into the Private folder in My Files may have to be opened in My Files.) As long as Private mode is enabled, all Private items are readily available to you in the same manner as non-Private items.

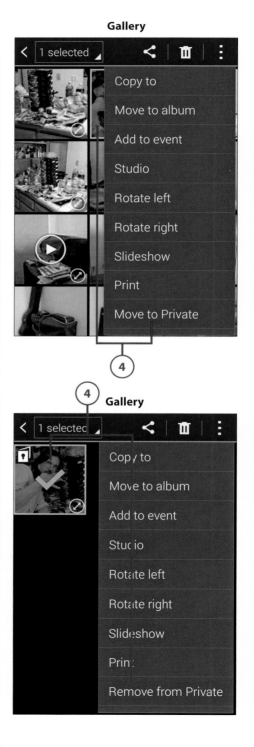

5. Hide all Private items by disabling Private mode. Tap its icon in Settings or the Private Mode item in the Notification panel, and then move the Private Mode slider to the Off position. Until you enable Private mode again, all items marked Private are hidden to all users—including you. When you want to view any file that you've marked as Private, you must re-enable Private mode.

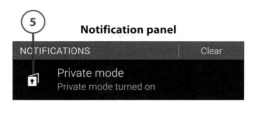

Notification panel

>>>Go Further
HEIGHTENED SECURITY

Securing the lock screen is as far as most users go to protect their phone and its data. However, just like your computer, your smartphone is susceptible to a variety of other threats. If you're concerned about security (or are *required* to have a secure phone by your company), here are some additional steps you can take:

- Review Security settings by opening Settings and tapping the Security icon. You can encrypt the device and external memory card, and verify apps to prevent installing known malware.

- Consider installing an antivirus app, such as Antivirus Security Free (AVG Mobile Technologies) or Norton Security Antivirus (NortonMobile). Both are available from the Google Play Store and are designed to protect the phone from viruses, malware, and theft.

- Corporate users can install Samsung KNOX 2 (www.samsungknox.com), a business security solution for the Galaxy S5.

- To prepare for the possibility of losing or misplacing your Galaxy S5, visit http://findmymobile.samsung.com for instructions on remotely ringing, locating, locking, or wiping your registered phone. However, some carriers don't currently support this feature.

- When you download a new app from the Play Store, a list of permissions appears. (*Permissions* are activities that the app is requesting your permission to perform whenever it's active.) Tap any permission entry to get a more thorough description of what it means. If you don't want to grant the specified permissions, don't download the app.

Permissions

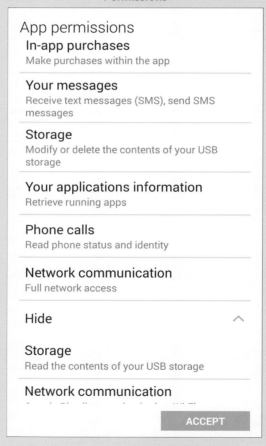

App permissions

In-app purchases
Make purchases within the app

Your messages
Receive text messages (SMS), send SMS messages

Storage
Modify or delete the contents of your USB storage

Your applications information
Retrieve running apps

Phone calls
Read phone status and identity

Network communication
Full network access

Hide ⌃

Storage
Read the contents of your USB storage

Network communication

ACCEPT

Smart Remote

In this chapter, you find out how to use your phone to provide Internet access for other devices and to control external devices. Topics include the following:

→ Using the S5 as a wireless modem for computers, tablets, and other devices
→ Controlling a television set and set-top box/DVR
→ Mirroring the phone's screen on a flat-screen TV

Powering Other Devices

If your laptop or desktop computer currently lacks Internet access (when traveling, at the beach, or during a provider outage, for example), you can temporarily convert your phone to a USB, Bluetooth, or wireless modem. Because the S5 has infrared capabilities, you can configure the included Smart Remote app to control your TV. And if you buy the optional MHL 2.0 HDTV Adapter, anything on the phone can be simultaneously displayed on your HDTV.

Creating a Mobile Hotspot for Wi-Fi Devices

Using the phone's Tethering and Mobile Hotspot settings in combination with a 3G or better data connection, your phone can become a *hotspot* through which up to 10 Wi-Fi devices can simultaneously connect to the Internet.

Carriers may call this a *mobile hotspot*, *portable hotspot*, or simply *hotspot*. Just as the name varies slightly among the carriers, the label and location of the hotspot and tethering icon(s) in Settings vary, too.

A Plan Add-On

Creating a hotspot and tethering may not be included in your data plan. They frequently cost extra and must be ordered from your carrier as needed. Although data transmitted when tethered or using the phone as a hotspot normally doesn't count against your data plan, there may be a maximum amount that you can use. Before trying these features, check with your carrier for details on the cost and the procedure for enabling/disabling this add-on service.

1. On the Home screen, tap Apps, followed by Settings. Go to the Network Connections section.

Or Launch the Carrier's App

Some carriers provide an app that—when launched—takes you directly to the Tethering and Hotspot settings.

2. Do the following:

    • *AT&T, U.S. Cellular:* Tap Tethering and Wi-Fi Hotspot.

    • *Metro PCS, T-Mobile:* Tap Tethering and Mobile Hotspot.

    • *Sprint:* Tap Hotspot.

    • *Verizon:* Tap More Networks, Mobile Hotspot.

3. Drag the Hotspot/Mobile Hotspot slider to the On position.

4. If Wi-Fi is currently enabled for the phone, an Attention dialog box appears. Tap OK to turn Wi-Fi off. (The hotspot runs only over a cellular data connection, not Wi-Fi.)

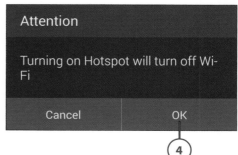

5. The hotspot is enabled. The screen explains how you and others can connect to it, and shows the names of the devices—if any—that are currently connected. The hotspot network's default name and log-in password are the phone's model and phone number—or the most recent name and password that you specified.

6. You can optionally edit the hotspot settings by opening the menu and choosing Configure. (You can do this before or after enabling hotspots.) Otherwise, go to Step 10.

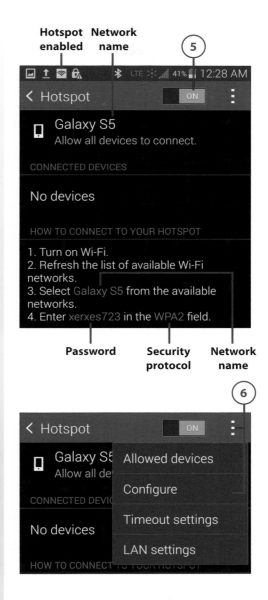

Hotspot enabled   Network name   5

< Hotspot   ON

Galaxy S5
Allow all devices to connect.

CONNECTED DEVICES

No devices

HOW TO CONNECT TO YOUR HOTSPOT

1. Turn on Wi-Fi.
2. Refresh the list of available Wi-Fi networks.
3. Select Galaxy S5 from the available networks.
4. Enter xerxes723 in the WPA2 field.

Password   Security protocol   Network name

6

< Hotspot   ON

Galaxy S5   Allowed devices
Allow all de

CONNECTED DEVIC   Configure

No devices   Timeout settings

HOW TO CONNECT   LAN settings

7. Make any desired changes to the network name, security protocol, and password. You can enable Show Password to see the password as you type or edit it.

Secure or Open Network?

Choosing Open for the Security setting eliminates the security protocol and password. Anyone within range can freely connect to your open hotspot. Just as you do with your home's wireless router, be sure to set a password and security protocol.

8. *Optional:* Tap Show Advanced Options to specify a broadcast frequency, select a specific channel number, and set the maximum number of allowed connections.

9. Tap Save to save the changed configuration settings or Cancel to ignore the changes.

10. Connect Wi-Fi-enabled devices (laptops, tablets, iPods, and so on) to the hotspot network by selecting the hotspot network's name on each device and entering the password when prompted.

Getting Connected

The command you choose or icon you click/tap to connect to a wireless network is specific to the device that's connecting. Use the same procedure that you use to connect to any new wireless network. While the hotspot is active, the Mobile Hotspot screen displays a list of all connected devices.

Channel number

Connecting with a MacBook Pro

Wi-Fi menu

11. When you finish, deactivate the hotspot by dragging the Hotspot/Mobile Hotspot slider to the Off position. The hotspot ends, all devices are disconnected, and Wi-Fi is automatically re-enabled (assuming a Wi-Fi network is available).

Connected devices

Data Used

Although Hotspot/tethered data is normally calculated separately from data transmitted on your monthly data plan, there may be a limit to it. To see how much data is being transmitted while the S5 is a hotspot or is tethered to a PC, open Settings, tap Data Usage, and view the Tethering entry beneath the graph.

It's Not All Good

Test Your Connection Speed

As with other cellular connections, the faster the network and the stronger your signal strength, the more usable a hotspot connection will be. If enabling a hotspot will incur an added fee, you might want to use your phone's current connection to run a speed test at http://speedtest.net (or get the Speedtest app). You should also consider where you'll be using the hotspot and what cellular networks will be available to you. Check your carrier's coverage map for information. If the data connection is less than 3G, a mobile hotspot will likely produce disappointing results. A good 4G connection, on the other hand, can produce exceptional speeds.

Tethering the Phone and a Computer

Another way to provide Internet access to a single computer is to connect the phone and computer with the phone's USB cable (referred to as *tethering*). Some carriers also support wireless tethering using Bluetooth. Of course, the latter feature only works with Bluetooth-equipped computers, such as Macs and some laptops. Unlike USB tethering (which is restricted to one computer), Bluetooth tethering can be used to simultaneously provide Internet access to multiple computers.

USB Tethering for Windows PCs

1. Visit the Support section of Samsung's site (www.samsung.com/us/support/) to download and install the USB driver for your carrier's Galaxy S5. Installing the device driver is a one-time process.

Finding Your Model Number

You can find your phone's carrier-specific model number by opening Settings and tapping About Device or About Phone.

2. Connect the phone's USB cable to the phone and to one of the PC's available USB ports.

An Extra Step

In Windows, you may see a notice that the necessary drivers are being installed. When installation finishes, an AutoPlay dialog box appears, asking what you want to do with the new connected device; that is, your phone. Click Open Device to View Files.

3. Open Settings on the phone, and do the following:

   - *AT&T, U.S. Cellular:* Tap Tethering and Wi-Fi Hotspot.

   - *Metro PCS, T-Mobile:* Tap Tethering and Mobile Hotspot.

   - *Sprint:* Tap Tethering.

   - *Verizon:* Tap More Networks, Tethering.

4. Enable USB Tethering by tapping its check box. After the computer recognizes the phone, you can use the PC's browser and other Internet applications.

5. When you're done using the phone as a USB modem, remove the check mark from USB tethering. If necessary, eject the phone hardware in the same way that you do with other connected USB devices. Disconnect the USB cable.

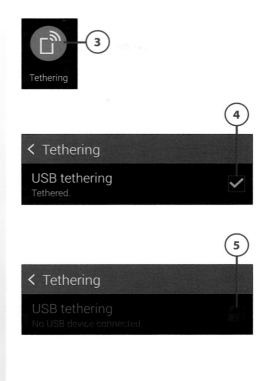

Disconnection Details

When possible, you should avoid simply unplugging USB data devices from a PC. If the Safely Remove Hardware icon is displayed at the right end of the Windows task bar, click the icon, choose the Eject *phone model* command from the pop-up menu that appears, and—when you're told that it's safe to do so—disconnect the USB cable. (If the Safely Remove Hardware icon isn't displayed, wait until you're certain that no data is being transferred between the phone and PC, and then disconnect the USB cable.)

It's Not All Good

USB Tethering for Macs

As described in the "USB Tethering for Windows PCs" task, USB tethering on a Mac isn't currently supported; that is, Samsung doesn't provide a driver as it does for Windows. To provide an unconnected Mac with Internet access, you can set up a mobile hotspot (see "Creating a Mobile Hotspot for Wi-Fi Devices," earlier in the chapter) or use Bluetooth tethering (see the next section).

Bluetooth Tethering

The following task explains how to tether a Mac to the S5 using Bluetooth. If your S5 hasn't previously been *paired* with the Mac, do so now. See the "Pairing the Phone with a Mac" sidebar at the end of Chapter 16, "Transferring and Sharing Files," for instructions.

Mac Versus PC

All recent Macs have built-in Bluetooth. To find out if your Windows PC or laptop has Bluetooth hardware, open the System control panel and click Device Manager.

1. On the phone, open Settings and tap the Bluetooth icon.

2. Enable Bluetooth by dragging its slider to the On position, ensure that the target computer is listed as a paired device, and then press the Back key.

3. On the Mac, open the Bluetooth menu on the menu bar and ensure that Bluetooth is enabled. If it's off, choose Turn Bluetooth On.

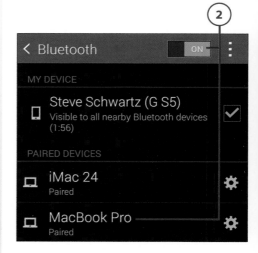

Bluetooth menu

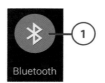

4. On the phone, go to the Network Connections section of Settings and do the following:

- *U.S. Cellular:* Tap Tethering and Wi-Fi Hotspot.

- *Sprint:* Tap Tethering.

- *Verizon:* Tap More Networks, Tethering.

The Other Carriers

At the S5's launch, AT&T, Metro PCS, and T-Mobile did not support Bluetooth tethering. If they later offer it, Step 4 will be similar to what's described for the other carriers.

5. Enable Bluetooth Tethering by tapping its check box.

6. Open the Bluetooth menu on the Mac's menu bar and choose *phone name*, Connect to Network. You can now use your computer's Internet apps as you normally do.

7. When you've completed your online activities, disable tethering by tapping the Bluetooth Tethering check box again. If you're no longer using Bluetooth on the phone for other activities, you can disable it.

Bluetooth menu   Phone

Mirroring the Phone on an HDTV

With Samsung's optional MHL 2.0 HDTV Adapter, you can use your flat-screen TV to display whatever is shown on the phone.

1. Plug an HDMI cable into the adapter.

2. Connect the other end of the HDMI cable to your flat-screen television.

3. Using your television's Input menu, select the HDMI input to which the adapter is connected.

4. Plug the other end of the adapter into your phone's USB port.

5. On the phone, run any application that you want to display on the TV.

>>>Go Further
MHL 2.0 HDTV ADAPTER TIPS

Note the following when using the adapter:

- *Playing music.* Depending on the quality of your television's speakers, stored and streamed songs may sound excellent.

- *Viewing videos and games.* Video quality can vary greatly, depending on its source and the app. For example, streamed video using an app, such as HBO Go, is generally encoded for playback on the phone's tiny screen rather than on a large, flat-screen TV. Expect the quality to be only passable. Games, on the other hand, may look wonderful. Experimentation should teach you what displays well and what doesn't.

- *Viewing photos.* Multi-megapixel photos may look fine when displayed on a TV. When viewing pictures, you can rotate the phone to switch between portrait and landscape display.

- *Viewing slide shows.* Slide shows don't have to be silent or dull. When playing a Gallery photo folder as a slide show, you can select a song to accompany the show and a transition effect to use when switching to a new slide.

- *Using the adapter with other phones.* When using the adapter with an MHL 2.0-compatible device such as the Galaxy S5 or an S 4, the necessary power can be supplied by the phone. However, if you use the adapter with the Samsung Galaxy S III or Note II, you *must* use the phone's USB cable/wall charger to power the adapter.

>>>Go Further
CONTROLLING YOUR TV WITH THE S5

In combination with the Galaxy S5's built-in infrared hardware, you can use the Smart Remote app as an intelligent remote control for one or more television sets and set-top boxes. Smart Remote supports most television and set-top box/DVR brands, as well as the major cable and satellite providers.

To configure Smart Remote, launch the app, and specify your zip code and provider. Then tap the remote control toolbar icon to configure the app to work with your television and set-top box. You can then use Smart Remote to do the following:

- Use the remote to turn the set on and off, adjust or mute the volume, change channels, change the input source, and display the TV's internal menu. You can access a basic version of the remote in the Notification panel and/or on the lock screen with which you can issue common commands to the TV or DVR.

- Open the Channel Guide to see a list of shows that are on. The guide can be scrolled by hour or day and used to select a show to watch. (The channel list can optionally be edited to display only channels to which you subscribe.) If you see an upcoming show that you want to watch, you can set a reminder for it that will appear in the Notification bar at the designated time.

- Tap the three-bar icon in the upper-left corner to select a subset of channels to display, such as Favorites, Movies, Sports, or Just for You (show recommendations, based on your viewing preferences).

- Use the remote to instruct your DVR to record the current show or play a previously recorded show.

Refresh

Remaining charge

Time operating on current charge

In this chapter, you learn to use your phone more efficiently by managing your plan, available storage, and memory; adding a memory card; updating system software; and performing basic troubleshooting. Topics include the following:

→ Using Task Manager to manage memory
→ Conserving the battery manually and by enabling special modes
→ Making the most of your talk and data plans
→ Viewing and expanding storage

Optimizing and Troubleshooting

There's more to understanding your Galaxy S5 than making phone calls and mastering a handful of favorite apps. This chapter delves into material that you don't need to commit to memory or even read immediately—but when you need it, you'll be happy to have it. Bonus content from this chapter can be viewed at the book's website, www.informit.com/title/9780789753496. (Look on the Downloads tab.) Information includes formatting and removing a memory card, installing and replacing the SIM card, checking for system updates, troubleshooting, and performing a Factory Data Reset.

Managing Memory

You've noticed that most apps don't have a Quit or Exit command. That's because the Android operating system is designed to handle memory management behind the scenes. If free memory is running low, for example, unnecessary processes automatically shut down. However, if you occasionally feel the need to take a hands-on approach to quitting apps and freeing memory, you can use the Task Manager.

1. Tap the Recent Apps key. A vertically scrolling list of apps that you've recently run or are currently running appears.

2. Launch the Task Manager by tapping its icon.

Other Actions

In addition to launching the Task Manager, you can tap any app thumbnail in the Recent Apps list to launch or switch to that app. To remove an item from the list, swipe it horizontally off-screen. To remove all items from the list, tap the Clear All icon.

3. Task Manager lists the currently running apps. To close an app, tap its End button. To simultaneously close all running apps, tap End All.

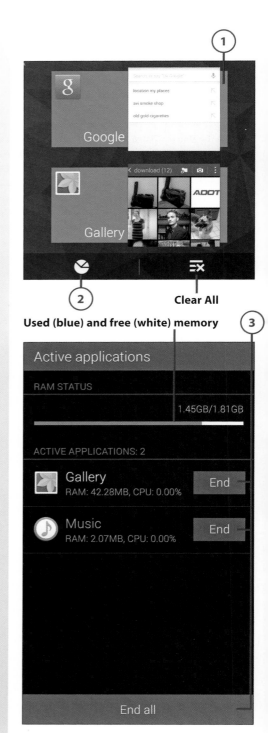

Clear All

Used (blue) and free (white) memory

4. Tap OK in the End or End All confirmation dialog box.

End

If you force stop an app, it may
cause errors.

Cancel   OK

④

Switch to a Running App

As in the Recent Apps list, you
can tap the name of any running
app—if its name is displayed in
white text—to switch to it.

Conserving the Battery

Depending on how frequently you use the phone and what you typically
do with it, there are several approaches to conserving the battery. First, you
can automatically conserve the remaining charge by enabling Power Saving
mode or the new Ultra Power Saving mode. Second, if you prefer to take the
manual approach, you can disable features that aren't currently needed or
change certain default settings so that less power is used. Finally, to monitor
how various apps and the operating system use the battery, you can open
Battery settings.

Configure and Enable Power Saving Mode

When Power Saving mode is enabled
and a low battery level is detected,
selected features are automatically
changed or disabled to extend the
remaining charge.

1. On the Home screen, tap
Apps, followed by Settings.
Alternatively, you can open the
Notification panel and tap the
Settings icon.

Notification panel ①

4:38 PM Tue, May 13

Wi-Fi   Location   Bluetooth   Sound   Multi
window

Quick Setting buttons

2. In the System section of Settings, tap the Power Saving icon.

3. Tap Power Saving Mode.

4. Move the Power Saving Mode slider to the On position. When Power Saving mode is enabled, you can selectively enable or disable options by tapping the Block Background Data check box and the Restrict Performance and Grayscale Mode text. Restrict Performance can be further customized by enabling and disabling particular options. Later when you elect to enable Power Saving mode, the settings specified here are applied collectively.

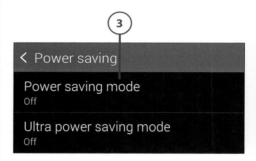

Using the Notification Panel

If you don't need to change the Power Saving mode settings, you can quickly enable or disable Power Saving mode by opening the Notification panel, scrolling the Quick Setting buttons to the right, and tapping the Power Saving icon. (If the icon isn't in the scrolling list, tap the Grid View icon to display *all* Quick Setting buttons.) If you want to change Power Saving mode settings, press and hold its button to go directly to the Power Saving mode screen in Settings.

If you frequently need to enable Power Saving mode, you should consider reconfiguring the Quick Setting buttons to add Power Saving as a primary button (see "Customize the Quick Setting Buttons" in Chapter 3, "Making the Phone Your Own"). Note that these comments apply equally to Ultra Power Saving mode.

Notification panel

List View/ Grid View toggle

Enable/disable Power Saving mode

Configure and Enable Ultra Power Saving Mode

When you're severely short on battery charge, you can squeeze even more work out of your phone by enabling Ultra Power Saving mode.

1. Perform Steps 1 and 2 of the "Configure and Enable Power Saving Mode" task, and tap Ultra Power Saving Mode.

2. Read the description and then move the Ultra Power Saving Mode slider to On.

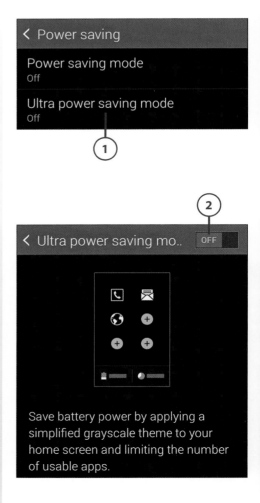

3. Read the mode restrictions that will be applied and tap OK. Ultra Power Saving mode is immediately applied to your phone and its temporary Home screen appears.

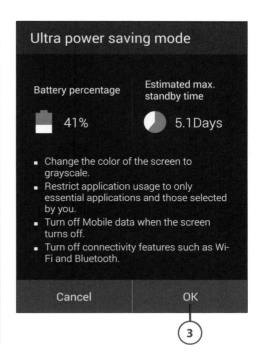

>>>Go Further
CONFIGURING ULTRA POWER SAVING MODE

When in Ultra Power Saving mode, you can access only the low-energy apps whose shortcuts appear on the one-page Home screen. To add apps beyond the initial three (Phone, Internet, and Messages), tap a + (plus) icon and select from among the handful of eligible apps. In addition to running any of these three to six essential apps, you can do the following:

- Modify a subset of system settings by tapping the menu icon and choosing Settings, or by opening the Notification panel and tapping the Settings icon.

- Exit from Ultra Power Saving mode by tapping the menu icon and choosing Disable Ultra Power Saving Mode.

Note that you cannot perform screen captures in Ultra Power Saving mode.

Tips for Manually Conserving the Remaining Charge

If the battery is commonly draining too quickly or you want to extend usage time when the battery is almost depleted, you can manually change certain settings as needed or set new defaults.

- If you aren't currently using some services, such as Location (GPS), Bluetooth, or Wi-Fi, disable them in the Notification panel by tapping their Quick Setting buttons. Turn them on again only when you need them.

- The phone's screen draws considerable power. Consider reducing the Screen Timeout value or the Brightness setting (Settings, Display). You can also adjust Brightness by dragging the slider near the top of the Notification panel. Whenever you're done using the phone for a bit, tap the Power button to instantly darken the display—rather than waiting for the Screen Timeout.

Disabled Enabled

Display settings

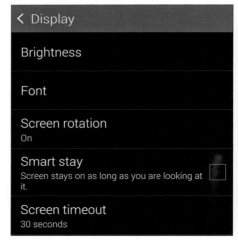

- Consider checking less frequently for new email. For unimportant email accounts, you could set the frequency to Once a Day or Manual, for example. You can still perform manual checks as often as you want. To change the retrieval frequency, launch Email, tap the menu icon, choose Settings, tap Manage Accounts, and select the account that you want to manage. Tap Sync Settings, Sync Schedule, and Set Sync Schedule; and then select a new sync/retrieval frequency.

- Avoid battery-intensive activities. Playing videos and games prevents the display from timing out. Streaming videos or music transfers large amounts of data to the phone, requiring that the connection be constantly active.

- In standby mode, the phone consumes little battery power. Although it may be sacrilege to suggest this, you can take things a step further by powering off the phone when you won't need it for an extended period. For instance, if you *never* answer the phone after you go to bed, consider turning it off nightly—or leave it on while you charge it during this period.

Email check frequency

Set sync schedule	
Manual	○
Every 15 minutes	○
Every 30 minutes	◉
Every hour	○
Every 2 hours	○
Every 4 hours	○
Once a day	○
Cancel	

Plug It In

Before the battery dies, you can continue a conversation and other activities by quickly plugging the phone into a wall outlet or USB port. The phone charges as you continue to work. When your call or app activity concludes, power off the phone and allow the battery to charge normally.

Because you never know when you'll need to recharge, you should consider buying an extra charging cable or two. Keep the spares at key locations—at work and in the car, for example.

It's Not All Good

Why Is This App Using GPS?

It's amazing and rather sad that so many apps now have a GPS component—given that it contributes to battery drain and data usage, and it frequently seems an unnecessary feature. For example, although a game might use GPS information to pair you with or show nearby players, is the feature essential? Will the app function without it? My attitude is that, unless enabling Location (GPS) benefits *me*, I'd rather not play "Where in the World Is Steve Schwartz?"

You have several options with GPS-enabled apps. First, turn off Location and see whether the app still functions or whether Location is forced back on. Second, if the app has a Settings command, you may be able to disable its GPS component or substitute a manually entered location. Third, enable Location while using the app and quickly disable it when you finish. Fourth, decide whether the app is *really* important to you. If not, uninstall it and search for a similar app that doesn't require GPS. Fifth, reconcile yourself to recharging more frequently. If an app is critical to your business or life, it's probably worth the battery drain.

View Battery Usage by Features and Apps

If you want to get a handle on which features and applications are draining your battery the most, you can find the answer in Settings.

Low Battery Indicator

If you want to be warned when the battery is extremely low, a blinking red LED can automatically appear when the screen is dark. Open Settings, tap the Display icon, tap LED Indicator, and ensure that Low Battery is checked.

1. Open Settings and tap the Battery icon (in the System section).

2. The scrolling summary lists the features, services, and apps that have been consuming the battery since the last time you charged the phone and shows the percentage of consumption attributable to each.

Refreshing the Data

While viewing the Battery screen, you can force a refresh to display up-to-date consumption figures.

3. *Optional:* Tap an entry to view additional information. Depending on the item, you may be able to alter its settings to reduce battery consumption, disable or execute a force stop for it, or uninstall it.

Show the Battery Percentage

Although the battery indicator in the status bar gives a rough indication of the remaining charge, you can alter it to show the percentage remaining. Ensure that Show Battery Percentage is checked (see the figure for Step 2).

Battery percentage   Refresh

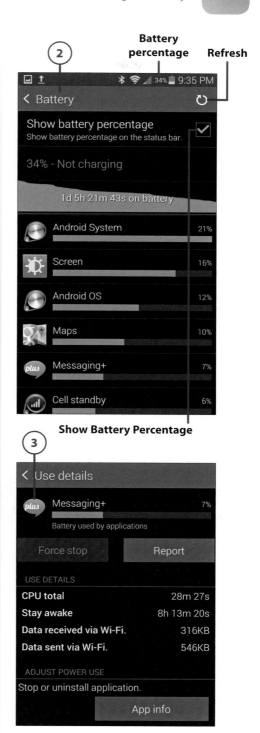

Show Battery Percentage

It's Not All Good

About Force Stop

Android is responsible for handling memory management, halting applications and processes as needed. In general, you should avoid using the Force Stop button for items that present it. (In Task Manager, tapping End is the same as performing a Force Stop.) Don't assume that Force Stop is the equivalent of a computer program's Quit or Exit command. Similar to the capability to force quit a misbehaving Mac or PC application, Force Stop's main purpose is to give you a way to semi-gracefully shut down an app or feature that isn't responding. (If Force Stop is grayed out on the Use Details screen, tap the App Info button. You may be able to execute a Force Stop from the App Info screen.)

When used as a means to temporarily halt battery consumption or free memory, the consequences may not always be what you intend. You may lose information; the phone, app, or feature may be left in an unstable state; or you might have difficulty restarting the application or feature.

Managing Talk Time and Data Usage

If you're on a limited talk, messaging, or data plan, the key to avoiding overage charges is relatively simple: Know and monitor your plan.

Checking Current Usage

Each carrier generally offers several ways for you to check the current month's usage, as well as manage your account. For example, depending upon your carrier, you might be able to take advantage of one of these built-in apps: AT&T (myAT&T), Sprint (Sprint Zone), T-Mobile (T-Mobile My Account), or Verizon (My Verizon Mobile).

Carriers typically provide a phone number that you can call to check your minutes and other usage. For example, Sprint users can dial ***4** from their cell phone; Verizon users can dial ***611**.

You can also check the carrier's website. At a minimum, you should see your usage for the current billing cycle. In addition, there might be an option to automatically receive a notification via text or email if you come close to exceeding a plan limit. *Forewarned is forearmed*. For example, when you discover or are notified that you're precariously close to hitting your monthly data limit, you can take steps to ensure that additional data-intensive activities (such as streaming videos or music) occur only over Wi-Fi. You may be able to request similar notification for other costly situations, such as international roaming.

Manage Data Usage

If your data plan has a monthly limit, you can enable the Data Usage setting on the phone to automatically warn you when you come close to exceeding your data limit—ignoring data transmitted over Wi-Fi, which doesn't count toward usage. You can also manually disable *mobile data* (using the cell network to transmit data) if you're close to exceeding your plan limit.

1. Open Settings and tap the Data Usage icon (in the Network Connections or Quick Settings section). The Data Usage screen appears.

2. The Mobile Data setting determines whether the cell network can be used to transfer data to and from the phone (checked) or whether you're restricting the phone to Wi-Fi data transfers (unchecked). If you're close to or have exceeded your monthly plan limit, remove the check mark to prevent additional overage charges.

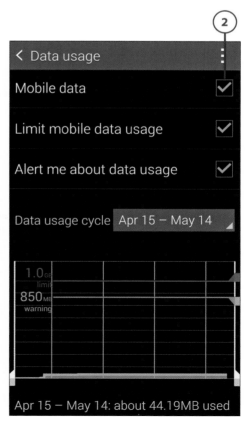

3. Tap the Limit Mobile Data Usage check box to instruct the phone to automatically disable mobile data when your plan limit is reached (red line). Read the explanatory material in the dialog box that appears and tap OK. When mobile data is disabled, you must do additional data transfers over Wi-Fi.

4. Tap the Alert Me About Data Usage check box to instruct the phone to warn when you're approaching your monthly limit (orange line). Read the explanatory material in the dialog box that appears and tap OK.

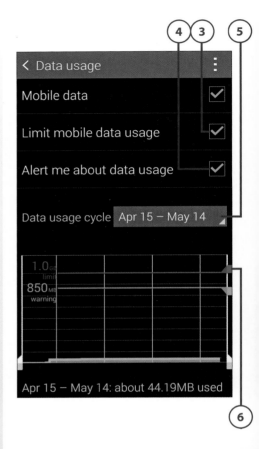

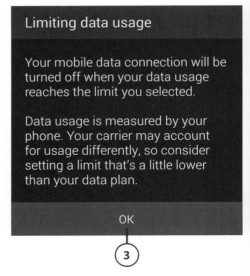

Limiting data usage

Your mobile data connection will be turned off when your data usage reaches the limit you selected.

Data usage is measured by your phone. Your carrier may account for usage differently, so consider setting a limit that's a little lower than your data plan.

OK

5. Ensure that the Data Usage Cycle matches your monthly billing cycle and represents the current cycle. If the billing period is incorrect, tap it, choose Change Cycle, specify the date when the usage cycle resets, and tap Set. If the cycle is incorrect, tap it to select a different 30-day period.

6. Set the red slider to match your plan's data limit (in gigabytes), set the orange slider to reflect the usage amount at which you want to be warned, and set the white bars to the period that you want to monitor.

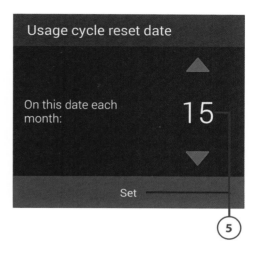

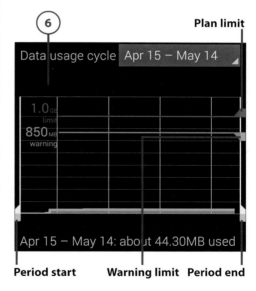

7. Tap the menu icon to enable or
   disable these additional Data
   Usage options:

   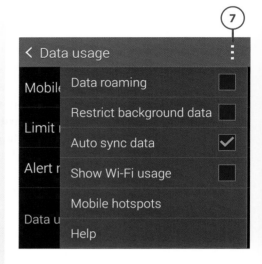

   - Enable Data Roaming to allow
     your phone to use other net-
     works for data access when
     roaming.

   - Enable Restrict Background
     Data to prevent background
     data access of apps and servic-
     es, restricting them to working
     only when a Wi-Fi connection
     is available.

   - Enable Auto Sync Data if you
     want your accounts to sync
     automatically—regardless of
     whether only a cellular con-
     nection is available.

   - Enable Show Wi-Fi Usage to
     add a separate Wi-Fi tab to
     the Data Usage screen, show-
     ing the last 30 days of Wi-Fi
     data usage and the apps that
     contributed to the usage. You
     aren't billed for Wi-Fi data
     usage, so it can be useful to
     see how much of your usage
     was free (Wi-Fi) versus paid
     (cellular).

   - Tap Mobile Hotspots to view
     enabled Wi-Fi hotspots within
     range of your phone.

What's Cheaper?

If you have unlimited or inexpensive text messaging, it may be advantageous
to send texts rather than make short calls. Conversely, if you're billed 25¢ per
message, it may be cheaper to call. Note that your carrier may allow you to
block incoming text messages (see your carrier's website for details). Received
text messages—including unwanted ones—may be billed to your account at
the same rate as messages that you send.

Can This Call Be Made Later?

The distinction between free and paid calls is typically determined by the time of day at the location where you make the call. If your free minutes begin at 7:00 p.m. each weeknight, for example, try to reserve lengthy, chatty calls for evenings and weekends.

If you're traveling and are in a different time zone, your daytime and evening calling periods generally change to match the local time. That is, free calling still begins at 7:00 PM—in whatever time zone you happen to be. Before heading out, check your plan to be sure. Similarly, if you're leaving the country, ask how out-of-country minutes are billed. Thinking that he was covered or that the rate would be reasonable, a friend didn't bother to check beforehand and returned to discover that his handful of international calls resulted in a bill of several hundred dollars.

Prorated Features

If your carrier plan allows you to add or remove features as needed, you might be able to save money by removing them as soon as you're finished using them rather than waiting until the end of the billing cycle. For example, I had to add the mobile hotspot and tethering feature to my plan in order to discuss how they worked in this book. When I finished a few days later, I immediately removed the feature from my plan. As a result, I was only charged one-tenth of the feature's full-month cost.

Faster Downloads with Download Booster

Although most U.S. carriers eliminated this highly touted feature before shipping their version of the S5, a few decided to support it—at least initially. When downloading files more than 30MB, Download Booster enables you to simultaneously use your Wi-Fi and cellular data connections to download the file faster. To enable Download Booster, open Settings, tap the Download Booster icon, move the slider to the On position, and then tap OK in the pop-up that appears.

Viewing and Expanding Storage

Although the 16GB version of the Galaxy S5 has approximately 11GB of internal memory available for storage, you can exhaust it with a combination of apps, photos, videos, music, and other data. You can expand your available storage by inserting a *microSD* (Secure Digital) or *microSDHC* (Secure Digital High Capacity) card into the phone's internal slot, adding as much as an additional 128GB.

View Used and Available Space

Storage

You can consult Storage to view the total, used, and available storage/memory on your phone.

1. Open Settings and tap the Storage icon (in the System section).

2. The Device Memory bar shows how the phone's built-in memory is being used. The colored sections of the bar represent the built-in storage that's currently in use, and the dark gray area on the right (Available Space) shows the amount of free space.

   - *Total Space* is the phone's built-in storage. It is used for the Android operating system, running apps, and storing all types of data (such as photos, music, videos, downloaded apps, and system files). Total Space does not include storage available on an add-in memory card, if you have one.

   - *System Memory* is the amount used by the Android operating system.

   - An *SD Card* section is shown at the bottom if there's an installed microSD or microSDHC card. Total Space is the amount of storage space available on the card after it has been formatted for use by the Android operating system. Available Space is the amount of free space on the card that can be used to store additional files.

3. *Optional:* Tap Used Space and Miscellaneous Files to view a breakdown of the storage space used by different types of data.

Storage Shrinkage

When viewing the information in Storage, you may think that the total space listed is less than the stated specs. Don't be alarmed; the figures are correct. Although the Galaxy S5 includes at least 16GB of internal storage, part of it is used as system memory. And when formatted for use, a 16GB microSDHC card has only 14.81GB of usable space, for example.

Adding a Memory Card

The Galaxy S5 can accommodate up to a 128GB memory card in its internal slot. When picking a card, take note of its *class* in the item description. The lower the class number (2–10), the slower the card. Under current class specifications, the class indicates the card's minimum sustained write speed in megabytes per second. Thus, a Class 2 card should be capable of writing data to the card at 2MBps (megabytes per second) or faster. (If a card's description or packaging doesn't mention a class, assume that it's Class 2 or slower. That frequently explains why such cards are so inexpensive.) Currently, you can purchase Class 10 cards for less than 75¢ per megabyte. Unless you already have an older, slower card, there's little monetary incentive to go slower than Class 10.

Next, determine the amount of storage you need. An 8GB or 16GB card suffices for most people. If you intend to pack it with videos and music or regularly shoot hundreds of photos or lengthy movies, go for the highest-capacity card you can afford—128GB is the max.

All Cards Aren't Equal

Even within a class, cards aren't identical. First, some Class 10 cards can sustain a minimum 10MBps *read* speed, as well as write speed. Second, the minimum speed on some of these cards is occasionally much faster than 10MBps. Third, based on reviews and ratings on sites such as Amazon.com and NewEgg.com, some cards appear to be knockoffs that are slower than their stated class, fail quickly, or don't work at all. When choosing a card from an online source, read the user comments, note the ratings, and check the seller's return policy.

Although it isn't necessary, make a note of whether your chosen card includes a microSD to SD adapter. If it does, you can slip your tiny card into the postage stamp–sized adapter and use it in devices that require an SD card rather than a microSD card. In the same vein, be sure that your chosen card is a *micro*SD or *micro*SDHC, not an SD or SDHC. Only a micro card will fit in the phone's slot.

Insert a Memory Card

Whether the card is new or being moved from another phone or device, the first step is to insert it into your phone.

1. Shut down the phone by holding down the Power button, tapping Power Off in the Device Options dialog box, and then tapping OK in the confirmation dialog box.

2. Remove the cover from the back of the phone by slipping your thumbnail into the tiny slot on the side (above the Power button) and prying off the back.

3. Grasp the memory card by its edges and turn the card so that its gold contact strips face down. The labeled side of the card should face up and be oriented as it is in the figure.

4. The top of the battery blocks the insertion or removal of memory and SIM cards. Carefully remove the battery by slipping your thumb into the slot at its bottom and prying gently upward.

5. The memory card slot sits atop the SIM card slot. Carefully push the memory card into its slot until it clicks into place, reinsert the battery, and replace the phone's back cover. Ensure that the cover is completely sealed around all edges.

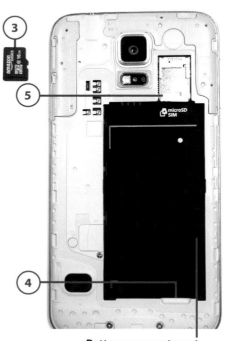

Battery compartment

Index

D

E

My
Samsung Galaxy S5

Steve Schwartz
with Craig James Johnston

que

FREE
Online Edition

Safari
Books Online

Your purchase of *My Samsung Galaxy S®5* includes access to a free online edition for 45 days through the **Safari Books Online** subscription service. Nearly every Que book is available online through **Safari Books Online**, along with thousands of books and videos from publishers such as Addison-Wesley Professional, Cisco Press, Exam Cram, IBM Press, O'Reilly Media, Prentice Hall, Sams, and VMware Press.

Safari Books Online is a digital library providing searchable, on-demand access to thousands of technology, digital media, and professional development books and videos from leading publishers. With one monthly or yearly subscription price, you get unlimited access to learning tools and information on topics including mobile app and software development, tips and tricks on using your favorite gadgets, networking, project management, graphic design, and much more.

Activate your FREE Online Edition at
informit.com/safarifree

STEP 1: Enter the coupon code: RIDZYBI.

STEP 2: New Safari users, complete the brief registration form.
Safari subscribers, just log in.

If you have difficulty registering on Safari or accessing the online edition,
please e-mail customer-service@safaribooksonline.com